Criminal Law in South Africa

Criminal Law in South Africa

Third Edition

Shannon Vaughn Hoctor

This book was originally published as a monograph in the International Encyclopaedia of Laws/Criminal Law.

Founding Editor: Roger Blanpain
General Editor: Frank Hendrickx
Volume Editors: Frank Verbruggen & Vanessa Franssen

Wolters Kluwer

Published by:
Kluwer Law International B.V.
PO Box 316
2400 AH Alphen aan den Rijn
The Netherlands
E-mail: lrs-sales@wolterskluwer.com
Website: www.wolterskluwer.com/en/solutions/kluwerlawinternational

Sold and distributed by:
Wolters Kluwer Legal & Regulatory U.S.
920 Links Avenue
Landisville, PA 17538
United States of America
E-mail: customer.service@wolterskluwer.com

ISBN 978-94-035-4469-4

e-Book: ISBN 978-94-035-4479-3
web-PDF: ISBN 978-94-035-4489-2

The Author

Professor Shannon Vaughn Hoctor (born 24 April 1967) obtained the degrees BA (1985–1987), LLB (1988–1989) and LLM (1992) from the University of Cape Town, South Africa. Professor Hoctor also holds a Postgraduate Diploma in Latin from the University of Wales Trinity Saint David (2014). He took the first steps in his academic career at the Faculty of Law at the University of Cape Town, *inter alia*, teaching a course in specific crimes, before proceeding to Leiden in the Netherlands to begin doctoral studies. After two years in Leiden, he took up a contract teaching post at the University of Port Elizabeth (UPE), South Africa, at the beginning of 1996. He was appointed to a senior lectureship at UPE from the beginning of 1997, teaching Criminal Law and Jurisprudence, and was awarded the degree DJuris by the University of Leiden in June 1997. After being promoted to Associate Professor at UPE, he took up a chair in Law at the University of Natal (now the University of KwaZulu-Natal) in Pietermaritzburg, where he taught from July 2002 until July 2021. He also served as Deputy Dean of the Faculty of Law at the University of KwaZulu-Natal in 2010–2011. In July 2021, Professor Hoctor moved to Stellenbosch University, where he teaches substantive criminal law at undergraduate and postgraduate levels, along with courses in international criminal law and sentencing.

Professor Hoctor has published numerous articles in law journals, along with several chapters in books, and has authored books in criminal law, statutory offences and road traffic law, along with five edited works. He has served as Editor-in-Chief of the *South African Journal of Criminal Justice* since 2010, as Editor-in-Chief of the legal-historical journal *Fundamina* since 2019 and as Assistant Editor of *Obiter* since 2002. He is also a member of the Academic Advisory Board for the *European Journal of Crime, Criminal Law and Criminal Justice* and the *Yearbook of International & European Criminal and Procedural Law*.

The Author

Table of Contents

List of Abbreviations

CPF	Community Policing Forum
DDPP	Deputy Director of Public Prosecutions
DEIC	Dutch East India Company
DNDPP	Deputy National Director of Public Prosecutions
DPP	Director of Public Prosecutions
MEC	Member of the Executive Council
NDPP	National Director of Public Prosecutions
SAPS	South African Police Service
SCA	Supreme Court of Appeal

List of Abbreviations

General Introduction

§1. The General Background of the Country

I. Geography

1. The Republic of South Africa occupies the southernmost portion of the African continent, stretching latitudinally from 22°S to 35°S and longitudinally from 17°E to 33°E. To the west and south, the country is bounded by the Atlantic Ocean and, to the east, by the Indian Ocean. Its northern boundaries are its borders with the republics of Namibia (in the west), Botswana (central), Zimbabwe and Mozambique (northeast) and the Kingdom of Eswatini (east). The Kingdom of Lesotho is completely enclosed by South African territory in the southeast. Some 1,920 km southeast of Cape Town in the Atlantic lie the Prince Edward and Marion islands, annexed by South Africa in 1947.

The country has a surface area of 1,220,813 km^2 (an area five times the size of the United Kingdom and equal to the combined area of Germany, France, Italy, the Netherlands and Belgium). Almost its entire area lies in the subtropical zone.

2. Geographically, the Republic can be divided into two major categories of physiographic natural regions: the interior plateau and the land between the plateau and the coast. The boundary of these regions is the Great Escarpment, an imposing line of mountain ranges, which varies in height above sea level from about 1,500 m in the south-west to 3,482 m in the KwaZulu-Natal Drakensberg. The interior plateau is the southward extension of the great African plateau, which rises in the middle of the Sahara desert, some 5,000 km to the northwest. The plateau region is characterised by wide plains with an average height of 1,200 m above sea level. The area between the Great Escarpment and the coast varies in width from 60 km in the west to 240 km in the east.

The western marginal zone is a desert area with little rain and high summer temperatures. The southwestern marginal zone has a Mediterranean climate with hot, dry summers and cool, rainy winters. Further east, along the Indian Ocean coastline, the climate is subtropical with humid, wet summers.

Most of the interior is semi-arid, with cool, dry winters and hot summers. The eastern parts of the plateau are more temperate and in the northeast, the climate is subtropical.[1]

1. www.gov.za (last accessed 31 Mar. 2025).

3. South Africa has an average annual rainfall of 464 mm (500 mm is considered the minimum annual rainfall required for successful dry-land farming). South Africa is highly vulnerable to climate variability and change due to the country's high dependence on rain-fed agriculture and natural resources. The high evaporation rate of already dry soils and the virtual absence of permanent surface water over large parts of the country make water a scarce resource.[2]

4. Because of South Africa's greater elevation above sea level, temperatures tend to be lower compared to regions in similar latitudes, due primarily to the greater elevation of the continent above sea level. There is a temperature variation of 6°C between the east and west coasts. Despite a latitudinal span of 13 degrees, average annual temperatures are remarkably uniform throughout the country. Whilst it might be expected that there should be an increase from south to north, this is offset by the increase in the height of the plateau towards the northeast. Summer temperatures in some parts may be as high as 32–38°C.[3]

5. The country consists of nine provinces: the Western Cape, the Eastern Cape, the Northern Cape, the Free State, KwaZulu-Natal, North West, Gauteng, Mpumalanga and Limpopo.

II. Population

6. The South African population is made up of people of diverse origin: the Nguni (comprising the Zulu, Xhosa, Ndebele and Swazi people); Sotho-Tswana (including the Southern, Northern and Western Sotho (Tswana) people); Tsonga; Venda; Afrikaners; English; coloureds (persons of mixed race); Indians (originally imported from India as indentured labour in the late nineteenth century); those who have immigrated to South Africa from the rest of Africa, Europe and Asia and maintain a strong cultural identity; and a small group of the Khoi and San peoples.

The diversity of the unique cultures of South Africa has been endorsed in recognition of eleven official languages: English, Afrikaans (a creole language derived from Dutch), isiXhosa, isiZulu, isiNdebele, Sesotho sa Leboa, Sesotho, Setswana, siSwati, Tshivenda and Xitsonga.[4] Although English is the mother tongue of only 8.7% of the population, it is the language most widely understood and is the second language of the majority of South Africans.[5]

The population of South Africa was estimated to be 62 million persons in the 2022 national census, of whom 51% were female. In terms of classification based on the 2022 census, 81.4% classified themselves as Africans,7.3% as white, 8.2%

2. https://climateknowledgeportal.worldbank.org/country/south-africa/climate-data-historical (last accessed 31 Mar. 2025).
3. www.gov.za (last accessed 31 Mar. 2025).
4. South African Sign Language has been included in this list by the Constitution Eighteenth Amendment Act 3 of 2023, the date of commencement of which has yet to be proclaimed.
5. According to the 2022 Census (https://census.statssa.gov.za/#/).

as coloured and 2.7% as Indian/Asian. Population estimates are: Africans 50.5 million, whites 4.5 million, 'coloured' 5.05 million and Asians 1.7 million.[6]

III. Economy

7. Until the last decades of the nineteenth century, the South African economy was based exclusively on agriculture, more or less self-sufficient but mainly at subsistence level. The discovery of diamonds (in 1871) and gold (in 1886) shifted the focus of the economy. Mining became a major industry, whilst agriculture changed from being subsistence-oriented to market-oriented. The mining industry stimulated commercial and industrial activity. By the middle of the twentieth century, South Africa had advanced from a mainly agrarian economy to a diversified economy in which agriculture, mining, secondary industry, commerce and a wide range of service establishments are the main components.

Industrial activity is concentrated in four metropolitan areas. These are in the Gauteng province, Durban-Pinetown in KwaZulu-Natal, Gqberha-Uitenhage in the Eastern Cape and the Cape Peninsula in the Western Cape. The hub is the city of Johannesburg, the home of the gold-mining industry and the centre of the Gauteng province, which accounts for about 33.9% of the gross domestic product.

These areas comprise only 3% of the geographical area of the country and produce 80% of all industrial products.

The South African economy is basically a free-market economy, allowing private enterprise and private ownership of resources.[7]

IV. Political System and Administrative Structure

A. *Constitutional Arrangements*

8. Prior to 1910, the erstwhile provinces of the Republic of South Africa were colonies under the British Crown. In 1910, the colonies were brought into a union under the British Crown.[8] The constitution of the Union of South Africa provided for a unitary state with organs of government in the Westminster model. The legislature (Parliament) was bicameral and vested with sovereign legislative power. The executive (the Cabinet) was drawn from the members of the party with a majority of seats in the lower house. The leader of the political party with the majority of seats became the Prime Minister.[9]

---

6. https://www.statssa.gov.za/ (last accessed 31 Mar. 2025).
7. https://www.britannica.com/place/South-Africa/Economy (last accessed 31 Mar. 2025). For further detail, *see* https://www.gov.za/about-sa/economy.
8. H.R. Hahlo & E. Kahn, *The Union of South Africa, The Development of its Laws and Constitution* (Stevens & Sons Ltd, London 1960) 51ff.
9. H.R. Hahlo & E. Kahn, *The Union of South Africa, The Development of its Laws and Constitution* (Stevens & Sons Ltd, London 1960) 128ff.

Under this constitution, the franchise was granted only to white adults; Africans, coloureds and Asiatics were not enfranchised and thus were precluded from participating in the government of the country.

9. The Union of South Africa endured until 1961, when, after a referendum of white citizens, a new constitution was adopted under which the Union became the Republic of South Africa, and independent of the British Crown. The Republic ceased to be a member of the British Commonwealth of Nations. Besides making the necessary changes for establishing a republic, the new constitution did not depart in any significant respect from the constitution of 1910.[10]

10. In 1983, after another referendum of white citizens, a new constitution was adopted which provided for a three-chamber legislature to which whites, coloureds and Asiatics elected (on separate voter rolls) representatives drawn from their respective racial groups. Africans continued to be excluded from membership of the South African Parliament.[11]

B. The Apartheid System

11. Since the time of their arrival in 1652, the Europeans dominated the indigenous peoples, subjugating them economically and by military force. This position of dominance hardened into a system of racial segregation that would become the universally despised system of apartheid.

12. Initially, segregation was mainly a social and economic practice (although from the colonial times, people of colour were denied the vote in whatever forms of representative government the European settlers introduced for themselves). In the mid-twentieth century, white Afrikaner nationalists gained political dominance in the country and instituted the legally enforced system of racial segregation that became known as apartheid. Apartheid was institutionalised by the enactment of various statutes which created a system for the classification of all citizens into various racial groups and, under pain of punishment, enforced residential, social, sexual and industrial segregation[12] according to these classifications.

13. Resistance by the unenfranchised South Africans to apartheid was manifested by public protests, marches, 'defiance' campaigns and ultimately the initiation of the 'armed struggle'. The government responded by police action, the banning of black political movements (notably the African National Congress and the Pan African Congress), and the detention and imprisonment of leaders of the resistance movements.

---

10. G. Carpenter, *Introduction to South African Constitutional Law* (Butterworths, Durban 1987) 216–219.
11. G. Carpenter, *Introduction to South African Constitutional Law* (Butterworths, Durban 1987) 280ff.
12. *See infra*, para. 66.

14. Police action, security laws and the proclamation, at various times, of states of emergency[13] failed to stamp out resistance to apartheid. In 1990, the government in effect abandoned its apartheid policy[14] and signified that it was prepared to negotiate with people of colour on a new constitutional dispensation which would be based on the principles of non-racialism, universal suffrage and full equality for all citizens.

C. *Full Democracy*

15. From 1990, a process for the negotiation of a new constitution was instituted, transforming South Africa from a non-democratic state to a full democracy. A negotiated settlement was enabled by the release of Nelson Mandela and the unbanning of the African National Congress and the Pan African Congress in 1990. Following multi-party negotiations, the 'interim' 1993 Constitution (with a limited lifespan) was adopted, which came into effect on the date of the first democratic election, on 27 April 1994. The 'interim' Constitution brought about sweeping changes, including: universal adult suffrage; the abolition of parliamentary sovereignty; a proportional voting system; the institution of the Constitutional Court; the division of the country into nine (previously four) provinces; and the division of legislative and executive competencies between national, provincial and local levels. After the 1994 election, the executive authority functioned as a government of national unity. The Constitutional Assembly, consisting of members of the National Assembly and Senate (i.e., Parliament), was tasked with drafting a final Constitution, which was adopted on 11 October 1996 and came into effect, upon certification by the Constitutional Court, on 4 February 1997. Although passed as Act 108 of 1996, the Citation of Constitutional Laws Act 5 of 2005 provided that the Constitution should not be referred to by means of an act or number, thus definitively establishing the uniqueness of the Constitution.

D. *Administrative Divisions*

16. The Union of South Africa was created from four colonies, which then occupied what is today the geographical area of the Republic of South Africa. The colonies, which had attained significant degrees of representative government (for their white inhabitants) and appropriate constitutional structures, each became a province of the new state, retaining its original boundaries. They retained to some measure of their former constitutional autonomy in the form of provincial legislatures (Provincial Councils) and executive organs (an Administrator-in-Executive-Committee). The former colonial judicial institutions were retained under the style

13. *See infra*, para. 68.
14. In the historic speech delivered on 2 Feb. 1990 by the State President (and head of government) at the opening of Parliament. In this speech, he announced the unbanning of the ANC and PAC, and the release of 'political' prisoners (including Nelson Mandela) (*see* Vol. 16, *Debates of Parliament*, 2 Feb. 1990, col. 12).

of 'provincial divisions' of the Supreme Court of South Africa. In 1986, a process of restructuring the system of provincial government began.

17. A pillar of the National Party government's apartheid system was the policy of 'separate development' in terms of which African people were to be provided with powers of self-government to be exercised in what the government called their 'homelands'. These homelands were designated areas within the Republic, which were identified and assigned formal boundaries. The government then set about establishing government structures within these homelands and enfranchising African people in relation to these homeland governments. The homeland governments, once established, were offered the opportunity to become constitutionally independent of the Republic of South Africa and its government. Some accepted this offer, and the South African Parliament enacted legislation which bestowed 'independence' upon these states and formally excised their land areas from the Republic of South Africa.[15] The 'independent' states so established were Transkei, Bophuthatswana, Ciskei and Venda. Other homelands declined to become independent and were conferred certain powers of self-government together with legislative and executive powers over their subjects. The self-governing territories were Lebowa, Gazankulu, KwaZulu, Qwaqwa, KaNgwane and KwaNdebele.

18. In terms of the new constitutional dispensation under the 1996 Constitution, three distinct, but interconnected, spheres of government are created at national, provincial and local levels, in terms of a system of co-operative government, which seeks to ensure that the functions of government are decentralised to levels closer to the people. The Constitution provides for legislative functions at national level to be performed by Parliament, which consists of the National Assembly and the National Council of Provinces. Each province has a provincial legislature. Whilst Parliament may pass legislation on any matter, some matters are 'functional areas of exclusive provincial competence' (i.e., provincial planning and provincial roads), where the national legislature will only interfere if it is in the national interest. There are also areas where both Parliament and provincial legislatures may pass legislation ('functional areas of concurrent national and provincial legislative competence', such as housing and public transport). Municipalities are the context for the local sphere of government, which consists of municipal councils (which may pass by-laws on matters such as building regulations and street trading).

19. Executive authority also functions in the national, provincial and local spheres. The President heads the national executive. The President, Deputy President and Ministers form the Cabinet. The provincial Premier heads the provincial executive (in the form of a provincial Executive Council, consisting of Members of the Executive Council (MECs)), whilst municipal councils perform executive functions at local level.

---

15. G. Carpenter, *Introduction to South African Constitutional Law* (Butterworths, Durban 1987) 402ff.

V. The Judicial System

20. For judicial purposes, South Africa is divided into provinces and magisterial districts.

21. There are nine judicial provinces, each of which has its own division of the High Court presided over by a judge president and so many judges of the High Court as may be appointed for the division.[16] In some provinces, there are 'local' divisions, which are areas for which a division (the 'local' division) of the 'provincial' division has been established[17] (judges of the 'provincial' division preside in the 'local' division). Within each province are 'circuit courts', itinerant courts presided over by judges of the High Court, which periodically visit areas in the province designated by the judge president for the purpose of trying criminal charges.[18]

Provincial and local divisions of the High Court have inherent criminal and civil jurisdiction for the province for which they have been established.[19]

22. In each province, there are a number of magisterial districts, each of which has a Magistrates' Court. Magistrates' courts have both civil and criminal jurisdiction.

The Minister of Justice may organise certain magisterial districts into regions. Each region has a Regional Magistrates' Court with criminal jurisdiction, which is greater than that of the district magistrates' courts.

23. The country is also divided into regions for the purpose of establishing small claims courts. By November 2024, there were 415 small claims courts.[20]

24. In areas controlled by African chiefs or headmen, traditional courts may exist[21] with criminal jurisdiction to try and punish any Black who has committed, in the area under the control of the chief or headman concerned, certain offences at common law or under Black law and custom and certain statutory offences.[22]

25. Every Provincial Division of the High Court can serve as a Court of Appeal from the chiefs', magistrates', regional and circuit courts in the province.

26. The Supreme Court of Appeal (SCA) of the High Court, previously known as the Appellate Division, is composed of Judges of Appeal and is presided over by the President of the SCA. The court has only appeal jurisdiction and hears civil and criminal appeals from decisions of the provincial divisions of the High Court.

---

16. Superior Courts Act 10 of 2013, s. 6; *see infra*, para. 414.
17. *See infra*, para. 415.
18. Superior Courts Act 10 of 2013, s. 7.
19. *See infra*, para. 413.
20. https://www.justice.gov.za/scc/scc.htm (last accessed 31 Mar. 2025).
21. Black Administration Act 38 of 1927, s. 20. This Act has been repealed, but this provision subsists until the legislation replacing it, the Traditional Courts Act 9 of 2022, comes into force.
22. The jurisdiction so conferred is severely limited by the exclusion of most of the common-law crimes (listed in the Third Schedule to the Act) and certain types of statutory offences (*ibid*).

27. The court with final jurisdiction in all matters is the Constitutional Court, which consists of the Chief Justice, Deputy Chief Justice and nine other judges.[23] It may decide on all constitutional matters – that is, a matter relating to the interpretation, protection or enforcement of the Constitution – as well as any factual or legal matter if it grants leave to appeal on the grounds that the matter raises an arguable point of law of general importance which ought to be considered by it, and it makes the final decision as to whether a matter falls within its ambit.[24] The Constitutional Court has the final decision whether a law is constitutional, and it is required that any order of invalidity (holding that a provision is unconstitutional) made by any High Court must be confirmed by the Constitutional Court before that order has any force.[25]

§2. Criminal Law, Criminal Justice and Criminal Science

I. Definitions of Criminal Law

A. *Criminal Law*

28. South African criminal law is that branch of South African national law which defines certain forms of human conduct as crimes and provides for judicial proceedings to be instituted against persons charged with committing a crime and the punishments that may be imposed.

29. South African criminal law is made up of substantive criminal law and adjectival or procedural criminal law. The substantive criminal law is given practical application and effect through the processes and mechanisms of the adjectival law.

B. *Substantive Criminal Law*

30. The substantive law is concerned with the determination and definition of the specific crimes and the formulation, synthesis and rationalisation of the principles of law and justice that must be applied in order to decide whether a person who has contravened the criminal law is deserving of punishment. This latter aspect of the substantive law comprises what is referred to as 'the general principles of liability'.

There is no formal codification of the substantive criminal law in South Africa.[26] The principles and definitions of the South African substantive criminal law are thus

23. In terms of s. 167(1) of the Constitution of the RSA, 1996.
24. Sections 167(3) and 167(7) of the Constitution of the RSA, 1996.
25. Section 167(5) of Constitution of the RSA, 1996.
26. At no stage in South African history has there been any serious consideration given to the idea of codification. However, the erstwhile 'independent' state of Transkei codified the general principles of liability and common-law crimes in the Transkeian Penal Code Act 9 of 1983. This code replaced an earlier provision, enacted during colonial times, on which *see infra*, para. 60.

to be found set out in the common-law sources, the judgments of the High Court and the expositions by academic writers.[27]

C. *Criminal Procedure*

31. The adjectival criminal law or procedural criminal law is concerned with the determination of the nature, organisation and functioning of the investigation, prosecution and adjudication in cases of crimes.

The South African law of criminal procedure is basically derived from the common law. However, various statutory provisions have supplemented and, on occasions, replaced the common law. Indeed, the principal source of South African procedural criminal law is the Criminal Procedure Act 51 of 1977. The Act though extensive in its scope and provisions[28] is however not a codification of the law and must be regarded as supplementary to the common law. The Constitution contains provisions which directly or indirectly govern the South African law of criminal procedure, and given the supremacy of the Constitution, such provisions must be regarded as the most important sources of criminal procedural rules.[29]

D. *Crimes and Offences*

32. In South African criminal law, the term 'crimes' is usually used to describe the crimes determined by the common law, whilst the term 'offences' is used to refer to crimes created by statute. However, for purposes of the principles of substantive and procedural law, there is no distinction of any significance between the categories of 'crime' and 'offence'.[30] South African law does not formally grade contraventions of the criminal law in any hierarchy of seriousness and thus for all technical and practical purposes, the terms 'crime' and 'offence' are synonymous.

II. Characteristics of Criminal Law

33. In South African law, crime is prosecuted at the instance of the state rather than at the instance of the victim and any punishment imposed is carried out by officials of the state rather than the victim or the victim's family. For these reasons, the criminal law in South Africa is classified as a branch of *public law.*

---

27. *See infra*, paras 74 et seq.
28. *See* the comprehensive commentary on the Act in E. du Toit et al., *Commentary on the Criminal Procedure Act* (Juta, Cape Town 1987).
29. J.J. Joubert et al., *Criminal Procedure Handbook* 13th ed. (Juta, Cape Town 2020) 24.
30. E.M. Burchell & P.M.A. Hunt, *South African Criminal Law and Procedure*, Vol. I *General Principles* 2nd ed. (Juta, Cape Town 1983) 82–84.

34. In accordance with the doctrine *nullum crimen sine lege,* only conduct proscribed by the *positive law* can be punished as a crime.[31] Thus, the mere fact that conduct is considered to be immoral will not justify the imposition of any form of public punishment upon the perpetrator.

At one time, the South African courts claimed to be *custos morum* and to enjoy the power to punish conduct on the ground of its immorality.[32] However, it is now clearly recognised that the courts are empowered to punish only conduct that is proscribed by a properly enacted statute of a competent legislature or because it is one of the pre-determined and closed lists of recognised common-law crimes.[33]

35. South African criminal law is essentially *punitive law.* The theme of retaliation is prominent in the sentencing policy and practices of the courts, although it is also so that the courts recognise that punishment can serve other purposes such as deterrence, incapacitation and reform and will determine punishment according to these objectives.[34]

III. Overview of the Criminal Justice System

36. As in other countries, the South African criminal law is administered through the medium of agencies for the enforcement of the law, prosecution of offenders, adjudication of charges brought and for the infliction of punishment. The agencies involved are: the police, the prosecution, the criminal courts and the Department of Correctional Services.

A. The Police

37. South Africa has a national police force, the South African Police Service (SAPS), established in terms of the SAPS Act of 1995, which is responsible for all aspects of the enforcement of the criminal law throughout the country. Responsibility for the SAPS falls to the Minister of Police.

Under the command and control of the national commissioner, the SAPS is charged, *inter alia,* with ensuring the safety and security of all persons and with ensuring cooperation between the service and the communities it serves in the combating of crime.[35]

The complement of police officers in SAPS, excluding civilians, was tallied as 178,708 in 2022–2023.[36] For administrative purposes, the country is divided into nine provincial regions, each headed by a provincial commissioner.

31. *See infra,* para. 88.
32. *R v. Marais* (1889) 6 SC 236. Cf. E.M. Burchell & P.M.A. Hunt, *South African Criminal Law and Procedure,* Vol. I *General Principles* 2nd ed. (Juta, Cape Town 1983) 58.
33. *See infra,* paras 89, 92.
34. *See infra,* paras 403 et seq.
35. South African Police Service Act 68 of 1995, preamble.
36. According to the 2023 SAPS annual performance plan 2023/2024 at https://www.saps.gov.za/ (last accessed 31 Mar. 2025).

The force operates in terms of a number of programmes. These include: (i) Administration, which provides for strategic leadership, management, and support. (ii) Visible Policing, which deals with the combating of crime and the maintenance of public order. (iii) Detective and Forensic Services, which is responsible for maintaining an effective crime-investigation service and which provides scientific support in the investigation of crime, along with the Directorate for Priority Crime Investigation, which targets financial crime, corruption, looting of infrastructure, and crime related to natural resources. (iv) Crime Intelligence, which manages crime intelligence and analyses crime information. (v) Protection and Security Services, which provides protection and security services to all identified dignitaries and government interests.[37]

Crime prevention in South Africa is based on the principles of community policing,[38] that is, partnerships between the community and the SAPS. Partnerships between police officers (who are appointed as sector managers) and communities strengthen existing community policing forums (CPFs), which have been in place since 1993. By the end of 2023, 1,152 functioning CPFs had been established at police stations. By October 2023, the Reserve Police Force stood at 3,502 active reservists. Sector policing was implemented at 1,078 police stations by the end of March 2014. It is a policing model that focuses on the geographical division of a police station area into smaller manageable sectors, based on the geographical constraints, the composition and diversity of communities and the specific interests and needs of a community.

B. The Prosecution Service

38. There is a single national prosecuting authority for the Republic,[39] headed by a National Director of Public Prosecutions (NDPP).[40] Other members of the National Office of the NDPP include: Deputy National Directors; Investigating Directors[41] and Special Directors;[42] other members of the prosecuting authority appointed at or assigned to the Office;[43] administrators; and investigators.

An office of the prosecuting authority has been established at the seat of each High Court and the head of the office is a Director (DPP) or Deputy Director of Public Prosecutions (DDPP).[44]

37. www.saps.gov.za (last accessed 31 Mar. 2025).
38. www.saps.gov.za (last accessed 31 Mar. 2025).
39. National Prosecuting Authority Act 32 of 1998.
40. National Prosecuting Authority Act 32 of 1998, s. 5.
41. Appointed to carry out investigations relating to, *inter alia*, corruption and commercial crime – s. 7.
42. In terms of s. 13(1)(*c*), appointed to carry out certain duties and functions as assigned by the President.
43. In terms of s. 1, 'members of the prosecuting authority' includes: prosecutors; investigators (s. 19D); financial investigators; administrators; those employed to perform work in specific cases (in terms of s. 38(1) or (3)); and persons performing services for the prosecuting authority in terms of a secondment or any other consultancy agreement in line with prosecutorial and investigation powers.
44. National Prosecuting Authority Act 32 of 1998, s. 6.

The power to institute and conduct criminal proceedings on behalf of the state, to carry out necessary functions incidental thereto and to discontinue criminal proceedings vests in the prosecuting authority. Any Director, subject to the control and directions of the National Director, exercises these powers in respect of the area of jurisdiction for which he or she has been appointed and in respect of any offences which have not been expressly excluded from his or her jurisdiction, either generally or in a specific case, by the National Director.[45]

C. The Judicial Service

39. The administration of criminal justice in South Africa is conducted according to the accusatorial method that is found in most Anglo-American jurisdictions. In the result, the judiciary in South Africa, as a general rule,[46] has no investigative role in the administration of justice and is confined to adjudication upon the guilt or innocence of accused persons.

40. Trials are before either the magistrates' court or the regional court or the High Court. Before which of these courts a charge will come to trial is determined by the Director of Public Prosecutions according to the penal jurisdiction enjoyed by the court.

D. Trial Jurisdictions

41. The courts of criminal jurisdiction in the first instance are magistrates' district and regional courts and provincial divisions of the High Court.[47]

A district court has jurisdiction over all crimes, except murder, treason, rape and compelled rape. A regional court has jurisdiction over all crimes except treason. However, a district court may not impose a sentence of imprisonment exceeding three years or a fine exceeding ZAR 120,000 (at exchange rates applicable at time of writing: GBP 5,040/USD 6,600/EUR 6,000). A regional court may not impose a sentence of imprisonment exceeding 15 years or a fine exceeding ZAR 600,000 (at exchange rates applicable at time of writing: GBP 25,200/USD 33,000/EUR 30,000).

A provincial division of the High Court has jurisdiction over all crimes committed within its area of jurisdiction. There are no limits upon the punishment that the High Court may impose.

42. Judgments of the magistrates' or regional courts may be taken on appeal to the provincial division of the High Court. Judgments in cases of first instance in the High Court may be appealed to the full bench of the division. Judgments of the provincial divisions on appeals from magistrates' or regional court decisions may be

45. National Prosecuting Authority Act 32 of 1998, s. 20.
46. In some circumstances, judicial officers may act in an inquisitorial way. *See infra*, para. 498.
47. *See* further *infra*, paras 413et seq.

further appealed to the SCA. An appeal from the judgment of the full bench may be taken to the SCA only with the special leave of that court. An appeal from a judgment of the SCA may be made to the Constitutional Court, and will be heard if the Constitutional Court permits such appeal to be heard.

E. Legal Representation

43. The right to legal representation is recognised by South African law. Thus, a person arrested, detained or brought to trial on a criminal charge is entitled to be represented by legal counsel.[48] The right to legal representation is entrenched in sections 35(2) and (3) of the Constitution, and is further confirmed by the provisions of section 73 of the Criminal Procedure Act. Indigent accused, who will be subject to a means test, may be represented by Legal Aid South Africa where 'substantial injustice' would otherwise result.[49] In terms of the Legal Practice Act 2014,[50] legal practitioners who have fulfilled the requirements of the Act may practice as attorneys, advocates, conveyancers and notaries. Based on its historical legal heritage, South Africa maintains a distinction between attorneys (known as solicitors in England and in the Commonwealth context) and advocates (known as barristers in England and in the Commonwealth context). Attorneys deal with members of the public directly and typically have more general practices, whereas advocates are specialist litigators, tasked with appearing in court.

F. Correctional Services

44. The country's prisons are administered by a department of state termed the Department of Correctional Services.[51] The Minister of Justice and Correctional Services is a member of the Cabinet. The National Commissioner of Correctional Services is charged with the management and control of the department.

45. There are 243 correctional centres in the country (nine exclusively for females), classified as maximum, medium or minimum security. The daily average correctional centre population is in the region of 160,000 prisoners. The latest most recent official statistics on overcrowding in South African prisons are 48%.[52]

---

48. *See infra*, para. 596.
49. *See* the Legal Aid South Africa Act 39 of 2014, and s. 35(3)(*g*) of the Constitution. In terms of the Legal Aid Manual 20 (available at https://legal-aid.co.za/wp-content/uploads/2018/11/Legal-Aid-Manual.pdf, last accessed 31 Mar. 2025), 'substantial injustice' is present when a person without legal aid would experience significant injustice by being sentenced, or having the possibility of being sentenced, to direct imprisonment of more than three months in a criminal case. *See* https://legal-aid.co.za/how-it-works (last accessed 31 Mar. 2025) for explanation of the means test.
50. Legal Practice Act 28 of 2014. The Act has been instituted to provide for the restructuring and transformation of the legal profession in South Africa.
51. *See* further *infra*, paras 681 et seq.
52. Annual Report of Judicial Inspectorate for Correctional Services 2023/2024 http://www.jics.gov.za/ (last accessed 31 Mar. 2025).

IV. Trends in the South African Criminal Justice System

46. A notable trend in the modern South African criminal justice system is the aggressively active role that the judiciary, particularly in the form of the judges of the SCA, play in the development and refinement of principles of criminal liability. During the last five decades or so, the South African judges have almost unilaterally eliminated the doctrine of strict liability from the South African criminal law;[53] abolished the doctrine *ignorantia juris neminem excusat*;[54] elaborated the *mens rea* so as to introduce the concept of *dolus eventualis*;[55] introduced the concept of criminal capacity as a separate and particular element of criminal liability[56] (and in the process introduced the defences of voluntary intoxication[57] and provocation (in the guise of 'non-pathological incapacity'[58])); and dealt with the setting aside of various unconstitutional rules.

47. , However the legislature has played a significant but more subdued and sometimes more conservative role in shaping the general nature of the substantive criminal law. Noteworthy in this regard is legislature's attempt to ameliorate the effects of the rule that voluntary intoxication is a defence to criminal liability;[59] its revision of the common-law crime of abortion;[60] its repeal of the common-law crime of bribery (substituting a statutory crime of 'corruption');[61] the introduction of a new regime for sexual offences, repealing and replacing a number of common-law offences;[62] and the introduction of legislation governing cybercrimes.[63] The introduction of a justiciable Bill of Rights has also had a significant impact on the South African criminal justice system.[64]

48. An important force in the shaping of the South African criminal justice system is the South African Law Reform Commission. Established in 1973, the Commission has conducted some important investigations into the South African criminal law and made significant recommendations for the reform of the South African criminal law. The principal reports of the Commission are listed in the bibliography (*infra*).

---

53. J. Burchell, *South African Criminal Law and Procedure*, Vol. I *General Principles* 4th ed. (Juta, Cape Town 2011) 451ff.
54. *See*, *S v. De Blom* 1977 (3) SA 513 (A), discussed in J. Burchell, *South African Criminal Law and Procedure*, Vol. I *General Principles* 4th ed. (Juta, Cape Town 2011) 400–403.
55. J. Burchell, *Principles of Criminal Law* 5th ed. (Juta, Cape Town 2016) 355.
56. J. Burchell, *Principles of Criminal Law* 5th ed. (Juta, Cape Town 2016) 251ff.; S.V. Hoctor, *Snyman's Criminal Law* 7th ed. (LexisNexis, Durban 2020) 136ff.
57. *S v. Chretien* 1981 (1) SA 1097 (A). *See infra*, para. 225.
58. J. Burchell, *Principles of Criminal Law* 5th ed. (Juta, Cape Town 2016) Ch. 22.
59. *See infra*, para. 227.
60. J.R.L. Milton, *South African Criminal Law and Procedure*, Vol. II *Common-Law Crimes* 3rd ed. (Juta, Cape Town 1996) 305ff.
61. *See*, J. Milton, 'Law Reform: Bribery and the Corruption Act 1992' 1993 *SACJ* 90.
62. Criminal Law (Sexual Offences and Related Matters) Amendment Act 32 of 2007.
63. *See infra*, para. 330. The Cybercrimes Act 19 of 2020 provides for an extensive regime for the regulation of cybercrime, which provides for broad extra-territorial application of the legislation. This replaces the previous piecemeal approach to regulation.
64. *See infra*, para. 70.

49. The main concentration of academic effort in South African law faculties regarding the criminal justice system is focused on the study and elucidation of the substantive and adjectival criminal law. Every South African university law faculty offers courses in the general principles of liability, specific crimes, criminal procedure and *capita selecta*.

This concentration upon criminal law in law faculties is largely to the exclusion of the study of criminology or penology. These subjects, if studied at a university, are offered in faculties other than the law faculty.

§3. Historical Background

50. South African criminal law has evolved out of a matrix of Roman-Dutch law and English law.[65]

I. The Roman-Dutch Law

51. The original criminal law practised in South Africa was the Roman-Dutch law of Holland (nowadays officially The Netherlands), which was brought to South Africa in 1652 by the Dutch colonial settlers.

52. The Roman-Dutch law, in turn, was a system that had evolved in Holland between the thirteenth and seventeenth centuries. It was called 'Roman-Dutch law'[66] because the name reflects the amalgamation of Roman and Dutch law, which occurred during this period. The reception of Roman law started slowly, but gradually gained momentum until in the sixteenth century a wholesale recourse to Roman law by jurists and judges was taking place. Roman law was officially regarded as a subsidiary common law, but in fact played an even more important role than this description suggests.

53. Roman criminal law began at an early date to influence criminal law in the Netherlands largely as a result of the knowledge which local officials and judicial officers had of the works of the Italian Commentators.

54. The famous *Caroli Constitutio Criminalis* of Charles V, which was enacted in 1532, though never formally promulgated in the Netherlands, nevertheless influenced the practice of the law. A first attempt at a systematic exposition of the criminal law of the Netherlands was contained in the *Praxis Rerum Criminalium* by Joost Damhouder (1507–1581), of Bruges, published in 1554. In the seventeenth century, the science of Dutch criminal law was much improved, principally as a result of the

65. Generally on the history of South African criminal law, *see* E.M. Burchell & P.M.A. Hunt, *South African Criminal Law and Procedure*, Vol. I. *General Principles* 2nd ed. (Juta, Cape Town 1983) Ch. 2.

66. The name was coined by the Dutch lawyer Simon van Leeuwen in the title of his book *Paratitula Juris Novissimi, dat is, Een Kort Begrip van het Rooms-Hollandts-Regt*, which was published in 1652. His most famous work he entitled *Het Roomsch-Hollandsch Recht* (1664).

publication of the famous treatise by Antonius Matthaeus II (1601–1654), *De Criminibus* (a detailed commentary on books 47 and 48 of Justinian's *Digest*). The '*Prolegomena*' to this work contained what amounts to the first attempt to formulate general principles of criminal liability.

Other important expositions of the Roman-Dutch criminal law included Pieter Bort's *Tractaet van Crimineele Saecken* (1652); Johannes Voet's exegesis in his *Commentarius ad Pandectas* (1698) upon Books 47 and 48 of Justinian's *Digest*;[67] J. Moorman, *Verhandelinge over de Misdaden* (1674); J. M. Barels, *Crimineele Advysen* (1778).

II. The Dutch Era

55. The Dutch established a settlement at the southern tip of Africa in 1652, at what was called the Cape of Good Hope. The settlement was under the aegis of the Dutch East India Company (DEIC), incorporated under a charter granted by the Estates-General of the United Netherlands.

Since Holland was the senior partner in the affairs of the DEIC, the Dutch settlers at the Cape practised and followed the Roman-Dutch law of Holland. In this way, the Roman-Dutch law became established as the common law of the European colonial settlements in South Africa.

56. The highest civil and criminal court at the Cape during the regime of the DEIC was the *Raad van Justitie*, the members of which were officials and *burghers* who were not required to have and very seldom did have legal qualifications. The public prosecutor was the *fiskaal.*

Criminal procedure was on the lines of Philip II's Criminal Procedure Ordinance of 1570 and was inquisitorial in form.

III. The British Era

57. In 1795 and again in 1806, the British occupied the Cape Colony. Although they did not formally replace the Roman-Dutch law with English law, the British disliked the inquisitorial form of procedure and soon initiated a process of replacing this feature of the Roman-Dutch law with the accusatorial form of procedure that applied in England.[68]

In 1813, a proclamation required judicial proceedings to be conducted in open court. In 1819, a criminal procedure code (known as the 'Crown Trial') was instituted, which showed considerable English influence, though it did not entirely

67. *See*, J.Ph. de Monte Verloren, *Geschiedenis van de Wetenschap van het Strafrecht en Strafprocesrecht in de Noordelike Nederlanden voor de Codificatie* (1942).
68. *See generally* on this process, C.J.R. Dugard, *South African Criminal Law and Procedure* Vol. IV *Introduction to Criminal Procedure* (Juta, Cape Town 1977) 20ff.

sweep away the old procedure. Ordinances of 1825[69] and 1826[70] decreed the replacement of Dutch by English as the language of the courts.

58. In 1827, a Charter of Justice[71] (which reaffirmed the retention of Roman-Dutch law as the law of the Cape) established a new Supreme Court, the judges to be drawn from the English, Irish or Scottish Bars, and provision was made, *inter alia*, for a system of appeals, the jury system, and an attorney-general in place of the *fiskaal*. The Bar was divided and advocates were to be of the United Kingdom Bar or Doctors of Law of Oxford, Cambridge or Dublin. A Criminal Procedure Ordinance of 1828[72] replaced the Crown Trial of 1819 and substantially assimilated criminal procedure in the Cape courts to that prevailing in England. Amongst other things, this Ordinance put an end to the practice of judicial interrogation of accused persons, who now became entitled to remain silent, whilst a confession was only admissible if made voluntarily. Later, the jury system and prosecution by way of a grand jury indictment were introduced.[73] An ordinance of 1830 adopted the English law of evidence.

59. By the latter decades of the nineteenth century, the situation regarding the system of criminal law applying at the Cape was that, as regards the adjectival law, English law had replaced the Dutch law almost entirely. As regards the substantive law, the Roman-Dutch law had been retained although some forms of English legal nomenclature and classification were to be observed, as with the recognition of crimes such as 'assault with intent to rape', 'receiving stolen goods' and 'manslaughter', which were quite foreign to Roman-Dutch law *eobus nominibus*.

60. The 1881–1883 *Commission on Native Laws and Customs* made a not inconsiderable contribution to the reception of English criminal law into South African common law.[74] The Commission produced a 'Draft Penal Code' which eventually became law under the name 'Native Territories' Penal Code'[75] (usually referred to in practice as the 'Transkeian Penal Code'). The great majority of sections of the Transkei Code were lifted word for word from the English Indictable Offences Bill, which had been drafted by the English jurist Sir James Stephen as a code of English criminal law.

Though the Transkeian Penal Code of 1886 became law only in the Transkei, its influence was felt far beyond the Transkei's borders. Some of its definitions came to be adopted *in toto* by the South African courts, and in other cases, it strongly

69. Ordinance 1 of 1825 (C).
70. Ordinance 27 of 1826 (C).
71. By letters patent of 24 Aug. 1827.
72. Ordinance 40 of 1828 (C).
73. The grand jury was however not a popular institution and was abolished in 1891.
74. *See*, D.S. Koyana, *The Influence of the Transkeian Penal Code on South African Criminal Law* (Lovedale Press, Lovedale 1990).
75. Act 24 of 1886 (C).

influenced the evolution of certain of the general principles of criminal liability and of the elements of some of the other particular crimes.[76]

61. By the time of the union of the colonies in 1910,[77] there had been a substantial measure of selective English law influence on the criminal law of the Cape, which was already best regarded as a 'mixed' system: a hybrid of Roman-Dutch and English criminal law. After the union, there was considerable development in the field of substantive law by the courts, who sought, in their judgments, to give order and system to the law as found in the writings of the Dutch jurists.[78]

62. By this time, the South African system of criminal law had acquired the values and institutions that characterised modern Anglo-American liberal democracy.[79]

The powers of arrest, search and seizure were, as in English law, exercised only under warrant duly issued by a judicial officer. Detained persons had to be released within forty-eight hours or brought before a judicial officer for a committal order. Detained persons were entitled to have access to their lawyer. The writ of habeas corpus[80] was available to obtain the release of persons unlawfully detained.

Trial was by jury (although trial by jury would be abolished in 1969). The onus was upon the prosecution to prove guilt 'beyond reasonable doubt'. The accused was entitled to be represented by a lawyer. An accused could not be required to make statements that incriminated himself, and a confession was only admitted as evidence if it was made 'freely and voluntarily'.

63. The seminal treatise on South African criminal law was published in 1917 by Frederick C. Gardiner and Charles W.H. Lansdown. Entitled *South African Criminal Law & Procedure*,[81] the work was widely relied upon by the courts as an authoritative exposition of the principles of modern South African criminal law. Although there was reference to Roman-Dutch authority, the work essentially reflected the principles and concepts of English common law.

64. The process of reception of the English criminal law was brought to an effective halt in the middle of the twentieth century. The cause was the rise of a spirit of nationalism, especially amongst the Afrikaans community, which created an atmosphere in which the contention that English law was not South African law could be, and was, advanced with some cogency. Whilst this was more true in respect of the civil law than the criminal law, the contention was given some force

---

76. *See* E.M. Burchell & P.M.A. Hunt, *South African Criminal Law and Procedure*, Vol. I *General Principles* 2nd ed. (Juta, Cape Town 1983) 37–40.
77. *Supra,* para. 8.
78. E.M. Burchell & P.M.A. Hunt, *South African Criminal Law and Procedure*, Vol. I *General Principles* 2nd ed. (Juta, Cape Town 1983) 43ff.
79. C.J.R. Dugard, *South African Criminal Law & Procedure*, Vol. IV *Introduction to Criminal Procedure* (Juta, Cape Town 1977) 33ff.
80. Taken over from the English law.
81. Juta, Cape Town 1917.

amongst the Afrikaans-speaking academic community by the appearance of treatises on South African criminal law which invoked Continental, especially German *Strafrechtswissenschaft* as the proper source and inspiration for the development of the South African criminal law.

65. The impetus for this development came from the writings of a number of South African academic lawyers trained in or conversant with Continental legal theory. Pre-eminent amongst these were Professors J. C. de Wet & H. L. Swanepoel, whose pioneering work *Strafreg* (1949)[82] would prove to be enormously influential in promoting the new direction for South African criminal law.[83]

IV. Criminal Law and Apartheid

66. In the course of the twentieth century, successive South African governments, pursuing policies of racial segregation, employed the sanctions of imprisonment and fines to enforce laws which imposed social and economic discrimination between the white and other races in this country. Under these laws, it became a crime for persons who were not white to enter urban areas;[84] to enter or use certain public facilities (public parks, beaches, theatres);[85] to occupy land in certain 'group' areas;[86] to be employed in certain jobs;[87] to possess intoxicating liquor;[88] and to marry or have a sexual relationship with a white person[89] (in this case the white person involved also committed a crime).

67. Resistance by the unenfranchised black people to discrimination, particularly in its guise as the official policy of 'apartheid', led to the enactment of various 'security' measures which conferred upon the police and the executive government extensive powers of arrest without warrant, detention without trial, indefinite incommunicado detention, house arrest and 'banning'.[90]

---

82. The latest edition of this work was J.C. de Wet, *De Wet & Swanepoel Strafreg* 4th ed. (Butterworths, Durban 1985).
83. For an appreciation of De Wet and his book, *see* 'Focus' (1991) 4 *SACJ* 123ff.
84. The offences were created by the Natives (Urban Areas) Act 25 of 1945.
85. The offences were created by the Reservation of Separate Amenities Act 49 of 1953. The Act was repealed in 1990.
86. The offences were created by the Group Areas Act 41 of 1950 and 36 of 1966. These Acts were repealed in 1991.
87. *See* C.J.R. Dugard, *Human Rights and the South African Legal Order* (Princeton, New Haven 1978) 86–87.
88. In terms of the Liquor Act 1928 and its successors.
89. *See* J.R.L. Milton, S.V. Hoctor & M.G. Cowling, *South African Criminal Law and Procedure*, Vol. III *Statutory Offences* 2nd ed. (Juta, Cape Town 1988) para. E3–2 for an account of this legislation, since repealed.
90. For a survey of these provisions, *see* A.S. Mathews, *Law, Order and Liberty* (Juta, Cape Town 1971); C.J.R. Dugard, *Human Rights and the South African Legal Order* (Princeton, New Haven, 1978); A.S. Mathews, *Freedom, State Security and the Rule of Law* (Juta, Cape Town 1986).

New 'security' crimes of 'sabotage', 'terrorism' and 'subversion' were created.[91] These were distinguished by excessively wide proscriptions and intractably vague language.[92] Their effect was to bring within the penal sanction a wide range of activities that would not otherwise be considered to be deserving of censure, never mind punishment.

68. By 1986, civil disorder had become endemic in some black townships and the government assumed greater powers by the declaration of a state of emergency. The police, aided in instances by militia, acted almost exclusively in terms of the extraordinary powers conferred under emergency regulations.[93]

In some areas, in the absence of a proper police force, vigilante groups emerged as surrogate agencies for law and order. Political and other disputes produced rival vigilante groups whose internecine differences exacerbated the violence and disorder within areas.[94] 'Peoples courts' emerged to undertake the administration of justice by way of settling disputes and punishing 'criminals'.[95]

69. In February 1990, a new era of political reform was introduced, which resulted not only in the termination of the state of emergency but also the removal of many of the racial crimes from the statute book.[96]

V. Post-Constitutional Jurisprudence

70. Since the dawn of constitutional supremacy in South Africa (in 1994),[97] the Bill of Rights has had a significant effect on criminal jurisprudence. In respect of sentencing, capital[98] and corporal[99] punishments have been struck down as unconstitutional forms of punishment, and it has been held that the inclusion of offenders aged 16 and 17 in the minimum sentencing legislation unjustifiably infringed the rights of a child in terms of section 28 of the Constitution.[100] Regarding procedural

91. For these crimes, *see* A.S. Mathews, *Freedom, State Security and the Rule of Law* (Juta, Cape Town 1971).
92. For further discussion of these crimes, *see* C.R. Snyman, *Criminal Law* (Butterworths, Durban 1984) 273ff, A.S. Mathews, *Freedom, State Security and the Rule of Law* (Juta, Cape Town 1971).
93. In terms of the Public Safety Act 1953. *See* E. Cameron & G. Marcus, 'The Administration of Justice, Law Reform and Jurisprudence' 1985 *Annual Survey of South African Law* 543ff.; E. Cameron, G. Marcus & D. Van Z. Smit, 'The Administration of Justice, Law Reform and Jurisprudence' 1986 *Annual Survey of South African Law* 545ff.
94. *See* C. Plasket, 'Sub-contracting the Dirty Work' 1989 *Acta Juridica* 165; N. Haysom et al., 'The Rise of Vigilantes' 1986 *SAJHR* 123–124, N. Haysom et al., 'Crossroads' 1986 *SAJHR* 256–257.
95. *See* W. Scharf, 'Community Policing in South Africa' 1989 *Acta Juridica* 225 et seq.; N. Haysom et al., 'People's Courts' 1986 *SAJHR* 113.
96. J. Burchell & J. Milton, *Principles of Criminal Law* (Juta, Cape Town 1991) 186.
97. *See infra*, para. 81.
98. *S v. Makwanyane* 1995 (2) SACR 1 (CC).
99. *S v. Williams* 1995 (2) SACR 251 (CC). *See*, *Christian Education South Africa v. Minister of Education* 2000 (4) SA 757 (CC) where a challenge to the prohibition on corporal punishment in schools, on the basis that this ban unjustifiably infringed the right to religious freedom, failed.
100. *Centre for Child Law v. Minister for Justice and Constitutional Development* 2009 (2) SACR 477 (CC).

criminal law, the rights of arrested, detained and accused persons are protected in terms of section 35 of the Constitution. In this regard, a number of statutory provisions which included a reverse onus have been struck down as unjustifiable breaches of the right to be presumed innocent until proven guilty.[101] The right to remain silent has been explicated by the Constitutional Court in *S v. Thebus*.[102] The exclusion of unconstitutionally obtained evidence is provided for in section 35(5) of the Constitution. Insofar as the substantive criminal law is concerned, the following provisions have been struck down as unconstitutional: the common-law crime of sodomy; the provisions of section 20A of the Sexual Offences Act of 1957;[103] the prohibition of the possession of indecent or obscene photographic matter;[104] the prohibition of public nudity on licensed premises;[105] the prohibition of deadly force in arrest;[106] the prohibition on the possession or cultivation of dagga for personal consumption by adults in private;[107] the imposition of criminal liability on children under the age of 16 years in relation to sections 15 and 16 of the Criminal Law (Sexual Offences and Related Matters) Amendment Act;[108] the criminalisation of the failure to give prior notice of a gathering;[109] aspects of the offence of incitement;[110] the defence of parental chastisement;[111] and the form of intimidation criminalised in section 1(1)(*b*) of the Intimidation Act.[112] In contrastthe constitutionality of the prohibition on making, distributing and possessing child pornography has been affirmed,[113] as have the crime of prostitution,[114] the crime of bestiality,[115] the common-purpose doctrine,[116] the crime of contempt of court *ex facie curiae* in the form of scandalising the court,[117] criminal defamation,[118] and fraud.[119] In respect of

---

101. *See* discussion by J. Burchell, *South African Criminal Law and Procedure*, Vol I *General Principles* 4th ed. (Juta, Cape Town 2011) 19–22.
102. *S v. Thebus* 2003 (6) SA 505 (CC); *see* P.J. Schwikkard, 'Arrested, Detained and Accused Persons' in I. Currie & J. de Waal, *The Bill of Rights Handbook* 6th ed. (Juta, Cape Town 2013) 758–768.
103. Act 23 of 1957.This provision criminalised homosexual conduct between males.
104. Indecent or Obscene Photographic Matter Act 37 of 1967, s. 2(1), in *Case v. Minister of Safety and Security; Curtis v. Minister of Safety and Security* 1996 (3) SACR 587 (CC).
105. Liquor Act 27 of 1989, s. 160(*d*), in *Phillips v. DPP, WLD* 2003 (1) SACR 425 (CC).
106. The original formulation was declared unconstitutional in *Ex parte Minister of Safety and Security: In re S v. Walters* 2002 (2) SACR 105 (CC).
107. In terms of ss 4(*b*) and 5(*b*) of the Drugs and Drug Trafficking Act 140 of 1992, in terms of *Minister of Justice and Constitutional Development v. Prince* 2019 (1) SACR 14 (CC).
108. Act 32 of 2007, in terms of *Teddy Bear Clinic for Abused Children v. Minister of Justice and Constitutional Development* 2014 (1) SACR 327 (CC).
109. Regulation of Gatherings Act 205 of 1993, s. 12(1)(*a*), in *S v. Mlungwana* 2019 (1) SACR 429 (CC).
110. In terms of the formulation in s. 18(2) of the Riotous Assemblies Act 17 of 1956, in terms of *Economic Freedom Fighters v. Minister of Justice and Correctional Services* [2020] ZACC 25.
111. *Freedom of Religion South Africa v. Minister of Justice and Constitutional Development* 2020 (1) SACR 113 (CC). *See infra*, para. 209.
112. *Moyo v. Minister of Police* 2020 (1) SACR 373 (CC).
113. Films and Publications Act 65 of 1996, s. 27, in *De Reuck v. DPP (WLD)* 2003 (2) SACR 445 (CC).
114. Sexual Offences Act 23 of 1957, s. 20(1)(*a*A), in *S v. Jordan* 2002 (2) SACR 499 (CC).
115. *S v. M* 2004 (1) SACR 228 (O).
116. *S v. Thebus supra; see infra*, paras 253–258.
117. *S v. Mamabolo* 2001 (1) SACR 686 (CC). The Constitutional Court however held that the summary procedure in terms of which a judge could summon a scandaliser to appear before him to answer the charge unjustifiably infringed the right to a fair trial.

the principle of legality, the Constitutional Court held in *Masiya v. DPP*[120] that the common-law crime of rape (defined in terms of vaginal penetration of a female) should be developed to include anal penetration of a female, but that this revised definition could not be applied retrospectively to the accused in this case.

§4. Sources of Criminal Law

I. International Sources

71. Customary international law forms part of South African law unless it is inconsistent with the Constitution or an Act of Parliament.[121] Thus, customary international law enjoys a status at least equal to that of legislation and the common law and should be treated accordingly by the courts.[122]

72. The negotiating and signing of all international agreements is the responsibility of the national executive.[123] An international agreement binds the Republic only after it has been approved by resolution in both the National Assembly and the National Council of Provinces.[124] The exception to this rule is if it is an international agreement of a technical, administrative or executive nature, or an agreement which does not require either ratification or accession, entered into by the national executive, which binds the Republic without approval by the National Assembly and the National Council of Provinces, but must be tabled in the Assembly and the Council within a reasonable time.[125] Any international agreement becomes law in the Republic when it is enacted into law by national legislation, but a self-executing provision of an agreement that has been approved by Parliament is law in the Republic unless it is inconsistent with the Constitution or an Act of Parliament.[126] The Republic is bound by international agreements which were binding on the Republic when the Constitution took effect.[127]

International treaties or conventions that are significant in relation to criminal law which have been incorporated into South African law are the conventions on

118. *S v. Hoho* 2009 (1) SACR 276 (SCA). This crime has however been repealed in terms of s. 34 of the Judicial Matters Amendment Act 15 of 2023.
119. *S v. Friedman* (1) 1996 (1) SACR 181 (W).
120. *Masiya v. DPP, Pretoria* 2007 (5) SA 30 (CC).
121. Constitution, 1996, s. 232; N.J. Botha, 'International Law' in W.A. Joubert (ed.), *Law of South Africa*, Vol. 11 2nd ed. (LexisNexis, Durban 2008) para. 452.
122. N.J. Botha, 'International Law' in W.A. Joubert (ed.), *Law of South Africa*, Vol. 11 2nd ed. (LexisNexis, Durban 2008) para. 452.
123. Constitution, 1996, s. 231(1).
124. Constitution, 1996, s. 231(2).
125. Constitution, 1996, s. 231(3).
126. Constitution, 1996, s. 231(4).
127. Constitution, 1996, s. 231(5).

offences committed aboard aircraft,[128] drug trafficking,[129] various extradition agreements[130] and those relating to the Rome Statute of the International Criminal Court.[131]

73. The South African government has acceded to the Charter of the United Nations, but the provisions of the charter have not been incorporated by legislation into South African law. South Africa has acceded to the Universal Declaration of Human Rights to the International Convention on Civil and Political Rights and the African Charter of Human and Peoples' Rights.

II. National Sources

74. The national sources of South African criminal law are the common law, the judgments of the High Court and the enactments of competent South African legislatures.

A. The Common Law

75. South African law is not codified. The principles and doctrines of the law are thus to be found in the common law. As regards the criminal law, the common law is the Roman-Dutch law as modified by English criminal law in the nineteenth century and expressed in the judgments of the courts and books of authority.

76. South African courts and academic writers, in expounding the criminal law, consult and cite as authoritative expositions of the common law the works of such writers as: J. Damhouder *Praxis Rerum Criminalium* (*Practycke in Criminele Saken*) (1660); A. Matthaeus II *De Criminibus* (1644); P. Bort *Tractaet van Crimineele Saecken* (1681); J. Moorman, *Verhandelinge over de Misdaden* (1674); J.M. Barels, *Crimineele Advysen* (1778); D.G. van der Keessel *Dicta ad Jus Criminale Libri 47 et 48 Digestorum* (c. 1770);[132] Johannes Voet *Commentarius ad Pandectas* (1698);[133] S. van Leeuwen *Het Roomsch-Hollandsch Recht* (1662);[134] Johannes van der Linden *Rechtsgeleerd Practicaal en Koopman's Handboek* (1806).[135]

---

128. Incorporated in the Civil Aviation Act 13 of 2009.
129. The Drug and Drug Trafficking Act 140 of 1992 gives effect to provisions of the United Nations Convention against Illicit Drug Traffic in Narcotic Drugs and Psychotropic Substances.
130. In terms of the Extradition Act 67 of 1962.
131. Ratified by South Africa on 10 Nov. 2000, *see* para. 371 *infra*.
132. These lectures were not published during Van der Keessel's lifetime. They were first published in an English translation, in six volumes, by B. Beinart and P. van Warmelo (Juta, Cape Town 1969–1981).
133. Translated into English under the title *The Selective Voet* by P.C. Gane (Butterworths, Durban 1955–1958).
134. Translated into English by J.G. Kotze under the title *Commentaries on Roman-Dutch Law* (Stevens and Sons, London 1886).
135. Translated into English by H. Juta under the title, *Institutes of Holland* (Juta, Cape Town 1891).

B. The Judgments of the High Court

77. Since South African criminal law is not codified, the doctrine of precedent (*stare decisis*) applies with full force in the South African judicial system. Judicial interpretations and applications of the common-law sources and penal statutory enactments are thus considered to be precedents binding upon lower courts. This is so only in the case of the decisions of the High Court; the judgments delivered in the inferior (i.e., magistrates' courts) are not considered to be precedents.[136]

As a result, the judgments of the various divisions of the High Court constitute an important and significant source of South African criminal law.

The judgments of the High Court in criminal cases are reported in the *South African Law Reports* and, since 1990, in the *South African Criminal Law Reports*. Previously, the *Prentice Hall Reports* contained criminal case reports; this series was discontinued in 1995. Criminal cases are also reported in the *All South African Law Reports* since 1996.

C. Legislation

78. The most prolific source of crimes in South African law is the legislation of various competent legislative organs.[137] These are:

1. the legislation of the legislatures of the colonies that in 1910 became the Union of South Africa;
2. the legislation of the Parliament of the Union and (after 1961) the Republic of South Africa;
3. the legislation of the Provincial Legislatures of the provinces of the Republic; and
4. the legislation of various subordinate legislatures exercising delegated powers of legislation.

79. Although various statutes were enacted during the period of the Dutch occupation of the Cape, none is any longer in force.

80. Legislation enacted by the various legislatures of the colonies and republics later formed into the Union of South Africa was and still is regarded as duly enacted legislation of a competent legislature.

Statutory offences enacted by these legislatures became part of the corpus of criminal law of the (Union and later the) Republic of South Africa. Much of the pre-Union legislation has now been repealed,[138] with the result that it is no longer a significant source of statutory offences.

136. *See* H.R. Hahlo & E. Kahn, *The South African Legal System and Its Background* (Juta, Cape Town 1968) 240ff.
137. *See*, on the legislative process, G.E. Devenish, *The South African Constitution* (LexisNexis, Durban 2005) 238ff.
138. Chiefly by the Pre-Union Statute Law Revision Acts of 1934, 1936, 1939, 1967, 1968, 1970, 1976, 1977, 1979.

81. The Parliament of the Union, later the Republic, of South Africa was established in 1910, since when it has enacted legislation in the form of Acts of Parliament. Constitutionally, the Republic of South Africa has, since the inception of constitutional democracy in 1994, abolished parliamentary sovereignty in favour of a system where the Constitution is supreme, and any legislation and executive conduct conflicting with the Constitution may be invalidated.

82. Provincial legislatures, termed provincial councils, were established in 1910 and abolished in 1986.[139] These councils were subordinate legislatures that exercised original plenary legislative powers. Termed 'ordinances', the enactments of a provincial council had the force of law only in the province in which enacted. Furthermore, provincial councils were empowered to legislate only in respect of certain determined matters. Provincial legislatures have been specifically empowered to legislate in certain areas of legislative competence in terms of the 1996 Constitution.

83. Parliament and the Provincial legislatures delegate legislative powers to various subordinate legislatures or officials. The legislation made by such subordinate legislators acting under the delegated authority takes the form of proclamations (normally made by the President) and regulations (normally made by Ministers for the implementation of acts of parliament).

84. A subordinate legislator, it has been held, may only enact criminal offences if the power to do so has been expressly included in the law-making powers devolved upon it.[140] The rationale of this restrictive construction of the effect of the delegation of law-making powers to subordinate legislators is a concern for the liberty of the subject.[141]

85. However, whether this means that there exists an inflexible principle that a subordinate legislator does not have the power to make non-compliance with its enactments a criminal offence unless expressly empowered to do so by the enabling legislation has been doubted.[142] It has been held in some cases that the power to enact criminal sanctions was a necessary implication of the delegation of legislative powers upon a subordinate legislature.[143]

§5. Classifications and Technique

86. South Africa has not codified its criminal law. As a result, it knows no distinction between general and specific criminal law. In the South African system,

139. By the Provincial Government Act 69 of 1986.
140. *R v. Magano* 1924 TPD 129; *R v. De Beer* 1930 TPD 329. *See* Constitution, 1996, s. 156.
141. *R v. De Beer* (*supra*) 334.
142. *R v. Parsotam* 1949 (4) SA 315 (N) 327.
143. As in *Hleka v. Johannesburg City Council* 1949 (1) SA 842 (A) 854–855; *Lekhari v. Johannesburg City Council* 1956 (1) SA 522 (A).

criminal law has its origins in either the common law or in the enactments of competent legislatures.[144] In South African law, there is nothing of any particular significance in the distinction between common law and statutory criminal law[145] and thus no particular techniques of construction or interpretation are required in this connection.

144. *Supra*, para. 74.
145. E.M. Burchell & P.M.A. Hunt, *South African Criminal Law and Procedure*, Vol. I *General Principles* 2nd ed. (Juta, Cape Town 1983) 93.

Part I. Substantive Criminal Law

Chapter 1. General Principles

§1. The Principle of Legality

87. The principle of legality as expressed in the maxim *nullum crimen, nulla poena sine lege* is fundamental to South African criminal law.[146] The principle is, moreover, recognised in the right to a fair trial set out in section 35 of the Constitution.[147] The principle is applied in the following forms.

I. Limitation on Penalisation

A. Nullum Crimen Sine Lege

88. The *nullum crimen sine lege* principle derives from European sources, and is at the core of the rule of law, and is basic to respect for human dignity.[148] Underlying this principle is the policy concern that criminal law rules should be as clear and precise as possible so that it is possible to find out, with reasonable ease and in advance, how to behave so as to avoid committing a crime.[149]

89. In South African criminal law, the principle *nullum crimen sine lege* applies insofar as it is commonly understood that there can be no conviction in a criminal court except if the conduct in question has previously been declared to be a crime either at common law or by statute. In practical terms, what the principle means is that the list of common-law crimes is closed. It follows that the courts thus lack the

146. *See*, J. Burchell, *Principles of Criminal Law* 5th ed. (Juta, Cape Town 2016) 35ff.; S.V. Hoctor, *Snyman's Criminal Law* 7th ed. (LexisNexis, Durban 2020) 31ff.
147. Constitution, 1996, s. 35(3)(*l*) provides for the right not to be convicted for an act or omission that was not an offence either under national or international law at the time it was committed or omitted (applied in *Masiya v. DPP, Pretoria* 2007 (5) SA 30 (CC)); and s. 35(3)(*n*) provides that an accused person has the right to the benefit of the least severe of the prescribed punishments if the prescribed punishment for the offence has been changed between the time that the offence was committed and the time of sentencing.
148. J. Burchell, *South African Criminal Law and Procedure*, Vol. 1 *General Principles of Criminal Law* 4th ed. (Juta, Cape Town 2011) 35.
149. S.V. Hoctor, *Snyman's Criminal Law* 7th ed. (LexisNexis, Durban 2020) 32.

power to create new crimes and, furthermore, there can be no conviction except under the provisions of a valid statute which explicitly creates a punishable offence.

90. The definitions of the common-law crimes find their authoritative expression in the decisions of the courts and books of authority. Since judges and scholars may differ in their interpretation or understanding of these sources as they relate to the existence of a crime, or definition of the elements of a crime, there always exists a measure of uncertainty as to the exact ambit or scope of a common-law crime.[150]

This presents a difficulty when it comes to the question of applying common-law crimes to novel situations. Thus, for instance, the common-law sources for definition of the crime of defeating the administration of justice, which are derived from early Roman law, make no provision for the obstruction of the police in the course of the performance of their duties. The South African courts have held that obstruction of the police amounts to the common-law offence of defeating the administration of justice,[151] though not without protest[152] that this amounts to a violation of the principle of legality.

91. In approaching the issue of the adaption of the common-law crimes to the needs of a modern society, the courts observe the following principles: the existing definitions of common-law crimes should not be replaced by new or different definitions;[153] in cases of conflict or uncertainty, the interpretation that favours the established definition of the crime or an element should be preferred;[154] the use of analogy so as to extend the definition of a crime to include similar conduct must be avoided; where there are lacunae in the law, the courts should not usurp the function of parliament nor rush in where the legislator declines to tread.[155] It remains to be seen to what extent courts in South Africa will go in developing the common law in order to bring it into line with the Constitution, remembering that the principle of legality is also an integral part of the Constitution.[156]

92. Furthermore, South African law treats the principle of legality as establishing the principle that only the legislature is capable of creating new crimes.[157] Thus, the only source of new crimes in modern South African law is a legislative act of a competent legislature.

It follows from this principle that in regard to statutory offences, *nullum crimen sine lege* means that in order for persons to be liable to punishment, they shall have contravened the provisions of an *existing* statute that is *in force* and has *expressly penalised* the contravention.

---

150. S.V. Hoctor, *Snyman's Criminal Law* 7th ed. (LexisNexis, Durban 2020) 38.
151. *S v. Greenstein* 1973 (3) SA 220 (RA); *S v. Burger* 1975 (2) SA 601 (C).
152. *S v. Burger* (*supra*) 622H–623.
153. *S v. Sibiya* 1955 (4) SA 247 (A) 256.
154. *Ex parte the Minister van Justisie: in re S v. von Molendorff* 1989 (4) SA 1028 (A).
155. *S v. Sibiya* 1955 (4) SA 247 (A) 256H.
156. *See*, J. Burchell, *Principles of Criminal Law* 5th ed. (Juta, Cape Town 2016) 41–46, and S.V. Hoctor, *Snyman's Criminal Law* 7th ed. (LexisNexis, Durban 2020) 39–41, for a discussion of this question in the light of the case of *Masiya v. DPP, Pretoria* 2007 (5) SA 30 (CC).
157. S.V. Hoctor, *Snyman's Criminal Law* 7th ed. (LexisNexis, Durban 2020) 34.

93. In principle, the absence of a criminalisation clause in a statutory offence indicates that the enactment in question does not create an offence. Unfortunately for the integrity of the principle of legality, the South African courts have on occasion been prepared to construe an enactment that lacks a criminalisation clause as nevertheless creating an offence where the act is definitely prohibited in a manner which renders it clear that the legislature was not exhorting or advising.[158]

This approach has, however, been much criticised[159] and is unlikely to be followed in the future.

B. Nullum Crimen Sine Poena

94. Since, without the liability to punishment, there would be no distinction between penal and non-penal laws, it has thus been held that 'to render any act criminal in our law, there must be some punishment affixed to the commission of the act and where no law exists affixing such punishment there is no crime in law'.[160]

Thus, the attachment of a penalty to a prohibited act has the effect of making it a crime even if the legislature does not call it such.[161] Accordingly, where the legislature merely prohibits an act or omission without expressly characterising it as an offence and does not provide a penalty for transgression, the prohibition will be considered not to create a crime.[162]

95. However, the fact that the legislature does not specify what the punishment is for an offence is not regarded as a serious flaw in the legislation. In such a case, it is presumed that the determination of the appropriate punishment has been left to the courts.[163]

C. Nulla Poena Sine Lege

96. The punishment for common-law crimes, according to South African law, is at the discretion of the judge. In this sense, South African law does not conform to the requirement of the principle of legality. However, there is a good reason for this:

---

158. *R v. Forlee* 1917 TPD 52.
159. *See* J. Burchell, *Principles of Criminal Law* 5th ed. (Juta, Cape Town 2016) 38; S.V. Hoctor, *Snyman's Criminal Law* 7th ed. (LexisNexis, Durban 2020) 36.
160. *R v. Carto* 1917 EDL 87 95.
161. *R v. Frederiks* 1923 TPD 350 353.
162. M.A. Rabie, 'Criteria for the Identification and Creation of Crimes' 1977 SACC 93 98.
163. Cf. *R v. Forlee* (*supra*) 55. In *DPP, Western Cape v. Prins* 2012 (2) SACR 183 (SCA) it was held that s. 276 of the Criminal Procedure Act 51 of 1977, which provides for a number of listed sentences which a person may receive upon conviction, is a general provision empowering courts to impose sentences in respect of all crimes, both common-law and statutory, where no other provision exists prescribing the sentence for a particular crime. Thus, it appears from this judgment that the principle of legality has been complied with in the absence of such a penalty clause, provided that it is clear that the prohibition is described as an offence and that parliament intended to create an offence. *See* S.V. Hoctor, *Snyman's Criminal Law* 7th ed. (LexisNexis, Durban 2020) 35.

the courts must have a discretion in sentencing an offender to take into account a variety of factors relating to his own and society's welfare and they must be free even to impose no punishment at all if that is desirable.[164]

97. In the case of statutory crimes, the maximum punishment that may be imposed is usually prescribed in the statute, a practice that at least ensures that the likely punishment for a contravention is known in advance.

Although statutory maxima may be desirable in order to prevent arbitrariness, compulsory minimum punishments have not found favour with the judiciary.[165]

II. Legality and Interpretation

98. The doctrine of legality, in relation to penal statutes, invokes the principle that in the interpretation of such statutes, a 'strict' construction ought to be adopted. The rationale for this approach is that strict construction is an aspect of the principle that the legislature and not the courts should create crimes. Under this rule, it is necessary for the courts to construe penal enactments strictly (rather than broadly) lest they create crimes not intended by the legislature. Further, the doctrine of legality in the form *nullum crimen sine lege* requires that persons not be subjected to penal sanctions without proper warning through duly enacted laws. Where an enactment is vague or ambiguous in this regard, a strict construction reveals whether the enactment provides proper notice of that which it purports to prohibit.

99. Although the modern approach to the interpretation of penal statutes rejects strict construction as an arbitrary requirement of the process of construction of penal statutes in favour of an approach that honestly seeks to give effect to the intention of the legislature (whatever that may be), this does not preclude the strict construction of penal enactments.[166]

§2. The Principle of the Individual Guilty Mind

100. As a general rule, South African law faithfully observes the general doctrine that '*actus non facit reum, nisi mens sit rea* '. *Mens rea* in the form of intention

164. J. Burchell, *Principles of Criminal Law* 3rd ed. (Juta, Cape Town 2005) 103; S.V. Hoctor, *Snyman's Criminal Law* 7th ed. (LexisNexis, Durban 2020) 41.
165. *See* the strong criticism of the mandatory penalties in the *Report of the Committee of Enquiry into the Penal System of South Africa* RP 78/1976 (Government Printer, Pretoria 1976) para. 5.1.4.3. 64–72, and the re-emphasis on the importance of judicial discretion in sentencing in *S v. Malgas* 2001 (1) SACR 469 (SCA) and *S v. Dodo* 2001 (3) SA 382 (CC). *See* J. Burchell, *Principles of Criminal Law* 3rd ed. (Juta, Cape Town 2005) 91–93. For discussion of mandatory and minimum sentence legislation, *see infra*, paras 393–396.
166. J.R.L. Milton, S.V. Hoctor & M.G. Cowling, *South African Criminal Law and Procedure*, Vol. III *Statutory Offences* 2nd ed. (Juta, Cape Town 1988) 1:29ff.

is recognised as an essential element of all common-law crimes, apart from culpable homicide[167] and where editors of newspapers are charged with contempt of court.[168]

In the case of statutory offences, the South African law, imitating English law, for some decades applied forms of strict liability in the case of so-called public welfare or regulatory offences. In recent times, the courts, in construing statutory offences, have turned against strict liability in the form of liability without proof of *mens rea* in favour of liability based on negligence.[169]

101. Notwithstanding the fact that a corporation has an artificial legal personality, it is possible in South African law to convict a corporation of a crime for which a guilty mind is required. This is achieved by imputing the guilty mind of the directors or servants of the corporation, to the corporation.[170]

§3. Vicarious Liability

102. The insistence on *mens rea* as an element of liability means that there is no vicarious liability for common-law crimes.[171] However, there are certain statutory provisions which impose vicarious liability upon certain employers for the acts of their employees.[172]

§4. The Principle of Proportionality

103. The principle that punishment should be proportional to the crime and the degree of culpability of the criminal is a feature of the South African criminal law. There is, however, no formal statutory statement of the principle and its application is found mainly in the expositions of judges and academics in relation to the nature of the sentencing process.[173] It has been held by the Constitutional Court that the concept of proportionality goes to the heart of the inquiry as to whether punishment is cruel, inhuman or degrading.[174] Thus, the principle of proportionality is central to an assessment of the constitutionality of a particular sentence.

---

167. *See infra*, para. 280.
168. *See infra*, para. 364.
169. J.R.L. Milton, S.V. Hoctor & M.G. Cowling, *South African Criminal Law and Procedure*, Vol. III *Statutory Offences* 2nd ed. (Juta & Co, Cape Town 1988) paras 2–22 to 2–26.
170. *See infra*, para. 113.
171. S.V. Hoctor, *Snyman's Criminal Law* 7th ed. (LexisNexis, Durban 2020) 212.
172. *See*, J.R.L. Milton, S.V. Hoctor & M.G. Cowling, *South African Criminal Law and Procedure*, Vol. III *Statutory Offences* 2nd ed. (Juta & Co., Cape Town 1988) paras 2–58ff.
173. Cf. M.A. Rabie & S.A. Strauss, *Punishment: An Introduction to Principles* 2nd ed. (Lex Patria, Pretoria 1985) Ch. 5; S.S. Terblanche, *Guide to Sentencing in South Africa* 3rd ed. (LexisNexis, Durban 2016) 182–183.
174. *S v. Dodo* 2001 (3) SA 382 (CC) para. 37.

Chapter 2. Scope of Application of Criminal Law

§1. Principles Concerning the Applicability of the Criminal Law with Respect to Time

I. Prohibition of Retroactive Criminal Law

104. South African law upholds the prohibition against *ex post facto* penal laws; there can be no punishment imposed *retrospectively*.

105. Judicial decisions concerning conduct are always made *ex post facto* and thus inevitably operate with retrospective effect. This being so, the invention or recognition by the courts of a crime that was not previously known to the legal system constitutes an instance of retrospective law-making.

In modern law, the courts generally recognise that the constitutional doctrine of separation of powers prohibits judges from making law and thus from creating new crimes.

106. Although the legislature is nowadays the sole crime-making organ of government, it is required by the principle of legality to observe the safeguard of prospectivity by abstaining from creating retrospective crimes.

Breaches of this branch of *nullum crimen sine lege* have been rare in South Africa. The right to a fair trial in the Constitution now specifically renders retroactive criminal provisions invalid.[175]

§2. Principles Concerning the Applicability of the Criminal Law with Respect to Space

I. Territoriality Principle

107. In principle, a violation of the South African criminal law (common law or statutory) committed by any person, whether a South African citizen or foreign national, within the geographical boundaries of the Republic of South Africa, is punishable by the South African courts of criminal jurisdiction. In this regard, the South African law observes the principle of territoriality.[176] Accordingly, and as a general rule, the criminal jurisdiction of the South African courts does not extend to encompass crimes committed outside the geographical boundaries of the country.

108. For these purposes, the boundaries of the country extend beyond the visible coastline to include the *territorial waters* which extend for a distance of 12 nautical miles from the baselines.[177]

---

175. Constitution, 1996, s. 35(3)(*l*).
176. A.V. Lansdown & J. Campbell, *South African Criminal Law and Procedure*, Vol. V *Criminal Procedure and Evidence* (Juta, Cape Town 1982) 7.
177. Maritime Zones Act, 15 of 1994, s. 4.

109. A version of the territoriality principle applies to the provincial divisions of the South African High Court. In principle, the High Court enjoys, at common law, inherent jurisdiction to try all criminal matters. This jurisdiction may be qualified by legislation. In South Africa, the criminal jurisdiction of each division is limited by the provisions of the Superior Courts Act 2013[178] to the area determined to be under the jurisdiction of a division by the Minister of Justice.[179]

110. The place where a crime is committed determines jurisdiction over the crime. Thus, if a crime is commenced in one province but completed in another, the latter will have jurisdiction in respect of the crime.[180]

111. Where an accused is arraigned before a division which has no territorial jurisdiction, he may plead lack of jurisdiction, and if the plea is upheld, the case must be adjourned to a court which has jurisdiction.[181] The NDPP may, if he 'deems it to be in the interests of the administration of justice', direct that an offence committed within one provincial jurisdiction should be transferred for trial to another provincial jurisdiction.[182]

II. Extra-Territorial Criminal Jurisdiction

112. The intra-territorial operation of the South African criminal law is, however, not absolute and certain common-law and statutory crimes have an extra-territorial application. The crimes concerned are.

Treason: Treason is an exception to the general rule that a State will punish only crimes committed within its own territory.[183] The rule is therefore that the South African courts have jurisdiction to try treason against the South African State committed anywhere in the world.

Official secrets: Under the Protection of Information Act,[184] any offence under the Act which is committed outside the Republic by any South African citizen or any person domiciled in the Republic is deemed to have been committed in the Republic.[185]

Terrorism offences: In terms of the Protection of Constitutional Democracy Against Terrorist and Related Activities Act 2004,[186] South African courts, *inter*

178. Act 10 of 2013, s. 6(3).
179. A similar principle applies in respect of magistrates' courts, but in a qualified form. *See infra*, para. 417.
180. A.V. Lansdown & J. Campbell, *South African Criminal Law and Procedure*, Vol. V *Criminal Procedure and Evidence* (Juta, Cape Town 1982) 5.
181. *Infra*, para. 424.
182. *See infra*, para. 425.; Criminal Procedure Act 51 of 1977, s. 111.
183. J.J. Joubert et al., *Criminal Procedure Handbook* 13th ed. (Juta, Cape Town 2020) 43.
184. The Protection of Information Act 84 of 1982.
185. Section 11(1).
186. Act 33 of 2004.

alia, have extra-territorial jurisdiction with regard to offences under the Act committed against the Republic, a citizen of the Republic or a person ordinarily resident in the Republic.[187]

Corruption: South African courts have jurisdiction in respect of any contravention of the Prevention and Combating of Corrupt Activities Act 2004[188] committed outside the Republic.[189]

Cybercrimes: In terms of the Cybercrimes Act 2020,[190] South African courts, *inter alia*, have extra-territorial jurisdiction with regard to offences under the Act committed against the Republic, a citizen of the Republic, a person ordinarily resident in the Republic, any company or body of persons in the Republic, and any restricted computer system contemplated in the Act.[191]

South African ships and aircraft: South African courts have jurisdiction in respect of offences committed aboard South African ships[192] or South African aircraft.[193]

Antarctica: South African courts have jurisdiction in respect of any crimes committed by a South African citizen in Antarctica.[194]

§3. Principles Concerning the Applicability of the Criminal Law with Respect to Person

I. Corporations

113. Since a company, as an artificial legal person, has neither body to be kicked nor soul to be damned, there is in principle a difficulty in subjecting companies (and other corporations) to the ordinary principles and procedures of the criminal process. South African law has overcome these problems by way of statutory provisions which enable the prosecution of corporations.

Section 332(1) of the Criminal Procedure Act 1977 provides that:

> For the purpose of imposing upon a corporate body criminal liability for any offence, whether under any law or at common law –
>
> > any act performed, with or without a particular intent, by or on instructions or with permission, express or implied, given by a director or servant of that corporate body; and

187. Section 15(1)(*b*)(iv).
188. Act 12 of 2004.
189. Section 35.
190. Act 19 of 2020.
191. Section 24(1)(*f*). The extra-territorial application of the Act recognises the inherently transnational nature of cybercrime. South Africa is a signatory to, and has been invited to accede to, the Budapest Convention – the Council of Europe Cybercrime Convention – but has yet to do so.
192. Merchant Shipping Act 57 of 1951, s. 327. *See*, A.V. Lansdown & J. Campbell, *South African Criminal Law & Procedure*, Vol. V *Criminal Procedure and Evidence* (Juta, Cape Town 1982) 14ff.
193. Civil Aviation Act 13 of 2009, s. 150.
194. South African Citizens in Antarctica Act 55 of 1962. *See*, Lansdown & Campbell, *supra* 18.

the omission, with or without a particular intent, of any act which ought to have been but was not performed by or on instructions given by a director or servant of that corporate body,

in the exercise of his powers or in the performance of his duties as such director or servant or in furthering or endeavouring to further the interests of that corporate body, shall be deemed to have been performed (and with the same intent, if any) by that corporate body or, as the case may be, to have been an omission (and with the same intent, if any) on the part of that corporate body.

What this means is that a company can be convicted of a crime on the basis that the unlawful conduct required for liability is supplied by the unlawful act or omission of its director or servant and the *mens rea* required is supplied by the guilty mind of the director or servant.[195]

II. Immunities Based on National Public Law

114. In South African law, in principle, all persons are obliged to obey the law and no persons are thus immune from prosecution for a contravention of the criminal law. In this regard, South African law does not subscribe to the English law doctrine of sovereign immunity from prosecution.[196] Accordingly, as a general principle, neither the head of state nor the servants of the state enjoy immunity from prosecution for contravention of the criminal law. An exception to this principle is where a crime is defined in terms that exclude the State or its agents as persons capable of committing the crime.[197] Likewise, a penal statute may not bind the State,[198] in which event the agents or servants of the State,[199] if authorised by the State, may contravene the statute with impunity.[200]

115. Members of the National Assembly, the National Council of Provinces and the provincial legislatures, by statute, enjoy special immunities from criminal proceedings in order to allow them to carry out their duties properly.

Section 6 of the Powers, Privileges and Immunities of Parliament and Provincial Legislatures Act[201] provides that there is freedom of speech in the proceedings of Parliament. In terms of section 58(1) of the Constitution, members of the National Assembly have freedom of speech in the House, and in terms of section 71(1) of

195. *See*, J. Burchell, *Principles of Criminal Law* 5th ed. (Juta, Cape Town 2016) 455–467.
196. *S v. Ohlenschlager* 1992 (1) SACR 695 (T) 757.
197. *S v. Ohlenschlager* (*supra*) 757.
198. There is a presumption in South African law that the state is not bound by a statute: *Administrator, Cape v. Raats, Röntgen & Vermeulen (Pty) Ltd* 1992 (1) SA 245 (A) 262A-D. The question has been raised whether this presumption should change in the light of the Constitution – *see*, L.M. du Plessis, 'Statutory Interpretation' 2nd ed. in W.A. Joubert (ed), *The Law of South Africa* Vol. 25(1) (LexisNexis, Durban 2011) para. 339.
199. *S v. Reed* 1972 (2) SA 35 (RA) 65.
200. *S v. De Bruin* 1975 (3) SA 56 (T).
201. Act 4 of 2004.

the Constitution, members of the National Council of Provinces enjoy similar privileges. Thus, in terms of these provisions of the Constitution those who have freedom of speech in the respective Houses and committees are not liable to civil or criminal proceedings, arrest, imprisonment or damages for: (i) anything that they have said in, produced before or submitted to the relevant House or any of its committees; or (ii) anything revealed as a result of anything that they have said in, produced before or submitted to the House or any of its committees.

116. It may happen that a person who is beyond the geographical jurisdiction of the South African courts is arrested and brought within the territory over which the court has jurisdiction. The South African Appellate Division decided, following the doctrines of the Roman-Dutch law, that if the detention and relocation of the subject are unlawful, his presence within the territory does not confer jurisdiction upon the court.[202]

III. Immunities Based on International Public Law

117. Foreign heads of state enjoy immunity from criminal proceedings in accordance with established custom of international law, enshrined in the Diplomatic Immunities and Privileges Act.[203]

118. Immunity from criminal prosecution is also granted to special envoys from any state or government or organisation and members of the diplomatic missions of foreign states.[204]

202. *Infra*, para. 423.
203. Act 37 of 2001, s. 4.
204. Determined by the provisions of the Diplomatic Immunities and Privileges Act 37 of 2001. In terms of s. 3 of the Act, the Vienna Convention on Diplomatic Relations of 1961 is applicable to diplomatic missions and members of such missions and the Vienna Convention on Consular Relations of 1963 is applicable to consular posts and members of such posts.

Chapter 3. General Principles of Liability

§1. Introduction: The Basic Elements of Criminal Offences

119. South African criminal law follows the traditional practice of the Western European legal systems in predicating liability to punishment as based upon certain general principles of liability which must rigorously be applied as the necessary means of determining whether (or not) an accused person is guilty of the crime charged and thus liable to be punished.

120. Historically, the South African law followed the usage, taken over specifically from the English law, of stating criminal liability to consist of the elements of an *actus reus* accompanied by *mens rea*. These concepts, in South African law, more or less exactly approximated the Continental concepts of the material and moral prerequisites for criminal liability. Thus, in South African law, the *actus reus* element requires a voluntary human act that brings about a consequence or is a circumstance prohibited by the criminal law. *Mens rea* requires a 'guilty' state of mind, which, for these purposes, is established by proving 'intention' or, in the case of certain crimes, 'negligence'.

121. In recent years, under the influence of Continental theories of criminal law, writers – and with increasing frequency, the courts – are postulating additional constitutive elements of liability in the form of a requirement of 'unlawfulness', an element which relates to the possibility that an *actus reus* might be legally justified or excused and thus not deserving of punishment. In addition, contemporary South African criminal law postulates as an essential element of liability, forming part of the *mens rea*, a requirement that the accused, at the time he performed the *actus reus*, should have possessed the mental quality of 'insight' into the unlawfulness of his conduct and the capacity to 'control' his conduct according to this insight. This latter element is conceived as something distinct from *mens rea* and is described as 'criminal capacity' (a concept better identified by the Afrikaans term *toerekenings-vatbaarheid*).

122. In the result the current doctrine in South African criminal law is that the general principles of criminal liability consist of the following more or less distinct and separable elements: (1) *actus reus*: a voluntary human act, (2) which act is unlawful, and (3) is performed by a person having criminal capacity (*mens rea*), and (4) with a mental element, consisting of intention (in some cases negligence) in which is incorporated a requirement of knowledge of the unlawfulness of the act (in Afrikaans: '*wederregtelikheidsbewussyn*').[205]

123. In this chapter, this fourfold division of the general principles of liability will be observed and the principles considered under the four headings here set out.

205. J. Burchell, *Principles of Criminal Law* 5th ed. (Juta, Cape Town 2016) 51; S.V. Hoctor, *Snyman's Criminal Law* 7th ed. (LexisNexis, Durban 2020) 25–30.

The next chapter will consider the 'defences' to liability in the sense of the factors or considerations which may excuse or justify the occurrence or presence of one or other element of liability.

§2. THE MATERIAL OR PHYSICAL ELEMENT (ACTUS REUS)

I. Description

124. In order for there to be criminal liability, it must be proved that the accused had performed an act voluntarily, which act brings about a consequence or creates a circumstance, which consequence or circumstance complies with the formal description of the prohibition penalised by common law or by statute.

125. The act will only give rise to criminal liability if it conforms with the description of the prohibition contained in the relevant definition of the crime. Thus, where a statute prohibits the possession of indecent 'photographic' matter, the possession of a *photocopy* that is indecent does not give rise to criminal liability since the accused did not possess what was forbidden by the statute.[206]

126. The description of the prohibition is a description of the act or omission that is prohibited (e.g., 'buying' drugs, 'driving' a vehicle, 'failing' to render a tax return).

127. The act constituting the description of the prohibition gives rise to liability only if it is *a voluntary human act*. This means that it is essential that the accused performed some physical bodily movement, which movement was directed by the free will of the actor.

II. Acts, Omissions and Causation

A. *Human Act*

128. In principle, an act constituting the description of the prohibition will only give rise to liability where it is performed by a *human being*. The question whether an artificial legal person such as a corporation or *universitas* could thus be convicted of a crime is resolved, in South African law, by a statutory provision which allows a corporate body to be convicted of crimes committed by persons acting in their capacities as directors or servants of the corporation.[207]

129. Apart from this exception allowing artificial legal persons to be held criminally liable, the act must be a human act; that is, the subject of the act must be a

206. *S v. Smith* 1973 (3) SA 945 (O).
207. *See supra,* para. 113.

human being. A human being can however be punished if she commits a crime through the instrumentality of an animal.[208]

B. Voluntary Act

130. To give rise to liability, a physical human movement must be voluntary in the sense that it is controlled by the accused's conscious will.[209] Involuntary movement is not an act for the purposes of criminal liability.[210]

An act is involuntary if it occurs during sleep,[211] black-out,[212] or is the result of concussion,[213] hypoglycaemia,[214] intoxication,[215] or provocation.[216]

These conditions are sometimes rather simplistically grouped under the heading of 'automatism', a term which is more descriptive of the symptoms of involuntary actions than definitive of the condition that produces involuntary acts. Automatism may be due to mental illness and the defence is then called 'insane' automatism.[217]

C. Commission and Omissions

131. As a general rule, criminal liability only arises in respect of a voluntary act of *commission*. However, South African law does, in certain circumstances, impose liability in the absence of a positive act. This is so where the person has omitted to act when under a duty to do so. South African law has identified a number of facts or relationships which are considered to give rise to a duty to act and, accordingly, criminal liability for an omission to act. These particular cases have been characterised as instances of a general duty to act which is determined by what is referred to as 'the legal convictions of the community'.[218]

132. An omission will give rise to liability under the following circumstances.

---

208. S.V. Hoctor, *Snyman's Criminal Law* 7th ed. (LexisNexis, Durban 2020) 45; *S v. Thody* 1971 (2) SA 213 (N).
209. *R v. Mkhize* 1959 (2) SA 260 (N). Thus, *vis absoluta* (absolute force), which exceeds one's ability to subject one's bodily movements to one's will, negates the voluntariness of an action – *see* S.V. Hoctor, *Snyman's Criminal Law* 7th ed. (LexisNexis, Durban 2020) 46.
210. *R v. Mkhize* (*supra*). Amnesia *ex post facto* is not determinative of involuntary conduct – *S v. Humphreys* 2013 (2) SACR 1 (SCA) paras 10–11; S.V. Hoctor, 'Amnesia and Criminal Responsibility' 2000 *SACJ* 273.
211. *S v. Naidoo* 1971 (3) SA 605 (N) 607E.
212. *R v. Du Plessis* 1950 (1) SA 297 (O); *S v. Evans* 1985 (2) SA 865 (ZS).
213. *R v. Smit* 1950 (4) 165 (O) 167–168.
214. *S v. Stellmacher* 1983 (2) SA 181 (SWA).
215. *S v. Chretien* 1981 (1) SA 1097 (A) 1104E–F.
216. *S v. Arnold* 1985 (3) SA 256 (C) 263.
217. This terminology does not accord with practice in psychiatry, and it is preferable to refer to this situation as automatism resulting from pathological causes – *see* J. Burchell, *South African Criminal Law and Procedure,* Vol. I 4th ed. (Juta, Cape Town 2011) 69.
218. *Minister van Polisie v. Ewels* 1975 (3) SA 590 (A); *S v. A* 1991 (2) SACR 247 (N).

A special or protective relationship towards another, such as that between parent and child,[219] policeman[220] (or gaoler)[221] and prisoner, may create liability for an omission to act. A person holding a public office may, by virtue of the office, be under a duty to act.[222]

The duty to act may be imposed by statute, as in the case of failure to support children,[223] to report instances of child abuse,[224] or the use of drugs or trafficking in drugs,[225] or failing to stop after a motor accident.[226]

Liability may arise from a prior dangerous act on the part of the offender. Where a person has through his own conduct created a potentially dangerous situation, a failure to prevent the danger from materialising (*omissio per commissionem*) may give rise to liability.[227] Similarly, the assumption of control of a potentially dangerous thing or animal which may cause harm unless precautions are taken gives rise to a duty to act in protection of third parties.[228]

Omission liability could also be based on a rule of the common law, an order of court, or an agreement.[229]

D. *Causation*

133. South African criminal law classifies descriptions of prohibitions contained in the material element of liability as proscribing either a particular factual circumstance (being drunk, being in possession of drugs) (so-called crimes of circumstance) or a particular condition (death, physical harm) which is the consequence of a voluntary human act (so-called crimes of consequence).

What distinguishes these two classes of crime from the point of view of the elements of criminal liability is that in the case of the crimes of consequence, it is necessary to prove that not only was there a voluntary human act but, in addition, that the act brought about the consequence which is proscribed in the definition of the crime in question. In short, it must be proved that the voluntary act of the accused 'caused' a prohibited consequence. If such a connection cannot be established, the voluntary act cannot give rise to criminal liability.

134. Thus, in South African law, in the case of crimes of consequence, it is an essential requirement for liability that it be proved that the accused's *actus* was the

---

219. *R v. Chenjere* 1960 (1) SA 473 (FC).
220. *Minister of Police v. Skosana* 1977 (1) SA 31 (A); *S v. A* 1991 (2) SACR 247 (N).
221. *Mtati v. Minister of Justice* 1958 (1) SA 221 (A).
222. *S v. Gaba* 1981 (3) SA 745 (O) (police officer deliberately failing to identify a criminal).
223. Children's Act 38 of 2005, s. 305(4).
224. Children's Act 38 of 2005, s. 110 (read with s. 305(1)(*c*)), requires, *inter alia*, a dentist, medical practitioner or nurse who suspects that a child has been ill-treated or abused to make a report to the authorities.
225. Drugs and Drug Trafficking Act 140 of 1992, s. 10. *See infra* para. 334.
226. National Road Traffic Act 93 of 1996, s. 61(1).
227. *S v. Russell* 1967 (3) SA 739 (N) 743H.
228. *S v. Fernandez* 1966 (2) SA 259 (A).
229. S.V. Hoctor, *Snyman's Criminal Law* 7th ed. (LexisNexis, Durban 2020) 50–51.

cause of the prohibited consequence. If such causation is not proved then, subject to one exception,[230] there can be no liability and the accused cannot be convicted.[231]

135. This being so, it becomes necessary, in any given case, to be able to determine whether a given consequence (say, death) was a result of the voluntary act of the accused person. South African law approaches this aspect of criminal liability by applying so-called tests of causation. The purpose of the test (or tests) is to provide the court with the forensic materials for analysing the factual complex so as to reach the conclusion whether the act of the accused was the cause of the prohibited consequence.

136. In South African law, there is general agreement that the principal test of causation is based on the doctrine of *condictio sine qua non*.[232] Also referred to as the test of 'factual causation', this test is applied as preliminary determinant of whether an act is the cause of a consequence. Where the conduct in question takes the form of a positive act, the test requires the court to ask whether 'but for' the act of the accused would the consequence in question have occurred at all or when it did? Put another way, the test is that an act is a cause of a consequence if the act cannot be notionally eliminated from the sequence of events, without the consequence also disappearing. The court has, therefore, to engage in a process of hypothetical elimination in order to determine whether a positive act is a factual cause of a consequence.[233] Where medical evidence is to be evaluated, the court must apply a judicial, and not a scientific, measure of proof.[234]

137. There is also general agreement that the *condictio sine qua non* test may, in some instances, lead to conclusions as to the criminal liability of persons that are unreasonable and not in accordance with justice. To cope with such instances, South African law applies a second or supplementary test of causation. This is the test of 'legal' causation which, though not assessed in terms of a single criterion, has on occasion been expressed in the form of the requirement of the 'adequate' cause, and, on occasion, been expressed as the absence of a *novus actus (or nova causa) interveniens.*[235]

138. The adequate cause test supplements the *condictio sine qua non* test by enquiring whether the consequence attributed by that test to the act of the accused was to be expected as normal in the light of human experience. If it was to be expected, the actor is liable; if not to be expected, there is no liability.

---

230. Namely, where the doctrine of common purpose is applied. *See infra*, para. 139.
231. S.V. Hoctor, *Snyman's Criminal Law* 7th ed. (LexisNexis, Durban 2020) 65–66.
232. *Minister of Police v. Skosana* 1977 (1) SA 31 (A); *S v. Daniëls* 1983 (3) SA 275 (A) 324, 331.
233. *S v. Skosana* 1977 (3) SA 31 (A); *S v. Daniëls* (*supra*) 331.
234. *S v. Maqubela* 2017 (2) SACR 690 (SCA).
235. *S v. Mokgethi* 1990 (1) SA 32 (A); *S v. Tembani* 2007 (1) SACR 355 (SCA) para. 10.

The *novus actus interveniens* test considers whether there has occurred an abnormal intervening act or event which, because of its abnormality, breaks the causal chain revealed after the application of the *condictio sine qua non* test.[236]

While these traditional tests for legal causation remain relevant, it was held in the Constitutional Court decision of *Du Plessis v. De Klerk* that constitutionally-based considerations of public policy, reasonableness, fairness and justice were most significant in resolving this matter.[237]

139. The rule that criminal liability in crimes of consequence is dependent upon proof that the accused's conduct was the effective cause of the prohibited consequence is, in South African law, subject to an important exception. In terms of the doctrine of common purpose, where two or more people agree to commit a crime or actively associate in a joint unlawful enterprise, it is not necessary for the prosecution to prove beyond a reasonable doubt that each participant committed conduct which causally contributed to the ultimate unlawful consequence. It is sufficient that it is established that they all agreed to commit a particular crime or actively associated themselves with the commission of the crime by one of their number with the requisite *mens rea.*[238]

This being so, the conduct of the participant who actually causes the consequence is imputed or attributed to the other participants. In the result, each will be guilty of the crime, even though their conduct cannot be established as an effective cause of the prohibited consequence.[239]

III. Classification of Offences by the Material Element

140. South African law does not practice any classification of offences according to the characteristics of the offence. In particular, there is no recognition of the classification of offences as occasional or habitual.[240] Nor, for most purposes, is the classification of offences as momentary or continuous of any importance in South African law. However, in regard to the latter classification, there is a recognition that theft is a 'continuing' crime.[241]

§3. The Element of Criminal Capacity (Insight and Self-Control)

141. Before an accused can be held liable for a contravention of the criminal law, it must be proved that the person was endowed with the intellectual capacity to

236. In *S v. Williams* 1986 (4) SA 1188 (A), it was held that the switching off of a life-support system did not amount to a *novus actus interveniens.*
237. *Du Plessis v. De Klerk* 2020 (1) SACR 1 (CC) para. 29.
238. *Infra*, para. 253.
239. *Infra*, para. 253.
240. Persons may be sentenced as 'habitual' offenders (*see infra*, para. 383), but this is a status brought about with the frequency with which the offender contravenes the law and is not related to the material definition of the crimes concerned.
241. *See infra*, para. 312.

distinguish right from wrong and, if possessed of that capacity, also the capacity to control his conduct in accordance with that insight.[242]

The possession of these capacities is a matter of fact which is determined by such personal circumstances of the accused as age, sanity, sobriety and emotional equilibrium. If, as a result of youth, mental illness, intoxication or emotional distress, a person lacks the capacity to appreciate the wrongfulness of an unlawful act, then there is no liability. So too, there is no liability if, as a result of the same factors, the person, whilst appreciating the wrongfulness of the act, is deprived of the ability to abstain from engaging in the conduct.

142. The element of capacity is recognised in South African law principally through the recognition by the courts of the defences to criminal liability known as youth, insanity, intoxication and provocation.[243]

§4. The Mental (or Moral) Element (Mens Rea)

I. Subjective Guilt or Culpability

143. In South African criminal law, as a general rule, criminal liability cannot arise merely from the performance of the objective act forbidden by the law or the failure to act (material or physical element). Subject to an exception to be stated, there must always be, in addition to the physical element and the *mens rea* element of capacity, a further mental element: the subjective guilt or culpability of the offender.[244] No unlawful behaviour can lead to punishment without a legally blameworthy state of mind of the accused in relation to his unlawful conduct. The exception to this rule is that, in relation to certain categories of statutory offences, *strict liability* (i.e., where it is irrelevant whether the state of mind of the offender is blameworthy) is allowed.[245]

144. In South African law, the modern approach to subjective guilt is to consider *mens rea* as consisting in the states of mind called 'intention' and 'negligence' ('fault'), and criminal capacity, as separate elements of *mens rea* liability.[246] This approach is followed here.

145. Thus, in modern South African criminal law, the general rule is that for there to be criminal liability for a prohibited act or omission, the accused must have

242. *S v. Laubscher* 1988 (1) SA 163 (A) 166H–167B; J. Burchell, *Principles of Criminal Law* 5th ed. (Juta, Cape Town 2016) 251ff.; S.V. Hoctor, *Snyman's Criminal Law* 7th ed. (LexisNexis, Durban 2020) 136ff.
243. For which, *see infra*, paras 212 et seq.
244. J. Burchell, *Principles of Criminal Law* 5th ed. (Juta, Cape Town 2016) 341.
245. *Infra*, para. 164.
246. J. Burchell, *Principles of Criminal Law* 5th ed. (Juta, Cape Town 2016) 347.

done that act intentionally or, in the case of certain crimes, negligently. Only in a few exceptional instances can there be liability without proof of such subjective fault.[247]

II. Intention

146. Intention in South African law is understood in the traditional sense as existing when an accused does what the law forbids him to do, or omits to do what the law commands him to do, knowing that his act or omission is unlawful.

147. South African law distinguishes motive from intent. Thus, merciful motive in euthanasia cases is considered to be irrelevant as it does not negate the intention to kill, which is required for murder.[248]

A. Degrees of Intent

148. In South African law, in all crimes for which intention is the required form of fault, it is necessary that the prosecution prove that the accused acted with the knowledge of the unlawfulness of his act or omission.[249] In some crimes, this will be sufficient to establish guilt on the part of the accused. However, in some cases, the definition of the crime indicates that, in addition, some special type of intention must be present. Thus, in the case of the crime of fraud, it must be proved that the accused intended to defraud;[250] in the case of housebreaking, the prosecution must not only prove that the accused intentionally broke into a house but also that he did so with the intent to commit some crime therein.[251] So too, various statutorily defined crimes contain formulations that require the prosecution to prove some special type of intent: the Intimidation Act of 1982[252] renders punishable certain activities if carried out 'with intent to compel or induce any person or persons of a particular nature, class or kind or persons in general to do or to abstain from doing any act or to assume or to abandon a particular standpoint'.[253]

B. Types of Intention with Reference to Their Consequences

149. The principal, and indeed prevailing, classification of intention in South African law, however, relates not so much to the volitional nature of intent as to the

247. J. Burchell, *Principles of Criminal Law* 5th ed. (Juta, Cape Town 2016) 341.
248. *R v. Peverett* 1940 AD 213; *S v. Hartmann* 1975 (3) SA 532 (C).
249. *See infra*, para. 159.
250. *See infra*, para. 321.
251. *See infra*, para. 327.
252. Act 72 of 1982. This offence is examined in J.R.L. Milton, S.V. Hoctor & M.G. Cowling, *South African Criminal Law and Procedure,* Vol III *Statutory Offences* 2nd ed. (Juta, Cape Town 1988) Ch. HA1.
253. Intimidation Act 72 of 1982, s. 1(1).

cognitive component of the state of mind of an accused person. In South African law, intention (usually identified by its Latin form *dolus*) is said to take the following forms: *dolus directus*, *dolus indirectus* and *dolus eventualis*.

1. Dolus Directus (Direct Intent) and Dolus Indirectus (Indirect Intent)

150. Direct intent is said to exist where the accused has the purpose or aim of committing a particular crime: the assassin who successfully kills his victim acts with *dolus directus.*[254]

Indirect intent (*dolus indirectus*) occurs where the commission of the crime in question was not the accused's actual aim or objective, but he nevertheless foresaw it as a certain or virtually certain consequence of achieving that objective and persisted anyway.[255]

For purposes of liability, no distinction is drawn between *dolus directus* and *dolus indirectus.*

2. Dolus Eventualis

151. Dolus eventualis is a generally recognised and widely applied form of intent in South African law.[256] It is premised upon an accused person's foresight of the *possible* consequences of his actions. Where a consequence (which is the result of an act which the law forbids him to do, or of an omission to do what the law commands) is subjectively foreseen by the actor at the time of the act or omission and he nevertheless proceeds to commit the act or to omit to do what he should do, it is said that, although the actor did not wish or desire to bring about the consequence, he nevertheless intended it and is thus liable.[257]

152. Where a common-law crime or statutory offence requires *mens rea* in the form of intention, *dolus eventualis* will suffice for guilt and direct intention (*dolus directus*) need not be proved.[258]

153. Dolus eventualis exists where the accused subjectively foresees the possibility that the prohibited consequence might occur or the prohibited circumstance might exist, and he accepts this possibility into the bargain (i.e., is reckless as regards this possibility).[259]

---

254. S.V. Hoctor, *Snyman's Criminal Law* 7th ed. (LexisNexis, Durban 2020) 160.
255. G. Kemp (ed.), *Criminal Law in South Africa* 4th ed. (Oxford University Press, Cape Town 2022) 225.
256. J. Burchell, *Principles of Criminal Law* 5th ed. (Juta, Cape Town 2016) 355ff.; S.V. Hoctor, *Snyman's Criminal Law* 7th ed. (LexisNexis, Durban 2020) 161ff.; 'Focus' (1988) 1 *SACJ* 415.
257. *S v. Mini* 1963 (3) SA 188 (A).
258. *S v. De Bruyn* 1968 (4) SA 498 (A); *Mkhwanazi v. S* [1998] 2 All SA 53 (SCA).
259. J. Burchell, *Principles of Criminal Law* 5th ed. (Juta, Cape Town 2016) 357; *R v. Horn* 1958 (3) SA 457 (A); S. Hoctor, 'The Degree of Foresight in *Dolus Eventualis*' 2013 SACJ 131.

In determining whether *dolus eventualis* exists, the courts enquire whether the accused himself subjectively foresaw the possibility of the consequence or circumstance. Provided the accused actually foresees the possibility of the consequence or circumstance, the degree of foresight is not relevant for the purposes of liability.[260] However, mere foresight does not suffice for liability, as the accused must also 'reconcile' himself to the occurrence of the consequence.[261]

III. Negligence

A. Definition

154. In South African criminal law, negligence is a sufficient degree of fault for certain crimes. These crimes are negligent homicide[262] (called 'culpable homicide' in South African law), contempt of court by the editor of a publication,[263] and a selection of statutory offences for which the legislature has explicitly prescribed negligence as the fault element.[264]

For these purposes, negligence exists where an accused person has failed to act with the degree of care or prudence which would have been displayed by a reasonable person in the same circumstances.

155. The test of negligence is traditionally stated[265] as a threefold enquiry:

1. Would a reasonable person, in the same circumstances as the accused, have foreseen the reasonable possibility of the occurrence of the consequence or the existence of the circumstance in question, including its unlawfulness?
2. Would a reasonable person have taken steps to guard against that possibility?
3. Did the accused fail to take the steps which he should reasonably have taken to guard against it?

If all three parts of this test receive an affirmative answer, then the accused's conduct can be regarded as negligent.

---

260. *S v. Ngubane* 1985 (3) SA 677 (A); S. Hoctor, 'The Degree of Foresight in *Dolus Eventualis*' 2013 SACJ 131.
261. *S v. Ngubane* 1985 (3) SA 677 (A) 685; *S v. Humphreys* 2013 (2) SACR 1 (SCA) 9; S.V. Hoctor, *Snyman's Criminal Law* 7th ed. (Butterworths, Durban 2020) 164. It was held in *S v. Goosen* 1989 (4) SA 1013 (A) that the consequence must occur in a way which is not markedly different to that which the accused foresaw, but this ruling has not been consistently followed in the law – *see S v. Nair* 1993 (1) SACR 451 (A); *S v. Lungile* 1999 (2) SACR 597 (SCA).
262. *See infra*, para. 280.
263. *See infra*, para. 364.
264. *See infra*, para. 163.
265. J. Burchell, *South African Criminal Law & Procedure,* Vol. I *General Principles* 4th ed. (Juta, Cape Town 2011) 426; S.V. Hoctor, *Snyman's Criminal Law* 7th ed. (LexisNexis, Durban 2020) 184.

B. An Evaluation of Negligence

156. In South African law, differing from the English law, criminal liability will result from negligence of any degree, and not only from 'gross' negligence.[266]

The test for liability is objective. That is to say, the personal or subjective features of the accused are not relevant to determining whether negligence is present; the sole issue is whether the accused failed to conform to the norm that would be observed by the reasonable man. A 'subjective' test of negligence for criminal liability, though mooted by some writers, has not been favoured by the courts.[267]

However, persons possessing, or professing, certain skills or proficiency in particular fields of activity are judged by the standard of the reasonable practitioner in that field rather than that of the ordinary reasonable person.[268] Moreover, in the application of the test for negligence, the reasonable person will be placed in the circumstances of the accused person.[269] It follows that negligence of children (who have the necessary criminal capacity) will be determined according to the standard of the reasonable child in the same circumstances.[270]

In the case of statutory offences, the test for liability is the same as for common-law crimes.

C. Types of Negligence

157. In South African law, negligence is traditionally conceived of as 'unconscious negligence', that is, negligence arising from a failure to foresee the consequence of conduct. 'Conscious negligence' (*luxuria*) is a form of fault that lies between *dolus eventualis* and unconscious negligence, comprising foresight of the prohibited result, followed by an unreasonable conclusion that it will not occur.[271]

158. 'Recklessness' is known in South African law only in the specific guise of a statutory prohibition upon reckless driving[272] and as a component of the *dolus eventualis* concept.[273] It does not exist as a separate category of fault as in the English or American law and has a distinct meaning from the Anglo-American concept.

266. *R v. Meiring* 1927 AD 41 45; G. Kemp (ed.), *Criminal Law in South Africa* 4th ed. (Oxford University Press, Cape Town 2022) 246.
267. *S v. Ngubane* 1985 (3) SA 677 (A) 686–687.
268. *S v. Kramer* 1987 (1) SA 887 (W).
269. G. Kemp (ed.), *Criminal Law in South Africa* 4th ed. (Oxford University Press, Cape Town 2022) 242.
270. S.V. Hoctor, *Snyman's Criminal Law* 7th ed. (LexisNexis, Durban 2020) 190.
271. S.V. Hoctor, *Snyman's Criminal Law* 7th ed. (LexisNexis, Durban 2020) 167, 191; J. Burchell, *Principles of Criminal Law* 5th ed. (Juta, Cape Town 2016) 380ff. For a judicial discussion of the concept, *see S v. Ngubane* 1985 (3) SA 677 (A) 686B–C.
272. *Infra*, para. 333.
273. *See supra*, para. 153.This understanding of recklessness is subjective in nature.

IV. Knowledge of Unlawfulness

159. Since 1977, following the decision of the Appellate Division in *S v. De Blom*,[274] the principle *ignorantia juris neminem excusat* has not applied in South African law.

It is thus a defence in South African criminal law that the accused was unaware that he was contravening the law or, in other words, that the accused was ignorant of the legal prohibition or mistaken as to its effect. It follows that in South African law, fault consists not only in an awareness of the prohibited act (or omission) but also in an awareness that the act is unlawful. Thus, it is incumbent upon the prosecution in every case to prove not only *dolus* (usually *directus or eventualis*) in relation to the facts of the case but also the knowledge, or foresight, on the part of the accused that his conduct was a contravention of the law.

It is not necessary to prove that the accused knew the detailed requirements of the offence charged, or the exact section or wording of the law in question, or the penalty for transgression, but merely that he knew, or at least foresaw the possibility, that what he was doing was contrary to law in the broad sense.[275]

160. Where negligence is the form of fault for an offence, ignorance may not be a defence if a reasonable person in the same circumstances would not have been ignorant of the unlawfulness of his conduct.[276]

V. The Required Form of Guilt

161. In South African law, intention is an essential prerequisite for criminal liability for almost all common-law crimes, and, as a general rule, for all statutory offences, except where the legislature has expressly provided that negligence is a sufficient fault for the offence, or that the offence is one of strict liability.

162. In relation to common-law crimes, negligence will serve to establish guilt on the part of an accused only where the crime charged is culpable homicide or the accused is the editor of publication and has been charged with contempt of court.[277] The negligent commission of any other common-law crime cannot result in criminal liability.[278]

163. In regard to statutory offences, negligence will provide the requisite fault for the offence in cases where negligence is not the gist of the offence charged, if

274. 1977 (3) SA 513 (A).
275. *S v. De Blom* (*supra*) 530A–B; *S v. Hlomza* 1987 (1) SA 25 (A) 31–32.
276. *S v. Du Toit* 1981 (2) SA 989 (C); *S v. Longdistance (Natal) (Pty) Ltd* 1990 (2) SA 277 (A).
277. *See supra,* para. 154.
278. Thus, in South African law, negligent wounding or injury cannot be charged as assault at common law.

there was a duty on the part of the person charged to be circumspect.[279] In other words, where a person has done an act which the law forbids and the scope and object of the legislation and the circumstances in which he did the act are such as to throw upon him a duty to take care, his failure to take care may furnish the element of fault which must be present before he can be convicted. The test whether negligence will provide the fault for a statutory offence is thus not whether the statute in question specifically prohibits negligent conduct but whether the Legislature required of the subject so high a degree of circumspection as to lead to the necessary conclusion that, despite the absence of express provision to that effect, it must have intended that a mere omission to exercise that degree of care which the law expects of a *bonus paterfamilias* is sufficient to render one guilty of the offence created by the statute.[280]

164. Liability in the absence of *mens rea* is not unknown in South African law. For some decades, the South African courts, influenced by the English law, construed certain 'public welfare' statutes as providing for strict liability for offenders.[281]

Since the 1960s, however, the South African courts have displayed considerable reluctance to construe penal statutes as imposing strict liability, a position expressed in *S v. Qumbella*[282] as follows:

> [T]he basic principle is that actus non facit reum, nisi mens sit rea. . . . Of course the lawmaker has it within its power to override this fundamental principle of fairness, and to make absolute the duty of compliance with its behests, thus rendering innocent violations punishable. But such an inroad into individual freedom should be made to appear very plainly, so that he who runs may read.

165. However, notwithstanding the judicial preference for treating statutory offences as offences involving *mens rea*, it is still possible for an offence to be designated as an offence of strict liability. The South African judges make this determination by reference to the intention of the legislature. This is established by means of construction of the statute in the light of what are termed 'other considerations'. These are 'the language or context of the prohibition or injunction, the scope and object of the statute, the nature and extent of the penalty, and the ease with which the prohibition or injunction could be evaded if reliance could be placed on the absence of *mens rea*'.[283] Applying these aids to construction of the statute,[284]

279. J. Burchell, *Principles of Criminal Law* 5th ed. (Juta, Cape Town 2016) 430; J.R.L. Milton, S.V. Hoctor & M.G. Cowling, *South African Criminal Law and Procedure*, Vol. III *Statutory Offences* (Juta, Cape Town 1988) paras 2–43ff.
280. *S v. Naidoo* 1974 (4) SA 574 (N) 596.
281. J.R.L. Milton, S.V. Hoctor & M.G. Cowling, *South African Criminal Law and Procedure*, Vol. III *Statutory Offences* (Juta, Cape Town 1988) paras 2–58ff.
282. 1966 (4) SA 356 (A) 364.
283. *S v. Arenstein* 1964 (1) SA 361 (A) 365.
284. Cf. J.R.L. Milton, S.V. Hoctor & M.G. Cowling, *South African Criminal Law and Procedure*, Vol. III *Statutory Offences* (Juta, Cape Town 1988) paras 2–16ff.

a judge may well conclude that the legislature intended to create an offence of strict liability.[285] It may be that the principle of strict liability may be regarded as unconstitutional, amounting to an unjustifiable limitation of the right to a fair trial and the right to freedom and security of the person.[286]

§5. The Coincidence of Acts and Mens Rea

166. South African law subscribes to the principle that where *mens rea* is an element of the crime charged, the unlawful act and the *mens rea* must occur and exist contemporaneously.[287] Accordingly, if a wrongdoer intending to kill does not cause the death of the victim, there can be no liability for murder. Equally, if the wrongdoer causes the death of the victim whilst not intending to kill (because, e.g., he believes the victim to be already dead), there can be no liability for murder.

However, the South African courts, in cases of homicide, have displayed a distinct reluctance strictly to abide by the exculpatory effects of the concurrence principle. In a number of cases, the courts have refused to regard an intentional but unsuccessful killing and the unintended but successful killing as separate and non-contemporaneous events, and convicted the wrongdoer of murder.[288]

This conclusion has been reached by regarding the homicide as not involving separate acts but rather a single transaction, thus obviating the necessity to consider the concurrence of *actus reus* and *mens rea.*[289] Alternatively, it has been held that the initial act of the accused is the *sine qua non* of the death of the victim, the subsequent conduct of the accused being considered not to be a *novus actus interveniens* that would terminate the causative link between the conduct of the accused and the death of the deceased.[290] A third approach has been to regard the accused's mistake as to the death of the deceased at the time that death is caused as not material for purposes of determining liability.[291]

---

285. As in *Amalgamated Beverage Industries Natal (Pty) Ltd. v. Durban City Council* 1992 (3) SA 562 (N).
286. Constitution of the RSA, 1996, ss 35(3) and 12(1) respectively; *see* further *S v. Coetzee* 1997 (1) SACR 379 (CC), particularly 442h–i.
287. J. Burchell, *Principles of Criminal Law* 5th ed. (Juta, Cape Town 2016) 445.
288. *R v. Thabo Meli* [1954] 1 All ER 373 (PC) (a case applying Roman-Dutch law); *S v. Masilela* 1968 (2) SA 558 (A); *S v. Mtombeni* 1993 (1) SACR 591 (ZS).
289. *R v. Thabo Meli* (*supra*); *S v. Masilela* (*supra*); *S v. Mtombeni* (*supra*).
290. *S v. Mtombeni* (*supra*) 595e.
291. *S v. Masilela* (*supra*) 573–574A.

Chapter 4. Grounds of Impunity or Defences (Justification and Excuse)

§1. General Principles

167. The intentional (or negligent) perpetration of an act (or omission) prohibited by the criminal law may not result in criminal liability if the law, for one reason or another, considers that the act or omission, in the circumstances, is justified or excused.

168. South African law follows the Anglo-American tradition of approaching the matter of impunity from the procedural point of view of whether the accused's excuse or justification for his wrongdoing is recognised by the law as a defence to criminal liability. The distinction between justification and excuse is thus not a matter of great significance in South African law;[292] the different manifestations of impunity being classified rather according to whether they are defences establishing an absence of either: (1) the voluntary nature of the *actus reus*, or (2) the unlawfulness of the *actus*, or (3) criminal capacity, or (4) fault (intention or negligence).

§2. Defences Showing the Actus Reus to Be Involuntary

169. Criminal liability depends upon the *actus* of the accused being voluntary.[293] Various conditions have been recognised by the South African courts as having the effect of depriving the accused of the freedom of will necessary to render conduct voluntary. These are somnambulism, black-out, concussion, hypoglycaemia, intoxication, provocation and *vis absoluta*.[294]

§3. Defences Showing the Actus Reus to Be Not Unlawful

170. South African law recognises the following circumstances attending the performance of a prohibited act as rendering the conduct not unlawful: private defence (self-defence and defence of property), necessity, impossibility, public authority, superior orders, consent.

I. Private Defence

171. Defence against crime is recognised in South African law as a defence to criminal liability under the name 'private' defence, which incorporates self-defence.

---

292. In *S v. Bailey* 1982 (3) SA 772 (A) 797A, the court raised but did not decide the question whether the defence of necessity (*see infra*, para. 192) was a defence of justification or a defence excluding *mens rea*.
293. *See supra*, para. 130.
294. *See supra*, para. 130.

A. Position in South African Law

172. South African law does not distinguish between self-defence and defence of another, such as a spouse, parent, or child.[295] The conditions for legitimate defence are the same, regardless of whether they relate to defence of one's self or defence of another.

The scope of the defence in South African law is not confined to defence of the person; private defence is a legitimate defence against attacks upon personal freedom,[296] sexual integrity,[297] chastity,[298] and dignity,[299] and private property.[300]

B. Conditions

1. Conditions Relating to the Attack

173. In order to succeed, private defence must have been a response to an unlawful commenced or imminent attack upon a legally protected interest that was unlawful.

174. The attack must have commenced or be imminent. The attack must not have been completed: any measures taken after the attack has ceased would be retaliatory rather than defensive and, therefore, unjustified.[301]

175. Private defence can only be resorted to in respect of an attack that is unlawful.[302]

Thus, a person may not defend himself against lawful arrest,[303] nor may one act to protect one's property from lawful search or seizure. Private defence cannot be raised against the spontaneous attack of an animal, since, in law, an animal cannot act unlawfully.[304]

2. Conditions Relating to the Defence

176. The defender must establish that the defence was necessary to avert the attack, a reasonable response to the attack and directed against the attacker.[305]

---

295. *R v. Patel* 1959 (3) SA 121 (A).
296. *R v. Hayes* 1904 TS 383; *R v. Mahomed* (1906) 27 NLR 396.
297. *R v. Nomahleki* 1928 GWL 8.
298. J. Moorman, *Verhandelinge over de Misdaden en der selve Straffen* (1764) 2.2.5 (who says *inter alia*, that a woman is entitled to kill a man endeavouring to rape her).
299. *S v. Van Vuuren* 1961 (3) SA 305 (E).
300. Private defence of property is discussed separately *infra*, para. 181.
301. Cf. *S v. Mogohlwane* 1982 (2) SA 587 (T).
302. *Ntanjana v. Vorster and Minister of Justice* 1950 (4) SA 398 (C) 404–405.
303. *R v. Ndara* 1955 (4) SA 182 (A) 184.
304. Cf. J van der Berg, 'The Curious Case of the Dog That Acted Lawfully' 1987 *SALJ* 22.
305. Some authorities maintain that the defender also be able to show that he was consciously acting in private defence (*see* D.W. Morkel & T. Verschoor, 'Oor die "bedoeling om te verdedig" by noodweer' 1981 *TRW* 73).

177. Where the threat is one of personal injury, a defence is not necessary if the attack can be avoided by retreat or escape[306] insofar as this is possible and would not expose the defender to even greater danger.[307] If retreat would expose the defender's chances of avoiding the injury, he is justified in standing his ground and defending himself.[308]

178. A defence that uses more force than is necessary is not justified. This principle is expressed in a requirement that the means used to avert the attack were reasonable in the circumstances.[309]

The principle that the amount of force used in the defence must be proportionate to that used in the attack has been rejected for South African law, at least insofar as it holds that the use of deadly force is inappropriate for the protection of interests other than human life.[310]

Although some South African cases have applied a version of the proportionality principle, namely whether the means used were commensurate with the danger apprehended,[311] the recent cases have favoured a test of reasonableness[312] in terms of which the test applied is whether, taking all the factors into account, the defender acted *reasonably* in the manner in which he defended himself. This test allows the court to assess the defence in the context of factors such as the nature of the attack, the interest threatened, the relationship of the parties, their respective age, sex, size and strength, the location of the incident, the nature of the means used in defence, the result of the defence.

The use of mechanical devices is admitted in South African law as a legitimate means of private defence of property, provided that proper and adequate public warning is given of the existence of the device and its nature.[313]

C. Exceeding the Bounds of Private Defence

179. Resort to self-defence is judged objectively. The courts, however, in determining whether, objectively speaking, resort to private defence was justified, 'adopt a robust attitude, not seeking to measure with nice intellectual callipers the precise bounds of legitimate self-defence'.[314] Thus, the test must be applied by the court putting itself in the position of the accused at the time of the attack.

---

306. *R v. Zikalala* 1953 (2) SA 568 (A) 572.
307. *R v. Zikalala* (*supra*) 572.
308. *R v. Manuele Sile* 1945 WLD 134 135; *S v. Steyn* 2010 (1) SACR 411 (SCA).
309. *R v. Jack Bob* 1929 SWA 32 34.
310. *Ex parte Minister van Justisie: In re S v. Van Wyk* 1967 (1) SA 488 (A) 497.
311. *R v. Stephen* 1928 WLD 170 172; *R v. Jack Bob* 1929 SWA 32.
312. *S v. Ntuli* 1975 (1) SA 429 (A) 436D, 437E; *S v. Motleleni* 1976 (1) SA 403 (A) 406; *S v. Trainor* 2003 (1) SACR 35 (SCA) 41–2.
313. *Infra*, para. 190.
314. *S v. Ntuli* 1975 (1) SA 429 (A) 437.

180. Where a person acts in defence against an unlawful attack, but exceeds the limits of private defence, either by continuing to defend himself after the attack had ceased or by using more force than was reasonable, the claim of private defence will not succeed.[315]

Where the defender has proceeded mistakenly or in ignorance of the true legal position regarding his resort to private defence, his ignorance or mistake serves to deprive him of the fault for the crime charged. Thus, although his defence of private defence may fail, the accused may nevertheless escape liability on the ground that he lacked the *intention* or *negligence* to act unlawfully.[316]

II. Private Defence of Property

A. *Position in South African Law*

181. In South African law, it has been held that a person may resort to force, including deadly force, in order to protect his property from damage, destruction or removal. It has been argued that this approach with regard to deadly force (followed in the leading case of *Ex parte Minister van Justisie: In re S v. Van Wyk*, discussed *infra*) would now be regarded as an unreasonable and unjustifiable infringement of the right to life, and thus unconstitutional.[317]

B. *Conditions*

1. Conditions Relating to the Attack

182. The defender must establish that: (1) property was (2) presently (3) in danger of damage or destruction (4) that was unlawful.

183. The property interests that are traditionally protected by private defence are: possession of movable property (interfered with by theft or robbery); intrusion upon immovable property, which may take the form of either a simple trespass or an unlawful invasion of a house (housebreaking); damage or destruction of movable or immovable property (malicious injury to property; arson). The types of interests involved may require particular defensive responses.

Private defence has succeeded in cases of an unlawful search,[318] entry into premises,[319] or remaining on property.[320]

---

315. *S v. Ngomane* 1979 (3) SA 859 (A).
316. *See infra*, para. 233.
317. J. Burchell, *South African Criminal Law and Procedure,* Vol. I *General Principles* 4th ed. (Juta, Cape Town 2011) 144, *sed contra* S.V. Hoctor, *Snyman's Criminal Law* 7th ed. (LexisNexis, Durban 2020) 91.
318. *R v. Thomas* 1928 EDL 401.
319. *R v. Stephen* 1928 WLD 170.
320. *S v. Botes* 1966 (3) SA 606 (O); *S v. Smart* 1971 (3) SA 75 (RAD) 78E–F.

184. The danger must be currently present: it must have existed at the time that the defence takes place.[321] If the danger has passed or the harm or damage that it threatened has occurred, the owner cannot justify any use of force upon the perpetrator.[322]

Unlike the case of self-defence, the danger need not necessarily be commenced or imminent. This is so in the case of defence of property by means of protective devices such as sharp objects, traps or trap-guns. Such devices are deployed not in response to a present danger but rather in respect of an anticipated danger. The use of such devices is admitted in South African law as a legitimate means of private defence of property,[323] provided that proper and adequate public warning is given of the existence of the device and its nature.[324]

185. Private defence of property can only be resorted to if there is serious danger to the property or the rights therein. The test of whether the danger existed is objective: the enquiry is whether there were 'reasonable grounds for the defender to think that because of the offender's unlawful conduct'[325] the danger existed.

186. The danger to property must arise from acts or conduct that are not lawful. Clearly, where the interference with property rights is authorised by law, the use of force to prevent the interference cannot amount to a legitimate private defence.

2. Conditions Relating to the Defence

187. In order to show that private defence was justified, the defender must establish that the defence was: (1) necessary to avert the danger, (2) a reasonable response to the attack, and (3) directed against the attacker.

188. The rule that a defence is not necessary if the attack could be avoided by retreating[326] has no application in the defence of property. Certainly, an owner, when confronted by a robber, is not expected to abandon his property and not resist the attempt to take it from him.[327] Likewise, the inhabitant of a dwelling is not expected to flee from his habitation, but rather to resist the intrusion of a burglar or thief.[328] In this situation, it seems that the attacker's intrusive invasion of the other's property rights terminates his right to life and releases the defender from the duty to retreat.

---

321. *S v. Moller* 1971 (4) SA 327 (T) 329.
322. *S v. Mogohlwane* 1982 (2) SA 590 (T).
323. *Ex parte Minister van Justisie: In re S v. Van Wyk* 1967 (1) SA 488 (A) 511ff.
324. *Ex parte Minister van Justisie: In re S v. Van Wyk* (*supra*) 509.
325. *Ex parte Minister van Justisie: In re S v. Van Wyk* (*supra*) 509.
326. *See supra,* para. 177.
327. *S v. Mogohlwane* 1982 (2) SA 587 (T).
328. *R v. Stephen* 1928 WLD 170.

189. The measures taken to protect the defender's proprietary interests must have been 'the only means whereby he could avoid the danger'.[329]

190. The setting or deployment of man-traps, trap-guns, spiked or electrified fencing is not per se unlawful and can constitute a necessary means of defending proprietary interests.[330]

191. The force used must have been a reasonable response to the threat of damage to the property. The test is whether the means of defending the property was reasonable 'having regard to all the circumstances, such as the nature and extent of the danger, the value of the property, the time and place of the occurrence'.[331]

In *Ex parte Minister van Justisie: In re S v. Van Wyk*,[332] it was decided that in appropriate circumstances, deadly force may be a reasonable response to an attack upon property interests.

III. Necessity

A. *The Position in South African Law*

192. South African law recognises that in an emergency situation in which a person is faced with a threat of serious harm that can only be avoided by contravening a prohibition of the criminal law, the person may use the emergency as a justification for the crime committed.

The defence, called necessity (sometimes 'compulsion'),[333] whilst generally recognised, 'must be confined within the strictest and narrowest limits because of the danger attendant upon allowing a plea of necessity to excuse criminal acts'.[334]

B. *Conditions*

193. For necessity to provide a defence, the following conditions must be satisfied:

1. A legal interest of the accused must have been endangered. Danger to life,[335] threat of bodily injury,[336] damage to property, and threat to personal

329. *Ex parte Minister van Justisie: In re S v. Van Wyk* 1967 (1) SA 488 (A) 509.
330. *See supra,* para. 184.
331. *Ex parte Minister van Justisie: In re S v. Van Wyk* 1967 (1) SA 488 (A) 509.
332. 1967 (1) SA 488 (A).
333. South African law does not attach any significance to the difference between necessity (pressure caused by events) and compulsion (duress) (pressure exerted by persons). Either form of pressure will be sufficient for establishing a defence excluding unlawfulness.
334. *R v. Mahomed* 1938 AD 30 36.
335. *S v. Alfeus* 1979 (3) SA 145 (A); *S v. Peterson* 1980 (1) SA 938 (A).
336. *S v. Pretorius* 1975 (2) SA 85 (SWA); *S v. Mtetwa* 1977 (3) SA 628 (E).

freedom[337] have been recognised as interests that support resort to necessary defence. However, the South African courts have not been prepared to recognise that acts done to avert a threat to economic or pecuniary interests will be justified by necessity.[338]

2. The threat must have commenced or have been imminent.[339]
3. The necessity must not be brought about by the actor's wrongful conduct.[340]
4. It must have been necessary for the accused to act unlawfully in order to avert the danger.
5. The means used to avoid the harm must have been reasonable under the circumstances.

(It has been suggested further that the accused must not have been legally obliged to endure the necessity situation.)[341]

194. As indicated above, South African law considers necessity as sufficient justification for the taking of human life.[342]

IV. Consent

195. South African law subscribes to the view that, since a crime is an affront to the community, the victim of a crime cannot relieve the wrongdoer of liability for the crime. Thus, in principle, the consent of the victim is not a defence to criminal liability. However, since there are certain crimes for which a lack of consent on the part of the victim is an essential element, it follows that in such cases, the accused can raise as a defence the fact that there was consent on the part of the victim.

196. The defence of consent is thus recognised in South African law in relation to crimes relating to the taking of another's property, crimes involving certain types of interference with the physical integrity of persons and certain crimes relating to sexual intercourse.[343]

197. Consent of the victim is, however, no defence in the case of homicide[344] (so that euthanasia is no defence).[345] Likewise, the consent of an employee to

---

337. In *S v. Mtetwa* 1977 (3) SA 628 (E).
338. *R v. Canestra* 1951 (2) SA 317 (A); *S v. Adams* 1979 (4) SA 793 (T) 799A; *S v. Adams*; *S v. Werner* 1981 (1) SA 187 (A) 221H.
339. *R v. Garnsworthy* 1923 WLD 17 21; *R v. Baxter* 1929 EDL 189.
340. *S v. Bradbury* 1967 (1) SA 387 (A) 393, 394, 399–400.
341. *S v. Kibi* 1978 (4) SA 173 (E). *See* J. Burchell, *Principles of Criminal Law* 5th ed. (Juta, Cape Town 2016) 173.
342. As decided in *S v. Goliath* 1972 (3) SA 1 (A); *see also Maimela v. Makhado Municipality* 2011 (2) SACR 339 (SCA) para. 23.
343. S.V. Hoctor, *Snyman's Criminal Law* 7th ed. (LexisNexis, Durban 2020) 103–104.
344. *R v. Peverett* 1940 AD 213 218; *S v. Robinson* 1968 (1) SA 666 (A) 678; *Ex parte Minister van Justisie: In re S v. Grotjohn* 1970 (2) SA 355 (A).
345. *S v. Hartmann* 1975 (3) SA 532 (C); *S v. De Bellocq* 1975 (3) SA 538 (T); *S v. Hibbert* 1979 (4) SA 717 (D). In *Stransham-Ford v. Minister of Justice and Correctional Services* 2015 (4) SA 50

chastisement[346] does not justify the assault nor does the consent of a female under 12 years of age provide a defence to a charge of rape.[347] It has been held that the victim's consent in the case of indecent assault is no defence where bodily harm is sustained.[348]

Consent legalises aggressions for religious, customary and superstitious purposes, unless the practice seriously offends public policy.[349]

198. Where the consent of the victim is a defence, the defence will only succeed if the consent was a real consent and it was given by a person capable in law of consenting.[350] It is settled that 'consent' induced by force or threats is not real consent for purposes of the criminal law.[351] Fraud, whether active or in the form of fraudulent non-disclosure, may nullify consent.[352]

V. Impossibility

199. In circumstances in which it is physically impossible for a citizen to comply with a positive injunction of the law, South African law considers the impossibility to deprive the failure to obey the law of any unlawfulness.[353]

200. It has been accepted that for the defence to succeed, there must be: (1) a positive obligation imposed by law, compliance with which was (2) physically impossible (3) through no fault on the part of the accused.[354]

201. The defence will succeed only if it was objectively impossible for the person in the position of the accused to comply with the injunction of the law.[355]

(GP), it was held that an absolute prohibition on assisted suicide by a medical practitioner is unconstitutional. However, in *Minister of Justice and Correctional Services v. Estate Stransham-Ford* 2017 (3) SA 152 (SCA), it was held that the circumstances of the case did not render a reconsideration of the common law relating to the crimes of murder and culpable homicide appropriate.

346. *R v. McCoy* 1953 (2) SA 4 (SR).
347. Criminal Law (Sexual Offences and Related Matters) Amendment Act 32 of 2007, s. 1(2)(*d*)(iv) and 57.
348. *S v. D* 1963 (3) SA 263(E) 265. *See infra* para. 289 for the statutory offence of sexual assault, which has replaced the common-law crime of indecent assault.
349. *S v. Sikunyana* 1961 (3) SA 549 (E); J. Burchell, *Principles of Criminal Law* 5th ed. (Juta, Cape Town 2016) 221–222. Cf. *R v. Phiri* 1963 R & N 395 (SR).
350. *See* J. Burchell, *Principles of Criminal Law* 5th ed. (Juta, Cape Town 2016) 226ff.
351. *Ex parte Minister of Justice: In re R v. Gesa*; *R v. De Jongh* 1959 (1) SA 234 (A).
352. *R v. C* 1952 (4) SA 117 (O); *R v. K* 1966 (1) SA 366 (RA).
353. For further discussion *see*, S.V. Hoctor, 'The Impossibility Defence in Criminal Law' in P.J. Schwikkard & S.V. Hoctor (eds), *Essays in Honour of Steph van der Merwe* (Juta, Cape Town 2023) 295ff.
354. G. Kemp (ed.), *Criminal Law in South Africa* 4th ed. (Oxford University Press, Cape Town 2022) 120.
355. *R v. Jetha* (1929) 50 NLR 91; *S v. Moeng* 1977 (3) SA 986 (O).

Great difficulty,[356] severe inconvenience or extreme economic hardship[357] are not sufficient grounds to establish impossibility.

202. The accused himself must not have brought about the circumstances that create the impossibility.[358]

VI. Superior Orders

203. Since 1900, South African law has recognised a defence to liability based upon obedience to superior orders.[359]

204. For the defence to succeed: (1) the order must emanate from a person lawfully placed in authority over the subordinate, (2) the subordinate must have been under a duty to obey the order, and (3) he must have done no more than was necessary to carry out the order.

205. The person giving the order must be authorised by the law of the land to issue orders and the person carrying out the order must be recognised by the law of the land as being obliged to obey orders.[360] Thus, the defence would not be available in respect of a member of a guerrilla force carrying out the order of an officer in that force.[361]

206. The duty to obey is determined by the law establishing the hierarchy of authority in the Defence Force and particularly the code of discipline established under the Defence Act 2002. So long as the order is a lawful order, the subordinate is duty-bound to obey. The problem arises where the order of the superior is not lawful either under civil or military law.

207. The South African courts have refused to concede that simple obedience to an order can be in itself a complete defence, whilst also recognising that it is unjust to punish a soldier for obeying the orders of a superior officer. They have thus devised a compromise solution which allows a defence of obedience to superior orders, provided the orders were not '*manifestly and palpably*'[362] unlawful.

Thus if the order is, say, that the soldier should massacre civilians or rape a woman, it would be manifestly and palpably unlawful and the law requires that the soldier should not obey and does not allow him to escape liability for a killing or

356. *S v. Leeuw* 1975 (1) SA 439 (O).
357. *Attorney-General v. Grieve* 1934 TPD 187.
358. *R v. Close Settlement Corporation Limited* 1922 AD 294; *R v. Korsten* 1927 NPD 12.
359. *R v. Smith* (1900) 17 SC 561. The defence covers commands issued in the police context as well as in the military; *see S v. Mostert* 2006 (1) SACR 560 (N).
360. *S v. Andreas* 1989 (2) PH H38 (SWA).
361. As in *S v. Andreas* (*supra*).
362. *S v. Banda* (1990) (3) SA 466 (B) 485B–C, 495E–G and 496C–D.

rape on the grounds of obedience to superior orders.[363] The test is whether, objectively viewed, the order is lawful or unlawful. If it would appear to a reasonable person (rather than a reasonable soldier)[364] that the order is unlawful, the soldier ought not to obey it and if he does, his act is unlawful and he is liable to punishment.[365]

208. The defence may take the form of a plea of lack of intention by reason of lack of knowledge of unlawfulness, if the accused genuinely[366] believed that the law required him to carry out the order.

VII. Parental Authority

209. In South African law, it was previously held that parents may inflict moderate corporal chastisement upon their children.[367] However, the defence was held to be unconstitutional by the Constitutional Court[368] as an unjustifiable infringement of the right to be free from all forms of violence,[369] and the right to dignity,[370] read with the Constitutional injunction requiring that a child's best interests be prioritised in all matters concerning the child.[371]

VIII. Public Authority

210. An act which would otherwise be unlawful is justified if it is perpetrated under the authority of some public office or public appointment. Thus, the public official who exceeds the speed limit in order to carry out his official duties is, by reason of his appointment, excused from liability.[372]

211. The present defence applies especially in respect of charges of assault or homicide arising from the arrest of persons suspected of having committed a criminal offence. The power to arrest is conferred upon 'arrestors' in respect of 'suspects' in terms of the Criminal Procedure Act 1977.[373]

---

363. Cf. *S v. Banda* (*supra*) 494.
364. *S v. Banda* (*supra*) 485E–H.
365. *S v. Banda* (*supra*); *S v. Andreas* 1989 (2) PH H38 (SWA).
366. *S v. Mule* 1990 (1) SACR 517 (SWA).
367. *R v. Janke and Janke* 1913 TPD 382. This defence also used to extend to teachers but was expressly abolished in this context – South African Schools Act 84 of 1996, s. 10.
368. *Freedom of Religion South Africa v. Minister of Justice and Constitutional Development* 2020 (1) SACR 113 (CC).
369. Constitution, 1996, s. 12(1)(*c*).
370. Constitution, 1996, s. 10.
371. Constitution, 1996, s. 28(2).
372. *S v. De Bruyn* 1975 (3) SA 56 (W); but *see S v. Fourie* 2001 (2) SACR 674 (C).
373. This use of force in relation to arrest is discussed *infra*, paras 514–515.

§4. Defences Showing the Absence of Criminal Capacity

212. South African law recognises the following circumstances attending the performance of a prohibited act as demonstrating an absence of criminal capacity on the part of the accused: youth, insanity, intoxication, and emotional stress (provocation).

I. Minority

213. Children because of their youth may lack intellectual and moral judgment and insight. The younger the child, the greater is his presumed lack of moral insight. The older the child, the more it can be assumed that he possesses this capacity. South African criminal law gives expression to this insight by way of a presumption that children cannot be blamed for crimes they might commit.

A. *Children under 12 Years*

214. In South African law, a child who has not yet completed the twelfth year of life is irrebuttably presumed to lack criminal capacity and thus cannot be held criminally responsible.[374]

B. *Children Between 12 and 14 Years*

215. In the case of a child between the ages of 12 and 14, the South African law likewise presumes that the child lacks criminal capacity. However, in this instance, on the basis that *malitia supplet aetatem*, the presumption is rebuttable and can be rebutted by proof that the child in fact possessed insight or self-control.[375]

C. *Children from 14 Years Upward*

216. On attaining the age of 14, a child is regarded as an adult for these purposes, and there is no presumption of lack of criminal capacity.

---

374. Child Justice Act 75 of 2008, s. 7(1). From an original age limit of 7 years, the Act initially adjusted the minimum age of capacity for a child to 10 years, and this limit was raised to 12 years in 2019, with a further periodic review of this issue provided for in the Act (s. 8). This development recognises the need to take account of modern views on the development of the brain of the child.
375. Child Justice Act 75 of 2008, s. 7(2); *R v. K* 1956 (3) SA 353 (A) 356.

II. Pathological Incapacity

217. In South African law, criminal responsibility is dependent upon the accused possessing that degree of mental health which enables the person to appreciate the wrongfulness of conduct and to control his actions according to this insight. A person who suffers from a mental illness or intellectual disability which deprives him of the cognitive or conative psychological capacities and thus of the insight or self-control required by the law can successfully raise the defence of pathological incapacity.[376]

A. Incapacity at the Moment of the Act or Omission

218. In terms of section 78 of the Criminal Procedure Act 51 of 1977:

> A person who commits an act or makes an omission which constitutes an offence and who at the time of such commission or omission suffers from a mental illness or intellectual disability which makes him or her incapable
>
> (a) of appreciating the wrongfulness of his or her act or omission; or
> (b) of acting in accordance with an appreciation of the wrongfulness of his or her act or omission, shall not be criminally responsible for such act or omission.

219. Although there is no formal definition of mental illness for purposes of the incapacity defence in South African law, in order for a mental disorder to constitute a mental illness or intellectual disability for these purposes, it must at least consist in 'a pathological disturbance of the accused's mental capacity and not a mere temporary mental confusion which is not attributable to a mental abnormality but rather to external stimuli such as alcohol, drugs or provocation'.[377]

Thus, a malfunctioning of the mind which is caused by a blow on the head resulting in concussion, the consumption of alcohol or drugs, or the administration of an anaesthetic is not an 'illness' or 'disease' of the mind since it is exogenous in its origin and not endogenous.[378] So too, a condition brought about by physiological changes in the body (such as hypoglycaemia)[379] will not qualify as a mental disease. The South African courts have refused to regard psychopathy as a form of mental illness, constituting pathological incapacity.[380]

---

376. *Report of the Commission of Enquiry into the Responsibility of Mentally Deranged Persons and Related Matters* (RP 60/1967) paras 9.30 et seq.
377. *S v. Stellmacher* 1982 (2) SA 181 (SWA) 187H (translation).
378. *See* J. Burchell, *Principles of Criminal Law* 5th ed. (Juta, Cape Town, 2016) 282.
379. *S v. Stellmacher* 1983 (2) SA 188 (SWA) where it was held that an accused was not insane when he committed a crime whilst in an abnormal state brought about by hypoglycaemia and a temporary epilepsy.
380. *R v. Von Zell* 1953 (3) SA (A) 308; *S v. Webb* (2) 1971 (2) SA 343 (T) 344–345; *S v. Mnyanda* 1976 (2) SA 751 (A).

220. Mere mental illness is not sufficient. It must be established that the illness had the effect of rendering the accused 'incapable of appreciating the wrongfulness of his or her act or omission' or of acting 'in accordance with an appreciation of the wrongfulness of his or her act or omission' at the time that the offence was committed.[381]

B. Incapacity at the Moment of Trial

221. An accused who suffers from mental illness or intellectual disability may not be fit to stand trial. An accused is not triable if the mental illness or intellectual disability renders him 'not capable of understanding the proceedings so as to make a proper defence'.[382]

The question of 'triability' is separate from that of responsibility: triability relates to the mental state of the accused at the time that he stands trial; responsibility relates to his mental state at the time he committed the crime charged. Thus, an accused may be triable[383] but found to lack capacity by reason of mental illness;[384] conversely, he may not lack capacity by reason of mental illness[385] but not be triable.[386] A person found to be not triable may be interned or released.[387]

C. Presumption of Capacity

222. Following English law, in South African law, 'every person is presumed not to suffer from a mental illness or intellectual disability so as not to be criminally responsible … until the contrary is proved on a balance of probabilities'.[388] The rule is an exception to the general principle that in criminal cases, the onus of proof rests upon the prosecution.[389]

Whenever an accused person's criminal responsibility is in issue, the burden of proof in this regard is on the party who raises the issue.[390]

381. J. Burchell, *Principles of Criminal Law* 5th ed. (Juta, Cape Town 2016) 287ff.
382. Criminal Procedure Act 1977, s. 77(1). The procedure for determining whether a person is mentally ill is set out in s. 79 of the Criminal Procedure Act 1977. *See infra*, paras 614 et seq.
383. Because he is not mentally ill at the time of standing trial.
384. Because he was mentally ill at the time of committing the crime.
385. Because he was not mentally ill at the time of committing the crime.
386. Because he is mentally ill at the time of standing trial.
387. *See infra*, paras 620–621.
388. Criminal Procedure Act 51 of 1977, s. 78(1A). *See infra*, para. 613.
389. *R v. Ndhlovu* 1945 AD 369 386–387. It has been argued that this rule constitutes an unjustifiable infringement of the right to be presumed innocent. *See* S.V. Hoctor, *Snyman's Criminal Law* 7th ed. (LexisNexis, Durban, 2020) 153; J. Burchell, *Principles of Criminal Law* 5th ed. (Juta, Cape Town, 2016) 294ff.
390. Criminal Procedure Act 51 of 1977, s. 78(1B).

D. Verdict

223. Originally, South African law used the 'guilty but insane' verdict of English law, but, in 1977, the verdict was changed to 'not guilty by reason of mental illness or intellectual disability'.[391]

E. Order of Internment or Release

224. If the court finds that the accused committed the act in question and that he at the time of such commission was by reason of mental illness or intellectual disability not criminally responsible for such act, the court must find the accused not guilty; or if the court so finds after the accused has been convicted of the offence charged but before sentence is passed, the court must set the conviction aside and find the accused not guilty, by reason of mental illness or intellectual disability, as the case may be.

The court is required to further direct, where the accused is charged with murder or culpable homicide or rape or compelled rape or another charge involving serious violence, or where the court deems it necessary in the public interest that the accused either: (i) be detained in a psychiatric hospital; or (ii) be temporarily detained in a correctional health facility of a prison where a bed is not immediately available in a psychiatric hospital and be transferred where a bed becomes available, if the court is of the opinion that it is necessary to do so on the grounds that the accused poses a serious danger or threat to himself or herself or to members of the public;[392] or (iii) be admitted to and detained in a designated health establishment and treated as if he or she were an involuntary mental health care user;[393] or (iv) be released subject to such conditions as the court considers appropriate; or (v) be released unconditionally; or (vi) be referred to a children's court,[394] pending which referral placement will take place in the care of a parent, guardian or another appropriate adult, or temporary safe care,[395] if such placement is not possible.[396]

Where the accused is charged with another offence, the court is required to direct that: (i) he or she be admitted to and detained in a specified institution and treated

391. Criminal Procedure Act 1977, s. 78(6). The verdict 'Not guilty' is not really an acquittal. This is because the Criminal Procedure Act 1977 allows an appeal *against* the finding of not guilty (s. 78(8)(*a*)).
392. In terms of s. 47 of the Mental Health Care Act 17 of 2002.
393. In terms of s. 37 of the Mental Health Care Act 17 of 2002.
394. As contemplated in s. 64 of the Child Justice Act 75 of 2008. In terms of s. 42 of the Children's Act 38 of 2005, every magistrate's court may function as a children's court.
395. In terms of s. 1 of the Children's Act 38 of 2005, 'temporary safe care', in relation to a child, means care of a child in an approved child and youth care centre, shelter or private home or any other place, where the child can safely be accommodated pending a decision or court order concerning the placement of the child, but excludes care of a child in a prison or police cell.
396. Criminal Procedure Act 51 of 1977, s. 78(6)(i).

as if he or she were an involuntary mental health care user;[397] or (ii) released, conditionally or unconditionally; or be referred to a children's court,[398] pending which referral placement will take place in the care of a parent, guardian or other appropriate adult, or temporary safe care,[399] if such placement is not possible.[400]

III. Intoxication

225. In South African law intoxication, whether voluntary or involuntary, and whether induced by the consumption of alcohol or the intake of drugs, if it has deprived a person of the capacity to appreciate the wrongfulness of his conduct or to act in accordance with such appreciation, is, in terms of the decision of the Appellate Division in *S v. Chretien*,[401] a complete defence to liability for any crime committed whilst so intoxicated.

226. South African law, however, applies the *actio libera in causa*[402] doctrine, with the result that a person who voluntarily and deliberately gets drunk in order to commit a crime is guilty of committing the crime even though at the time he commits the prohibited act, he is so drunk that he has acted involuntarily.[403]

227. Following the *Chretien* case, the Criminal Law Amendment Act 1 of 1988 was enacted. Section 1(1) of the Act provides as follows:

> Any person who consumes or uses any substance which impairs his faculties to appreciate the wrongfulness of his acts or to act in accordance with that appreciation, while knowing that such substance has that effect, and who while such faculties are thus impaired commits any act prohibited by law under any penalty, but is not criminally liable because his faculties were impaired as aforesaid, shall be guilty of an offence and shall be liable on conviction to the penalty, except the death penalty, which may be imposed in respect of the commission of that act.

The true nature of this offence is far from evident. Thus, it is not clear whether a contravention of section 1(1) is merely a competent verdict to the crime which the accused committed whilst intoxicated.[404] Or is a contravention of section 1(1) a substantive and autonomous offence? In which case, it is difficult to know how an

397. In terms of s. 37 of the Mental Health Care Act 17 of 2002.
398. As contemplated in s. 64 of the Child Justice Act 75 of 2008. In terms of s. 42 of the Children's Act 38 of 2005, every magistrate's court may function as a children's court.
399. *See* definition of 'temporary safe care' in note 395 *supra*.
400. Criminal Procedure Act, s. 78(6)(ii).
401. 1981 (1) SA 1097 (A); followed, *inter alia*, in *S v. Ramdass* 2017 (1) SACR 30 (KZD).
402. *Actio non in se, sed tamen in sua causa libera.*
403. Cf. *S v. Baartman* 1983 (4) SA 395 (NC).
404. *S v. Oliphant* 1989 (4) 169 (O).

accused can be convicted of it since by definition at the time he contravened the section of he was so drunk that, in terms of *Chretien*, he has a complete defence to criminal liability.[405]

IV. Non-pathological Incapacity (Provocation and Emotional Stress)

228. South African law, besides recognising that a lack of capacity may be induced by mental illness ('pathological incapacity'),[406] also recognises that a state of incapacity may arise from causes not of a pathological nature. Instances of so-called non-pathological incapacity brought about by emotional stress induced by provocation have been held by the South African courts to establish lack of capacity and thus an absence of criminal responsibility.[407]

229. The conclusion that severe emotional stress may deprive a person of the capacity to appreciate the wrongfulness of his or her conduct or to act in accordance with this appreciation was arrived at as a logical conclusion of the decision in *S v. Chretien* that intoxication may establish a lack of criminal capacity.[408]

230. In the result, then, in South African law, severe emotional stress may deprive a person of the capacity to appreciate the wrongfulness of his conduct or to act in accordance with this appreciation and for this reason constitute a complete defence to criminal liability.[409]

§5. Defences Showing Absence of Mens Rea

I. Ignorance or Mistake

231. In South African law, ignorance or mistake concerning an essential element of the crime serves to establish an absence of fault on the part of the accused.

---

405. *See* J. Burchell, *Principles of Criminal Law* 5th ed. (Juta, Cape Town 2016) 312ff.; S.V. Hoctor, *Snyman's Criminal Law* 7th ed. (LexisNexis, Durban 2020) 199ff.; 'Focus' 1990 *SACJ* 268ff.
406. *See supra,* para. 217.
407. This development is traced in J. Burchell & J. Milton, *Principles of Criminal Law* 2nd ed. (Juta, Cape Town 1997) 278ff.; C.R. Snyman, *Criminal Law* 4th ed. (Butterworths, Durban, 2002) 235–239.
408. *S v. Van Vuuren* 1983 (1) SA 12 (A) 17G–H.
409. *S v. Arnold* 1985 (3) SA 256 (C); *S v. Campher* 1987 (1) SA 940 (A); *S v. Laubscher* 1988 (1) SA 163 (A); *S v. Wiid* 1990 (1) SA 561 (A). *See* however the problematic judgment of the SCA in *S v. Eadie* 2002 (1) SACR 663 (SCA) which asserts that there is no distinction between the notions of conative capacity and automatism, and in the light of which it seems that it would have to be established that an accused was acting involuntarily in order for the defence based on lack of conative capacity to prevail. For a critical discussion of this judgment, *see* S.V. Hoctor, 'A Peregrination Through the Law of Provocation' in J.J. Joubert (ed.), *Essays in Honour of C.R. Snyman* (Unisa Press, Pretoria, 2008) 110ff.

A. Ignorance or Mistake of Law

232. Since the decision of the Appellate Division in *S v. De Blom*,[410] the rule that '*ignorantia juris neminem excusat*' has had no application in South African law.

It is thus a defence under South African criminal law for the accused to prove that he was genuinely ignorant that his conduct was unlawful. South African criminal law has not sought to limit the scope of this defence by requiring that the ignorance should have been insurmountable or reasonable.[411]

However, in the case of offences for which negligence suffices for the fault requirement,[412] ignorance of the law which is unreasonable is no excuse. Indeed, since the reasonable man would not have displayed such ignorance, the accused's *ignorantia juris* will provide the required fault for such offences.[413] Reliance upon incorrect legal advice does not necessarily prevent a mistake from being unreasonable: 'Legal advice has no magic which justifies the recipient in jettisoning his common sense.'[414]

233. Mistake as to the existence of a defence excluding the unlawfulness of an act, known as 'putative defence', will establish an absence of intention on the part of the accused.[415] Thus, if a person mistakenly believes he is acting in lawful self-defence,[416] or defence of his property, or in circumstances of necessity, or obedience to superior orders,[417] or with the consent of the victim,[418] he will lack the intention to act unlawfully. Accordingly, even though the defence of absence of unlawfulness fails, the offender will be acquitted on the ground of absence of intention to commit the crime.

B. Ignorance or Mistake of Fact

234. Ignorance or mistake of fact in the form that a person, whilst fully aware that a particular act is against the law, is unaware that the conduct he has engaged in violates the law serves as a defence in South African law by establishing an

410. 1977 (3) SA 513 (A).
411. S.V. Hoctor, *Snyman's Criminal Law* 7th ed. (LexisNexis, Durban 2020) 181.
412. *See supra,* para. 154.
413. *S v. De Blom* (*supra*) 531–532. *See supra,* para. 163.
414. *S v. Longdistance (Natal) (Pty) Ltd* 1990 (2) 277 (A) 283. In *S v. Claassens* 1992 (2) SACR 434 (T) 440, it was held that a client should be able to rely on legal advice unless there are indications that the advice may be unreliable, that is, where reliance on such advice is unreasonable.
415. J. Burchell, *Principles of Criminal Law* 5th ed. (Juta, Cape Town 2016) 409ff. In evaluating the issue of knowledge of unlawfulness, it has been held in *S v. Sam* 1980 (4) SA 289 (T) 294 that there is no difference between a mistake of fact and a mistake of law. *See* further *S v. De Blom* (*supra*) 530ff.
416. *S v. Botes* 1966 (3) SA 606 (O); *S v. Mokoena* 1967 (4) SA 162 (O); *S v. De Oliveira* 1993 (2) SACR 59 (A).
417. *S v. Andreas* 1989 (1) PH H38 (SWA).
418. *R v. Z* 1960 (1) SA 739 (A); *S v. S* 1971 (2) SA 591 (A).

absence of intention on the part of the accused. Because the accused has misunderstood the nature or significance of his act or omission, he lacks the intention to do the act or omission.

235. Clearly, ignorance or mistake of fact will be a defence to all crimes for which intention is the prescribed form of fault. Conversely, in the case of crimes of strict liability, ignorance or mistake of fact is no defence at all.[419] In crimes for which negligence suffices for the fault requirement, only mistakes of fact which are not unreasonable in the circumstances will provide a defence.[420]

II. Youthfulness, Insanity, Intoxication, Provocation

236. Conditions such as youth, mental illness, intoxication or provocation are usually considered defences that show that a person was deprived of the capacity for insight or self-control. However, it is conceivable that these conditions might equally deprive the person of the ability to form the intention to commit the crime charged.[421]

§6. Other Grounds of Impunity

I. *De Minimis Non Curat Lex*

237. In South African law, an accused charged with an offence may obtain an acquittal by raising the trivial nature of the contravention. This doctrine of *de minimis non curat lex*, borrowed from the English law, is usually presented as a 'defence' to criminal liability.[422]

Strictly speaking, the triviality of a contravention of the law is not a defence which excludes the unlawfulness or otherwise of the accused's conduct, but rather a decision of a court to allow unlawful conduct to go unpunished on account of its triviality.

419. J.R.L. Milton, 'Reasonable Mistake of Fact as a Defence in Statutory Offences' 1971 *SALJ* 70.
420. *S v. De Blom* 1977 (3) SA 513 (A). Cf. *S v. Du Toit* 1981 (3) SA 33 (C).
421. J. Burchell, *Principles of Criminal Law* 5th ed. (Juta, Cape Town 2016) 407–409.
422. *S v. Kgogong* 1980 (3) SA 600 (A); *S v. Nedzamba* 1993 (1) SACR 672 (V). For discussion, *see* S.V. Hoctor, 'Assessing the *de minimis non curat lex* defence in South African law'in P.J. Schwikkard & S.V. Hoctor (eds), *A Reasonable Man: Essays in Honour of Jonathan Burchell* (Juta, Cape Town 2019) 119ff.

Chapter 5. Incomplete or Partly Perpetrated Crimes

§1. Criminal Attempt

238. In the Roman-Dutch law, an attempt to commit a crime was punishable.[423] The South African common law has, accordingly, always regarded an attempt to commit a crime as itself a crime, punishable at the discretion of the court.

239. At one time there was some doubt whether an attempt to commit a statutory – as opposed to a common law – crime was punishable. This doubt has been removed by the enactment of legislation, presently section 18(1) of the Riotous Assemblies Act 1956,[424] which provides that any person who attempts to commit an offence against a statute or a statutory regulation is guilty of an offence. The Act further provides that the punishment for the attempt is the punishment prescribed by the statute in question for the offence which the accused has attempted to commit.

I. *Actus Reus*

240. Since in the case of attempt there is no completed crime, liability for an attempt to commit a crime depends largely upon the fact that the accused intended to commit the crime. However, in this regard, South African law eschews a simple subjective approach to the determination of liability and requires at least some physical manifestation of the intention to commit the crime. In the result, as a general rule, it is essential to prove that the accused had performed some physical act which objectively manifests the accused's intention to commit the crime in question.

In this regard, attempts fall into two categories: completed and uncompleted.[425]

A. Completed Attempts

241. A completed attempt occurs where the actor has done all that he can do in order to commit the crime but, for one reason or another, does not succeed in bringing about the proscribed circumstance or consequence. However, the conduct of the actor provides the *actus reus* for liability for an attempt to commit the crime attempted.[426]

423. *R v. Nlhovo* 1921 AD 485 495–498, 504; *R v. Schoombie* 1945 AD 541 545.
424. Act 17 of 1956.
425. *R v. Schoombie* 1945 AD 541 545–546.
426. *R v. Nhlovo* 1921 AD 485; *S v. Laurence* 1975 (4) SA 825 (A).

B. Interrupted (Incomplete) Attempts

242. This type of attempt occurs when the actor is interrupted in the course of conduct that would otherwise give rise to the circumstance or consequence that constitutes the completed crime. In this case, the question arises whether the actor's conduct, prior to the stage of interruption, was in its nature or extent sufficiently proximate to the choate crime to justify punishment as an attempt to commit the crime. The court must determine the line between 'the end of the beginning and the beginning of the end'[427] and decide on which side of the line the accused's conduct falls.

243. The principal test applied in South African law for this purpose is whether the attempt has reached the 'commencement of the consummation'.[428] Under this test, the commencement of the consummation constitutes 'the last series of acts which would constitute a continuous operation, unbroken by intervals of time which might give an opportunity for reconsideration'.[429]

C. Interruption by Reason of Voluntary Withdrawal

244. South African law does not subscribe to the principle that a voluntary withdrawal from an attempt should result in impunity for the accused. The approach taken by the courts[430] is that once the conduct of the accused reaches the stage of the commencement of the consummation, the accused is guilty of an attempt and thus a subsequent voluntary withdrawal from the attempt does not affect the matter of liability[431] (although it might mitigate punishment). On this reasoning, it follows that if the voluntary withdrawal occurs prior to the commencement of the consummation, there is no liability since there is no attempt.[432]

II. *Mens Rea*

245. The mental element of attempt liability consists in intention to commit the crime that the accused is charged to have attempted;[433] the intention of an attempter

427. *R v. B* 1958 (1) SA 199 (A) 202.
428. This test was taken over, in *R v. Sharpe* 1903 TS 868, from the American case of *Hicks v. Commonwealth* (1889) 19 American State Reports 892, and applied in *R v. Lionda* 1944 AD 348. *See* further S.V. Hoctor, 'The (Surprising) Roots of the Test for Criminal Liability for Interrupted Attempt in South African Law' 2015 *SACJ* 363.
429. *R v. Schoombie* 1945 AD 541 547.
430. *S v. Du Plessis* 1981 (3) SA 382 (A) 400D.
431. C.R. Snyman, *Criminal Law* 6th ed. (LexisNexis, Durban 2014) 284–286 considers voluntary withdrawal to be a good defence even after the commencement of the consummation. Aliter M.A. Rabie, 'Die verweer van vrywillige terugtrede by poging – 'n tweede mening' 1981 *SACC* 56; S.V. Hoctor, 'Voluntary Withdrawal in the Context of Attempt: A Defence?' 2021 *Obiter* 148.
432. *S v. Kudangirana* 1976 (3) SA 563 (RA).
433. *R v. Katz* 1959 (3) SA 408 (C) 423–424; *S v. Palmos* 1979 (2) SA 82 (A) 94G.

is the same as that required of a perpetrator of the completed crime. *Dolus eventualis* suffices.[434]

Since the *mens rea* of attempt consists in intention, it follows that it is not possible to attempt a crime for which negligence is the *mens rea*.[435]

III. Attempting the Impossible

246. In South African law, the fact that an attempt to commit a crime could not be achieved whether because the means used were, in the existing or in all conceivable circumstances, inadequate or because the object was, in the existing or in all conceivable circumstances, unattainable does not prevent the endeavour from amounting to an attempt.[436] In short, there can be liability for an attempt to commit the impossible.

247. South African law has rejected the distinction between absolute and relative impossibility as 'logically unsatisfactory'.[437] Accordingly, attempt liability will arise even though the crime in question was absolutely incapable of commission.

248. The rule regarding attempts to commit the impossible is subject to two qualifications:

1. in statutory crimes, the language of the statute may preclude a conviction of attempt;[438] and
2. it is not legally possible to commit the crime attempted.

The principle that a person can be convicted of a crime that is impossible to commit cannot apply where the impossibility arises from the fact that no such crime exists in the law. Thus, since adultery is not a crime in South African law, a couple who believe that it is a crime to commit adultery and nevertheless attempt to do so cannot be convicted. Moreover, a mistake as to the definition of a crime, as opposed to a mistake about the factual circumstances of the crime, falls within the exception to liability for attempting the impossible.[439]

§2. Participation in, or Parties to, Criminal Offences

I. General Remarks

249. In relation to the situation in which a number of persons cooperate in the commission of the same crime, South African law draws a broad distinction

434. *S v. Palmos* (*supra*) 94G.
435. *S v. Ntanzi* 1981 (2) SA 477 (N).
436. *R v. Davies* 1956 (3) SA 52 (A).
437. *R v. Davies* (*supra*) 62, 75–76.
438. *R v. Davies* 1956 (3) SA 52 (A) 64.
439. S.V. Hoctor, *Snyman's Criminal Law* 7th ed. (LexisNexis, Durban, 2020) 248; S.V. Hoctor, 'Assessing Attempt at the Impossible in South African Criminal Law' 2006 *JJS* 130.

between perpetrators, accomplices and accessories after the fact.[440] Notwithstanding the significant influence of English law upon the South African criminal law, the South African law does not distinguish between principals in the first and second degrees and principals in the second degree and accessories.

250. The perpetrator (or co-perpetrator) is someone who satisfies the definitional elements of a particular crime. An accomplice is someone who knowingly associates himself with the commission of the crime by the perpetrator and furthers the commission of the crime. An accessory is one who assists the perpetrator after the completion of the crime.[441]

II. Perpetrators and Co-perpetrators

251. Perpetrators are principal offenders: persons who directly engage in the criminal act or omission as described by the law. Their liability is dependent upon the proof of their commission of the *actus reus* with the necessary *mens rea*.[442]

252. South African law invokes the concept of the co-perpetrator in cases where a number of persons have co-operated in the commission of a crime and each, in so doing, has satisfied the definitional elements for liability for the crime.

Strictly speaking, this is not a case of participation since each co-perpetrator is a perpetrator (principal offender) in his own right and his liability is in no way accessory or dependent on the conduct of another person. However, it does happen that where a number of persons cooperate to commit a crime, it is not always possible to prove that each participant personally performed every act required for liability for the offence. South African law, instead of treating such a situation as an inevitable ground for the acquittal of the particular accused rather, recognises that in appropriate circumstances, the proved conduct of another member of the group may be imputed or attributed to the accused so as to render him liable in his own right. This device of attribution of the *actus* of one person to another creates a special category of co-perpetration.[443] In it, a person is deemed to be a perpetrator by reason of his mere involvement with a person or persons who actually perpetrate a crime. This is achieved by the application of the doctrine of common purpose.

---

440. *S v. Williams* 1980 (1) SA 60 (A).
441. *S v. Williams* 1980 (1) SA 60 (A) 63. *See* J. Burchell, *Principles of Criminal Law* 5th ed. (Juta, Cape Town 2016) 475ff.; S.V. Hoctor, *Snyman's Criminal Law* 7th ed. (LexisNexis, Durban, 2020) 219ff.
442. J. Burchell, *Principles of Criminal Law* 5th ed. (Juta, Cape Town 2016) 475; S.V. Hoctor, *Snyman's Criminal Law* 7th ed. (LexisNexis, Durban, 2020) 220.
443. J. Burchell, *Principles of Criminal Law* 5th ed. (Juta, Cape Town 2016) 477; S.V. Hoctor, *Snyman's Criminal Law* 7th ed. (LexisNexis, Durban, 2020) 225–226.

A. The Doctrine of Common Purpose

253. The doctrine of common purpose holds that where two or more people agree to commit a crime or actively associate in a joint unlawful enterprise, each will be responsible for specific criminal conduct committed by one of their number, which falls within their common design. Liability arises from their 'common purpose' to commit the crime.[444]

If the participants are charged with having committed a 'consequence crime', it is not necessary for the prosecution to prove beyond reasonable doubt that each participant committed conduct which causally contributed to the ultimate unlawful consequence. It is sufficient that it is established that they all agreed to commit a particular crime or actively associated themselves with the commission of the crime by one of their number with the requisite *mens rea.* If this is established, then the conduct of the participant who actually causes the consequence is imputed or attributed to the other participants.[445]

Furthermore, it is not necessary to establish precisely which member of the common purpose caused the consequence, provided that it is established that one of the group brought about this result.[446]

254. One of the earliest applications of the doctrine in South Africa was to convict 200 students engaged in protest action.[447] The doctrine came to be used in murder cases in which it was not possible to establish which of a number of assailants had struck the fatal blow.[448] Then, the doctrine came to be applied to murder cases where it was known who inflicted the fatal blow in order to convict as a perpetrator one who had not struck the blow.[449] A notable application of the doctrine has been to convict a member of a group set up to commit acts of sabotage against the state of the murder of a person slain by another member of the group on the basis that the accused knew when he joined the group, that its members might use deadly force against its opponents.[450]

255. Liability under the common-purpose doctrine arises upon proof of: (a) *actus reus* and (b) *mens rea.*[451]

256. (a) The *actus reus* required to render a person liable in terms of the common-purpose doctrine consists in the conclusion of an agreement, whether

---

444. *S v. Safatsa* 1988 (1) SA 868 (A) (*see* 'Focus' 1988 *SACJ* 225); *S v. Mgedezi* 1989 (1) SA 687 (A); *S v. Nzo* 1990 (3) SA 1 (A).
445. *S v. Safatsa* (*supra*); *S v. Mgedezi* (*supra*); *S v. Nzo* (*supra*). It was held by the Constitutional Court in *S v. Tshabalala* 2020 (2) SACR 38 (CC) that the doctrine even applies to the autographic (i.e., committed only through the instrumentality of one's own body) crime of common-law rape.
446. *S v. Safatsa* (*supra*).
447. *R v. Taylor* 1920 EDL 318.
448. *R v. Ngcobo* 1928 AD 732; *S v. Safatsa* 1988 (1) SA 868 (A).
449. *R v. Nsele* 1955 (2) 145 (A). This enabled the imposition of the death sentence upon those participants in the fatal assault who had not causally contributed to the death of the victim.
450. *S v. Nzo* 1990 (3) SA 1 (A).
451. J. Burchell, *Principles of Criminal Law* 5th ed. (Juta, Cape Town 2016) 495ff.

express or implied, to commit a crime and some form of participation in the criminal activity.[452] It is in this regard that the doctrine of common purpose departs from ordinary principles of liability: the form that the participation takes does not have to causally contribute to the unlawful consequence in order for the participant to be convicted of the consequence crime in question. Thus, the member of a mob who throws a stone harmlessly at the person who is ultimately slain by the mob is guilty of the murder of the victim by reason of his participation in the attack of the mob.[453]

The doctrine does not require that there be a formal prior agreement between the participants in order for liability to arise; it is sufficient if collaboration begins without premeditation and on the spur of the moment.[454] A person may make common purpose with others simply by actively associating himself with their unlawful purpose. Association in the common purpose need not be express; it may be implied from conduct.

However, where no prior agreement has been reached, there are certain prerequisites which must be satisfied before the principle of imputation, which lies at the heart of the common purpose, can apply. These are:

i. presence at the scene of the violence;
ii. awareness of the criminal act;
iii. intention to make common cause with those who were actually perpetrating the assault;
iv. manifestation of a sharing of a common purpose with the perpetrators of the assault by performing 'some act of association with the conduct of the others'[455] and possession of the requisite *mens rea*.

257. (b) *Mens rea*. In order to be liable under the doctrine of common purpose, the participant must intend to commit the crime, which is the object of the common purpose. In respect of this element, there is no imputation of the *mens rea* of other participants. Liability depends upon the individual participant having himself formed the necessary *mens rea*.[456] If he has not done so, there can be no liability, regardless of the state of mind of the other parties to the common purpose.

258. The essence of common-purpose liability is the act of association with the commission of the crime by the other participants. The converse of association is dissociation and it is clear that a party to a common purpose will avoid liability under this doctrine by timeous dissociation from the common purpose.[457] Insofar as

452. *S v. Mgedezi* 1989 (1) SA 687 (A) 706.
453. *S v. Safatsa* 1988 (1) SA 868 (A).
454. *S v. Khoza* 1982 (3) SA 1019 (A) 1053D–H.
455. *S v. Mgedezi* 1989 (1) SA 687 (A) 706. The decision in *Mgedezi's* case and the principles set out therein do not infringe the constitutional rights to dignity, freedom or security of the person or the right to be presumed innocent – *Thebus v. S* 2003 (6) SA 505 (CC).
456. J. Burchell, *Principles of Criminal Law* 5th ed. (Juta, Cape Town 2016) 495.
457. *S v. Singo* 1993 (1) SACR 226 (A). Cf. Focus: 'Common Purpose' 1992 *SACJ* 160.

common-purpose liability is dependent upon the intention to commit the crime contemplated and an active association with the conduct of the other parties, where a party either ceases to so intend or ceases to actively associate himself, there is dissociation from the common purpose.[458]

B. Joining-In

259. To be distinguished from the participant in a common purpose is the 'joiner-in'. This term is used in South African homicide law to describe a person who is not a party to a common purpose but who 'joins-in' with a crime. Typically, a joining-in happens when the joiner comes upon the scene of a murderous assault and, without making common purpose with the perpetrator of the assault, himself assaults the victim. Clearly, if this assault is the cause of the death of the victim, the joiner-in commits murder. The question which has troubled South African courts is what is the liability of the joiner-in where his conduct does *not* cause death (or other prohibited consequence)?

260. In some cases, the joiner-in was held to be liable on the basis that he had 'ratified' the conduct of the initial perpetrator of the harm.[459] However, this approach was criticised as resting criminal liability not upon the principle of causation but rather upon the unacceptable principle of ratification.[460] The currently accepted view[461] is that the liability of the joiner-in must be determined by the principle of causation. Thus, if a person joins in a fatal assault upon another *after* the fatal blow has been administered, and his assault does not causally contribute to death, he cannot be convicted of murder but, at most, attempted murder.[462]

III. Accomplices

261. An accomplice is one, other than the perpetrator(s) and other than the accessory after the fact, who takes part in the commission of the crime. Accomplice liability is distinct from that of the perpetrator, being based on the accomplice's own *actus reus* and *mens rea*.

A. Requirement of a Principal Offence

262. It is, however, of the essence of accomplice liability that there should be a principal offence to which the act of the accomplice is accessory: a person cannot be an accomplice to his or her own crime.

---

458. *S v. Singo* (*supra*); S.V. Hoctor, *Snyman's Criminal Law* 7th ed. (LexisNexis, Durban, 2020) 231–232.
459. *R v. Mgxwiti* 1954 (1) SA 370 (A); *S v. Dlamini* 1984 (3) SA 360 (N).
460. *S v. Thomo* 1969 (1) SA 381 (A).
461. *S v. Motaung* 1990 (4) SA 485 (A); followed in *S v. Tsotetsi* 2019 (2) SACR 594 (WCC).
462. *S v. Motaung* (*supra*).

Thus, there can be no question of an accomplice without a perpetrator or co-perpetrator who commits the crime. An accomplice associates himself wittingly with the commission of the crime by the perpetrator or co-perpetrator in that he knowingly affords the perpetrator or co-perpetrator the opportunity, the means or the information which furthers the commission of the crime.[463]

263. The *actus reus* of an accomplice consists in 'furthering' or 'assisting' the commission of the crime.[464]

It is not clear whether, for these purposes, 'further' means 'causally further'.[465] If it does, then, in relation to crimes of consequence at least, there would be no distinction between perpetrators and accomplices, since an accomplice who causally furthers, say, the killing of a person causes death and is thus a perpetrator.

264. The *actus reus* of the accomplice is the voluntary act which furthers or assists; accomplice liability is thus not a form of vicarious liability. There must be fault in the form of an intention to further or assist in the commission of the crime of the perpetrator. For these purposes, negligence does not suffice for accomplice liability.[466]

IV. Accessory after the Fact

265. In South African law, a person who intentionally assists the perpetrator *after* the completion of the crime is not an accomplice because he or she does not further the commission of the crime. It is, however, conventional to characterise such a person as an accessory after the fact.

266. There are two views as to the basis of this form of liability. One defines the accessory as a person who associates himself with the crime of the principal offender.[467] This approach may lead to an assumption that somebody who merely approves, condones or ratifies a crime after it has been completed is an accessory after the fact and, for this reason, has been criticised as vague and too wide.[468] The other approach defines the accessory as one who, with the intention to defeat the administration of justice, assists the principal offender after the completion of the crime. Since such conduct would constitute the crime of defeating or obstructing the course of justice,[469] this approach makes it unnecessary to postulate a separate form of liability. It has, thus, been suggested that there is no need in South African law for accessory liability.[470]

---

463. *S v. Williams* 1980 (1) SA 60 (A).
464. *S v. Williams* (*supra*) 63.
465. R.C. Whiting, 'Principals and Accessories in Crime' 1980 *SALJ* 199; S.V. Hoctor, *Snyman's Criminal Law* 7th ed. (LexisNexis, Durban, 2020) 236–237.
466. S.V. Hoctor, *Snyman's Criminal Law* 7th ed. (LexisNexis, Durban, 2020) 236.
467. *R v. Nkau Majara* [1954] AC 235 (PC).
468. J. Burchell, *Principles of Criminal Law* 5th ed. (Juta, Cape Town 2016) 517–519.
469. *See infra*, para. 366.
470. S.V. Hoctor, *Snyman's Criminal Law* 7th ed. (LexisNexis, Durban, 2020) 240.

267. The liability of an accessory after the fact is, like that of an accomplice, accessory in nature. There can only be an accessory after the fact if somebody else has committed the crime or attempted to do so. Accordingly, a person cannot be an accessory after the fact to his or her own crime, except where the person makes himself an accomplice to the act of the accessory after the fact. For instance, Y has murdered Z; X acts as an accessory by concealing the truth from the police. If Y were to assist X in this concealment, it has been held that he can be convicted as an accomplice to the crime of X.[471]

V. Special Cases

A. Entrapment

268. In South African law, an act of entrapment by law enforcement authorities does not justify the conduct of the person entrapped.[472] There may however be a defence based on the fact that the evidence obtained through the trap is inadmissible.[473] The police official who sets the trap may not be held criminally liable on the basis of his conduct relating to the trap as long as he acted in good faith.[474]

§3. Incitement and Conspiracy to Commit Crime

I. Incitement

269. In South African law, incitement to commit a crime is made punishable by section 18(2)(*b*) of the Riotous Assemblies Act,[475] which provides that '[a]ny person who . . . incites, instigates, commands, or procures any other person to commit any offence, whether at common law or against a statute or statutory regulation, shall be guilty of an offence and liable on conviction to the punishment to which a person convicted of actually committing that offence would be liable'.

270. The unlawful conduct element of incitement consists in communication by the accused to the incitee. It is immaterial, however, whether the incitee acts upon the communication or not.[476]

---

471. *R v. Gani* 1957 (2) SA 212 (A); *S v. Jonathan* 1987 (1) SA 633 (A).
472. S.V. Hoctor, *Snyman's Criminal Law* 7th ed. (LexisNexis, Durban, 2020) 122.
473. This area of the law is regulated by s. 252A of the Criminal Procedure Act 51 of 1977. Evidence obtained through entrapment may be excluded if the conduct of the law enforcement official goes 'beyond providing an opportunity to commit an offence', by using improper or unfair means to obtain such evidence. *See infra* para. 502.
474. Criminal Procedure Act 51 of 1977, s. 252A(5)(*a*).
475. Act 17 of 1956. In the Constitutional Court case of *Economic Freedom Fighters v. Minister of Justice and Correctional Services* [2020] ZACC 25, it was held that the infringement of the right to freedom of expression, protected in s. 16 of the Constitution, 1996, was not justifiable, and that the term 'any offence' should be replaced by 'serious offence'. Incitement can therefore only be committed in respect of 'serious' offences.
476. *R v. O* 1952 (3) SA 184 (T).

The approach to the other's mind may take various forms, such as suggestion, proposal, request, exhortation, gesture, argument, persuasion, inducement, goading or the arousal of cupidity. The list is not exhaustive. The means employed are of secondary importance; the decisive question in each case is whether the accused reached and sought to influence the mind of the other person towards the commission of a crime.[477]

II. Conspiracy

271. Conspiracy to commit a crime is an offence in South African Law in terms of section 18(2)(*a*) of the Riotous Assemblies Act 17 of 1956, which provides that '[a]ny person who . . . conspires with any other person to aid or procure the commission of or to commit . . . any offence, whether at common law or against a statute or statutory regulation, shall be guilty of an offence and liable on conviction to the punishment to which a person convicted of actually committing that offence would be liable'.

The agreement between the parties constitutes the unlawful conduct element of conspiracy.[478] Liability is based on the intention to commit the crime in question.[479]

477. *S v. Nkosiyana* 1966 (4) SA 655 (A).
478. *R v. Harris* (1927) 48 NLR 330 347; *S v. Cooper* 1976 (2) SA 875 (T). It has been held that where a party only pretends to enter into a conspiracy, even though he cannot be convicted of conspiracy, his overt manifestation of assent to the conspiracy would suffice to establish conspiracy liability for the other party – *see S v. Ngobese* 2019 (1) SACR 575 (GJ).
479. *R v. S* 1959 (1) SA 680 (C) 683–684; *S v. Alexander* 1965 (2) SA 818 (C) 822.

Chapter 6. Classification and Survey of Specific Crimes

§1. Classification of Crimes

272. Notwithstanding the influence of the English law, South African criminal law does not classify crimes according to their relative seriousness ('felonies' and 'misdemeanours'). A prevalent classification is according to the origin of crimes ('common law' or 'statutory').[480] Academic writers tend, however, to classify crimes (whether common law or statutory) according to the nature of the social interests that the crimes are designed to protect.[481] Classification according to the interests protected has no substantive or procedural significance and is merely a matter of convenience. It is preferred by writers in that it is a useful method of focusing attention on the nature and purpose of the crime.

273. The usual classification on this basis is: Crimes against the Person, Crimes against Property, Crimes against the State and Crimes against the Community.

§2. Crimes Against the Person

I. Abortion

274. Abortion, though a crime by South African common law, is now proscribed by statute. In terms of the Choice on Termination of Pregnancy Act, it is an offence for any person who is not a medical practitioner to procure the termination of a pregnancy.[482]

Termination of a pregnancy may only take place with the informed consent of the woman, and no other consent is required.[483] The Act[484] provides that the requirements for a lawful termination vary according to the stage ('gestational period') which the pregnancy has reached: (i) in the first twelve weeks, the abortion may be performed by a registered medical practitioner (or registered midwife) at the request of the mother; (ii) in weeks thirteen to twenty, termination may only take place by a registered medical practitioner, after consultation with the woman, for certain specified therapeutic, eugenic or humanitarian grounds; and (iii) after twenty weeks, termination may only occur if a registered medical practitioner, having consulted with another medical practitioner or registered midwife, believes that the woman's life would be in danger or that there would be severe malformation of the foetus.

480. Cf. E.M. Burchell & P.M.A. Hunt, *South African Criminal Law and Procedure*, Vol. I *General Principles* 2nd ed. (Juta, Cape Town 1983) 93.
481. Cf. E.M. Burchell & P.M.A. Hunt, *South African Criminal Law and Procedure*, Vol. I *General Principles* 2nd ed. (Juta, Cape Town 1983) 96 et seq.
482. Choice on Termination of Pregnancy Act 92 of 1996, s. 10(1)(*a*)(*b*). 'Termination of pregnancy' is defined as the separation and expulsion, by medical or surgical means, of the contents of a pregnant uterus (s. 1).
483. Choice on Termination of Pregnancy Act 92 of 1996, s. 5.
484. Choice on Termination of Pregnancy Act 92 of 1996, s. 2.

The offence can only be committed intentionally.[485]

II. Homicide

275. Homicide is punished, if it is intentional (murder), or negligent (culpable homicide). The intentional killing of infants, though separately recognised in law (infanticide), is punished as murder. Euthanasia is murder.

A. *Murder*

276. Murder is the unlawful and intentional killing of another person.[486]

An intentional killing of a human being is not unlawful if done in defence of person,[487] or in circumstances of necessity,[488] or under superior orders.[489] There are no other grounds for justification: euthanasia is unlawful,[490] as is killing at the request or with the consent of the victim.[491]

Intent to kill is tested subjectively: the State must prove either *dolus directus or dolus eventualis*: negligence (or even recklessness) is insufficient for murder. *Dolus eventualis* exists where the fatal conduct is done, foreseeing the possibility that it may cause the death of a person.[492]

277. In 1917, capital punishment became the mandatory punishment for murder. In 1990, after expressions of concern at the high number of executions carried out in South Africa,[493] the law was amended so as to allow the court an almost complete discretion as to whether to pass the sentence of death for murder.[494] The death penalty was held to be unconstitutional in that it unjustifiably infringed on the right to life, the right to dignity and the right not to be subjected to cruel, inhuman or degrading punishment in *S v. Makwanyane*.[495]

---

485. J. Burchell, *Principles of Criminal Law* 5th ed. (Juta, Cape Town 2016) 575.
486. J.R.L. Milton, *South African Criminal Law and Procedure*, Vol. II *Common-Law Crimes* 3rd ed. (Juta, Cape Town 1996) 310; S.V. Hoctor, *Snyman's Criminal Law* 7th ed. (LexisNexis, Durban, 2020) 387.
487. *See supra,* para. 172.
488. *See supra,* para. 194.
489. *See supra,* para. 203.
490. *S v. Hartmann* 1975 (3) SA 532 (C); *S v. De Bellocq* 1975 (3) SA 538 (T); *S v. Hibbert* 1979 (4) 717 (D).
491. *R v. Peverett* 1940 AD 213; *S v. Robinson* 1968 (1) SA 666 (A) 678. *See supra,* para. 197.
492. *See supra,* para. 151.
493. Between 1979 and 1988 there was an annual average of 120 executions in South Africa. *See* 'The Death Penalty in South Africa' 1989 *SACJ* 251 253.
494. *See infra*, para. 377.
495. 1995 (2) SACR 1 (CC).

B. Suicide

278. Neither suicide nor attempted suicide is a crime.[496] Assisting another person to commit suicide may however result in a murder conviction for the person providing assistance.[497]

C. Infanticide

279. In Roman-Dutch law, there existed the crime of *crimen expositionis infantis*, which took two forms: abandoning a child in the expectation that it would die and abandoning a child in a place where it was likely to be fostered. The former was punishable by death; the latter, more leniently.

Crimen expositionis infantis which causes death is, it seems, a separate crime in South African law.[498] (The other form of the Roman-Dutch crime is now punished by statute.)[499] There is no need for such a crime since every instance of the intentional killing of an infant is murder.

D. Culpable Homicide

280. Culpable homicide is the unlawful, negligent killing of another human being.[500]

In South African law, culpable homicide initially included not only negligent homicide but also (under the application of the *versari in re illicita* (felony-murder) doctrine) unintended death arising from an illegal activity[501] and also *intentional* homicide committed in circumstances of 'partial excuse'.[502] South African law has since abandoned both the *versari* and partial excuse[503] doctrines so that culpable homicide consists simply and exclusively of the *negligent* killing of a person.[504]

281. Even if the accused was negligent, it is open to him to raise a defence excluding unlawfulness. Thus, the accused could show that the negligent killing was

---

496. *S v. Grotjohn* 1970 (2) SA 355 (A) 363D, 366.
497. *S v. Grotjohn* (*supra*).
498. *R v. Adams* (1903) 21 SC 556. Cf. *S v. Bengu* 1965 (1) SA 298 (N).
499. Children's Act 38 of 2005, s. 305(3).
500. J.R.L. Milton, *South African Criminal Law and Procedure*, Vol. II *Common-Law Crimes* 3rd ed. (Juta, Cape Town 1996) 364; S.V. Hoctor, *Snyman's Criminal Law* 7th ed. (LexisNexis, Durban, 2020) 391.
501. J.R.L. Milton, *South African Criminal Law and Procedure*, Vol. II *Common-Law Crimes* 3rd ed. (Juta, Cape Town 1996) 371.
502. J.R.L. Milton, *South African Criminal Law and Procedure*, Vol. II *Common-Law Crimes* 3rd ed. (Juta, Cape Town 1996) 370. Examples of partially excused murder were killings under severe provocation or killing in private defence where the defender had exceeded the limits allowed by the law.
503. *S v. Bailey* 1982 (3) SA 772 (A) 798G; *S v. Ngubane* 1985 (3) SA 677 (A) 684C.
504. *S v. Ntuli* 1975 (1) SA 429 (A) 436; *S v. Burger* 1975 (4) SA 877 (A) 878.

done in the course of private defence[505] or carrying out superior orders[506] or an arrest in terms of section 49 of the Criminal Procedure Act 1977.[507] Indeed, any defence that would justify an intentional killing should be available where the killing is merely unintended.

282. The test of negligence is that of whether a reasonable person in the circumstances would have foreseen that death might be the result of a proposed course of conduct *and* would have taken steps to guard against death occurring.[508]

If the court concludes that a reasonable man would not have foreseen death, then it will conclude that the accused had not been negligent and thus that he or she had not committed culpable homicide. Conversely, if the court finds that a reasonable person would have foreseen death,[509] it will conclude that the accused, by failing to foresee that death would result from the course of conduct he embarked upon, had been negligent and thus guilty of culpable homicide.

Likewise, if the court were to conclude that even if a reasonable person might have foreseen that death might eventuate but that the reasonable person would nevertheless have proceeded with the conduct, then again, it would conclude that there was no negligence on the part of the accused. Of course, if the reasonable person would not have proceeded, then the accused – who did proceed – is clearly guilty of negligence.

III. Crimes Against Bodily Integrity

283. Physical harm or injury to the body of a human being is called assault in South African law, a crime which has a variety of forms. The basic offence is called common assault, involving the application of simple force to the body of another (or inspiring fear that such force is about to be applied). Where the force potentially involves what is called 'grievous bodily harm', it is punishable as a separate form of assault. Where the force applied to the body involves or is intended to involve the sexual parts of the body, the assault is also treated as a separate assault crime, called 'sexual assault'.

A. Common Assault

284. Common assault consists in unlawfully and intentionally: (1) applying force to the person of another, or (2) inspiring a belief in that other person that force is immediately to be applied to him.[510]

505. *See supra,* para. 172.
506. *See supra,* para. 203.
507. *See supra,* para. 211.
508. *See supra,* para. 155.
509. What must be foreseen is death and not merely injury: *S v. Bernardus* 1965 (3) SA 287 (A).
510. J.R.L. Milton, *South African Criminal Law and Procedure*, Vol. II *Common-Law Crimes* 3rd ed. (Juta, Cape Town 1996) 406; S.V. Hoctor, *Snyman's Criminal Law* 7th ed. (LexisNexis, Durban, 2020) 395. Assault can also be committed by omission – *S v. B* 1994 (2) SACR 237 (E).

This type of assault occurs where violent force is applied to the person of another, causing bruising, wounding, breaking or mutilation. This may occur directly as where the offender attacks the victim with a weapon or indirectly as where X derails a train in which Y is travelling[511] or causes him to drink a harmful liquid such as alcohol[512] or urine.[513]

285. South African law, following the English law, has recognised that touching a person's body without inflicting any sort of physical harm may constitute an assault.

Generally, touching is considered to be an assault where the manner or nature of the touch is in some way insulting to the victim.[514] Touching that has a sexual motivation, however gentle or affectionate, is an assault if done without the consent of the person touched.[515]

286. The mere inspiring of an apprehension in the mind of a person that he or she is about to be touched or beaten is in itself an assault for which punishment may be imposed.[516]

The gist of this form of assault is the creation of apprehension in the mind of the victim of the assault. An assault is thus any act or gesture which induces in the mind of another an apprehension that he or she is about to suffer a battery.

287. The crime is committed by the act, gesture or words,[517] causing a belief that the attack will occur. It is not necessary that the victim should also have experienced any emotion of fear.

B. Assault with Intent to Do Grievous Bodily Harm

288. Assaults involving serious physical injury have always been regarded as more serious than those that merely inspire fear or involve mere touching or only slight bodily injury. In South African law, this type of assault is identified by the description 'assault with intent to do grievous bodily harm'.[518] Grievous bodily harm is 'harm which in itself is such as seriously to interfere with health'.[519]

511. *R v. Jolly* 1923 AD 176 179.
512. *S v. Marx* 1962 (1) SA 848 (N) 853.
513. *S v. A* 1993 (1) SACR 600 (A).
514. *R v. Herbert* (1900) 10 CTR 424.
515. *See infra*, para. 289.
516. *S v. Mtimunye* 1994 (2) SACR 482 (T) 485a-b.
517. J. Burchell, *Principles of Criminal Law* 5th ed. (Juta, Cape Town 2016) 597–598; S.V. Hoctor, *Snyman's Criminal Law* 7th ed. (LexisNexis, Durban, 2020) 399.
518. J.R.L. Milton, *South African Criminal Law and Procedure*, Vol. II *Common-Law Crimes* 3rd ed. (Juta, Cape Town 1996) 431.
519. J.R.L. Milton, *South African Criminal Law and Procedure*, Vol. II *Common-Law Crimes* 3rd ed. (Juta, Cape Town 1996) 433.

C. Sexual Assault, Compelled Sexual Assault and Compelled Self-Sexual Assault

289. Sexually motivated touching or fondling of persons is punished in South African law as the separate crime of sexual assault, which has replaced the common-law crime of indecent assault.

Sexual assault is committed by any person who: (i) unlawfully and intentionally sexually violates a complainant without the complainant's consent; or (ii) unlawfully and intentionally inspires the belief in a complainant that such complainant will be sexually violated.[520]

A person who unlawfully and intentionally compels a third person, without his or her consent, to commit an act of sexual violation with a complainant, without the complainant's consent, is guilty of the offence of compelled sexual assault.[521]

The offence of compelled self-sexual assault is committed by a person who unlawfully and intentionally compels a complainant, without the complainant's consent, to: (a) engage in masturbation; any form of arousal or stimulation of a sexual nature of the female breasts; or sexually suggestive or lewd acts, with the complainant him- or herself; or (b) engage in any act which has or may have the effect of sexually arousing or sexually degrading the complainant; or (c) cause the complainant to penetrate in any manner whatsoever his or her own genital organs or anus.[522]

D. Rape and Compelled Rape

290. The common-law definition of rape was defined as the unlawful, intentional sexual intercourse with a woman without her consent.[523]

The common-law crime of rape has now been repealed in favour of the statutory version of the crime to be found in the codification of sex offences in South African law contained in the Criminal Law (Sexual Offences and Related Matters) Amendment Act.[524]

---

520. Criminal Law (Sexual Offences and Related Matters) Amendment Act 32 of 2007, s. 5; S.V. Hoctor, *Snyman's Criminal Law* 7th ed. (LexisNexis, Durban 2020) 320. 'Sexual violation' is defined in s. 1 of this Act as excluding an act of sexual penetration, but including: masturbation of one person by another; the insertion of any object resembling or representing human or animal sexual organs into or beyond the mouth of another person; or any act causing direct or indirect contact: (i) between the genital organs or anus of a person (or in the case of a female, her breasts) and any part of the body of another person or animal or any object; (ii) between the mouth of one person and the genital organs or anus (or in the case of a female, her breasts); or between the mouth of one person and the mouth of another person; or between the mouth of one person and any other part of the body of another person which could be associated with sexual arousal or stimulation or any object resembling erogenous body areas; or (iii) between the mouth of the complainant and the genital organs or anus of an animal.
521. Criminal Law (Sexual Offences and Related Matters) Amendment Act 32 of 2007, s. 6.
522. Criminal Law (Sexual Offences and Related Matters) Amendment Act 32 of 2007, s. 7.
523. J.R.L. Milton, *South African Criminal Law and Procedure*, Vol. II *Common-Law Crimes* 3rd ed. (Juta, Cape Town 1996) 439.
524. Criminal Law (Sexual Offences and Related Matters) Amendment Act 32 of 2007.

291. The statutory crime of rape has been expanded to include all forms of non-consensual sexual penetration and makes no distinction in terms of gender with regard to perpetrator or victim.[525]

292. The crime is committed by any person who unlawfully and intentionally commits an act of sexual penetration with a complainant, without the consent of such complainant.[526]

'Sexual penetration' includes any act which causes penetration to any extent whatsoever by: (a) the genital organs of one person into or beyond the genital organs, anus or mouth of another person; (b) any other part of the body of one person or, any object, including any part of the body of an animal, into or beyond the genital organs or anus of another person; or (c) the genital organs of an animal, into or beyond the mouth of another person.[527]

293. Consent is described in the Act as voluntary or uncoerced agreement.[528] Absence of consent is further described in terms of particular sets of circumstances: (a) where B (the complainant) submits or is subjected to such a sexual act (including an act of sexual penetration) as a result of: (i) the use of force or intimidation by A (the accused person) against B, C (a third person) or D (another person) or against the property of B, C or D; or (ii) a threat of harm by A against B, C or D or against the property of B, C or D; (b) where there is an abuse of power or authority by A to the extent that B is inhibited from indicating his or her unwillingness or resistance to the sexual act, or unwillingness to participate in such a sexual act; (c) where the sexual act is committed under false pretences or by fraudulent means, including where B is led to believe by A that: (i) B is committing such a sexual act with a particular person who is in fact a different person; or (ii) such a sexual act is something other than that act; or (d) where B is incapable in law of appreciating the nature of the sexual act, including where B is, at the time of the commission of such sexual act: (i) asleep; (ii) unconscious; (iii) in an altered state of consciousness, including under the influence of any medicine, drug, alcohol or other substance, to the extent that B's consciousness or judgment is adversely affected; (iv) a child below the age of 12; or (v) a person who is mentally disabled.[529]

294. Rape can only be committed intentionally (as with the common-law crime).[530]

295. Any person who unlawfully and intentionally compels a third person, without the consent of such third person, to commit an act of sexual penetration with a complainant, without the complainant's consent, commits the crime of compelled rape.[531]

---

525. *See* generally S.V. Hoctor, *Snyman's Criminal Law* 7th ed. (LexisNexis, Durban 2020) 307–319.
526. Criminal Law (Sexual Offences and Related Matters) Amendment Act 32 of 2007, s. 3.
527. Criminal Law (Sexual Offences and Related Matters) Amendment Act 32 of 2007, s. 1.
528. Criminal Law (Sexual Offences and Related Matters) Amendment Act 32 of 2007, s. 1(2).
529. Criminal Law (Sexual Offences and Related Matters) Amendment Act 32 of 2007, s. 1(3).
530. *R v. Z* 1960 (1) SA 739 (A) 742–743, 745.
531. Criminal Law (Sexual Offences and Related Matters) Amendment Act 32 of 2007, s. 4.

E. Crimen Injuria

296. Crimen injuria consists in unlawfully and intentionally impairing the dignitas of another.[532]

Dignitas can be described negatively in terms of the person's right to freedom from insulting, degrading, offensive or humiliating treatment or from invasions of privacy. Acts that have been held to constitute *crimen injuria* include indecent exposure of the person, communications or other conduct which invite or propose sexual impropriety, indecent assault, inducing engagement to marry or sexual intercourse by fraud, vulgar abuse, gross impertinence,[533] insults,[534] and humiliation,[535] invasions of privacy (including voyeuristic 'peeping',[536] eavesdropping, telephone tapping, 'bugging' and other forms of electronic surveillance).[537]

An *iniuria* is unlawful only when objectively considered in the light of the prevailing norms of society, it is insulting. This requirement is sometimes expressed in the form that the impairment of another's *dignitas* must be serious.[538] The basis for judging gravity is largely the court's conception of contemporary *boni mores.*

F. Kidnapping

297. Kidnapping consists in unlawfully and intentionally depriving a person of liberty of movement and/or his custodians of control.[539]

The crime may take the form of physically carrying a person off, or imprisoning the person without physically moving him[540] from one place to another, or enticing away by craft or cunning, or some other act by which the person is deprived of liberty.

---

532. J.R.L. Milton, *South African Criminal Law and Procedure*, Vol. II *Common-Law Crimes* 3rd ed. (Juta, Cape Town 1996) 492; S.V. Hoctor, *Snyman's Criminal Law* 7th ed. (LexisNexis, Durban 2020) 407.
533. *R v. Walton* 1958 (3) SA 693 (SR).
534. *S v. M* 1979 (2) SA 25 (A) ('white bitch'); *S v. Bugwandeen* 1987 (1) SA 787 (N) ('black bastard'). In *S v. Sharp* 2002 (1) SACR 360 (Ck), it was however held that calling a policewoman a 'bitch' did not amount to an impairment of dignity.
535. *R v. Sethuntsa* 1945 EDL 128 (complainant forced to carry his own excrement in his hands through the streets of a town).
536. *R v. Holliday* 1927 CPD 395.
537. Cf. *S v. A* 1971 (2) SA 293 (T); *S v. I* 1976 (2) SA 781 (RA).
538. *See*, however, *S v. Bugwandeen* 1987 (1) SA 787 (N) where the 'serious' requirement is rejected as imprecise and nebulous. *Contra*, J.R.L. Milton, *South African Criminal Law and Procedure,* Vol. II *Common-Law Crimes* 3rd ed. (Juta, Cape Town 1996) 501; S.V. Hoctor, *Snyman's Criminal Law* 7th ed. (LexisNexis, Durban 2020) 411.
539. J.R.L Milton, *South African Criminal Law and Procedure*, Vol. II *Common-Law Crimes* 3rd ed. (Juta, Cape Town 1996) 539; S.V. Hoctor, *Snyman's Criminal Law* 7th ed. (LexisNexis, Durban 2020) 417.
540. *S v. Mellors* 1990 (1) SACR 347 (W).

In principle, there seems no reason to require that the deprivation of liberty or custody should endure for any length of time. In the light of the prevailing case-law,[541] the view is justified that there is a deprivation of liberty or custody when there is any substantial interference with freedom of movement.

G. Hijacking

298. The Civil Aviation Act 2009[542] gives effect to the provisions of various international conventions for combating hijacking.

In terms of the Act, any person who on board any aircraft in flight by force or threat of force or by any other form of intimidation and without lawful reason seizes or exercises control of that aircraft commits an offence.[543]

Any person who destroys an aircraft in service or wilfully causes damage to such an aircraft which renders it incapable of flight or which is likely to endanger its safety in flight commits an offence.[544]

Any person who places on an aircraft in service a device or substance which is likely to destroy that aircraft or to cause damage to it which renders it incapable of flight or is likely to endanger its safety in flight, commits an offence.[545]

The Act, following the provisions of the Hague Convention, confers jurisdiction over offences committed aboard aircraft registered in South Africa.[546]

§3. Crimes Against the Family

I. Abduction

299. Abduction is defined as unlawfully taking a minor out of the control of his or her custodian with the intention of enabling someone to marry or have sexual intercourse with that minor.[547]

Abduction is committed only where the abduction is for the purposes of marriage or a sexual liaison with the abductee. This feature distinguishes abduction from kidnapping.

Tribal custom amongst certain African peoples in South Africa recognises a form of abduction ('*ukuthwala*') as a legitimate means of obtaining the hand of a girl in marriage.[548] However, it has been held abduction by way of '*thwala*' is unlawful.[549]

---

541. *S v. Blanche* 1969 (2) SA 359 (W) 360; *S v. Mellors* 1990 (1) SACR 347 (W).
542. Act 13 of 2009.
543. Civil Aviation Act 13 of 2009, s. 133(*a*). Any person who commits an act of violence which is likely to endanger the aircraft's safety or wilfully interferes with any crew member of the aircraft in the performance of their duties also commits an offence in terms of this provision.
544. Civil Aviation Act 13 of 2009, s. 133(*b*).
545. Civil Aviation Act 13 of 2009, s. 133(*c*).
546. Civil Aviation Act 13 of 2009, s. 150.
547. J.R.L. Milton, *South African Criminal Law and Procedure*, Vol. II *Common-Law Crimes* 3rd ed. (Juta, Cape Town 1996) 554.
548. J.C. Bekker, *Seymour's Customary Law in South Africa* 5th ed. (Juta, Cape Town 1989) 98.

Seduction is not abduction and a taking merely to facilitate a seduction will not constitute abduction.[550] The test as to whether the removal was for purposes of seduction or abduction is whether the removal was for a substantial period of time.

The person abducted must be an unmarried minor.[551]

It is not clear what social purpose the crime of abduction serves in the twenty-first century. It does not prevent the sexual seduction of young women, and the crime of kidnapping is available to punish men who take and detain young girls for immoral or other purposes. The specific effect of the crime is simply to protect a parent's power to consent to the marriage of a child.

300. It is an offence under the Sexual Offences Act 1957 for any person to take or detain a female against her will to or in or upon a house or place with intent that she may be unlawfully carnally known by any male, whether a particular male or not.[552]

II. Bigamy

301. Bigamy consists in unlawfully and intentionally entering into what purports to be a lawful marriage ceremony with one person whilst lawfully married to another.[553]

The African customary law institution of marriage is polygamous in nature. In terms of the Recognition of Customary Marriages Act, a valid customary marriage is recognised as a marriage.[554] Therefore, it follows that if a person, being married in terms of customary law, enters into a civil marriage (or being married in terms of civil law, enters into a customary marriage), he commits bigamy.[555]

III. Incest

302. Persons who, on account of consanguinity, affinity or adoptive relationship, may not marry one another, who unlawfully and intentionally engage in an act of sexual penetration with each other, or in sexual violation with each other where one of them is a child, and the act of sexual violation was of such a nature that it was

549. *R v. Sita* 1954 (4) SA 20 (E). In *S v. Jezile* 2015 (2) SACR 452 (WCC) the court rejected the appellant's reliance on an aberrant form of *ukuthwala* as a form of 'living customary law' that justified abduction and rape.
550. *R v. Hanna* 1937 TPD 236 239.
551. *R v. Jorgensen* 1935 EDL 219 223.
552. Sexual Offences Act 23 of 1957 s. 12(1)(*a*).
553. J.R.L. Milton, *South African Criminal Law and Procedure*, Vol. II *Common-Law Crimes* 3rd ed. (Juta, Cape Town 1996) 259.
554. Recognition of Customary Marriages Act 120 of 1998, s. 2(1).
555. S.V. Hoctor, *Snyman's Criminal Law* 7th ed. (LexisNexis, Durban 2020) 350.

reprehensible for the adult person to have acted in that manner under the circumstances concerned are, despite their mutual consent to engage in such act, guilty of the offence of incest.[556]

The relationships of consanguinity, affinity and adoption which determine whether incest is committed are co-extensive with those accepted by the private law as determining legal capacity to marry.[557] The prohibition extends to all ascendants and descendants in the direct line *ad infinitum* and to collaterals, if either of them is related to their common ancestor in the first degree of descent (thus, the prohibition does not extend to cousins). In relation to affines, only those related in the ascending and descending line *ad infinitum* are prohibited from marrying. An adoptive parent may not marry an adopted child. Adopted children are however not related by blood or affinity to the biological children of the adoptive parents and thus intercourse between the adopted child and a child of the adoptive parents is not incest.

§4. Crimes Against Property

I. Theft

303. The South African law of theft has evolved as a mixture of Roman-Dutch law and English law. It has followed Roman-Dutch law in adopting a single comprehensive definition of theft, avoiding the proliferation of theft crimes that one finds in English law. It has also preferred the Roman concept of *contrectatio* to the English concept of asportation. At the same time, the English law has exercised considerable influence on the development of the South African law of theft, especially in the definition of the *mens rea* of the crime; the *animus furandi* (intention to steal) of South African theft law is a creature of the English law and not the law of Rome.

304. In South African law, theft consists in an unlawful appropriation with intent to steal a thing capable of being stolen.[558]

305. The South African law, following Roman-Dutch law, adopted the *contrectatio* concept as the definition of the taking element of theft. Under the construction placed upon the *contrectatio* concept in South African law, a removal (asportation) of the res is not necessary.[559] Thus, persons who 'shoplift' in self-service stores

---

556. Criminal Law (Sexual Offences and Related Matters) Amendment Act 32 of 2007, s. 12(1). For the meaning of 'sexual penetration' in the context of Act 32 of 2007, *see* para. 292 *supra*.
557. Criminal Law (Sexual Offences and Related Matters) Amendment Act 32 of 2007, s. 12(2); S.V. Hoctor, *Snyman's Criminal Law* 7th ed. (LexisNexis, Durban 2020) 335–338. In terms of s. 2(1) of the Recognition of Customary Marriages Act 120 of 1998, a valid customary marriage is recognised as a marriage.
558. J. Burchell, *Principles of Criminal Law* 5th ed. (Juta, Cape Town 2016) 689; S.V. Hoctor, *Snyman's Criminal Law* 7th ed. (LexisNexis, Durban 2020) 421.
559. *R v. Mlooi* 1925 AD 131 152.

commit theft when they take the goods from the shelf[560] (provided there is the necessary intention to steal) and it is not relevant that the shoplifter had not yet approached the till or removed the goods from the store.[561]

A mere touching of the thing is not a *contrectatio*, unless it amounts to an assumption of control.[562]

306. The South African case-law concerning *contrectatio* can be interpreted as having adopted as the criterion for the taking element of theft, the concept of 'appropriation'.[563] It would be to the advantage of South African law if the fully developed 'appropriation' concept of the taking element of theft were to replace the simplistic and antiquated *contrectatio* concept.[564] The act of appropriation consists in any act in respect of property whereby a person: (i) deprives the lawful owner or possessor of his or her property, and (ii) himself exercises the rights of an owner in respect of the property.[565]

307. Immovable property is incapable of being stolen. However, parts of an immovable (e.g., trees or crops, or drainpipes from a house) that are separated from it can be stolen.

308. The Roman and Roman-Dutch law's insistence upon actual handling (*contrectatio*) of a thing in order for there to be theft led to the logical conclusion that an 'incorporeal' thing could not be stolen. Thus, it is the South African law that only corporeal movable things are capable of being stolen.[566] However, money where it is not corporeal cash but is represented by a credit entry in books of account is capable of being stolen.[567] It is not clear whether this is merely an exception to the general rule demanded by the realities of modern financial transactions or whether it represents a general principle that incorporeal things are capable of being stolen.

309. *Res communes* and *res publicae* cannot be stolen. Wild animals are *res nullius* and as such cannot be stolen even if they are running on private property[568] unless they have already been captured and are still under control.

Since an owner can devolve the right to possess a thing upon another without ceasing to be the owner, it follows that if the owner takes his property from the possessor, thereby depriving him of the possession of it, the owner has committed *furtum possessionis*. Thus, by taking his own property, the owner has committed theft;

560. *S v. Dlamini* 1984 (3) SA 196 (N).
561. *S v. Dlamini* (*supra*); *S v. Chaba* 2019 (3) All SA 103 (FB) para. 54.
562. *R v. Brand* 1960 (3) SA 637 (A).
563. S.V. Hoctor, *Snyman's Criminal Law* 7th ed. (LexisNexis, Durban 2020) 424–426.
564. Cf. *S v. Harper* 1981 (2) SA 638 (D) 665. In *S v. Boesak* 2000 (1) SACR 633 (SCA) para. 97 it was held that 'appropriation' was part of the definition of theft.
565. S.V. Hoctor, *Snyman's Criminal Law* 7th ed. (LexisNexis, Durban 2020) 424.
566. *R v. Cheeseborough* 1948 (3) SA 756 (T); *R v. Renaud* 1922 CPD 322. In *S v. Ndebele* 2012 (1) SACR 245 (GSJ) it was held, contrary to the earlier decision in *S v. Mintoor* 1996 (1) SACR 514 (C), that electricity could be stolen.
567. *S v. Graham* 1975 (3) SA 569 (A) 576H.
568. *S v. Monomiya* 1970 (1) SA 66 (N).

his crime though lies not in the taking of his property but in the theft of the possessory interest that the other person enjoyed in the thing concerned.[569]

310. The South African courts have decided that the ownership at different points of time of individual banknotes or coins is not important in deciding whether a theft of them has been committed.[570]

311. The *mens rea* of theft consists in an intention to deprive the owner permanently of 'the whole benefit of his ownership'.[571] The principal significance of this is that a person who takes another's property without permission and uses it and then returns it (an 'unauthorised borrowing') does not commit theft because he does not have the intention permanently to deprive the owner of his rights in the property.

312. In South African law, theft is a 'continuing crime'.[572] This means that the theft continues as long as the stolen property is in the possession of the thief or of some person who was a party to the theft.[573] The consequences of this doctrine are that even though the original *contrectatio* took place outside the court's jurisdiction, the thief may be tried at the place where he is found with the property,[574] and that persons who assist the thief after the initial *contrectatio* but whilst the theft 'continues' are guilty not merely as accessories after the fact but of theft itself.[575]

II. Theft by False Pretences

313. The crime of theft by false pretences is committed by any person who unlawfully, with intent to steal and by means of misrepresentation, effects an appropriation of property capable of being stolen.[576]

This crime occupies a position between the crime of theft and fraud. Its purpose is to punish cases in which a villain manages to effect a *contrectatio* of another's property by way of making some false representation to the other, thereby obtaining consent to the taking or at least, preventing any resistance to the taking.

III. Theft of Trust Money

314. Roman and Roman-Dutch law did not consider the unfaithful use of trust money by a trustee to be theft. This was because it was believed that the ownership of the money had passed to the trustee.

---

569. *R v. Janoo* 1959 (3) SA 107 (A).
570. *R v. Manuel* 1953 (4) SA 523 (A).
571. *R v. Sibiya* 1955 (4) SA 247 (A).
572. *S v. Dayizana* 1989 (1) SA 919 (E); *S v. Cassiem* 2001 (1) SACR 489 (SCA).
573. *R v. Attia* 1937 TPD 102 106.
574. *S v. Kruger* 1989 (1) SA 785 (A).
575. J.R.L. Milton, *South African Criminal Law and Procedure*, Vol. II *Common-Law Crimes* 3rd ed. (Juta, Cape Town 1996) 629.
576. J.R.L.Milton, *South African Criminal Law and Procedure*, Vol. II *Common-Law Crimes* 3rd ed. (Juta, Cape Town 1996) 754.

However, since the South African courts do not consider that the question of the ownership of cash necessarily affects the question of whether there has been a theft of money,[577] it follows that where money is received and held in trust, the recipient's ownership of the coins or notes is qualified (for the purposes of criminal law) and the money is capable of being stolen.

South African law distinguishes for these purposes between 'trust' relationships and 'debtor-creditor' relationships. If money is handed over in a debtor-creditor relationship, the expenditure of the money for purposes other than that for which it was given will not amount to theft. This is because essentially what has happened is that the parties have entered into a commercial relationship in which the person giving the money has relied upon the promise of the recipient to repay the money. If it turns out that he is unable to pay, the lender's redress is in the law of contract.[578]

A trustee will usually effect a *contrectatio* of trust money simply by drawing the money and spending it.[579] An expenditure, however, will not constitute theft if the trustee at the time has sufficient funds (in the form of an '*equivalent liquid fund*') at his disposal to cover the amount expended.[580]

IV. Receiving Stolen Property

315. The crime of receiving consists in unlawfully receiving possession of stolen property while knowing it to have been stolen.[581]

V. Unauthorised Borrowing

316. Under the General Law Amendment Act 1956, it is a crime to borrow property belonging to another without the consent of the owner.[582]

Roman law recognised two forms of improper dealing with the property of another: unauthorised borrowing (*furtum usus*) and extra-contractual user (exceeding one's contractual rights in using property entrusted to one by way of deposit, loan or some other contract). The South African courts, however, decided that no such crimes existed in the South African common law.[583]

---

577. *See supra* para. 310.
578. *See* M.M. Loubser, *Theft of Money in South African Law* (Stellenbosch, 1978); S.V. Hoctor, *Snyman's Criminal Law* 7th ed. (LexisNexis, Durban) 439–440.
579. In *S v. Boesak* 2000 (1) SACR 633 (SCA), it was held that where a person entrusted with money for one purpose uses it for another, unrelated, purpose, or appropriates it for his own use, theft of trust money is committed.
580. *S v. Visagie* 1991 (1) SA 177 (A).
581. J.R.L. Milton, *South African Criminal Law and Procedure*, Vol. II *Common-Law Crimes* 3rd ed. (Juta, Cape Town 1996) 662.
582. 'removes … property from the control of the owner': General Law Amendment Act 50 of 1956, s. 1(1).
583. *R v. Sibiya* 1955 (4) SA 247 (A).

The General Law Amendment Act 1956 inexplicably criminalises only unauthorised borrowing, leaving extra-contractual user beyond the reach of the criminal law.[584]

VI. Game Theft

317. In South African law, wild animals are not capable of being stolen.[585]
This principle meant that the owner of a game farm did not own the wild animals on the farm (unless each was acquired by an act of *occupatio*). The Game Theft Act 1991 was enacted to regulate the ownership of game in certain instances and to combat the theft and wrongful and unlawful hunting, catching and taking into possession of game.[586]

VII. Robbery

318. Robbery consists in the theft of property by intentionally using violence or threats of violence to induce submission to the taking of it from another.[587]

319. The violence should be such as to have the effect of overcoming the victim's resistance to the taking and cause submission to the taking.[588]
It follows from this that if the violence is merely incidental, it will not cause the taking to be robbery. Bag-snatching is, however, robbery since the force used in snatching the bag from an unsuspecting or unresisting victim's grasp is intended to cause submission to the taking.[589]
Whilst it is logical to say that in order for violence to cause submission to the taking of the property, it must precede (and not succeed) the taking, there is no hard

584. S.V. Hoctor, *Snyman's Criminal Law* 7th ed. (LexisNexis, Durban 2020) 444. In *S v. Rheeder* 2000 (2) SACR 558 (SCA) the court interpreted the term 'control' in the provision strictly to mean not only mere physical possession, but *complete* control, i.e., physical possession together with legitimate final discretion as to its use. As Snyman points out (*ibid.,* 446), this interpretation makes it easier for the state to obtain a conviction in cases of extra-contractual use.
585. *See supra* para. 309.
586. Act 105 of 1991. *See* J.R.L. Milton, S.V. Hoctor & M.G. Cowling, *South African Criminal Law and Procedure*, Vol. III *Statutory Offences* 2nd ed. (Juta, Cape Town 1988) J2–34ff.
587. J.R.L. Milton, *South African Criminal Law and Procedure*, Vol. II *Common-Law Crimes* 3rd ed. (Juta, Cape Town 1996) 642; S.V. Hoctor, *Snyman's Criminal Law* 7th ed. (LexisNexis, Durban 2020) 448. Robbery typically occurs in respect of corporeal property, but can be committed by the theft of an incorporeal through force and violence – *S v. Sishuba* 2018 (1) SACR 402 (WCC).
588. *S v. Malinga* 1962 (3) SA 589 (T).
589. *S v. Sithole* 1981 (1) SA 1186 (N); *see also S v. Salmans* 2006 (1) SACR 328 (C), where a similar approach is adopted in respect of cellphone-snatching, and *S v. Mogala* 1978 (2) SA 412 (A) 415–416. *See* further S.V. Hoctor, 'Examining the Expanding Crime of Robbery' 2012 *SACJ* 361.

and fast rule to this effect in South African law.[590] The test is whether, in the circumstances of the case, there was such a close connection between the taking and the violence that they can be regarded as connecting components of what was substantially one event.[591]

VIII. Extortion (Blackmail)

320. Extortion consists in taking from another some advantage by intentionally and unlawfully subjecting him to pressure, which induces him to submit to the taking.[592]

There must be something in the nature of a threat: something which is intended to inspire fear and which does inspire fear.

Any kind of threat will suffice,[593] including that of damage to property;[594] arrest or prosecution;[595] dismissal;[596] or civil proceedings.[597]

The advantage obtained is usually money, but it may be other property, corporeal or incorporeal, movable or immovable, or services. Whilst the common-law rule was that it was essential that the advantage should be of a proprietary nature and capable of being assessed in terms of money,[598] any advantage is now sufficient for the purposes of extortion liability.[599]

IX. Fraud

321. Fraud consists in unlawfully making, with intent to defraud, a misrepresentation which causes actual prejudice or which is potentially prejudicial to another.[600]

The essence of fraud is the deceiving or misleading of the victim of the crime by way of a misrepresentation of fact or law made by one person to another.

---

590. *S v. Yolelo* 1981 (1) SA 1002 (A).
591. *S v. Yolelo* 1981 (1) SA 1002 (A).
592. J.R.L. Milton, *South African Criminal Law and Procedure*, Vol. II *Common-Law Crimes* 3rd ed. (Juta, Cape Town 1996) 681; S.V. Hoctor, *Snyman's Criminal Law* 7th ed. (LexisNexis, Durban 2020) 369.
593. *R v. Notaris* 1903 TS 484 485.
594. *R v. Nggandu* 1939 EDL 213.
595. *R v. N* 1955 (2) SA 647 (T).
596. *R v. Farndon* 1937 EDL 180.
597. *R v. Neta* 1937 (2) PH H187 (A).
598. *Ex parte the Minister van Justisie: in re S v. J en S v. Von Molendorff* 1989 (4) SA 1028 (A).
599. In terms of the General Law Amendment Act 139 of 1992, s. 1.
600. J.R.L. Milton, *South African Criminal Law and Procedure*, Vol. II *Common-Law Crimes* 3rd ed. (Juta, Cape Town 1996) 702; S.V. Hoctor, *Snyman's Criminal Law* 7th ed. (LexisNexis, Durban 2020) 461.

The misrepresentation must cause prejudice to the victim. The prejudice need not be proprietary; it can be non-proprietary.[601] Further, there need not be any actual prejudice suffered; mere potential prejudice flowing from the misrepresentation suffices.

Non-proprietary prejudice takes the form of prejudice to personal interests such as reputation[602] and the interests of the public administration, as, for instance, obtaining permits or licences by misrepresentation or cheating in examinations.[603]

'Potential prejudice' means that the making of the misrepresentation looked at objectively must have involved a risk of prejudice, proprietary or non-proprietary (in the sense described above).[604] The test is whether it is reasonably possible that prejudice would occur.[605] The question is not whether the representor intended to cause prejudice but rather whether, on an objective assessment, his misrepresentation would have brought about the prejudice.[606]

The concept of potential prejudice imparts a very wide scope to the South African crime of fraud. It causes to be the crime of fraud, the paying of an existing debt by a bad cheque,[607] or lying about the reason for obtaining a loan,[608] or placing a false coin in a parking meter.[609]

Intent to defraud has two principal aspects: an intention to deceive and an intention to defraud.[610]

X. Forgery and Counterfeiting Offences

322. Forgery, at common law, consists in unlawfully making with intent to defraud, a false document which causes actual or potential prejudice to another.[611]

Forgery is committed only in respect of 'documents'. For these purposes, a document is any writing in any form, on any material, which communicates to some person or persons a human statement, whether of fact or fiction.[612] From this, it follows

601. *R v. Heyne* 1956 (3) SA 604 (A).
602. *R v. Seabe* 1927 AD 28 33.
603. *R v. Thabeta* 1948 (3) SA 218 (T).
604. *R v. Seabe* 1927 AD 28. In *S v. Friedman* 1996 (1) SACR 181 (W), the court confirmed that potential prejudice suffices for liability, and moreover that the breadth of this requirement does not unjustifiably infringe the Constitution of the RSA, 1996. *See also S v. Mngqibisa* 2008 (1) SACR 92 (SCA).
605. *R v. Seabe* (*supra*) 32, 34.
606. *R v. Kruse* 1946 AD 524 533.
607. Cf. *S v. Moodie* 1983 (1) SA 1161 (C).
608. *S v. Huijzers* 1988 (2) SA 503 (A).
609. *S v. Myeza* 1985 (4) SA 30 (T).
610. *S v. Isaacs* 1968 (2) SA 187 (D).
611. J.R.L. Milton, *South African Criminal Law and Procedure*, Vol. II *Common-Law Crimes* 3rd ed. (Juta, Cape Town 1996) 740; S.V. Hoctor, *Snyman's Criminal Law* 7th ed. (LexisNexis, Durban 2020) 469.
612. J.R.L. Milton, *South African Criminal Law and Procedure*, Vol. II *Common-Law Crimes* 3rd ed. (Juta, Cape Town 1996) 744.

that it does not matter what substance the writing appears, whether paper, stone, wood, cloth or earth. Nor does it matter in what medium the writing is done, whether ink, type, paint or blood.[613]

The writing must convey the message of the spoken word and must convey the same message to all persons. Thus, forgery is only committed in respect of documents containing writing or marks which can be interpreted into the spoken word. Since visual and musical art conveys different messages to different persons, a painting or musical performance is not a 'document' and thus cannot be forged. But an artist's signature or the musician's composition can be forged.

To be a forgery, the document must tell a lie *about itself*.[614] As with fraud, forgery is only a crime if it causes prejudice (actual or potential, proprietary or non-proprietary) to someone.

323. Section 2 of the Prevention of Counterfeiting of Currency Act 1965 makes it an offence for any person to forge a banknote or counterfeit any current coin.[615]

The South African Reserve Bank Act makes it an offence for any person to forge any note of the bank.[616]

324. At common law, it is a crime to utter any forged document. Uttering consists in unlawfully putting off a forged document with intent to defraud to the prejudice or potential prejudice of another.

By statute,[617] any person who utters, tenders or accepts any counterfeit coin, knowing it to be counterfeit, or a forged or altered banknote, knowing it to be forged or altered, commits an offence. It is an offence for any person to utter, tender or accept any forged, altered or unlawfully issued note of the Reserve Bank or any coin, knowing it to be forged, altered or unlawfully issued.[618]

XI. Malicious Injury to Property

325. At common law, it is a crime to unlawfully and intentionally damage the property of another.[619]

Property is damaged where it is destroyed or lost or permanently damaged, or damaged with the result that it reasonably requires repair. All kinds of corporeal movable or immovable property may be the subject of this crime. The property must, however, belong to another person, and the crime is not committed in respect of property owned by the accused.

---

613. J.R.L. Milton, *South African Criminal Law and Procedure*, Vol. II *Common-Law Crimes* 3rd ed. (Juta, Cape Town 1996) 745.
614. *S v. Banur Investments (Pty) Ltd* 1970 (3) SA 767 (A) 772.
615. Prevention of Counterfeiting of Currency Act 16 of 1965, s. 2.
616. South African Reserve Bank Act 90 of 1989, s. 34(1)(*a*).
617. Prevention of Counterfeiting of Currency Act 16 of 1965, s. 2(*c*).
618. South African Reserve Bank Act 90 of 1989, s. 34(1)(*b*).
619. J.R.L. Milton, *South African Criminal Law and Procedure*, Vol. II *Common-Law Crimes* 3rd ed. (Juta, Cape Town 1996) 765; S.V. Hoctor, *Snyman's Criminal Law* 7th ed. (LexisNexis, Durban 2020) 475.

XII. Arson

326. Arson consists in unlawfully setting an immovable structure on fire with intent to injure another.[620]

It is not sufficient that the fire be lit; the structure must actually be set on fire.[621] It would seem that there is no 'setting on fire' unless some part of the structure actually burns[622] and is damaged by that burning. The crime is only committed by the setting on fire of immovable property.

There is authority that an owner does not commit arson by setting fire to that which is owned by him.[623] However, there is authority which holds that an owner who sets fire to a house owned by him but occupied by another commits arson.[624] This latter proposition is consistent with the premise that crime exists to protect human habitation. If this is so, the fact that the arsonist owns the structure concerned is irrelevant.

The arsonist must intend to set property on fire and intend to cause patrimonial harm to some other person.[625] Thus, the intent with which the act of burning is committed is central, converting an ostensibly lawful act (burning one's own property) into an unlawful act.[626]

XIII. Housebreaking

327. In South African law, housebreaking with intent to commit a crime is a common-law crime.

The offence consists in unlawfully breaking and entering premises with intent to commit a crime.[627]

'House' in the word 'housebreaking' has a special meaning. Thus, it has been held that the following are premises: a store-room;[628] a garage;[629] a shop;[630] a permanently occupied tent;[631] an office;[632] an immovable display cabinet separate from

620. J.R.L. Milton, *South African Criminal Law and Procedure*, Vol. II *Common-Law Crimes* 3rd ed. (Juta, Cape Town 1996) 777; S.V. Hoctor, *Snyman's Criminal Law* 7th ed. (LexisNexis, Durban 2020) 478.
621. *R v. Schoombie* 1945 AD 541 548.
622. *R v. Schoombie* (*supra*) 548.
623. *R v. van Vliet* (1892) 9 SC 273.
624. *S v. Van Zyl* 1987 (1) SA 497 (O).
625. *R v. Mavros* 1921 AD 19.
626. *S v. Dalindyebo* 2016 (1) SACR 329 (SCA) paras 61–66.
627. J.R.L Milton, *South African Criminal Law and Procedure*, Vol. II *Common-Law Crimes* 3rd ed. (Juta, Cape Town 1996) 792; S.V. Hoctor, *Snyman's Criminal Law* 7th ed. (LexisNexis, Durban 2020) 479.
628. *R v. Chalala* 1947 (3) SA 62 (O).
629. *R v. Dorfling* 1954 (2) SA 125 (E).
630. *R v. Van Boven* 1917 CPD 204.
631. *R v. Thompson* 1905 ORC 127.
632. *R v. Coetzee* 1958 (2) SA 8 (T).

but forming an integral portion of a shop;[633] a cabin on board ship;[634] and a small but heavily built concrete mine dynamite magazine.[635]

The crime is committed not merely by entering the 'house': there must be a '*breaking*' into the premises.[636]

To 'break' premises means to create a way into those premises by displacing some obstruction which forms part of those premises.[637] The breaking must involve some displacement of some part of the building. The offender does not 'break' if he enters through an open door or window or puts his arm through an existing opening in the structure.[638]

To commit the crime, the intruder must not only break into the premises but must also *enter* them: a mere 'breaking' without such an entry is not enough.[639]

Furthermore, it is not sufficient that the accused should have intentionally broken and entered; the crime is only committed if the housebreaker breaks and enters with the intention to commit some specific crime on the premises. It is thus incumbent on the prosecution to prove that the accused broke and entered with the intention of committing, e.g., theft, rape, or assault. Where it is not known what crime the housebreaker intended to commit, the prosecution may allege that he intended 'to commit a crime to the prosecutor unknown'.[640]

XIV. Trespass

328. At South African common law, trespass is not a crime,[641] although intrusion upon another's home could be punished as a criminal *iniuria*.[642] A series of statutes intended to suppress vagrancy and squatting were enacted, explicitly penalising 'trespass' upon land. A uniform trespass offence was created by the Trespass Act of 1959. The offence has two forms: trespassing upon *occupied* land or buildings and trespassing upon *unoccupied* land or buildings.[643]

---

633. *S v. Ndhlovu* 1963 (1) SA 926 (T). In relation to a caravan used for storage, *see S v. Madyo* 1990 (1) SACR 292 (E); *S v. Temmers* 1994 (1) SACR 357 (C).
634. *R v. Lawrence* 1954 (2) SA 408 (C). But not a ship '*qua*' ship: *R v. Smith* 1959 (4) SA 524 (N) 526.
635. *R v. Botha* 1960 (2) SA 147 (T).
636. *S v. Rudman* 1989 (3) SA 368 (E) 385.
637. *R v. Mososa* 1931 CPD 348 351; *S v. Small* 2005 (2) SACR 300 (C).
638. *R v. Chalala* 1947 (3) SA 62 (O).
639. *R v. George* 1921 EDL 125.
640. Criminal Procedure Act 51 of 1977, ss 95(12), 262; *S v. Slabb* 2007 (1) SACR 77 (C).
641. *R v. Tamplin* (1886) 4 HCG 241.
642. *R v. Schonken* 1929 AD 36 45. *See supra,* para. 296.
643. Trespass Act 6 of 1959, s. 2. *See*, J.R.L. Milton, S.V. Hoctor & M.G. Cowling, *South African Criminal Law and Procedure*, Vol. III *Statutory Offences* (Juta, Cape Town 1988) Ch. J1.

XV. Crimes Against Intellectual Property

329. In South African law, copyright is unique amongst the various forms of intellectual property in that the sanctions of the criminal law are deployed as part of the protection the law affords to copyright.[644]

The criminalisation of copyright infringement is effected by the provisions of section 27 of the Copyright Act 1978. Any person who, at a time when copyright subsists in a work, without the authority of the owner of the copyright makes for sale or hire, sells or lets, or, for purposes of trade, exhibits in public, imports, distributes articles which he knows to be infringing copies of the work commits an offence.[645]

XVI. Cybercrime

330. Cybercrime, or computer crime, has been defined as that area of criminality covering 'all sets of circumstances where electronic data processing forms the means for the commission and/or the object of an offence and represents the basis for the suspicion that an offence has been committed'.[646] While computers may be used to commit both common-law crimes (such as theft) and statutory offences (such as money laundering) relating to property, the legislature has further made provision, in two statutes, for a number of offences in which computers are specifically used for the purposes of committing the offence. The first important statute is the Cybercrimes Act,[647] which contains the following offences: unlawful access of a computer system or computer data storage medium;[648] unlawful interception of data;[649] unlawful acts in respect of software or hardware tool;[650] unlawful interference with data or computer program;[651] unlawful interference with computer data

644. *See* O.H. Dean, 'Copyright Infringement as a Criminal Offence' 1988 *De Rebus* 203; J.R.L. Milton, S.V. Hoctor & M.G. Cowling, *South African Criminal Law and Procedure*, Vol. III *Statutory Offences* (Juta, Cape Town 1988) Ch. J3.
645. Copyright Act 98 of 1978, s. 27(1).
646. D.P. van der Merwe, *Computers and the Law* 2ed. (Juta, Cape Town 2000) 188. *See*, J.R.L. Milton, S.V. Hoctor & M.G. Cowling, *South African Criminal Law and Procedure*, Vol. III *Statutory Offences* (Juta, Cape Town 1988) Ch. G8.
647. Act 19 of 2020. This legislation reflects the need to take account of the challenge of cybercrime as a transnational phenomenon. The Council of Europe Convention on Cybercrime (Budapest Convention) has provided a framework for such legislation, with the aim of harmonising domestic criminal law offences. The aim of providing an African Union response to cybercrime and violations of personal data has been adopted by the African Union Convention on Cyber Security and Personal Data Protection, and the Southern African Development Community Model Law on Computer Crime and Cybercrime is also aimed at addressing the problem of cybercrime. All these instruments form the antecedents to the South African Act.
648. Cybercrimes Act 19 of 2020, s. 2(1). In terms of s. 1, a computer system is a single computer or two or more inter-connected or related computers, which exchange data or any other function with each other or another computer or computer system. A computer data storage medium is defined in s.1 as any device from which data or a computer program is capable of being reproduced or on which data or a computer program is capable of being stored, by a computer system.
649. Cybercrimes Act 19 of 2020, s. 3(1).
650. Cybercrimes Act 19 of 2020, s. 4(1).
651. Cybercrimes Act 19 of 2020, s. 5(1).

storage medium or computer system;[652] unlawful acquisition, possession, provision, receipt or use of password, access code or similar data or device;[653] cyber fraud;[654] cyber forgery and uttering;[655] cyber extortion;[656] disclosing a data message which incites damage to property or violence;[657] disclosing a data message which threatens persons with damage to property or violence;[658] disclosure of a data message of an intimate image;[659] or attempting, conspiring, aiding, abetting, inducing, inciting, instigating, instructing, commanding or procuring a person to commit an offence, in relation to any of these offences.[660]

The Regulation of Interception of Communications and Provision of Communication-related Information Act 70 of 2002 prohibits the interception and monitoring of certain communications.[661] Under this Act, it is an offence for any person to intentionally intercept or attempt to intercept or authorise or procure any other person to intercept any communication in the course of its occurrence or transmission at any place in the Republic.[662]

§5. Crimes Against Community Interests

I. Public Indecency

331. South African courts invented the common-law crime of 'public indecency'[663] consisting in unlawfully, intentionally and publicly committing an act which tends to deprive the morals of others or which outrages the public's sense of decency and propriety.[664]

The crime is committed only if the indecent conduct takes place in public. Nudity, exposure of the genitalia, and sexual intercourse are the types of conduct punished by this crime.

652. Cybercrimes Act 19 of 2020, s. 6(1).
653. Cybercrimes Act 19 of 2020, s. 7.
654. Cybercrimes Act 19 of 2020, s. 8.
655. Cybercrimes Act 19 of 2020, s. 9.
656. Cybercrimes Act 19 of 2020, s. 10.
657. Cybercrimes Act 19 of 2020, s. 14.
658. Cybercrimes Act 19 of 2020, s. 15.
659. Cybercrimes Act 19 of 2020, s. 16.
660. Cybercrimes Act 19 of 2020, s. 17.
661. The Act also authorises such conduct in certain circumstances. *See infra*, para. 504.
662. Regulation of Interception of Communications and Provision of Communication-related Information Act 70 of 2002, s. 49.
663. In *R v. Marais* (1889) 6 SC 367.
664. J.R.L. Milton, *South African Criminal Law and Procedure*, Vol. II *Common-Law Crimes* 3rd ed. (Juta, Cape Town 1996) 271; S.V. Hoctor, *Snyman's Criminal Law* 7th ed. (LexisNexis, Durban 2020) 383.

II. Blasphemy

332. The contention that the common-law crime of blasphemy had been abrogated by disuse in South Africa has been rejected.[665]

Blasphemy is thus a crime in South African law. It is defined as unlawfully, intentionally and publicly acting contemptuously towards God.[666]

It seems that it is only Christian beliefs and feelings that are protected by the crime.[667]

III. Road Traffic Offences

333. The National Road Traffic Act 1996 regulates the licensing of vehicles and drivers using 'public' roads and also the manner in which vehicles are driven on the roads. The criminal sanction is extensively deployed to enforce the regulatory provisions of this Act.[668] Certain driving offences are the subject of severe penalties. The principal driving offences are: driving without consideration for any other person using the road;[669] driving recklessly or negligently;[670] driving whilst under the influence of intoxicating liquor or a drug having a narcotic effect;[671] or with an excessive blood/alcohol ratio;[672] or with an excessive breath/alcohol ratio.[673] Hit-and-run drivers,[674] unlicensed drivers,[675] 'joy' riders[676] and speedsters[677] are also punished under the Act.

665. *R v. Webb* 1934 AD 493. The ensuing lack of prosecutions is, however, indicative that such a challenge today may be successful.
666. J.R.L. Milton, *South African Criminal Law and Procedure*, Vol. II *Common-Law Crimes* 3rd ed. (Juta, Cape Town 1996) 293; J. Burchell, *Principles of Criminal Law* 5th ed. (Juta, Cape Town 2016) 790.
667. *R v. Webb* (*supra*). It has therefore been argued that the crime is unconstitutional, in that it unjustifiably infringes on both the right to freedom of expression and the right to equality – *see*, J. Burchell, *Principles of Criminal Law* 5th ed. (Juta, Cape Town 2016) 790–791.
668. Act 93 of 1996. *See* for a survey, J.R.L. Milton, S.V. Hoctor & M.G. Cowling, *South African Criminal Law and Procedure*, Vol. III *Statutory Offences* (Juta, Cape Town 1988) Ch. G3; *see*, further S.V. Hoctor, *Cooper's Motor Law* 2nd ed. (Juta, Cape Town 2007).
669. National Road Traffic Act 93 of 1996, s. 64.
670. National Road Traffic Act 93 of 1996, s. 63.
671. National Road Traffic Act 93 of 1996, s. 65(1).
672. National Road Traffic Act 93 of 1996, s. 65(2). The offence is committed if the concentration of alcohol exceeds 0.05 grams per 100 millilitres.
673. National Road Traffic Act 93 of 1996, s. 65(5). The offence is committed if the concentration of alcohol in the breath exceeds 0.24 milligrams per 1,000 millilitres.
674. National Road Traffic Act 93 of 1996, s. 61.
675. National Road Traffic Act 93 of 1996, s. 12.
676. National Road Traffic Act 93 of 1996, s. 66(2).
677. National Road Traffic Act 93 of 1996, s. 59(4).

IV. Drug Offences

334. The Drugs and Drug Trafficking Act 1992 prohibits the possession or use or dealing in 'dependence-producing' substances.[678] Further, the Act makes provision for the suppression of trafficking in drugs in accordance with the provisions of the United Nations Convention against Illicit Drug Traffic in Narcotics Drugs and Psychotropic Substances.

Financial houses and stockbrokers are required, on pain of punishment, to report suspicions that persons are dealing in funds obtained from drug trafficking.[679] Duties of secrecy imposed by law are waived.[680]

Employers and principals are vicariously criminally liable for the acts of their employees or agents in respect of any of the offences committed under the Act.[681]

Persons suspected of having information regarding drug offences may be detained for interrogation until such time as they have satisfactorily answered questions.[682]

V. Witchcraft

335. The Witchcraft Suppression Act 1957 contains extensive prohibitions upon the divination or 'smelling out' of witches[683] and the employment of sorcerers or practitioners of 'black' magic.[684] The provisions of the Act, generally speaking, do not affect practices of 'medicinal' magic or 'ceremonial' or cult magic. Nor are the various occult sciences proscribed, though the practice of certain of these (such as fortune-telling) for the purpose of gain is penalised.[685]

VI. Arms and Weapons

336. *3*The right to have or carry arms is regulated in South African law by the Firearms Control Act 2000. The fundamental principle of the Act is that persons may possess arms and ammunition only if licensed to do so in terms of the Act.[686]

---

678. Drugs and Drug Trafficking Act 140 of 1992, ss 4, 5. For a survey of the offences *see*, J.R.L. Milton, S.V. Hoctor & M.G. Cowling, *South African Criminal Law and Procedure*, Vol. III *Statutory Offences* (Juta, Cape Town 1988) Ch. F3. Aspects of these offences were declared to be unconstitutional in *Minister of Justice and Constitutional Development v. Prince* 2019 (1) SACR 14 (CC) with regard to the drug cannabis, based on the unjustifiable limitation on the right to privacy that they create. In relation to cannabis, possession of this substance for personal consumption in private by an adult is no longer unlawful. Moreover, cultivation of cannabis by an adult in a private place for such adult's personal consumption in private is not unlawful.
679. Drugs and Drug Trafficking Act 140 of 1992, s. 10.
680. Drugs and Drug Trafficking Act 140 of 1992, s. 10.
681. Drugs and Drug Trafficking Act 140 of 1992, s. 24.
682. Drugs and Drug Trafficking Act 140 of 1992, s. 12.
683. *See S v. Mafunisa* 1986 (3) SA 495 (V).
684. Witchcraft Suppression Act 3 of 1957, s. 1. For a survey of the offences, *see* J.R.L. Milton, S.V. Hoctor & M.G. Cowling, *South African Criminal Law and Procedure*, Vol. III *Statutory Offences* (Juta, Cape Town 1988) Ch. E2.
685. Witchcraft Suppression Act 3 of 1957, s. 1(*f*).
686. J.R.L. Milton, S.V. Hoctor & M.G. Cowling, *South African Criminal Law and Procedure*, Vol. III *Statutory Offences* 2nd ed. (Juta, Cape Town 1988) Ch. B1.

Unlicensed possession of a firearm is an offence under the Act.[687] A firearm which falls within the category of a 'prohibited firearm' may not be possessed or licensed except under certain conditions.[688] Unlicensed dealing in firearms or ammunition is likewise an offence.[689]

The Act also imposes strict duties upon persons lawfully in possession of arms to safeguard them. It is an offence to fail to safeguard or negligently lose a firearm[690] as it is not to report the theft or loss of an armament.[691]

Any person who intentionally points any firearm, antique firearm or air gun, or anything which is likely to lead a person to believe that it is a firearm, antique firearm or air gun, at any other person commits an offence.[692]

337. The Dangerous Weapons Act 2013 provides for the punishment of persons who possess dangerous weapons.[693] The concept of a dangerous weapon is wide enough to embrace any object of whatever character or shape which can cause bodily harm to a human being.[694]

VII. Protection of the Environment

338. The criminal sanction is widely used as a means of enforcing measures enacted for the protection of the natural environment. Notable enactments which penalise forms of environmental damage and serve to enforce the regulation of the environment are the Hazardous Substances Act 15 of 1973; Marine Pollution (Control and Civil Liability) Act 6 of 1981; Mountain Catchment Areas Act 63 of 1970; Conservation of Agricultural Resources Act 43 of 1983; National Water Act 36 of 1998; National Heritage Resources Act 25 of 1999; Nuclear Energy Act 46 of 1999; Fertilizers, Farm Feeds, Agricultural Remedies and Stock Remedies Act 36 of 1947; National Environmental Management: Biodiversity Act 10 of 2004; National Environmental Management: Protected Areas Act 57 of 2003; National Environmental Management: Air Quality Act 39 of 2004; National Environmental Management: Waste Act 59 of 2008; National Environmental Management: Integrated Coastal Management Act 24 of 2008; and various provincial nature conservation ordinances (which largely regulate the protection and conservation of wildlife and flora).[695]

---

687. Firearms Control Act 60 of 2000, s. 3. There is a list of devices not regarded as firearms for the purposes of the Act in s. 5.
688. Firearms Control Act 60 of 2000, s. 4(1).
689. Firearms Control Act 60 of 2000, s. 31.
690. Firearms Control Act 60 of 2000, s. 120(8).
691. Firearms Control Act 60 of 2000, s. 120(11).
692. Firearms Control Act 60 of 2000, s. 120(6).
693. Dangerous Weapons Act 15 of 2013, s. 3(1).
694. *See* Dangerous Weapons Act 15 of 2013, s. 1 where a dangerous weapon is defined as any object other than a firearm, capable of causing death or inflicting serious bodily harm, if it was used for an unlawful purpose. *See* M. Carnelley & S.V. Hoctor, 'Some Comments on the Dangerous Weapons Act 15 of 2013' 2013 SACJ 354.
695. For a comprehensive survey, *see* H.A. Strydom & N.D. King (eds), *Fuggle & Rabie's Environmental Management in South Africa* (Juta, Cape Town 2009).

VIII. Money Laundering and Organised Crime

339. The Financial Intelligence Centre Act[696] established a Financial Intelligence Centre in order to combat money laundering activities.

Money laundering[697] or money laundering activity means an activity which has or is likely to have the effect of concealing or disguising the nature, source, location, disposition or movement of the proceeds of unlawful activities or any interest which anyone has in such proceeds and includes any activity which constitutes an offence in terms of section 64 of the Act or sections 4, 5 and 6 of the Prevention of Organised Crime Act of 1998

340. The Prevention of Organised Crime Act[698] deals with racketeering, gangsterism, confiscation orders, civil forfeiture orders, and money laundering.[699]

Any person who in terms of section 2(1) of the Act:

(a) (i) receives or retains any property derived, directly or indirectly, from a pattern of racketeering activity;[700] and
  (ii) knows or ought reasonably to have known that such property is so derived; and
  (iii) uses or invests, directly or indirectly, any part of such property in acquisition or any interest in, or the establishment or operation or activities or, any enterprise;

(b) (i) receives or retains any property, directly or indirectly, on behalf of any enterprise; and
  (ii) knows or ought reasonably to have known that such property derived or is derived from or through a pattern of racketeering activity;

(c) (i) uses or invests any property, directly or indirectly, on behalf of any enterprise or in the acquisition of any interest in, or the establishment or operation or activities of any enterprise; and
  (ii) knows or ought reasonably to have known that such property is derived from or through a pattern of racketeering activity;

(d) acquires or maintains, directly or indirectly, any interest in or control of any enterprise through a pattern of racketeering activity;

(e) whilst managing or being employed by, or associated with any enterprise, conducts or participates in the conduct, directly or indirectly, of such enterprise's affairs through a pattern of racketeering activity;

(f) manages the operation or activities of an enterprise and who knows or ought reasonably to have known that any person, whilst employed by or associated with that enterprise, conducts or participates in the conduct, directly or indirectly, of such enterprise's affairs through a pattern of racketeering activity; or

---

696. Financial Intelligence Centre Act 38 of 2001.
697. Financial Intelligence Centre Act 38 of 2001, s. 1.
698. Prevention of Organised Crime Act 121 of 1998.
699. Prevention of Organised Crime Act 121 of 1998, s. 2.
700. In terms of s. 1 'pattern of racketeering activity' means the planned, ongoing, continuous or repeated participation or involvement in any offence referred to in Schedule 1.

(g) conspires or attempts to violate any of the provisions of paragraphs (*a*), (*b*), (*c*), (*d*), (*e*) or (*f*), within the Republic or elsewhere, is guilty of an offence.

The court may hear evidence, including evidence with regard to hearsay, similar facts or previous convictions relating to the offences above, notwithstanding that such evidence might otherwise be inadmissible, provided that such evidence would not render a trial unfair.[701] For purposes of proving a previous conviction during a trial in respect of an offence above, it will be sufficient to prove the original record of judicial proceedings if a certified is produced, and it will be prima facie proof that any matter recorded thereon was correctly recorded.[702]

341. The offence of money laundering in the Prevention of Organised Crime Act of 1998 provides that any person who knows or ought reasonably to have known that property is or forms part of the proceeds of unlawful activities and:

a. enters into any agreement or engages in any arrangement or transaction with anyone in connection with that property, whether such agreement, arrangement or transaction is legally enforceable or not;
b. performs any other act in connection with such property, whether it is performed independently or in concert with any other person, which has or is likely to have the effect:
   i. of concealing or disguising the nature, source, location, disposition or movement of the said property or the ownership thereof or any interest which anyone may have in respect thereof;
   ii. of enabling or assisting any person who has committed or commits an offence, whether in the Republic or elsewhere:
   – to avoid prosecution; or
   – to remove or diminish any property acquired directly or indirectly, as a result of the commission of an offence, is guilty of an offence.[703]

Any person who knows or ought reasonably to have known that another person obtained the proceeds of unlawful activities and who enters into an agreement with anyone or engages in any arrangement or transaction whereby:

a. the retention or the control by or on behalf of the said other person of the proceeds of unlawful activities[704] is facilitated; or

701. Prevention of Organised Crime Act 121 of 1998, s. 2(2).
702. Prevention of Organised Crime Act 121 of 1998, s. 2(3).
703. Prevention of Organised Crime Act 121 of 1998, s. 4. Property is defined in s. 1 to mean money or any other movable, immovable, corporeal or incorporeal thing and includes any rights, privileges, claims and securities and any interest therein and all proceeds thereof.
704. 'Proceeds of unlawful activities' means any property or any service, advantage, benefit or reward which was derived, received or retained, directly or indirectly, in the Republic or elsewhere, at any time before or after the commencement of the Act, in connection with or as a result of any unlawful activity carried on by any person, and includes any property representing property so derived.

b. the said proceeds of unlawful activities are used to make funds available to the said other person or to acquire property on his or her behalf or to benefit him or her in any other way, is guilty of an offence.[705]

Any person who:

a. acquires;
b. uses; or
c. has possession of,

property and who knows or ought reasonably to have known that it is or forms part of the proceeds of unlawful activities of another person is guilty of an offence.[706]

If a person is charged with committing an offence under sections 2(1)(a) or (b), 4, 5, or 6, that person may raise as a defence the fact that he or she had reported a knowledge or suspicion in terms of section 29 of the Financial Intelligence Centre Act.[707]

If a person who is an employee of an accountable institution as defined in the Financial Intelligence Centre Act is charged with committing an offence under sections 2(1)(a) or (b), 4, 5, or 6, that person may also raise as a defence the fact that he or she had:

a. complied with the applicable obligations in terms of the internal rules relating to the reporting of information of the accountable institution; or
b. reported the matter to the person charged with the responsibility of ensuring compliance by the accountable institution with its duties under the Act; or
c. reported a suspicion to his or her superior, if any, if:
    1. the accountable institution had not appointed such a person or established such rules;
    2. the accountable institution had not complied with its obligations in section 42(3) of the Act in respect of the person; or
    3. those rules were not applicable to that person.[708]

342. Any person who actively participates in or is a member of a criminal gang[709] and who:

a. wilfully aids and abets any criminal activity committed for the benefit of, at the direction of, or in association with any criminal gang;

705. Prevention of Organised Crime Act 121 of 1998, s. 5.
706. Prevention of Organised Crime Act 121 of 1998, s. 6.
707. Financial Intelligence Centre Act 38 of 2001, s. 29.
708. Prevention of Organised Crime Act 121 of 1998, s. 7A(2).
709. 'Criminal gang' includes any formal or informal ongoing organisation, association, or group of three or more persons, which has as one of its activities the commission of one or more criminal offences, which has an identifiable name or identifying sign or symbol, and whose members individually or collectively engage in or have engaged in a pattern of criminal gang activity.

b. threatens to commit, bring about or perform any act of violence or any criminal activity by a criminal gang or with the assistance of a criminal gang; or
c. threatens any specific person or persons in general, with retaliation in any manner or by any means whatsoever, in response to any act or alleged act of violence, is guilty of an offence.[710]

Any person who:

a. performs any act which is aimed at causing, bringing about, promoting or contributing towards a pattern of criminal gang activity;
b. incites, instigates, commands, aids, advises, encourages or procures any other person to commit, bring about, perform or participate in a pattern of criminal gang activity; or
c. intentionally causes, encourages, recruits, incites, instigates, commands, aids or advises another person to join a criminal gang, is guilty of an offence.[711]

In considering whether a person is a member of a criminal gang, the court may have regard to the following factors, namely that such person:

a. admits to criminal gang membership;
b. is identified as a member of a criminal gang by a parent or guardian;
c. resides in or frequents a particular criminal gang's area and adopts their style of dress, their use of hand signs, language or tattoos, and associates with known members of a criminal gang;
d. has been arrested more than once in the company of identified members of a criminal gang for offences which are consistent with usual criminal gang activities;
e. is identified as a member of a criminal gang by physical evidence such as photographs or other documentation.[712]

IX. Corruption

343. The Prevention and Combating of Corrupt Activities Act provides for both a general corruption offence as well as a number of specific offences.[713] The general corruption offence may be summarised in the following terms (according to Snyman): 'Anybody who (a) accepts any gratification from anybody else, or (b) gives any gratification to anybody else in order to influence the receiver to conduct herself in a way which amounts to the unlawful exercise of any duties, commits corruption.'[714] The specific corruption offences created by the Act include: corruption

710. Prevention of Organised Crime Act 121 of 1998, s. 9(1).
711. Prevention of Organised Crime Act 121 of 1998, s. 9(2).
712. Prevention of Organised Crime Act 121 of 1998, s. 11.
713. Act 12 of 2004.
714. Prevention and Combating of Corrupt Activities Act 12 of 2004, s. 3. *See* S.V. Hoctor, *Snyman's Criminal Law* 7th ed. (LexisNexis, Durban 2020) 357, approved in *S v. Scholtz* 2018 (2) SACR

in respect of public officers;[715] corruption in respect of foreign public officials;[716] corruption in respect of agents;[717] corruption in respect of members of the legislative authority;[718] corruption in respect of judicial officers;[719] corruption in respect of the prosecuting authority;[720] the receiving or offering of unauthorised gratification by a party to an employment relationship;[721] corruption in respect of witnesses;[722] corruption in respect of contracts;[723] corruption in respect of the granting of tenders;[724] corruption in respect of auctions;[725] corruption in respect of sporting events;[726] and corruption in respect of gambling or games of chance.[727] In addition, the following conduct is criminalised by the Act:[728] acquisition of a private interest in a contract, agreement or investment by a public officer connected with the public body in which such public officer is employed;[729] unacceptable conduct relating to witnesses;[730] intentional interference with the investigation of an offence;[731] failure by a person in a position of authority to report a corrupt transaction;[732] and failure by members of the private sector or incorporated state-owned entities to prevent corrupt activities.[733]

§6. Crimes Against Sexual Morality

I. Offences Relating to Adults

344. It is an offence under the Sexual Offences Act 1957 for any person to have unlawful carnal intercourse or commit an act of indecency with any other person for reward.[734,735]

---

526 (SCA) para. 123. The term 'gratification' is very broadly defined in the Act, and courts may take account of possible meanings of the term not indicated in the Act.
715. Prevention and Combating of Corrupt Activities Act 12 of 2004, s. 4.
716. Prevention and Combating of Corrupt Activities Act 12 of 2004, s. 5.
717. Prevention and Combating of Corrupt Activities Act 12 of 2004, s. 6.
718. Prevention and Combating of Corrupt Activities Act 12 of 2004, s. 7.
719. Prevention and Combating of Corrupt Activities Act 12 of 2004, s. 8.
720. Prevention and Combating of Corrupt Activities Act 12 of 2004, s. 9.
721. Prevention and Combating of Corrupt Activities Act 12 of 2004, s. 10.
722. Prevention and Combating of Corrupt Activities Act 12 of 2004, s. 11.
723. Prevention and Combating of Corrupt Activities Act 12 of 2004, s. 12.
724. Prevention and Combating of Corrupt Activities Act 12 of 2004, s. 13.
725. Prevention and Combating of Corrupt Activities Act 12 of 2004, s. 14.
726. Prevention and Combating of Corrupt Activities Act 12 of 2004, s. 15.
727. Prevention and Combating of Corrupt Activities Act 12 of 2004, s. 16.
728. Prevention and Combating of Corrupt Activities Act 12 of 2004.
729. Section 17(1). Section 17(2) provides for certain exceptions to liability.
730. Section 18.
731. Section 19.
732. Section 34(1), read with s. 34(2). The term 'position of authority' is defined in s. 34(4).
733. Section 34A.
734. J. Burchell, *Principles of Criminal Law* 5th ed. (Juta, Cape Town 2016) 797–800.
735. Sexual Offences Act 1957, s. 20(1A)(*a*). The constitutionality of this provision was affirmed by the Constitutional Court in *S v. Jordan* 2002 (2) SACR 499 (CC).

Solicitation[736] and procuring[737] for prostitution are offences under the Act, as is living on the earnings of prostitution[738] and keeping a brothel.[739]

The offence of engaging in the sexual services of a person 18 years or older is committed by a person who unlawfully and intentionally engages in the services of a person 18 years or older for financial or other reward, favour or compensation to such person or another person.[740]

It is further an offence for any person to unlawfully and intentionally disclose, by means of an electronic communications service, a data message of an intimate image of a person, without the consent of such person.[741]

II. Sexual Offences Against Children

345. In terms of section 15 of the Criminal Law (Sexual Offences and Related Matters) Amendment Act 32 of 2007, a person who commits an act of sexual *penetration*[742] with a child who is 12 years of age or older but under the age of 16 is, despite the consent of the child to the commission of such an act, guilty of the offence of having committed an act of consensual sexual penetration with a child.[743] Unless the accused person is related to the child within the prohibited incest degrees of blood, affinity or an adoptive relationship,[744] it is a valid defence to such a charge to contend that the child deceived the accused person into believing that he or she was 16 years or older at the time of the alleged commission of the offence and the accused person reasonably believed that the child was 16 years or older.[745]

A person who commits an act of sexual *violation* with a child who is 12 years of age or older but under the age of 16 is, despite the consent of such child to the commission of such an act, guilty of the offence of having committed an act of consensual sexual violation with a child.[746] Again, unless the accused person is related to

736. Sexual Offences Act 23 of 1957, s. 19(1).
737. Sexual Offences Act 23 of 1957, s. 10(a).
738. Sexual Offences Act 23 of 1957, s. 20(1)(a).
739. Sexual Offences Act 23 of 1957, s. 2.
740. Criminal Law (Sexual Offences and Related Matters) Amendment Act 32 of 2007; s. 11.
741. Cybercrimes Act 19 of 2020, s. 16.
742. For the definition of 'sexual penetration', *see supra* para. 292.
743. Unless such person, at the time of the alleged commission of such act was: (i) 12 years of age or older but under the age of 16 years; or (ii) either 16 or 17 years of age and the age difference between the parties was not more than two years. In terms of s. 15(2)(*b*) of Act 32 of 2007, the Director of Public Prosecutions may delegate his or her power to institute a prosecution under s. 15. Such prosecution must be authorised in writing by the Director of Public Prosecutions if the accused was either 16 or 17 years of age at the time of the alleged commission of the offence and the age difference between the parties was more than two years (s. 15(2)(*a*)). Section 15 has been amended following the decision in *Teddy Bear Clinic for Abused Children v. Minister of Justice and Constitutional Development* [2013] ZACC 35, in terms of the Criminal Law (Sexual Offences and Related Matters) Amendment Act Amendment Act 5 of 2015.
744. In which case this defence does not apply: s. 56(3) of Act 32 of 2007.
745. Criminal Law (Sexual Offences and Related Matters) Amendment Act 32 of 2007, s. 56(2)(*a*).
746. Criminal Law (Sexual Offences and Related Matters) Amendment Act 32 of 2007, s. 16(1). There is no liability under the section where such person, at the time of the alleged commission of such

the child within the prohibited incest degrees of blood, affinity or an adoptive relationship,[747] it is a valid defence to such a charge to contend that the child deceived the accused person into believing that he or she was 16 years or older at the time of the alleged commission of the offence and the accused person reasonably believed that the child was 16 years or older.[748]

Other offences created by Act 32 of 2007 relating to children are: sexual exploitation of children;[749] sexual grooming of children;[750] displaying pornography to children;[751] using children for or benefiting from child pornography;[752] and offences relating to creation, possession and distribution of child pornography.[753]

III. Bestiality

346. Once a crime at common law, bestiality is now a statutory offence.[754] There must be penetration of the body of the animal or the person or masturbation of the animal. It has been submitted that this type of behaviour ought no longer be the subject of prosecution in criminal law, but the constitutionality of this offence has been confirmed in the case of *S v. M.*[755]

§7. Crimes Against the State

I. Treason

347. Treason consists in any overt act unlawfully committed by a person owing allegiance to a State with intent to overthrow, impair, violate, threaten or endanger

act was: (i) 12 years of age or older but under the age of 16 years; or (ii) either 16 or 17 years of age and the age difference between the parties was not more than two years. In terms of s. 2 of Act 32 of 2007, the Director of Public Prosecutions may delegate his or her power to institute a prosecution under s. 15. Such prosecution must be authorised in writing by the Director of Public Prosecutions if the accused was either 16 or 17 years of age at the time of the alleged commission of the offence and the age difference between the parties was more than two years. For the definition of 'sexual violation', *see supra* para. 289. Section 16 has been amended following the decision in *Teddy Bear Clinic for Abused Children v. Minister of Justice and Constitutional Development* [2013] ZACC 35, in terms of the Criminal Law (Sexual Offences and Related Matters) Amendment Act Amendment Act 5 of 2015.

747. In which case this defence does not apply: s. 56(3) of Act 32 of 2007.
748. Criminal Law (Sexual Offences and Related Matters) Amendment Act 32 of 2007, s. 56(2)(*a*).
749. Criminal Law (Sexual Offences and Related Matters) Amendment Act 32 of 2007, s. 17(1).
750. Criminal Law (Sexual Offences and Related Matters) Amendment Act 32 of 2007, s. 18.
751. Criminal Law (Sexual Offences and Related Matters) Amendment Act 32 of 2007, s. 19.
752. Criminal Law (Sexual Offences and Related Matters) Amendment Act 32 of 2007, s. 20.
753. Criminal Law (Sexual Offences and Related Matters) Amendment Act 32 of 2007, s. 19A.
754. Criminal Law (Sexual Offences and Related Matters) Amendment Act 32 of 2007, s. 13.
755. 2004 (1) SACR 228 (O); *see* M. Carnelley & S.V.Hoctor, 'Bestiality: The Paradox of the "Paragon of Animals"' 2004 *Obiter* 506.

the existence, independence or security of the State or to overthrow or coerce the Government of the State or change the constitutional structure of the State.[756]

Although it is the general rule that treason is only committed by an 'overt' act, it is treason for any person to fail to report an act of treason being committed or about to be committed.[757]

Treason is committed only by persons who owe allegiance to the State.[758] Not only citizens owe allegiance but also persons who are domiciled in the country or even resident there.[759]

The common-law definitions of treason describe the intention for the crime in the phrase *animus hostilis* or 'hostile intent'.[760]

The exact meaning to be given to this phrase is the subject of some controversy. It is agreed that an intention to overthrow the State (which includes the government) amounts to a hostile intent. The question is however whether a person who intends to pressurise or coerce the government into a course of action has a 'hostile' intent. It would seem that this is the case.[761]

South African courts have jurisdiction to try treason against the South African State committed anywhere in the world.

II. Espionage

348. South Africa, following the model developed in Britain early in the twentieth century, has enacted legislation designed to penalise espionage and thereanent the disclosure of 'official secrets' by traitorous citizens or others.

349. In terms of the Protection of Information Act 1982,[762] it is for any person to approach, inspect, pass over, be in the neighbourhood of, or enter any prohibited place for any purpose prejudicial to the security or interests of the Republic.[763]

It is an offence to obtain or receive any secret official code or password kept, made or obtained in any prohibited place for purpose of disclosure to any foreign state.[764]

It is an offence[765] to prepare, compile or make for purpose of disclosure to any foreign state any documents, model, article or information relating to:

1. any prohibited place, or to armaments; or

756. *S v. Banda* 1990 (3) SA 466 (B); J.R.L. Milton, *South African Criminal Law and Procedure*, Vol. II *Common-Law Crimes* 3rd ed. (Juta, Cape Town 1996) 2.
757. *S v. Banda* 1990 (3) SA 466 (B) 511.
758. *R v. Prozesky* (1900) 21 NLR 216 at 218; *S v. Pastoors* 1986 (unreported) (discussed by C.R. Snyman, 'Die trouvereiste by hoogverraad' 1988 *SACJ* 1ff).
759. *S v. Pastoors* (*supra*).
760. *See R v. Erasmus* 1923 AD 73 80, 84; *R v. Viljoen* 1923 AD 90 97; *R v. Christian* 1924 AD 101 133–134, *S v. Zwane* 1989 (3) SA 253 (W).
761. *R v. Erasmus* 1923 AD 73 82; *S v. Banda* 1990 (3) SA 466 (B) 478.
762. Act 84 of 1982.
763. Protection of Information Act 84 of 1982, s. 2.
764. Protection of Information Act 84 of 1982, s. 3(*a*).
765. Protection of Information Act 84 of 1982, s. 3(*b*).

2. the defence of the Republic, any military or security matter; or
3. any other matter or article which may directly or indirectly be of use to any foreign state.

350. It is an offence for a person to retain for a purpose prejudicial to the security or interests of the Republic any official document.[766]

351. It is an offence to harbour or conceal any person who has committed or intends to commit an offence under the Protection of Information Act.[767]

III. Sedition

352. Sedition consists in unlawfully gathering, together with a number of people, with the intention of impairing the authority of the State by defying or subverting the authority of its Government, but without the intention of overthrowing or coercing that Government.[768]

The purpose of the gathering must be to challenge, resist or defy the authority of the State. This can be done by organising mass marches and protest meetings,[769] convening 'peoples' courts and assuming the law enforcement functions of the police.[770]

The intent required for sedition is not an intent to disturb the public peace and order but an intent to defy or subvert the Government's authority.[771]

IV. Terrorism and Sabotage

353. Any person who engages in a terrorist activity is guilty of the offence of terrorism.[772] Any person who: (i) does anything which will, or is likely to, enhance the ability of any entity to engage in a terrorist activity, including to provide or offer to provide a skill or an expertise; (ii) enters or remains in any country; or (iii) makes himself or herself available, for the benefit of, at the direction of, or in association with any entity engaging in a terrorist activity, and who knows or ought reasonably

766. Protection of Information Act 84 of 1982, s. 5(2)(*a*).
767. Protection of Information Act 84 of 1982, s. 7.
768. J. Burchell, *Principles of Criminal Law* 5th ed. (Juta, Cape Town 2016) 850.
769. *S v. Twala* 1979 (3) SA 864 (T).
770. *S v. Zwane (3)* 1989 (3) SA 253 (W).
771. *S v. Zwane (3)* 1989 (3) SA 253 (W) 261E.
772. Protection of Constitutional Democracy against Terrorist and Related Activity Act 33 of 2004, s. 2. In terms of s. 1, 'engages in a terrorist activity', includes: (a) the commission, performance or carrying out of; (b) the facilitation of, participation or assistance in, or contribution to the commission, performance or carrying out of; (c) the performance of an act in preparation for or planning of; or (d) instructing, directly or indirectly, the: (i) commission, performance, carrying out of; (ii) facilitation of, participation or assistance in, or contribution to the commission, performance or carrying out of; or (iii) performance of an act in preparation for or planning of, a terrorist activity, and the expressions 'to engage in a terrorist activity', 'engaging in a terrorist activity' and 'engagement in a terrorist activity' must be construed accordingly. *See S v. Okah* 2018 (4) BCLR 456 (CC).

to have known or suspected, that such act was done for the purpose of enhancing the ability of such entity to engage in a terrorist activity, is guilty of the offence associated with a terrorist activity.[773] Any person who: (i) provides or offers to provide any weapon to any other person for use by or for the benefit of an entity; (ii) solicits support for or gives support to an entity; (iii) provides, receives or participates in training or instruction, or recruits an entity to receive training or instruction; (iv) recruits any entity; (v) collects or makes a document; or (vi) possesses a thing, connected with the engagement in a terrorist activity, and who knows or ought reasonably to have known or suspected that such weapons, soliciting, training, recruitment, document or thing is so connected is guilty of an offence connected with terrorist activities.[774]

354. Certain offences, called 'convention offences', have been created in relation to the financing of specified offences.[775] It is an offence[776] to directly or indirectly, in whole or in part, and by any means or method acquire property; collect property; use property; possess property; own property; provides or make available, or invite a person to provide or make available property; provide or make available, or invite a person to provide or make available any financial or other service; provide or make available, or invite a person to provide or make available economic support; or facilitate the acquisition, collection, use or provision of property, or the provision of any financial or other service, or the provision of economic support, whilst intending that the property, financial or other service or economic support, as the case may be, be used, or whilst such person knows or ought reasonably to have known or suspected that the property, service or support concerned will be used, directly or indirectly, in whole or in part: (i) to commit or facilitate the commission of a specified offence; (ii) for the benefit of, or on behalf of, or at the direction of, or under the control of an entity which commits or attempts to commit or facilitates the commission of a specified offence; or (iii) for the benefit of a specific entity identified in an order made under section 23; or (iv) for the benefit of a specific entity related to terrorist activity identified pursuant to a resolution of the United Nations Security Council and announced in a notice as specified.[777]

It is further a 'convention offence' for any person to, directly or indirectly, in whole or in part, and by any means or method deal with, enter into or facilitate any transaction or perform any other act in connection with property which such person

773. Protection of Constitutional Democracy against Terrorist and Related Activity Act 33 of 2004, s. 3(1).
774. Protection of Constitutional Democracy against Terrorist and Related Activity Act 33 of 2004, s. 3(2).
775. In terms of s. 1 'Convention offence' means: (a) an offence, created in fulfilment of the Republic's international obligations in terms of instruments dealing with terrorist and related activities, referred to in Part 2 of Ch. 2; (b) an offence referred to in s. 56(1)(h) of the Nuclear Energy Act 46 of 1999; or (c) an offence referred to in s. 133 or s. 142(6) of the Civil Aviation Act 13 of 2009.
776. Protection of Constitutional Democracy against Terrorist and Related Activity Act 33 of 2004, s. 4(1).
777. In s. 26A (3) of the Financial Intelligence Centre Act 38 of 2001.

knows or ought reasonably to have known or suspected to have been acquired, collected, used, possessed, owned or provided: (i) to commit or facilitate the commission of a specified offence; (ii) for the benefit of, or on behalf of, or at the direction of, or under the control of an entity which commits or attempts to commit or facilitates the commission of a specified offence; (iii) for the benefit of a specific entity identified in an order made under section 23; or (iv) for the benefit of a specific entity related to terrorist activity identified pursuant to a resolution of the United Nations Security Council and announced in a notice as specified.[778] It is further an offence to provide financial or other services in respect of such property.[779] Moreover, an offence is committed by any person who knows or ought reasonably to have known or suspected that property is such property (in terms of section 2(a) of the Act) and enters into, or becomes concerned in, an arrangement which in any way has or is likely to have the effect of facilitating the retention or control of such property by or on behalf of: (i) an entity which commits or attempts to commit or facilitates the commission of a specified offence; or (ii) a specific entity identified in an order made under section 23; or (iv) for the benefit of a specific entity related to terrorist activity identified pursuant to a resolution of the United Nations Security Council and announced in a notice as specified; converting such property; concealing or disguising the nature, source, location, disposition or movement of such property, the ownership thereof or any interest anyone may have therein; removing such property from a jurisdiction; or transferring such property to a nominee.[780]

355. Act 33 of 2004 further provides for offences relating to hostages, causing harm to internationally protected persons and explosive or other lethal devices. Any person who intentionally seizes or detains, and threatens to kill, injure or continue to detain, any other person (i.e., a hostage) in order to compel a third party, namely a state, an intergovernmental organisation, a natural or juridical person, or a group of persons to do or abstain from doing any act as an explicit or implicit condition for the release of the hostage is guilty of an offence of taking a hostage.[781]

Any person who, knowing that a person is an internationally protected person, intentionally murders or kidnaps or otherwise violently attacks the person or liberty of that person or executes a violent attack upon the official premises, the private accommodation or the means of transport of that person, which attack is likely to endanger his or her person or liberty, is guilty of an offence relating to causing harm to an internationally protected person.[782]

---

778. Protection of Constitutional Democracy against Terrorist and Related Activity Act 33 of 2004, s. 4(2)(*a*). The notice is as referred to in s. 26A (3) of the Financial Intelligence Centre Act 38 of 2001.
779. Protection of Constitutional Democracy against Terrorist and Related Activity Act 33 of 2004, s. 4(2)(*b*).
780. Protection of Constitutional Democracy against Terrorist and Related Activity Act 33 of 2004, s. 4(3).
781. Protection of Constitutional Democracy against Terrorist and Related Activity Act 33 of 2004, s. 7.
782. Protection of Constitutional Democracy against Terrorist and Related Activity Act 33 of 2004, s. 8. In terms of s. 1 of the Act, an 'internationally protected person' means a Head of State, including any member of a collegial body performing the functions of a Head of State under the constitution of the State concerned, a Head of Government or a Minister for Foreign Affairs, whenever any such person is in the Republic, as well as members of his or her family accompanying him or her; or

Any person who intentionally delivers, places, discharges or detonates an explosive or other lethal device in, into or against a place of private or public use, a state or government facility, a public transport facility, a public transportation system, or an infrastructure facility, with the purpose, amongst others, of causing death or serious bodily injury; or extensive damage to, or destruction of such a place, facility or system, where such destruction results in or is likely to result in major economic loss, is guilty of an offence relating to explosive or other lethal devices.[783]

Other offences listed in the Act include: offences relating to hoaxes; offences relating to fixed platforms; offences relating to hijacking aircraft; offences relating to hijacking or endangering the safety of maritime navigation; offences relating to harbouring or concealing persons; offences relating to leaving the Republic for the purposes of involvement in a terrorist activity; and failure to fulfil the duty to report a person suspected of involvement in terrorist activity.

V. Public Violence

356. Public violence consists in the unlawful and intentional commission of a number of people acting in concert with acts of sufficiently serious dimensions which are intended forcibly to disturb the public peace or security or to invade the rights of others.[784]

The 'number of people' must act in concert. They must evolve a common purpose[785] forcibly to disturb the public peace or to invade the rights of others.

Examples of conduct held to be public violence include faction fighting,[786] riots,[787] violent resistance to the police acting lawfully,[788] forcible coercion by strikers of other workers,[789] and breaking up or taking over a meeting.[790] The crime is committed by persons who are members of the gathering. It is thus an essential element of the crime that the particular accused should have unlawfully and intentionally been a member of a gathering that engaged in public violence.

---

any representative or official of a State or any official or other agent of an international organisation or intergovernmental organisation or of an intergovernmental character who, at the time when and in the place where a crime against him or her, or his or her official premises, his or her private accommodation, or his or her means of transport is committed, is entitled, pursuant to international law to special protection from any attack on his or her person, freedom or dignity, as well as members of his or her family forming part of his or her household.

783. Protection of Constitutional Democracy against Terrorist and Related Activity Act 33 of 2004, s. 5. *See S v. Okah* (*supra*).

784. J.R.L. Milton, *South African Criminal Law and Procedure*, Vol. II *Common-Law Crimes* 3rd ed. (Juta, Cape Town 1996) 74; S.V. Hoctor, *Snyman's Criminal Law* 7th ed. (LexisNexis, Durban 2020) 277.

785. *See supra,* para. 253.

786. *R v. Tshayitsheni* 1918 TPD 23.

787. *R v. Taylor* 1920 EDL 318.

788. *R v. Ndwardwa* 1937 TPD 165; *R v. Marthinus* 1941 CPD 319.

789. *R v. Cele* 1958 (1) SA 144 (N).

790. *R v. Wilkens* 1941 TPD 276; *R v. Claassens* 1959 (3) SA 292 (T).

VI. Offences Relating to Essential Infrastructure

357. Any person who tampers with or destroys essential infrastructure, or colludes with or assists another person in such act, and who knows or ought reasonably to have known or suspected that it is essential infrastructure commits an offence.[791]

§8. Crimes Against the Administration of Justice

I. Contempt of Court

358. Contempt of court consists in unlawfully and intentionally violating the dignity, repute or authority of a judicial body or interfering in the administration of justice in a matter pending before it.[792]

The crime as applied in South African law follows the approach of the English law in subordinating freedom of expression to the interests of the administration of justice.[793]

Fair and legitimate criticism of the judiciary is lawful, and reasonable argument or expostulation may be offered against any judicial act as contrary to law or the public good.[794] A litigant is entitled to apply for the recusal of the judicial officer without being exposed to a charge of contempt of the officer.[795]

359. Contempts of court are classified as:

1. Contempts in facie curiae.
2. Contempts ex facie curiae with reference to pending judicial proceedings.
3. Contempts ex facie curiae which do not refer to pending proceedings.

360. Contempt *in facie curiae* is contempt committed in the presence of the court whilst it is sitting. It may take the form of adopting an insulting, contemptuous or defiant demeanour towards the court;[796] using insulting language towards the court;[797] refusing to obey the court's lawful orders; appearing in court seriously

---

791. Criminal Matters Amendment Act 18 of 2015, s. 3. 'Essential infrastructure' means any installation, structure, facility or system, whether publicly or privately owned, which if lost or damaged or tampered with would interfere with the provision or distribution of a basic service to the public.
792. J.R.L. Milton, *South African Criminal Law and Procedure*, Vol. II *Common-Law Crimes* 3rd ed. (Juta, Cape Town 1996) 164.; S.V. Hoctor, *Snyman's Criminal Law* 7th ed. (LexisNexis, Durban 2020) 281.
793. Cf. *S v. Harber* 1988 (3) SA 396 (A) 422H.
794. Cf. *S v. Van Niekerk* 1970 (3) SA 655 (T) 656–657; J. Burchell, *Principles of Criminal Law* 5th ed. (Juta, Cape Town 2016) 866–867.
795. *R v. Silber* 1952 (2) SA 475 (A) 481–484.
796. *R v. Baby* 1924 TPD 426; *S v. Mabheka* 1980 (2) PH H177 (O).
797. *S v. Poswa* 1986 (1) 215 (NC); *S v. Zungo* 1966 (1) 268 (N) 272.

improperly dressed;[798] being drunk in court;[799] shouting or singing.[800] Merely forgetting to switch off a cell phone, which subsequently rings in court, does not constitute a crime.[801]

361. Contempt *ex facie curiae* with reference to pending judicial proceedings pertains to the publication of matter concerning pending judicial proceedings which has the tendency to prejudice the outcome of the proceedings.

The effect of this form of contempt of court is to prohibit the publication in the press or other media of any information or commentary upon a matter which is *sub judice* and of course constitutes a major inroad upon the freedom of the press and the right of freedom of speech and information. It is justified on the grounds that it prevents 'trial by newspaper'.[802] However, in the light of the indispensability of a free press to democracy, it has been held by the SCA that before a ban on publication would be considered, what is required is 'a demonstrable relationship between the publication and the prejudice that it might cause to the administration of justice, substantial prejudice if it occurs, and a real risk that prejudice will occur'.[803]

362. Contempt *ex facie curiae* which do not refer to pending proceedings is committed by publications which violate the dignity, repute or authority of a judicial officer or the judiciary by unfair and improper criticism. Traditionally, this species of contempt is committed where a person:

1. scurrilously abuses a judge or the judiciary as a whole; or
2. imputes bias, partiality or improper motives to a judge or the courts in their administration of justice.[804]

Imputations of partiality (by far the commonest form of scandalising the court)[805] are contempt because they have the potential effect of lowering the repute of the judiciary and the courts and thereby undermine the public confidence in the administration of justice.

---

798. *S v. Bukwana* 1983 (1) PH H53 (NC).
799. *R v. Lloyd* 1905 (22) SC 347; *Duffey v. Munnik* 1957 (4) SA 390 (T).
800. *S v. Senyane; S v. Hlapane* 1993 (1) SACR 643 (O).
801. *S v. Sonpra* 2004 (1) SACR 278 (T).
802. *S v. Harber; in re S v. Baleka* 1986 (4) SA 214 (T) 221F.
803. *Midi Television (Pty) Ltd v. Director of Public Prosecutions (WC)* 2007 (9) BCLR 958 (SCA) para. 5.
804. For an extended examination of the history of scandalisation contempt in South African law, *see* A.E. van Blerk, *Judge and Be Judged* (Juta, Cape Town 1988). For an instance, *see S v. van Niekerk* 1970 (3) SA 655 (T); *S v. van Niekerk* 1972 (3) SA 279 (D), 1972 (3) SA 711 (A). An attack on the competence of certain racial groups to be magistrates is contempt of court – *S v. Bresler* 2002 (2) SACR 18 (C). In *S v. Mamabolo* 2001 (1) SACR 686 (CC), the Constitutional Court held that the offence of contempt of court by scandalising the court was not a constitutional violation of the right to freedom of expression. However, interference with the functioning of the courts is in itself unconstitutional – *Nelson Mandela Bay Municipality v. Gcora* 2019 (2) SACR 451 (ECP).
805. *R v. Torch Printing & Publishing Co* 1956 (1) SA 815 (C); *S v. Van Niekerk* 1970 (3) SA 655 (T) (these cases involved imputations of racial bias to judges).

363. Contempt of court concerns itself only with that conduct which impinges upon the administration of justice in or by the courts and not the part played by the executive government, its officials, employees and servants.[806]

364. In the case of contempt in terms of the *sub judice* rule,[807] where the accused is the editor or publisher of a newspaper or other medium, negligence is sufficient to establish the *mens rea* for the crime.[808]

365. In South African law, contempt of court may be prosecuted summarily. In this procedure, the court before whom the contempt is committed may there and then sentence the contemnor. In cases of contempt committed *in facie curiae*, the court can act immediately and without any other formality than informing the contemnor of the contempt[809] and affording an opportunity to answer the complaint.[810] In contempts committed *ex facie curia*, the offender is summoned on notice of motion to appear before the court to show cause why he should not be summarily punished for contempt.[811]

II. Defeating or Obstructing the Course of Justice

366. Defeating or obstructing the course of justice consists in unlawfully doing an act which is intended to defeat or obstruct and which does defeat or obstruct the due administration of justice.[812]

The conduct of this crime takes two principal forms: defeating the administration of justice or obstructing the administration of justice. Defeating is more serious than obstructing, since it means that justice has not been done (but defeated). Obstructing does not imply that justice is not done but rather that the process of doing justice has been delayed or made more difficult. Every case of defeating will include an obstructing of justice, but an obstruction cannot amount to defeating.[813]

The crime may be committed *before* proceedings are 'pending', as where the police are put to the trouble of investigating the truth of a false statement which is

806. *S v. Tromp* 1966 (1) SA 646 (N) 653.
807. *See supra*, para. 361.
808. *S v. Harber* 1988 (3) SA 396 (A) 418. For comment on this extraordinary view, *see* J. Burchell, 'Contempt of Court by the Media: Another Opportunity to Extend Press Freedom is Lost' 1988 *SAJHR* 375.
809. *S v. Pillay* 1990 (2) SACR 410 (CkA).
810. *S v. Nel* 1991 (1) SA 731 (A). There should only be a departure from the *audi alteram partem* rule in exceptional cases – *S v. James* 2019 (1) SACR 95 (ECB).
811. On this procedure and its possible unconstitutionality, *see* J. Burchell, *Principles of Criminal Law* 5th ed. (Juta, Cape Town 2016) 874. The summary procedure for scandalisation contempt was held to be an unconstitutional infringement of the right to a fair trial in *S v. Mamabolo* 2001 (1) SACR 686 (CC).
812. J.R.L. Milton, *South African Criminal Law and Procedure*, Vol. II *Common-Law Crimes* 3rd ed. (Juta, Cape Town 1996) 102; S.V. Hoctor, *Snyman's Criminal Law* 7th ed. (LexisNexis, Durban 2020) 292.
813. *R v. Cowan & Davies* 1903 TS 798.

made to them in connection with a matter which is being investigated[814] or is interfered with in the execution of their duties.[815]

'Administration of justice' means the *judicial* administration of justice in civil or criminal proceedings. If what is obstructed or defeated are quasi-judicial or administrative proceedings, the crime is not committed.[816]

III. Perjury

367. Perjury consists in the unlawful and intentional making, upon oath, affirmation or admonition and in the course of judicial proceedings before a competent tribunal, of a statement which the maker knows to be or foresees may be false.[817]

The statement must be false. The falsity may be an explicit untruth, or it may lie in inference or evasion. Whether concealment of fact is a falsehood is not clear.[818]

It is not only the ordinary courts of law before which common-law perjury can be committed,[819] for the term 'judicial proceedings' here also connotes proceedings of a judicial character before tribunals of various kinds other than courts of justice in the narrow sense.

A false statement made under oath outside the courtroom cannot amount to perjury.[820]

IV. Subornation of Perjury

368. 'Suborning' perjury is a crime in South African common law. The crime consists in unlawfully and intentionally inducing another person to commit perjury.[821]

V. Conflicting Statements on Oath

369. By statute, it is an offence to make conflicting statements under oath.[822]

---

814. *S v. Burger* 1975 (2) SA 601 (C); *S v. Mene* 1988 (3) SA 641 (A).
815. *S v. Naidoo* 1977 (2) SA 123 (N). Where the accused falsely informed the police that he had kidnapped a girl whom he would kill unless a ransom was paid, it was held that the offence had not been committed – *S v. Bazzard* 1992 (1) SACR 302 (NC).
816. *S v. Mdakani* 1964 (3) SA 311 (T).
817. J.R.L. Milton, *South African Criminal Law and Procedure*, Vol. II *Common-Law Crimes* 3rd ed. (Juta, Cape Town 1996) 131; S.V. Hoctor, *Snyman's Criminal Law* 7th ed. (LexisNexis, Durban 2020) 296.
818. *See* Milton (*supra*) 138.
819. *R v. Beukman* 1950 (4) SA 261 (O) 263; *S v. Carse* 1967 (2) SA 659 (C) 665.
820. *R v. Beukman* (*supra*).
821. J.R.L. Milton, *South African Criminal Law and Procedure*, Vol. II *Common-Law Crimes* 3rd ed. (Juta, Cape Town 1996) 151; S.V. Hoctor, *Snyman's Criminal Law* 7th ed. (LexisNexis, Durban 2020) 299.
822. Criminal Procedure Act 56 of 1955, s. 319(3). *See*, J.R.L. Milton, *South African Law and Procedure*, Vol. II *Common-Law Crimes* 3rd ed. (Juta, Cape Town 1996) 155ff.; S.V. Hoctor, *Snyman's Criminal Law* 7th ed. (LexisNexis, Durban 2020) 299.

The offence is committed if there are two different statements made at different times under different oaths. It is only necessary for the State to prove that the statements conflict with each other and it is not necessary to prove which, if any, statement is untrue.[823]

VI. Compounding

370. Compounding consists in unlawfully and intentionally agreeing for reward not to prosecute a crime.[824]

South African law does not punish the compounding of a crime punishable only by a fine.[825] Furthermore, certain statutes authorise the compounding of offences. A notable example is the compounding[826] of certain defined traffic and municipal offences[827] (by payment of 'admission of guilt' fines before a prosecution is launched for the offence).[828]

§9. International Crimes

I. Rome Statute

371. The Implementation of the Rome Statute of the International Criminal Court Act[829] provides for a framework to ensure the effective implementation of the Rome Statute of the International Criminal Court and to ensure that anything done in terms of the Act conforms with the obligations of the Republic in terms of the Statute.

The fact that a person is or was a head of state or government, a member of a government or Parliament, an elected representative or a government official or a member of a security service or armed force who was under a legal obligation to obey a manifestly unlawful order of a government or superior is neither a defence to a crime nor a ground for any possible reduction of a sentence if convicted.[830] For the purposes of the Act, the term 'crime' means the crime of genocide, crimes against humanity and war crimes.[831]

In order to secure the jurisdiction of local courts, any person who commits one of these crimes outside the territory of the Republic is deemed to have committed that crime in the territory of the Republic if: (a) that person is a South African citizen; or (b) if not a citizen is ordinarily resident in the Republic; or (c) that person, after

---

823. *R v. Mohamed* 1951 (1) SA 439 (T).
824. J.R.L. Milton, *South African Criminal Law and Procedure*, Vol. II *Common-Law Crimes* 3rd ed. (Juta, Cape Town 1996) 204.
825. *R v. Thomas* (1883) 1 Buch AC 205.
826. Criminal Procedure Act 51 of 1977, s. 341.
827. These are set out in the third Schedule to the Criminal Procedure Act 51 of 1977.
828. *See supra*, para. 569.
829. Implementation of the Rome Statute of the International Criminal Court Act 27 of 2002.
830. Implementation of the Rome Statute of the International Criminal Court Act 27 of 2002, s. 4(2).
831. Implementation of the Rome Statute of the International Criminal Court Act 27 of 2002, s. 1(vii).

the commission of the crime, is present in the Republic; or (d) that person has committed the crime against a South African citizen or against a person who is ordinarily resident in the Republic.[832]

II. Torture

372. The Prevention and Combating of Torture of Persons Act[833] seeks to give effect to South Africa's international obligations under the United Nations Convention against Torture and Other Cruel, Inhuman or Degrading Treatment or Punishment of 1984. The Act is underpinned by the right to freedom and security of the person, which includes the right not to be tortured in any way.[834] This Act should be read with the relevant implementation of the Rome Statute of the International Criminal Court Act,[835] which provides that torture can also be a crime under international law, as incorporated in this legislation, where it is committed in a particular context.[836]

Any person who commits torture, attempts to commit torture, or incites, instigates, commands or procures any person to commit torture is guilty of the offence of torture.[837] Furthermore, any person who participates in torture or who conspires with a public official to aid or procure the commission of or to commit torture is guilty of the offence of torture.[838]

III. Trafficking

373. The offence of trafficking in persons is committed by any person who delivers, recruits, transports, transfers, harbours, sells, exchanges, leases or receives another person within or across the borders of the Republic, using various means, aimed at either such person, an immediate family member of that person or any other person in close relationship to that person, for the purpose of any form or manner of exploitation.[839]

---

832. Implementation of the Rome Statute of the International Criminal Court Act 27 of 2002, s. 4(3).
833. Act 13 of 2013.
834. Constitution 1996; s. 12(1)(*d*).
835. *See supra,* para. 371.
836. The Torture Act provides for criminal liability for torture where this would not be covered by Act 27 of 2002 (G. Kemp et al., *Criminal Law in South Africa* 4th ed. (Oxford University Press, Cape Town 2022) 675).
837. The Prevention and Combating of Torture of Persons Act 13 of 2013, s. 4(1). In terms of s. 3 of this Act, torture means any act by which severe pain or suffering, whether physical or mental, is intentionally inflicted on a person, either: (i) to obtain information or a confession, or to punish a person, or to intimidate or coercing a person; or (ii) for any reason based on discrimination of any kind, where the torture is inflicted with the consent or at the instigation of a public official or someone acting in an official capacity.
838. The Prevention and Combating of Torture of Persons Act 13 of 2013, s. 4(2).
839. Prevention and Combating of Trafficking in Persons Act 7 of 2013, s. 4(1). *See S v. Jezile* 2015 (2) SACR 452 (WCC).

The means identified in this provision are: a threat of harm; the threat or use of force or other forms of coercion; the abuse of vulnerability; fraud; deception; abduction; kidnapping; the abuse of power; the direct or indirect giving or receiving of payments or benefits to obtain the consent of a person having control or authority over another person; or the direct or indirect giving or receiving of payments, compensation, rewards, benefits or any other advantage. Furthermore, in terms of the prohibition on trafficking in persons, an offence is committed by any person who adopts a child, facilitated or secured through legal or illegal means, or concludes a forced marriage with another person, within or across the borders of the Republic, for the purpose of the exploitation of that child or other person in any form or manner.[840]

These offences, along with other related offences, are created by the Prevention and Combating of Trafficking in Persons Act, 2013,[841] which is aimed at giving effect to the international obligations on South Africa to combat and ultimately eradicate trafficking in persons by virtue of international instruments such as the United Nations Protocol to Prevent, Suppress and Punish Trafficking in Persons, especially Women and Children, Supplementing the United Nations Convention against Transnational Organised Crime of 2000. The Act further seeks to give specific effect to the rights not to be arbitrarily or without just cause deprived of freedom and not to be treated in a cruel, inhuman or degrading way;[842] the right not to be subjected to slavery, servitude or forced labour;[843] and the right of children to be protected from maltreatment, neglect, abuse or degradation.[844]

840. Prevention and Combating of Trafficking in Persons Act 7 of 2013, s. 4(2).
841. Act 7 of 2013.
842. Constitution, 1996, s. 12(1).
843. Constitution, 1996, s. 13.
844. Constitution, 1996, s. 28(1)(*d*).

Chapter 7. The Sanctioning System

§1. The General Sanctioning System

I. Types of Sanctions

374. There is no single legislative provision governing the whole South African sanctioning system.[845] The most general provision is section 276(1) of the Criminal Procedure Act 51 of 1977 which specifies the sentences which courts may impose. These are: imprisonment, including life imprisonment and imprisonment for an indefinite period as a dangerous criminal; periodical imprisonment; imprisonment from which a person may be placed under correctional supervision; declaration as a habitual criminal; committal to any institution established by law; a fine; and correctional supervision.

This list of sanctions is qualified in the same section by declaring it '[s]ubject to the provisions of the [Criminal Procedure] Act and any other law and the common law'. In practice, these qualifications take two forms. First, they can be read as referring to the limited punishment jurisdiction of the various courts. Second, there is the possibility that there might be provision in other legislation for a type of punishment not included in the list in section 276. Thus, for example, the Correctional Services Act 111 of 1998 makes provision for the imposition of segregation and loss of amenities.[846] Such exceptional provisions are relatively rare. In practice, the courts do not use the common law as a justification for imposing sentences other than those contained in the list or specific statutory provisions.

375. There is also a range of orders which courts may make in the context of sentencing, either in terms of general legislation, such as compensation orders, or in terms of specific legislation, such as the revocation of driving licenses in terms of road traffic legislation.[847] Such orders, strictly speaking, are not punishments but nevertheless, in practice, may have the effect of penalising the offender.

With regard to the sentencing of corporate entities, a court may not impose any punishment other than a fine.[848]

II. Role of the Constitution

376. The role of the Constitution is visible in almost every aspect of sentencing.[849] Capital punishment[850] and corporal punishment[851] have been declared

845. The leading South African textbook on the subject is S.S. Terblanche, *Guide to Sentencing in South Africa* 3rd ed. (LexisNexis, Durban 2016). A great deal of useful information on the system of sanctions is also contained in E. Du Toit (ed.), *Commentary on the Criminal Procedure Act* (Juta, Cape Town (loose-leaf) original service 1987) and A. Kruger, *Hiemstra*'s *Criminal Procedure* (LexisNexis, Durban 2008 (loose-leaf)).
846. *See infra*, para. 693.
847. *See infra*, para. 399.
848. Criminal Procedure Act 51 of 1977, s. 332(2)(*c*).
849. S.S. Terblanche, *Guide to Sentencing in South Africa* 3rd ed. (LexisNexis, Durban 2016) 14.

unconstitutional. In assessing whether the right to freedom and security of the person, which includes the right not to be treated or punished in a cruel, inhuman or degrading way,[852] has been unjustifiably infringed, the key assessment relates to the proportionality between the seriousness of the offence and the extent of the punishment.[853] The issue of proportionality also relates to the right not to be deprived of freedom 'without just cause', where the offence is the 'cause' justifying an offender's incarceration.[854] Deprivation of the offender's freedom can only be justified by a sentence in proportion to the offence.[855] The requirement of proportionality is also linked to the right to dignity.[856] Moreover the right to a fair trial, contained in section 35(3) of the Constitution, clearly extends to the sentencing phase of the trial.[857]

§2. PUNISHMENTS

I. The Sentence of Death

377. The sentence of death was a controversial part of the sanctioning system in South Africa for many years. In addition to being a discretionary sentence for a number of crimes, it was, until 1990, a mandatory sentence for murder where the accused was older than 18 years and where there were no extenuating circumstances. In 1990, mandatory death sentences were abolished and the list of offences, set out in section 277(1) of the Criminal Procedure Act, for which the sentence of death may be imposed was reduced. However, the Constitutional Court in *S v. Makwanyane*[858] held that the imposition of the death penalty was unconstitutional.[859] Capital punishment is thus no longer a valid punishment in South Africa.

II. Imprisonment

378. Since the abolition of the sentence of imprisonment with hard labour in 1959, courts have not had the general power to impose imprisonment, which must

---

850. *See infra*, para. 377.
851. *See infra*, para. 389.
852. Constitution, 1996, s. 12(1)(*e*).
853. It was held by the Constitutional Court in *S v. Dodo* 2001 (1) SACR 594 (CC) para. 37 that this goes 'to the heart of the inquiry as to whether punishment is cruel, inhuman or degrading'.
854. Constitution, 1996, s. 12(1)(*a*).
855. S.S. Terblanche, *Guide to Sentencing in South Africa* 3rd ed. (LexisNexis, Durban 2016) 12.
856. Constitution, 1996, s. 10; *S v. Dodo* 2001 (1) SACR 594 (CC) para. 38.
857. *S v. Dzukuda* 2000 (2) SACR 443 (CC) paras 11–12; S.S. Terblanche, *Guide to Sentencing in South Africa* 3rd ed. (LexisNexis, Durban 2016) 13.
858. *S v. Makwanyane* 1995 (2) SACR 1 (CC).
859. All eleven justices agreed that the imposition of the death penalty unjustifiably infringed the right not to be subject to cruel, inhuman or degrading punishment (s. 11(2) of the interim Constitution), and eight justices also specifically held that its imposition unjustifiably infringed the right to life (s. 9 of the interim Constitution).

be served under more or less punitive conditions. Other than the limits on the punishment jurisdiction of the lower courts and maximum sentences which may be prescribed for statutory offences, there is no general restriction on the length of prison sentences that the courts may impose. Sentences in excess of twenty-five years imprisonment for a single offence are extremely rare, however. The minimum sentence of imprisonment is four days, but a court may sentence an offender to be detained until the rising of the court.[860]

379. In 1990, the general provision relating to imprisonment was amended also to specify life imprisonment for the first time. This amendment was enacted by the same Act, which introduced the changes to the law relating to the sentence of death. Prior to 1990, life imprisonment was a competent sentence, but it was imposed extremely rarely. Since 1990, there have been indications that life imprisonment will be imposed in instances where, previously, the sentence of death would have been regarded as appropriate.[861] It has been held that life imprisonment should only be imposed in exceptional cases.[862] Life imprisonment is mandatory for certain serious offences.[863]

380. The courts have developed general guidelines in relation to the imposition of imprisonment. The guidelines are very broad and reveal the wide discretion which courts have in deciding whether to impose a sentence of imprisonment.

381. Imprisonment is regarded as a serious form of punishment which should not be imposed lightly where the objectives of punishment can be met by another sentence.[864] In particular, first offenders[865] and young offenders[866] should be kept out of prison as far as possible, although there is no absolute prohibition on sending offenders of either category to prison.[867] Imprisonment is also an inappropriate punishment for petty offences, no matter how often they are repeated.[868] An offender should only be imprisoned if he needs to be removed from society.[869] The courts have also recognised that, notwithstanding the statutory function of the Department of Correctional Services to treat and train sentenced prisoners, conditions for the effective rehabilitation of prisoners do not exist and that this should be borne in mind when sentences are imposed.[870]

---

860. Criminal Procedure Act 51 of 1977, s. 284.
861. *S v. Mdau* 1991 (1) SA 169 (A).
862. *S v. Martin* 1996 (1) SACR 172 (W); *S v. Dodo* 2001 (1) SACR 301 (E).
863. *See supra* para. 393.
864. *S v. Benetti* 1975 (3) SA 603 (T).
865. *S v. Makkahela* 1975 (3) SA 788 (C).
866. *Persadh v. R* 1944 NPD 357.
867. *S v. Holder* 1979 (2) SA 70 (A).
868. *S. v. Adams* 1962 (1) SA 162 (C).
869. *S v. R* 1993 (1) SACR 209 (A).
870. *S v. Jensen* 1990 (1) SACR 694 (C).

III. Periodical Imprisonment

382. Section 285 of the Criminal Procedure Act empowers courts generally to impose, *in lieu* of any other punishment, a sentence of periodical imprisonment of not less than 100 and not more than 2,000 hours. The only exception to this general power is that periodical imprisonment may not be imposed in those instances where a statutory minimum punishment is prescribed for an offence. The purpose of periodical imprisonment is to allow an offender to serve his sentence for short periods, for example, over weekends, and thus to enable him to maintain his work and contact with his family. However, in practice, there are difficulties with the effective implementation of this sentence.

IV. Declaration as a Habitual Criminal

383. If a superior or regional court is satisfied that a convicted person habitually commits offences and that the community should be protected against him, such a court may declare him a habitual criminal.[871] The effect of such a declaration is that the offender is imprisoned. In theory, the term of imprisonment is indefinite, but in practice, the minimum term to be served by a habitual criminal is seven years and the maximum fifteen years.[872] Declaration as a habitual criminal cannot be combined with any other sentence. The sentence may not be imposed on an accused person under the age of 18 or in cases where the court is of the view that the offence warrants imprisonment for longer than fifteen years.

384. The courts which have the jurisdiction to declare someone a habitual criminal exercise a very wide discretion in deciding whether the person concerned habitually commits offences and is a threat to the community. In coming to a conclusion in this regard, the court must consider the previous convictions of the offender. Whilst there is no longer a legally specified period after which previous convictions must be disregarded, the lapse of time should not be too great. Although it is not prescribed by statute, the courts have insisted that an offender should have been warned when sentenced on a previous occasion that he may be declared a habitual offender before such an order is made. This judge-made law does not entirely remove the discretion of the sentencing court to declare an offender a habitual criminal even where no warning has previously been given.[873]

871. Criminal Procedure Act 51 of 1977, s. 286.
872. The minimum period is prescribed by s. 73(6)(*c*) of the Correctional Services Act 111 of 1998, whilst the maximum period is deduced from the provision in s. 286(2)(*c*) of the Criminal Procedure Act, that no one should be declared an habitual criminal if the offence warrants a sentence of more than fifteen years. In *S v. Niemand* 2001 (2) SACR 654 (CC), the Constitutional Court confirmed the constitutionality of s. 286, provided that no offender be detained for a period exceeding fifteen years.
873. *S v. Erasmus* 1987 (4) SA 685 (C). The lack of a previous warning would however have to be taken into account – *S v. Shabalala* 1984 (2) SA 234 (N).

V. Committal to an Institution Established by Law

385. Any court which convicts a person of any offence may, if certain requirements are met, order the committal of the convicted person to a treatment centre.[874] Such a committal may be *in lieu* of, or in addition to, any sentence except a sentence of imprisonment. The key substantive requirement is that the court must be satisfied that the person to be committed is someone as described in section 21 of the Prevention and Treatment of Drug Dependency Act 20 of 1992. This section refers primarily to alcohol and drug dependence, but it can also be used to detain persons who are a danger to themselves or others or a threat to the peace or spendthrift. These provisions are very wide but in comparison with imprisonment are used relatively rarely.

386. In terms of the Child Justice Act 75 of 2008, a child may be sentenced to compulsory residence in a child and youth care centre.[875]

VI. Fines

387. A fine may be imposed as a sentence for any offence for which no penalty is prescribed. A fine may be imposed on its own as a primary penalty or with imprisonment as an alternative.[876] In practice, in the case of most statutory offences, there is provision both for a maximum fine and for imprisonment, which can be imposed as a separate or an additional punishment or as an alternative to a fine. The usual procedure is for the court to impose a fine, with a term of imprisonment as an alternative, to be brought into operation only if the fine is not paid. However, where a sentence of imprisonment has not been imposed as an alternative, there is a procedure for having the matter brought before the court again for reconsideration. Where there is no statutory maximum fine, the sentencing court is limited only to the maximum of its sentencing jurisdiction (except for punishment jurisdiction).

388. In many circumstances, a fine is regarded as the ideal form of punishment as it penalises the offender without having the negative effects (and expense) of imprisonment. It is therefore regarded as particularly appropriate for first offenders. The fine is used both as a formal punishment for minor traffic offences, for example, and as a substantive punishment for more serious offences.[877] In the former instance, in practice, fines are set according to a scale or tariff, but in the latter, the courts have to determine the quantum of the fine and usually its relationship to an alternative period of imprisonment. The principles according to which these decisions should be made are not entirely clear. There is agreement in the jurisprudence that the courts should always enquire carefully into the financial position of the accused

874. Criminal Procedure Act 1977, s. 296.
875. *See infra*, para. 397.
876. Criminal Procedure Act 51 of 1977, s. 287.
877. S.S. Terblanche, *Guide to Sentencing in South Africa* 3rd ed. (LexisNexis, Durban 2016) 297ff.

and his ability to pay.[878] There is also consensus that the amount should bear some relationship to the ability of the accused to pay.[879] However, there is a division of opinion about whether the amount of the fine should not sometimes be set at a level which the accused may not be able to afford in order to indicate, for example, the particular seriousness of the offence.[880] There is no formal provision in South African law for the calculations to be based on a day-fine system of the kind which exists in many European countries.

VII. Corporal Punishment

389. In *S v. Williams*,[881] the Constitutional Court determined that the provisions of section 294 of the Criminal Procedure Act, which provided for corporal punishment as a sentencing option, unjustifiably infringed the rights to dignity and the right not to be subject to cruel, inhuman and degrading punishment.[882] Corporal punishment has therefore been abolished as a sentencing option.[883]

VIII. Correctional Supervision

390. In 1991, a further primary sentencing option, correctional supervision, was added to the list in the Criminal Procedure Act.[884] In essence, correctional supervision is a community-based punishment administered by the Department of Correctional Services.[885]

391. The sentence of correctional supervision may be imposed directly, but it may also be imposed indirectly in a number of ways. A court may impose a sentence of imprisonment but indicate at the time of its imposition that the Commissioner of Correctional Services has the discretion to change the imprisonment to correctional supervision.[886] Correctional supervision may be set as a condition on which the passing of sentence is postponed or its implementation suspended.[887] The Commissioner of Correctional Services also has the power to approach a court which has passed a sentence of imprisonment of less than five years or which has

878. *S v. Sithole* 1979 (2) SA 67 (A).
879. *S v. Zwane* 1997 (1) SACR 326 (W).
880. D.P. van der Merwe, *Sentencing* (Juta, Cape Town 1991) 4–34–36; E. Du Toit, *Straf in Suid-Afrika* (Juta, Cape Town 1981) 306–310; S.S. Terblanche, *Guide to Sentencing in South Africa* 3rd ed. (LexisNexis, Durban 2016) 299–302.
881. *S v. Williams* 1995 (2) SACR 251 (CC).
882. Respectively ss 10 and 11(2) of the interim Constitution.
883. Abolition of Corporal Punishment Act 33 of 1997.
884. Criminal Procedure Act 1977. ss 276(1)(h), 276A. For discussion, *see* S.S. Terblanche, *Guide to Sentencing in South Africa* 3rd ed. (LexisNexis, Durban 2016) 317ff.
885. *See infra*, para. 697.
886. Criminal Procedure Act 51 of 1977, s. 276(1)(*i*).
887. Criminal Procedure Act 51 of 1977, s. 297(1)(*a*)(i)(*cc*A).

passed a longer sentence of which the prisoner has less than five years to serve and ask the court to convert the imprisonment into a sentence of correctional supervision.[888]

IX. Declaration as Dangerous Criminal

392. A High Court or regional court which convicts a person of one or more offences may, if it is satisfied that the person represents a danger to the physical and mental well-being of other persons and that the community should be protected against him or her, declare such offender a dangerous criminal.[889] If it appears to such a court or if it is alleged before such court that the accused is a dangerous criminal, the court may after conviction direct that the matter be inquired into and reported on.[890] The court which declares an offender to be a dangerous criminal must: (a) sentence such offender to imprisonment for an indefinite period, and (b) direct that upon expiration of such period determined by it, which should not exceed its jurisdiction, the offender should again be brought before the court.[891] It has been held that this form of punishment is not unconstitutional, as it is not so vague as infringing the legality principle, and moreover, provided the punishment is not grossly disproportionate to the crime, declaration as a dangerous criminal is not unconstitutional on the basis of its indeterminacy.[892]

§3. Mandatory and Minimum Sentencing

I. Mandatory Sentencing Provisions

393. Along with the minimum sentencing provisions discussed below, the mandatory sentencing provisions were introduced into South African law in an attempt by the legislature to combat the prevalence of violent crime in South Africa and to address high crime rates, essentially by mandating heavy punishments as a means of deterrence.[893] Though the legislation was intended as a temporary measure, it has now become permanent, and given the high level of serious crime in South Africa, it has become a significant feature of sentencing practice in the regional magistrates' courts and high courts.

Section 51 of the Criminal Law Amendment Act 105 of 1997 provides for mandatory sentences for certain serious offences. A high court or regional court must, if

---

888. Criminal Procedure Act 51 of 1977, s. 276A(3).
889. Criminal Procedure Act 51 of 1977, s. 286A(1). 'Dangerous' is assessed as a prediction of future behaviour, based on past behaviour and the offender's character and circumstances – *S v. Bull* 2001 (2) SACR 681 (SCA).
890. For the details of such inquiry, *see* Criminal Procedure Act 51 of 1977, s. 286A(2), (3), (4).
891. Criminal Procedure Act 51 of 1977, s. 286B(1). For the further sentencing options when the court engages in a consideration of such sentence, *see* Criminal Procedure Act 51 of 1977, s. 286B(4), (5).
892. *S v. Bull* 2001 (2) SACR 681 (SCA).
893. S.S. Terblanche, *Guide to Sentencing in South Africa* 3rd ed. (LexisNexis, Durban 2016) 50.

it has convicted a person of certain scheduled offences, sentence the person to life imprisonment.[894] Life imprisonment is mandatory for murder or attempted murder when: (a) it was planned or premeditated; (b) the victim was a law enforcement officer performing his function as such, whether on duty or not, or was a person who has or was likely to give material evidence with reference to any offence referred to in Schedule 1 of the Criminal Procedure Act at criminal proceedings in any court, or was a person under the age of 18 years; (c) the death of the victim was caused by the accused in committing or attempting to commit or after having committed or attempted to commit rape or compelled rape or robbery with aggravating circumstances; or (d) the offence was committed by a person, group of persons or syndicate acting in the execution of furtherance of a common purpose or conspiracy; or (e) the victim was killed in order to unlawfully remove any body part of the victim, or as a result of such unlawful removal of a body part of the victim; or (f) the death of the victim resulted from, or is directly related to, certain offences relating to the practice of witchcraft;[895] or the death of the victim resulted from physical abuse or sexual abuse, by the accused who is or was in a domestic relationship with the victim.[896]

Life imprisonment is also mandatory for rape[897] and compelled rape,[898] when it is committed in the following circumstances: (a) where the accused is convicted of the offence of rape and evidence adduced at the trial of the accused proves that the victim was also raped by any co-perpetrator or accomplice; or a person, who was compelled by any co-perpetrator or accomplice, to rape the victim;[899] (b) where the accused is convicted of the offence of rape on the basis that the accused acted in the execution or furtherance of a common purpose or conspiracy and evidence adduced at the trial of the accused proves that the victim was raped by more than one person who acted in the execution or furtherance of a common purpose or conspiracy to rape the victim; (c) by the accused who: (i) has previously been convicted of the offence of rape or compelled rape; or (ii) has been convicted by the trial court of two or more offences of rape or the offences of rape and compelled rape, irrespective of whether the rape of which the accused has so been convicted constitutes a common law or statutory offence; or the date of the commission of any such offence of which the accused has so been convicted; or whether the accused has been sentenced in respect of any such offence of which the accused has so been convicted; or whether any such offence of which the accused has so been convicted was committed in respect of the same victim or any other victim; or whether any such offence of which the accused has so been convicted was committed as part of the same chain of events, on a single occasion or on different occasions; or (d) by a person, knowing that he has the acquired immune deficiency syndrome or the human

---

894. Criminal Law Amendment Act 105 of 1997, s. 51(1); Schedule 2, Part 1.
895. Witchcraft Suppression Act 3 of 1957, s. 1(*a*)–(*e*).
896. As contemplated in the definitions of 'domestic violence' and 'domestic relationship' in s. 1 of the Domestic Violence Act 116 of 1998.
897. Criminal Law (Sexual Offences and Related Matters) Amendment Act 32 of 2007, s. 3.
898. Criminal Law (Sexual Offences and Related Matters) Amendment Act 32 of 2007, s. 4.
899. As contemplated in the Criminal Law (Sexual Offences and Related Matters) Amendment Act 32 of 2007, s. 4.

immunodeficiency virus. Life imprisonment is further mandatory for rape and compelled rape, where the rape was accompanied by the infliction of grievous bodily harm or where the victim is: (i) a person under the age of 18 years; (ii) is an older person as defined in section 1 of the Older Persons Act 13 of 2006; (iii) a person with a disability who, due to his or her disability, is rendered vulnerable; (iv) a person who is mentally disabled as contemplated in section 1 of the Criminal Law (Sexual Offences and Related Matters) Amendment Act, 2007; or (v) is or was in a domestic relationship, as defined in section 1 of the Domestic Violence Act, 1998, with the accused.

Moreover, life imprisonment is obligatory with regard to a range of offences, including terrorism, hijacking and hostage-taking, set out in the Protection of Constitutional Democracy against Terrorist and Related Activities Act.[900] Trafficking in persons[901] is visited with mandatory life imprisonment, as too is genocide and any conduct falling within the category of a crime against humanity.[902]

II. Minimum Sentencing Provisions

394. Minimum sentences are sentences with a lower limit, allowing the court to impose a higher sentence by exercising its discretion.[903] A range of minimum sentences was introduced into South African law by legislation[904] with the aim of these provisions functioning as a drastic but temporary measure to deal with the upsurge in serious crime. Though initially intended to be temporary, the temporary regime has now become permanent.[905] Minimum sentences apply to all accused persons of 18 years or older.[906]

395. In terms of the Criminal Law Amendment Act of 1997,[907] when a regional court or a high court has convicted a person for a Part II Schedule 2 offence, that is to say:

a. murder or attempted murder in circumstances other than those mentioned above;[908]

---

900. Protection of Constitutional Democracy against Terrorism and Related Activities Act 33 of 2004. *See supra,* para. 353.
901. Prevention and Combating of Trafficking in Persons Act 7 of 2013. Involvement in the offence as provided for in s. 10 of Act 7 of 2013 attracts the same punishment. *See supra,* para. 373.
902. Offences referred to in the Implementation of the Rome Statute of the International Criminal Court Act 27 of 2002, Schedule 1, Parts 1 and 2. *See supra,* para. 371.
903. S.S. Terblanche, *Guide to Sentencing in South Africa* 3rd ed. (LexisNexis, Durban 2016) 48.
904. By the Criminal Law Amendment Act 105 of 1997.
905. In terms of the Criminal Law (Sentencing) Amendment Act 38 of 2007.
906. *Centre for Child Law v. Minister of Justice and Constitutional Development* 2009 (2) SACR 477 (CC), where the provision in s. 51(6) of Act 105 of 1997 allowing minimum sentences to apply to offenders over sixteen years was struck down as unconstitutional. The state bears the onus of proving age beyond reasonable doubt – s. 51(7) of Act 105 of 1997.
907. Criminal Law Amendment Act 105 of 1997, s. 51(2).
908. *See supra,* para. 393.

b. rape or compelled rape in circumstances other than those mentioned above;[909]
c. robbery where there are aggravating circumstances or involving the taking of a motor vehicle;
d. an offence referred to in section 13(f) of the Drugs and Drug Trafficking Act[910] if it is proved that the value of the dependence-producing substance in question is more than ZAR 50,000 (at exchange rates applicable at time of writing: GBP 2,100/USD 2,750/EUR 2,500) or the value of the dependence-producing substance is more than ZAR 10,000 (at exchange rates applicable at time of writing: GBP 420/USD 550/EUR 500) and the offence was committed by a person, a group of persons, syndicate or any enterprise acting in the execution or furtherance of a common purpose or conspiracy or where the offence was committed by any law enforcement officer;
e. any offence relating to the dealing in or smuggling of ammunition, firearms, explosives or armament or the possession of an automatic or semi-automatic firearm, explosives or armament;
f. any offence relating to exchange control, corruption, extortion, fraud, forgery, uttering, theft or corruption involving amounts of ZAR 500,000 (at exchange rates applicable at time of writing: GBP 21,000/USD 27,500/EUR 25,000) or more, or involving amounts of more than ZAR 100,000 (at exchange rates applicable at time of writing: GBP 4,200/USD 5,500/EUR 5,000) if it is proved that the offence was committed by a person, group of persons, syndicate or any enterprise acting in the execution or furtherance of a common purpose or conspiracy or if it is proved that the offence was committed by any law enforcement officer, where it involves amounts of more than ZAR 10,000 (for exchange rates *see* above) or where the officer was acting as a member of a group of persons, syndicate or any enterprise acting in the execution or furtherance of a common purpose or conspiracy;
g. any one of a range of offences, including terrorism, hijacking and hostage-taking, set out in the Protection of Constitutional Democracy against Terrorist and Related Activities Act in circumstances other than those mentioned above,[911] as well as contraventions of the sections in this Act prohibiting financing of specified offences and hoaxes;
h. any offence referred to in sections 2, 4, 5 or 6 of the Prevention of Organised Crime Act 121 of 1998, which relates to an offence involving ferrous or non-ferrous metal which formed part of the essential infrastructure, as defined in section 1 of the Criminal Matters Amendment Act 18 of 2015;
i. theft of ferrous or non-ferrous metal which formed part of essential infrastructure, as defined in section 1 of the Criminal Matters Amendment Act 18 of 2015: (*a*) if it caused: (i) interference with or disruption of any basic service, as defined in section 1 of the aforementioned Act, to the public; or (ii) damage to such essential infrastructure; or (*b*) if the offence was committed by or with the collusion or assistance of: (i) a law enforcement officer as defined in section 51(8) of the Act; (ii) a security officer, as defined in section 1 of the Private

909. *See, supra,* para. 393.
910. Drugs and Drug Trafficking Act 140 of 1992.
911. *See supra*, para. 393.

Security Industry Regulation Act 56 of 2001, who was required to protect or safeguard such essential infrastructure; (iii) an employee of, or contractor appointed by, the owner or the person in charge of such essential infrastructure; or (iv) a group of persons, syndicate or any enterprise acting in the execution or furtherance of a common purpose or conspiracy;

j. an offence referred to in section 3 of the Criminal Matters Amendment Act 18 of 2015;
k. any offence referred to in sections 8, 9 or 10 of the Cybercrimes Act 19 of 2020, committed in the following circumstances (for exchange rates *see supra*): (i) where the amount involved exceeded ZAR 500,000; or (ii) where the amount involved exceeded R10,000,000, if it is proven that the offence was committed by a person, group of persons, syndicate or any enterprise acting in the execution or furtherance of a common purpose or conspiracy or by a person or with the collusion or assistance of another person, who as part of his or her duties, functions or lawful authority was in charge of, in control of, or had access to data, a computer program, a computer data storage medium or a computer system of another person in respect of which the offence in question was committed; or (iii) if it is proven that the offence was committed by any law enforcement officer involving amounts of more than ZAR 10,000, or as a member of a group of persons, syndicate or any enterprise acting in the execution or furtherance of a common purpose or conspiracy; or with the collusion or assistance of another person, who as part of his or her duties, functions or lawful authority was in charge of, in control of, or had access to data, a computer program, a computer data storage medium or a computer system of another person in respect of which the offence in question was committed;
l. sexual exploitation of a child or sexual exploitation of a person who is mentally disabled as contemplated in section 17 or 23 or using a child for child pornography or using a person who is mentally disabled for pornographic purposes, as contemplated in section 20 (1) or 26 (1) of the Criminal Law (Sexual Offences and Related Matters) Amendment Act, 2007, respectively;

then such person must be sentenced:

1. in the case of a first offender to imprisonment for a period of not less than fifteen years;
2. in the case of a second offender of any such offence to imprisonment for a period not less than twenty years; and
3. in the case of a third or subsequent offender for any such offence to imprisonment for a period of not less than twenty-five years.

In the case of assault with intent to do grievous bodily harm on a child under the age of 16, or on a child of 16 or 17 years of age and the age difference between the child and the person who has been convicted of the offence is more than four years; or where the victim is or was in a domestic relationship, as defined in section 1 of the Domestic Violence Act, 1998, with the accused, and in respect of any offence in contravention of section 36 of the Arms and Ammunition Act,[912] on account of having in possession more than 1,000 rounds of ammunition intended for firing in an arm, a regional court or a high court must sentence:

a. a first offender to a period of imprisonment of not less than ten years;
b. a second offender of any such offence to imprisonment for a period of not less than fifteen years; and
c. a third or subsequent offender to imprisonment for a period of not less than twenty years.[913]

A regional court or a high court must sentence the person in the case of:

a. a first offender, to imprisonment of not less than five years;
b. a second offender of any such offence, to imprisonment for a period of not less than seven years; and
c. a third or subsequent offender of any such offence for a period of not less than ten years; in respect of the following crimes and offences: treason, sedition, public violence, robbery (other than a robbery mentioned above), kidnapping, an offence involving an assault where a dangerous wound is inflicted with a firearm (other than an offence mentioned above), breaking or entering any premises with intent to commit an offence, and escaping from lawful custody, if the accused has with him at the time a firearm which was intended for use as such in the commission of such offence. The same minima apply to any offence involving ferrous or non-ferrous metal which formed part of essential infrastructure, as defined in section 1 of the Criminal Matters Amendment Act 18 of 2015, referred to in (*a*) section 54(1) of the International Trade Administration Act 71 of 2002; or (*b*) section 32(1)(*a*), (*b*), (*c*), (*d*), (*k*) in so far as that paragraph relates to section 21(1), (*l*), (*m*) or (*o*) of the Second-Hand Goods Act 6 of 2009.[914]

In the case of any offence referred to in section 36 or 37 of the General Law Amendment Act 62 of 1955, involving ferrous or non-ferrous metal which formed part of essential infrastructure, as defined in section 1 of the Criminal Matters Amendment Act 18 of 2015; or theft, involving ferrous or non-ferrous metal which formed part of essential infrastructure, as defined in section 1 of the Criminal Matters Amendment Act 18 of 2015, which is not covered in Part II of Schedule 2 of the Act, a regional or a high court must sentence:[915]

a. a first offender, to imprisonment for a period not less than three years;
b. a second offender of any such offence, to imprisonment for a period not less than five years; and

912. Act 75 of 1969, repealed and replaced by the Firearms Control Act 60 of 2000.
913. Criminal Law Amendment Act 105 of 1997, Schedule 2, Part III; read with s. 51(2)(*b*).
914. Criminal Law Amendment Act 105 of 1997, Schedule 2, Part IV, read with s. 51(2)(*c*).
915. Criminal Law Amendment Act 105 of 1997, Schedule 2, Part V, read with s. 51(2)(*d*).

c. a third or subsequent offender of any such offence, to imprisonment for a period not less than seven years.

The maximum sentence that a regional court may impose may not be more than five years longer than the minimum sentence that it may impose.[916] The operation of a sentence imposed may not be suspended.[917] Where there is no reference to the minimum sentencing legislation in the charge sheet, then the facts of each case should be examined to determine whether the omission could be said to result in an unfair trial.[918]

If a court is satisfied that substantial and compelling circumstances exist which justify the imposition of a lesser sentence than the prescribed sentence, it must enter those circumstances on the record of the proceedings and must thereafter impose such lesser sentence.[919]

III. Substantial and Compelling Circumstances in Minimum Sentencing

396. As discussed in the previous section, the Criminal Law Amendment Act of 1997[920] provides for the minimum sentences for certain offences. However, the sentencing regime in the Act has been criticised for its disproportionality between the various offences and the prescribed sentences.[921] Concerns about the possible unconstitutionality of the Act, given these difficulties, have been allayed by the approach adopted by the SCA in *S v. Malgas*,[922] which was approved by the Constitutional Court in *S v. Dodo*,[923] in respect of the test for deciding whether a prescribed sentence may be departed from.

This approach links the process of ensuring proportionality to the provision of the Act, which states that if the court is satisfied that substantial and compelling circumstances exist which justify the imposition of a lesser sentence than the prescribed sentence, it must enter these circumstances on the record and then impose such lesser sentence.[924] It was held in *S v. Malgas*[925] that:

a. section 51 has limited but not eliminated the courts' discretion in imposing sentence in respect of offences referred to in part 1 of Schedule 2 (or imprisonment for other specified periods for offences listed in other parts of Schedule 2);

916. Criminal Law Amendment Act 105 of 1997, s. 51(2).
917. Criminal Law Amendment Act 105 of 1997, s. 51(5), as contemplated in the Criminal Procedure Act 51 of 1977, s. 297(4).
918. *S v. MT* 2018 (2) SACR 592 (CC).
919. Criminal Law Amendment Act 105 of 1997, s. 51(3)(*a*).
920. Criminal Law Amendment Act 105 of 1997, s. 51(1).
921. S.S. Terblanche, *Guide to Sentencing in South Africa* 3rd ed. (LexisNexis, Durban 2016) 90; *S v. Vilakazi* 2009 (1) SACR 552 (SCA) paras 11–13.
922. *S v. Malgas* 2001 (1) SACR 469 (SCA).
923. *S v. Dodo* 2001 (1) SACR 594 (CC) paras 11, 40.
924. Criminal Law Amendment Act 105 of 1997, s. 51(3)(*a*).
925. *S v. Malgas* 2001 (1) SACR 469 (SCA) para. 25.

b. courts are required to approach the imposition of sentence conscious that the Legislature has ordained life imprisonment (or the particular prescribed period of imprisonment) as the sentence that should *ordinarily* and in the absence of weighty justification be imposed for the listed crimes in the specified circumstances;
c. unless there are, and can be seen to be, truly convincing reasons for a different response, the crimes in question are therefore required to elicit a severe, standardised and consistent response from the courts;
d. the specified sentences are not to be departed from lightly and for flimsy reasons, and therefore, speculative hypotheses favourable to the offender, undue sympathy, aversion to imprisoning first offenders, personal doubts as to the efficacy of the policy underlying the legislation, and marginal differences in personal circumstances or degrees of participation between co-offenders are to be excluded;
e. the Legislature has deliberately left it to the courts to decide whether the circumstances of any particular case call for a departure from the prescribed sentence, and whilst the emphasis has shifted to the objective gravity of the type of crime and the need for effective sanctions against it, this does not mean that all other considerations are to be ignored;
f. all factors (other than those set out in (d)) traditionally taken into account in sentencing (whether or not they diminish moral guilt) thus continue to play a role, and none is excluded at the outset from consideration in the sentencing process;
g. the ultimate impact of all the circumstances relevant to sentencing must be measured against the composite yardstick ('substantial and compelling') and must be such as cumulatively justify a departure from the standardised response that the Legislature has ordained;
h. in applying the statutory provisions, it is inappropriately constricting to use the concepts developed in dealing with appeals against sentence as the sole criterion;
i. if the sentencing court on consideration of the circumstances of the particular case is satisfied that they render the prescribed sentence unjust in that it would be disproportionate to the crime, the criminal and the needs of society, so that an injustice would be done by imposing that sentence, it is entitled to impose a lesser sentence; and
j. in so doing, account must be taken of the fact that crime of that particular kind has been singled out for severe punishment and that the sentence to be imposed in lieu of the prescribed sentence should be assessed paying due regard to the benchmark which the Legislature has provided.

Paragraph (i) above, described by the Constitutional Court in *S v. Dodo* as the 'determinative test', was held to make it plain that the power of the court to impose a lesser sentence than the sentence prescribed can be exercised well before the disproportionality between the mandated sentence and the nature of the offence becomes so great that it can be typified as gross.[926] Thus the sentencing court is not

926. *S v. Dodo* 2001 (1) SACR 594 (CC) para. 40.

required to impose a sentence which would limit the offender's right not to be punished in a cruel, inhuman or degrading way as a result of its disproportionality.[927]

It is incumbent upon a court in every case, before it imposes a prescribed sentence, to assess, upon a consideration of all the circumstances of the particular case, whether the prescribed sentence is proportionate to the particular offence.[928] Should a court be satisfied that a lesser sentence is called for in a particular case, justifying a departure from the prescribed sentence, then the court is obliged to impose that lesser sentence.[929] To fail to do so would be unjust.

A prescribed sentence cannot be assumed *a priori* to be proportionate, or indeed constitutionally permissible, in a given case. Whether this is so falls to be determined upon a consideration of the circumstances of the particular case.[930] The statement in *S v. Malgas* that a court should be conscious that the legislatively determined prescribed sentence should 'ordinarily and in the absence of weighty justification' be imposed should be interpreted in the light of the judgment and the 'determinative test' such that any circumstances which would render that prescribed sentence disproportionate to the offence would constitute the requisite 'weighty justification' for the imposition of a lesser sentence.[931] Once the court has found substantial and compelling circumstances to be present, its discretion is unfettered by the provisions of section 51.

When imposing a sentence in respect of rape, the following shall not constitute substantial and compelling circumstances justifying the imposition of a lesser sentence: (i) the complainant's previous sexual history; (ii) an apparent lack of physical injury to the complainant; (iii) an accused person's cultural or religious beliefs about rape; or (iv) any relationship between the accused person and the complainant prior to the offence being committed.[932]

§4. Other Measures Related to Punishment

I. Measures Applicable to Children

397. Having convicted a child (any person under the age of 18), a child justice court must impose a sentence in accordance with the Child Justice Act.[933] This Act provides for the following sentencing options: a community-based sentence;[934] a

927. Constitution, 1996, s. 12(1)(*e*); *S v. Vilakazi* 2009 (1) SACR 552 (SCA) para. 14.
928. *S v. Vilakazi* 2009 (1) SACR 552 (SCA) para. 15.
929. *S v. Vilakazi* 2009 (1) SACR 552 (SCA) para. 15; *S v. Malgas* 2001 (1) SACR 469 (SCA) para. 14.
930. *S v. Vilakazi* 2009 (1) SACR 552 (SCA) para. 18.
931. *S v. Vilakazi* 2009 (1) SACR 552 (SCA) para. 16; *DPP, KwaZulu-Natal v. Ngcobo* 2009 (2) SACR 361 (SCA).
932. Criminal Law Amendment Act 105 of 1997, s. 51(3)(*a*A).
933. Child Justice Act 75 of 2008, s. 68. The prosecutor may make furnish the child justice court with a victim impact statement to adduce evidence of the impact of the crime (s. 70(2) of Act 75 of 2008). A child justice court imposing sentence must request a pre-sentence report prepared by a probation officer prior to doing so (s. 71(1)(*a*) of Act 75 of 2008). *See* generally S.V. Hoctor, 'Sentencing' in W.A. Joubert (ed.), *The Law of South Africa* Vol. 24 2nd ed. (LexisNexis, Durban 2010) paras 528–529.
934. Child Justice Act 75 of 2008, s. 72.

restorative justice sentence;[935] a fine or alternatives to a fine;[936] correctional supervision;[937] compulsory residence in a child and youth care centre;[938] and imprisonment.[939]

II. Compensation Order

398. The Criminal Procedure Act provides (independently of civil claims) for the making of compensation orders against offenders where the offence causes damage to or loss of property[940] and in order to recompense the innocent purchaser of property unlawfully obtained.[941] Strictly speaking, such orders are not punishments but are a cheap alternative means of compensating the party which suffered the loss rather than requiring him to bring an action at civil law. Compensation can also be effected by making its payment a condition of suspension of sentence.[942]

III. Forfeiture

399. Section 35 of the Criminal Procedure Act makes detailed provisions for the forfeiture of articles to the state after the conviction of the accused. It deals in particular with weapons with which an offence was committed and with vehicles which were used in the commission of an offence. Other more specialised legislation provides for the cancellation or suspension of driving licences[943] or firearm licences[944] after conviction of specific offences. A convicted person can also be declared unfit to hold such a licence in the future.

§5. Modes of Punishment

I. Introduction

400. In South African law, there is extensive provision for delaying the implementation of all or part of the punishment. Sentences can be postponed conditionally or unconditionally, or they can be imposed and their implementation

935. Child Justice Act 75 of 2008, s. 73.
936. Child Justice Act 75 of 2008, s. 74.
937. Child Justice Act 75 of 2008, s. 75.
938. Child Justice Act 75 of 2008, s. 76. Such centre must provide a programme referred to in s. 191(2)(*j*) of the Children's Act 38 of 2005.
939. Child Justice Act 75 of 2008, s. 77. This sentence may be imposed provided that the child must not be under the age of 14 years at the time of being sentenced for the offence, and that the court must impose this sentence as a measure of last resort and for the shortest appropriate period of time. Such a sentence may only be imposed in respect of the commission of certain offences, and on certain conditions.
940. Criminal Procedure Act 51 of 1977, s. 300.
941. Criminal Procedure Act 51 of 1977, s. 301.
942. Criminal Procedure Act 51 of 1977, s. 297(1)(*a*)(i)(*aa*).
943. National Road Traffic Act 93 of 1996, ss 34, 35, which provide for endorsement, suspension or cancellation of a licence or permit or disqualification from obtaining a licence or permit.
944. Firearms Control Act 60 of 2000, s. 103.

suspended conditionally.[945] The conditions provide a mechanism for the courts to extend their range of sentencing options by ordering the accused to do or refrain from doing certain things.

II. The Postponement of Sentence

401. A court may postpone the passing of sentence for any offence, except for an offence where the legislation stipulates a compulsory minimum for up to five years.[946] Such postponement may be conditional or unconditional. The conditions on which the passing of sentence may be postponed are the same as those on which a sentence may be suspended and are discussed below. Postponement of sentence is regarded as particularly appropriate in order to keep juveniles and first offenders out of prison.

III. The Suspension of Sentence

402. Sentences may be suspended in whole or in part for up to five years.[947] Compulsory minimum sentences may only be suspended in part,[948] but as the minimum period of suspension may be until the rising of the court, this is no effective bar on suspending a sentence. Suspension is always conditional and the Criminal Procedure Act specifies a number of such conditions, whilst at the same time leaving the court the scope to set conditions of its own. The specified conditions relate to compensation, rendering of a service to an aggrieved person *in lieu* of compensation, performance of community service, submission to correctional supervision, submission to instruction or treatment, compulsory attendance or residence at some specified centre for a specified purpose, and submission to the supervision and control of a probation officer.[949] Suspension of sentence can also be used as a mechanism to ensure that fines are paid by instalment.[950]

§6. Principles and Rules Concerning Sentencing

I. The General Principles

403. The common-law basis of South African criminal law is reflected also in sentencing law in the sense that there has been no legislative attempt to state the general principles applicable to sentencing.[951]

---

945. Criminal Procedure Act 51 of 1977, s. 297.
946. Criminal Procedure Act 51 of 1977, s. 297(1).
947. Criminal Procedure Act 51 of 1977, s. 297(1)(*b*).
948. Criminal Procedure Act 51 of 1977, s. 297(4).
949. Criminal Procedure Act 51 of 1977, s. 297(1)(*a*)(i).
950. Criminal Procedure Act 51 of 1977, s. 297(5).
951. J.R. Lund, 'Discretion, Principles and Precedent in Sentencing (Part One)' 1979 *SACC* 203; 'Discretion, Principles and Precedent in Sentencing (Part Two)' 1980 *SACC* 36; S.S. Terblanche, *Guide to Sentencing in South Africa* 3rd ed. (LexisNexis, Durban 2016) 151ff.

The leading South African writers on the subject discuss philosophical arguments on punishment as an introduction to the principles of sentencing.[952] The broad consensus is that a modified retributive theory of punishment underlies the approach to sentencing. The notion of just deserts, that punishment should fit the crime, is seen as a point of departure which cannot be rejected. This is the case not only because it reflects the views of society at large but because inherent in it is an element of the principle of legality. A system of sentencing which is based primarily on an evaluation of the seriousness of the offence protects the person being sentenced from being punished for something he did not do. It also ensures some proportionality between the crime and the sentence.

404. Utilitarian theories of punishment, such as theories of individual or general deterrence, or of rehabilitation of the offender are also considered, but only as modifying or ameliorating the primary retributive approach. They cannot be primary, as this could result in sentences which were significantly harsher than justified by the offence and would thus offend the principle of legality. However, in practice, the rehabilitative theory in particular can operate as a mitigating factor, for example, in the argument that younger offenders should not be given excessively harsh sentences as this would undermine the opportunity they might otherwise have to reform themselves.

405. Because of the wide scope which the courts are allowed in determining sentence, they are expected to give judgments in which they justify the sentences they impose. Sentences are open to appeal and also review by superior courts[953] and the reasons for their imposition are considered carefully, thus providing for the possibility of the development of a sentencing jurisprudence. Statements of sentencing principle are often cast in very general terms. Perhaps the most oft-quoted is an exhortation that the sentencing court should consider the triad of the crime, the criminal and the interests of society.[954] To this was added the further exhortation that sentencing should be blended with a measure of mercy.[955] In practice, specific factors have been recognised which are generally regarded as mitigating or aggravating and of which a sentencing court must take note in appropriate cases. These are often dealt with on an ad hoc basis, which cuts across principled arguments about the philosophy of punishment. In the section which follows the more important of these factors are outlined.

952. M.A. Rabie & S.A. Strauss, *Punishment: An Introduction to Principles* 4th ed. (Lex Patria, Cape Town 1985) 1–59; D.P. van der Merwe, *Sentencing* (Juta, Cape Town 1991) 3–1–29; S.S. Terblanche, *Guide to Sentencing in South Africa* 3rd ed. (LexisNexis, Durban 2016) 171–190; *see also*, J. Burchell, *Principles of Criminal Law* 3rd ed. (Juta, Cape Town 2005) 68–81. Only E. Du Toit, *Straf in Suid-Afrika* (Juta, Cape Town 1981) does not adopt this approach.
953. *See infra*, paras 664 et seq.
954. *S v. Zinn* 1969 (2) SA 537 (A). *See also*, V.G. Hiemstra, 'Die trits in *Zinn*' 1980 *SACC* 203.
955. *S v. Kumalo* 1973 (3) SA 697 (A).

II. Specific Factors

406. Section 78(7) of the Criminal Procedure Act of 1977 provides specifically that if someone is criminally liable for his conduct but if his criminal capacity is reduced as a result of mental illness or intellectual disability, that diminished responsibility may be taken into account in sentencing. It is clear that the courts are being invited to recognise diminished responsibility as a mitigating factor.

407. Not only are there specific punishments prescribed for juveniles but youth in general is regarded as a mitigating factor.[956] This factor is particularly significant where it can be shown that the youth of the accused was related to the lack of judgment which led to the commission of the offence. Old age too can be mitigating in appropriate circumstances.[957]

408. Other factors which are regarded as mitigating because they reduce the moral blameworthiness of the accused in relation to the offence with which they are charged include provocation[958] and entrapment,[959] intoxication as a result of the use of alcohol or drugs[960] and coercion or intimidation.[961] A genuine belief in witchcraft may also be a mitigating factor.[962]

409. Factors which increase the moral blameworthiness of the accused in relation to the offence can be regarded as aggravating. These include the calculated commission of the offence,[963] particular cruelty,[964] and abuse of trust.[965]

410. Factors which relate to the character of the accused are also of importance. Thus, good character in general may be considered in mitigation. This is linked to an absence of previous convictions and also to remorse for the commission of the offence.[966] The latter is often regarded as indicated by a willingness to make reparation[967] or even to assist the police.[968] Conversely, bad character, as reflected in a long list of previous convictions, a lack of remorse or a failure to cooperate may be an aggravating factor. A range of other personal factors, such as the poor health or difficult family circumstances of the accused, may be considered.

411. The interests of society as a sentencing factor are difficult to specify. Sometimes, it is expressed in mitigation, in the sense that society only requires a light

956. *S v. Lehnberg* 1975 (4) SA 553 (A).
957. *S v. Heller* 1971 (2) SA 29 (A).
958. *S v. Mokonto* 1971 (2) SA 319 (A).
959. *S v. Van Pittius* 1973 (3) SA 814 (C).
960. *S v. Cele* 1990 (1) SACR 251 (A).
961. *S v. De Boer* 1968 (4) SA 866 (A).
962. *S v. Nxele* 1973 (3) SA 753 (A); *S v. Latha* 2012 (2) SACR 30 (ECG).
963. *S v. Mafela* 1980 (3) SA 825 (A); *S v. Andhee* 1996 (1) SACR 419 (A).
964. *S v. Du Toit* 1979 (3) SA 846 (A). *S v. Mnguni* 1994 (1) SACR 579 (A).
965. *S v. Reddy* 1975 (3) SA 757 (A).
966. *S v. Seegers* 1970 (2) SA 506 (A).
967. *S v. Charlie* 1976 (2) SA 596 (A).
968. *S v. Deal Enterprises (Pty) Ltd* 1978 (3) SA 302 (W).

sentence in a particular case. Conversely, a long-term imprisonment might be regarded as necessary in order to protect society.[969] An exemplary heavy sentence may also be imposed because of the societal interest in combating a form of crime prevalent in a particular district. Although the courts have accepted this latter consideration, there is a danger that it might result in a heavier sentence than is justified by the offence,[970] thus threatening the protection which the modified retributive approach offers to the individual offender.

III. Cumulative and Concurrent Sentences

412. When a person is convicted of two or more offences or when a person who is under sentence is convicted of another offence, the court may sentence him or her to several punishments for the offences or to such punishment for the other offence as the court may competently impose.[971] If the punishments consist of imprisonment, the one sentence commences after the expiration, setting aside or remission of the other, in such order as the court may direct, unless the court directs that the punishments run concurrently.[972] Where such punishments consist of correctional supervision, they will commence the one after the expiration, setting aside or remission of the other, in such order as the court may direct, unless the court directs that such punishments of correctional supervision will run concurrently.[973] Concurrence does not apply to punishments of fines,[974] nor may a fine with an alternative period of imprisonment run concurrently with any other form of detention.[975] Where two offences are closely related in time and place and in reality form part of the same transaction, concurrent sentences should be passed.[976]

969. *S v. Mzwakala* 1957 (4) SA 273 (A).
970. *S v. September* 1969 (1) SA 148 (C).
971. Criminal Procedure Act 51 of 1977, s. 280(1). *See*, on the approach of an appeal court to the question whether the cumulative effect of sentences was excessive, *Johaar v. S* [2009] 3 All SA 520 (SCA).
972. Criminal Procedure Act 51 of 1977, s. 280(2). *See*, on imprisonment, *supra* paras 378 et seq.
973. Criminal Procedure Act 51 of 1977, s. 280(3). *See*, on correctional supervision, *supra* paras 390–394.
974. *R v. Makina* 1961 (3) SA 174 (SR); *S v. Khambule* 1968 (2) PH H336 (N); *S v. Lukhwarelu* 1978 (2) PH H164 (T).
975. *S v. Bouwer* 1977 (2) SA 444 (O).
976. *Mia v. S* [2009] 4 All SA 33 (SCA).

Part II. Criminal Procedure

Chapter 1. General Characteristics

§1. Organisation of Criminal Jurisdiction

I. Criminal Trial Courts

413. The following courts have jurisdiction to try criminal cases: the nine provincial and six local divisions of the High Court, as established in terms of the Superior Courts Act 10 of 2013; the lower courts comprising the magistrates' courts and regional courts created in terms of the Magistrates' Court Act 32 of 1944; and the traditional courts operating under section 20 of the Black Administration Act 38 of 1927.[977] It should be noted that the SCA of the High Court[978] – which has its seat in Bloemfontein – has appellate jurisdiction only. It is not a trial court (except in cases of contempt of court *in facie curiae*).[979]

The various divisions of the High Court and the magistrates' courts and regional courts (the latter two are known as 'lower courts') are the most important criminal trial courts. The rest of the discussion is confined to these courts.

414. The nine 'provincial' divisions of the High Court[980] and their respective seats are: Gauteng (Pretoria); KwaZulu-Natal (Pietermaritzburg); Free State (Bloemfontein); Western Cape (Cape Town); Northern Cape (Kimberley) Limpopo (Polokwane); Mpumalanga (Nelspruit); North West (Mahikeng); and Eastern Cape (Grahamstown). The provincial divisions have original jurisdiction in respect of all crimes committed within their area as demarcated by law, and each area comprises several magisterial districts.

415. The six local divisions of the High Court and their respective seats are: Gauteng, Johannesburg; KwaZulu-Natal, Durban; Limpopo, Thohoyandou; Eastern Cape, Bisho; Eastern Cape, Mthatha; and Eastern Cape, Port Elizabeth. The area of each local division also consists of a number of magisterial districts. A *provincial* division has concurrent jurisdiction in the area of its local division.

---

977. *See supra,* para. 24.
978. *See supra,* para. 26.
979. *See supra,* para. 360.
980. The High Court was previously known as the Supreme Court, but since the implementation of the 1996 Constitution, where this court is referred to as the High Court in s. 166, the nomenclature has changed. The Renaming of the High Courts Act 30 of 2008 changed the names of the high courts.

416. Both provincial and local divisions may sit as 'circuit courts', that is, at places within their area but not at their seat.

417. Section 90 of the Magistrates' Court Act 32 of 1944 determines that magistrates' courts and regional courts shall have jurisdiction to hear cases of persons who are charged with an offence committed within the magisterial districts or within the regional divisions, respectively. A regional division consists of a number of magisterial districts.

418. Criminal jurisdiction has three elements: substantive, territorial and punitive (penal).

II. Substantive Jurisdiction of Criminal Courts

419. There are no limits to the substantive jurisdiction of the High Court. It may try any kind of crime,[981] but does in practice only deal with the most serious offences. The regional court can try all cases except high treason,[982] and the magistrates' court may try all cases except murder, rape, compelled rape and high treason.[983]

III. Territorial Jurisdiction of Criminal Courts

420. Territorial jurisdiction applies to all criminal trial courts. This means that in principle the offence must have been committed at a place falling within the area demarcated by law as that over which the relevant court has jurisdiction.

421. But in South Africa, a rigid approach to territorial jurisdiction is not always followed. The High Court may, for example, try a person for a crime committed outside the international boundaries of South Africa.[984] Section 90(2) of the Magistrates' Courts Act 32 of 1944 provides that when any person is charged with any offence committed within a distance of 4 km beyond the boundary of the magisterial district or of the regional division, such person may be tried by the court of this district or of this regional division, as the case may be, as if he had been charged with an offence committed within the district or within the regional division respectively. Further, section 90(3) provides that where it is uncertain in which of several jurisdictions an offence has been committed, such offence may be tried in any of such jurisdictions. Special provisions also exist with regard to crimes committed on aircraft and on board any vessel on a voyage within or beyond the territorial waters of South Africa.[985]

981. *See supra,* para. 21.
982. Magistrates' Court Act 32 of 1944, s. 89(2).
983. Magistrates' Court Act 32 of 1944, s. 89(1).
984. *See supra,* para. 112.
985. *See supra,* para. 112.

422. Section 90(8) of the Magistrates' Court Act 32 of 1944 also makes it possible to consolidate crimes committed in various jurisdictions to be tried in a single jurisdiction.

423. A Court does not have territorial jurisdiction in respect of an accused who is illegally removed from a foreign state and then brought into South Africa to stand trial in respect of a crime committed in South Africa. This rule, it would seem, applies only to the situation where the South African state itself is directly or through its agents involved in the abduction.[986] The state cannot secure territorial jurisdiction through its own illegal activities. It must come to court with clean hands. This rule, which excludes territorial jurisdiction, should be understood in light of the doctrine of procedural legality[987] and the State's obligation to respect international sovereignty and promote international relations and the maintenance of human rights.

The prosecuting state should obtain jurisdiction by making use of extradition, as governed by the Extradition Act 67 of 1962.

Extra-territorial jurisdiction for South African courts has been instituted in respect of a number of types of offences, including cybercrimes,[988] sexual offences,[989] and offences relating to terrorism.[990]

IV. Procedural Matters Governing Territorial Jurisdiction

424. Procedural matters pertaining to territorial jurisdiction are also governed by the Criminal Procedure Act 1977. Where an accused pleads that the court has no territorial jurisdiction[991] and the plea is upheld, the court must adjourn the case to the court which has jurisdiction. Where an accused has pleaded and his plea does not involve the absence of territorial jurisdiction, the court is deemed to have territorial jurisdiction.[992]

425. Section 111 of the Criminal Procedure Act 1977, read with section 22(3) of the National Prosecuting Authority Act 32 of 1998, provides that if it is deemed in the interests of the administration of justice that an offence committed within the area of jurisdiction of one Director of Public Prosecutions (DPP) be tried within the area of jurisdiction of another DPP, the NDPP may in writing direct that criminal

986. *S v. Ebrahim* 1991 (2) SA 553 (A). Cf. M.G. Cowling, 'Recent Cases – Criminal Procedure' 1991 *SACJ* 384.
987. *See infra*, para. 444.
988. Cybercrimes Act 19 of 2020, s. 24.
989. Criminal Law (Sexual Offences and Related Offences) Amendment Act 32 of 2007, s. 61.
990. Protection of Constitutional Democracy against Terrorist and Related Activities Act 33 of 2004, s. 15.
991. Criminal Procedure Act 51 of 1977, s. 110(2).
992. Criminal Procedure Act 51 of 1977, s. 110(1).

proceedings in respect of such offence be commenced within the area of jurisdiction of such other DPP.[993] This peculiar provision has been invoked in matters allegedly affecting the security of the state and in an attempt to avoid possible riots or disturbances at the ordinary trial venue. The direction of the NDPP is final and not subject to appeal to any court, although it may as an administrative decision be reviewed by the Supreme Court.

V. Punitive Jurisdiction of Criminal Courts

426. The punitive (or penal) jurisdiction of the High Court is extensive in the sense that it may impose all legally possible sentences as specified in section 276(1) of the Criminal Procedure Act 1977. These sentences are enumerated in paragraph 374 *supra*. Imprisonment and fines imposed by the High Court have no limits, subject to maxima that may be specified by statute in respect of certain offences.

427. The regional court may impose all sentences specified in section 276 of the Criminal Procedure Act. However, imprisonment is limited to fifteen years and fines of ZAR 600,000 (at exchange rates applicable at the time of writing: GBP 25,200/ USD 33,000/EUR 30,000) except in so far as other statutory provisions may specifically grant a higher penal jurisdiction.

428. The magistrates' court may impose all sentences stated in section 276(1) of the Criminal Procedure Act 1977, except declaration as a habitual or dangerous criminal. However, imprisonment is limited to three years and fines of ZAR 120,000.00 (at exchange rates applicable at the time of writing: GBP 5,040/USD 6,600/ EUR 6,000). These maxima may be exceeded where a higher penal jurisdiction is specifically authorised by a statute dealing with statutory offences.

VI. Compensatory Orders

429. Criminal courts may in certain circumstances make compensatory orders.[994] Where a person is convicted by a High Court, regional court or magistrates' court of an offence which has caused damage to or loss of property – including money – belonging to some other person, the court in question may, upon the application of the injured person or of the prosecutor acting on the instructions of the injured person, forthwith award the injured person compensation for such damage or loss. However, the proviso is that a regional court or a magistrates' court shall not make any such award if the compensation applied for exceeds ZAR 1,000,000.00 or ZAR 300,000.00, respectively.

In the case of the High Court, the compensation order can extend to the actual damage suffered and sought to be recovered. A compensatory order made in a criminal matter has the effect of a civil judgment. Obviously, a compensatory order can

993. *S v. De Vries and others* 2008 (4) SA 441 (C).
994. Criminal Procedure Act 51 of 1977, s. 300.

only be made in the event of a conviction and if the accused was afforded an adequate opportunity to address the court on the matter and to lead evidence.[995]

§2. Stages of the Penal Process

430. The three basic stages are the pre-trial, trial and post-trial stages.

431. The *pre-trial stage* includes the police investigation of the alleged crime and such matters as search and seizure – as well as the ascertainment of the bodily conditions or physical features of a suspect. These matters are dealt with *infra* in Chapter 2 which focuses on the powers and methods concerning the investigation of crime.

432. South African criminal procedure does not make use of investigating judges or magistrates. The police force is in principle responsible for the investigation of crime. They submit the docket (dossier, file) containing the result of their investigations, as well as statements obtained from available witnesses, to the public prosecutor. The latter can then direct further investigations or decide to prosecute if satisfied that the investigation is complete and that there are reasonable prospects of a conviction should the matter go to trial.

433. The methods of securing the attendance of an accused in court are arrest, summons, written notice and indictment in accordance with the relevant provisions of the Criminal Procedure Act 1977.

434. The extensive preparatory examination provided for in terms of sections 123–143 of the Act is hardly ever used. Summary trials are the norm. These trials, however, are often preceded by various committal proceedings during which the accused may be asked to plead and during which the presiding judicial officer has the power to question the accused. An accused may, for example, be asked to plead in a magistrates' court and may then be questioned by a magistrate even though the matter would ultimately be tried by the regional court or High Court. The magistrate does not have access to the prosecution's file. The prosecution also does not adduce any evidence during these committal proceedings and may also not question the accused. The record of committal proceedings may be proved during the trial stage. Further aspects concerning pre-trial judicial examination during committal proceedings are discussed in paragraph 551 *infra.*

435. The *trial stage* commences as soon as the accused has pleaded to the charge(s) in the court which has jurisdiction and which will finally dispose of the matter. The accused pleads afresh in the trial court and is questioned by the trial court even if the accused has also been questioned during earlier pre-trial committal proceedings. Upon completion of the judicial questioning of the accused, the trial

995. E. du Toit, *Straf in Suid-Afrika* (Juta, Cape Town 1981) 350; S.S. Terblanche, *Guide to Sentencing in South* Africa 3rd ed. (LexisNexis, Durban 2016) 462.

takes its course as set out in Chapter 4 *infra.* Once the accused has reached the trial court and has pleaded in this court, he is entitled to demand finality, namely, that he be acquitted or convicted[996] – a right which does not exist in respect of committal proceedings.[997]

436. The *post-trial stage* is reached after conviction and sentence and is dealt with in Chapter 5 *infra.* Appeal and review are the most important post-trial remedies.

437. In certain circumstances, the penal process may be deviated from, for example, where the court refers an accused who is under 18 years old to the so-called children's court[998] and where the trial of a drug addict is converted into an enquiry.[999] These deviations are only permitted in limited circumstances.

§3. Different Forms of Trial

I. A Single Form of Trial

438. South African criminal procedure does not as a rule distinguish between different forms of trial. And committal procedures are not a form of trial. Such differences as do exist between the High Court, regional court and magistrates' court trials relate to technical matters which do not alter the basic common form of trial as described in Chapter 4 *infra.*

There are, however, substantial differences between the procedure to be followed upon a plea of guilty and the procedure to be followed upon a plea of not guilty. These are discussed in paragraphs 604 et seq. in Chapter 4, which deals with arraignment and plea.

II. Trial by Judge and Assessors

439. In a High Court criminal trial, the judge may sit alone or with one or two assessors.[1000] The assessors must be a person or persons experienced in the administration of justice (such as advocates, attorneys, and law lecturers) or who have skill in any matter which may be considered at the trial (such as accountants or pathologists, as the case may be).[1001] Assessors are members of the court and the finding of the majority on questions of *fact* (as opposed to questions of law) shall be the decision of the court.[1002] The finding of the judge takes preference if there is

996. Criminal Procedure Act 51 of 1977, s. 108 as read with s. 106(4).
997. *S v. Hendrix* 1979 (3) SA 816 (D); *S v. Singh* 1990 (1) SA 123 (A).
998. Child Justice Act 75 of 2008, ss 50 and 64.
999. Criminal Procedure Act 51 of 1977, s. 255.
1000. *See generally*, D. van Zyl Smit & N.M. Isakow, 'Assessors and Criminal Justice' 1985 *SAJHR* 218.
1001. Criminal Procedure Act 51 of 1977, s. 145.
1002. Criminal Procedure Act 51 of 1977, s. 145(4)(*a*).

only one assessor. Any decision concerning questions of law and the appropriate sentence is the sole duty or province of the judge, even though the judge may ask the assessors for their opinion regarding sentence. Trial by judge and assessors does not affect the normal trial procedure, except that the judge has a discretion to decide certain evidential matters (such as the admissibility of confessions) in the absence of the assessors, who are then temporarily excused.[1003]

III. Trial by Magistrate (or Regional Magistrate) and Assessors

440. A magistrate or regional magistrate – that is, those judicial officers who preside in the lower courts – may also call upon the assistance of one or two assessors. But these assessors need not necessarily be lawyers, nor is it required that they should necessarily have special skills relevant to the possible issues which might arise during the course of the trial. Section 93*ter*(2)(*a*) of the Magistrates' Court Act 32 of 1944 provides that a magistrate or regional magistrate shall take the following factors into account in determining whether the summoning of assessors would be expedient for the administration of justice:

1. the cultural and social environment from which the accused originates;
2. the educational background of the accused;
3. the nature and seriousness of the offence;
4. the extent or probable extent of the punishment to which the accused will be exposed upon conviction; and
5. any other matter or circumstance which the magistrate or regional magistrate may deem indicative of the desirability of summoning an assessor or assessors.

441. The appointment of assessors in the lower courts is therefore – unlike the appointment of assessors in the Supreme Court – to a large extent aimed at promoting the idea of lay participation in the adjudication of facts in criminal cases.

A magistrate or regional magistrate who has sat alone and who has convicted an accused may also summon one or two assessors to assist in considering a community-based punishment (e.g., a community service order).[1004]

§4. Principles Concerning Procedures

I. A Crime Control Versus Due Process Perspective

442. South African criminal procedure can be described as a system which contains crime control as well as due process elements. However, in respect of certain alleged criminal activity, there is a marked tendency to legislate along lines which give obvious preference to crime control values – most notably in regard to pre-trial

1003. Criminal Procedure Act 51 of 1977, s. 145(4)(*b*).
1004. Magistrates' Court Act 32 of 1944, s. 93*ter*(1)(*b*).

police and prosecutorial powers concerning crimes against the security of the state[1005] and drug trafficking.[1006] These aspects are dealt with more fully in Chapter 2 *infra,* which deals with the investigation of crime. In other respects, however, police and prosecutorial activities are governed by legislation which seeks to uphold principles of restraint, proportionality and accountability, in the light of the values of the Constitution.

443. The general due process character of ordinary proceedings in the South African criminal justice system is reflected in:

- the right to legal representation[1007] and the right to be given a reasonable opportunity to obtain legal representation;[1008]
- the passive defence right, that is, the right to silence during the investigative,[1009] pleading[1010] and trial[1011] stages of the criminal process;
- the right to have an opportunity to apply for bail,[1012] underpinned by the Constitution;[1013]
- the right to have access to an independent court;[1014]
- the right to a fair and public[1015] trial by an impartial court;[1016]
- the right to be informed of the reason for an arrest;[1017]
- the right to invoke and rely upon the *interdictum de libero homine exhibendo* (writ of habeas corpus) against unlawful deprivation of liberty;[1018]

1005. *See* e.g., Protection of Constitutional Democracy Against Terrorist and Related Activities Act 33 of 2004, Ch. 4.

1006. *See* e.g., Drugs and Drug Trafficking Act 140 of 1992, ss 11 and 12.

1007. Criminal Procedure Act 51 of 1977, s. 73. Detainees and accused (and inevitably arrested persons, who are detained at the moment of arrest) have the right to choose and to consult with a legal practitioner, and to be informed of this right promptly (ss 35(2)(*b*) and 35(3)(*f*) of the Constitution), and must also be informed of the right to have a legal practitioner assigned to them by the state and at state expense, if substantial injustice would otherwise result (ss 35(2)(*c*) and 35(3)(*g*)).

1008. *R v. Zackey* 1945 AD 505 511; *S v. Yelani* 1986 (3) SA 802 (E); *S v. Yantolo* 1977 (2) SA 146 (E). *See* previous note.

1009. *S v. Maritz* 1974 (1) SA 266 (NC). The right to remain silent in relation to pre-trial procedures is set out in s. 35(1)(*a*) of the Constitution. An arrested person must be promptly informed of such right and of the consequences of not remaining silent (s. 35(1)(*b*) of the Constitution).

1010. *S v. Daniëls* 1983 (3) SA 275 (A).

1011. Criminal Procedure Act 51 of 1977, s. 196(1)(*a*). The right to remain silent in relation to trial procedures is set out in s. 35(3)(h) of the Constitution.

1012. *See* Criminal Procedure Act 51 of 1977, ss 59 and 60.

1013. Section 35(1)(*f*) of the Constitution states the right of every arrested person to be released from detention if the interests of justice permit, subject to reasonable conditions.

1014. *S v. Ramgobin* 1985 (4) SA 130 (N).

1015. *See* Criminal Procedure Act 51 of 1977, s. 152 as qualified by s. 153. *See* further s. 35(3)(*c*) of the Constitution.

1016. A.V. Lansdown & J. Campbell, *South African Criminal Law and Procedure*, Vol. V *Criminal Procedure and Evidence* (Juta, Cape Town 1982) 482–489.

1017. Criminal Procedure Act 51 of 1977, s. 39(2). *See* further s. 35(1)(*e*) of the Constitution.

1018. *Ganyile v. Minister of Justice* 1962 (1) SA 647 (E); *Wood v. Ondangwa Tribal Authority* 1975 (2) 294 (A).

- the right to appear within (normally) forty-eight hours after having been arrested;[1019]
- the right to have pre-trial access to a copy of a statement made by the accused to the police;[1020]
- the right of the accused to be given a copy of the written statement of a prosecution witness in circumstances where there is a material discrepancy between such written statement and the oral testimony of such a witness;[1021]
- the right to be present at trial;[1022]
- the right to be informed by the court of procedural rights,[1023] especially the right to legal representation[1024] and the right to silence;[1025] the right to compulsory process to obtain witnesses for the defence[1026] and to call such witnesses;[1027]
- the right to have a trial within a reasonable period;[1028]
- the right to have a proper opportunity to prepare for trial;[1029]
- the right to cross-examine witnesses called by the prosecution[1030] or a co-accused;[1031]
- the right to testify[1032] and the right to refuse to testify;[1033]
- the right to have a trial based upon accusatorial principles;[1034]
- the right to object to a vague or incorrect or defective indictment;[1035]
- the right not to be convicted of any crime of which the accused himself has previously been convicted or acquitted,[1036] save in the course of appeal or review proceedings relating to that conviction or acquittal;
- the right not to be convicted of a crime in respect of any act or omission which, at the time of such act or omission, was not a crime;[1037]
- the right not to be given a sentence more severe than that which was by law applicable at the time when the crime was committed;[1038]
- the right to receive only such a sentence as is permitted by law;[1039]

1019. Criminal Procedure Act 51 of 1977, s. 50. *See* further s. 35(1)(*d*) of the Constitution.
1020. Criminal Procedure Act 51 of 1977, s. 335.
1021. *S v. Xaba* 1983 (3) SA 717 (A).
1022. Criminal Procedure Act 51 of 1977, s. 158. *See* further s. 35(3)(*e*) of the Constitution.
1023. *See generally*, S.E. van der Merwe, G.A. Barton & K.J. Kemp, *Plea Procedures in Summary Criminal Trials* (Butterworths, Durban 1984) para. 6.6.4.
1024. *S v. Mabaso* 1990 (3) SA 185 (A).
1025. *S v. Lwane* 1966 (2) SA 433 (A).
1026. *S v. Hlongwane* 1982 (4) SA 321 (N).
1027. Criminal Procedure Act 51 of 1977, s. 151(2)(*a*).
1028. *S v. Magoda* 1984 (4) SA 462 (C). *See* s. 35(3)(*d*) of the Constitution.
1029. *S v. Yantolo* 1977 (2) SA 146 (E). *See* s. 35(3)(*b*) of the Constitution.
1030. Criminal Procedure Act 51 of 1977, s. 166(1).
1031. Criminal Procedure Act 51 of 1977, s. 166(1).
1032. Constitution, 1996, s. 35(3)(*i*).
1033. Criminal Procedure Act 51 of 1977, s. 196(1).
1034. *S v. Mpetha* (1) 1983 1 SA 493 (C) 494A.
1035. Criminal Procedure Act 51 of 1977, s. 85. *See* s. 35(3)(*a*) of the Constitution.
1036. *S v. Ndou* 1971 (1) SA 668 (A); *see* further Constitution, 1996, s. 35(3)(*m*).
1037. Constitution, 1996, s. 35(3)(*l*). *See* further J. Burchell, *Principles of Criminal Law* 5th ed. (Juta, Cape Town, 2016) 35.
1038. Constitution, 1996, s. 35(3)(*n*). *See* further J. Burchell, *Principles of Criminal Law* 5th ed. (Juta, Cape Town, 2016) 41.
1039. J. Burchell, *Principles of Criminal Law* 5th ed. (Juta, Cape Town, 2016) 40.

- the right to demand finality, that is, the right to demand a verdict;[1040]
- the right to address the court on the merits[1041] and on sentencing;[1042]
- the right not to be convicted unless guilt has been proved by the prosecution beyond a reasonable doubt[1043] on the basis of admissible evidence[1044] and in terms of a regular procedure;[1045]
- the *right* of appeal against any conviction or sentence of any lower court;[1046]
- the right to apply to the High Court for leave to appeal against a conviction and/or sentence of this court;[1047]
- the right to petition the President of the SCA for leave to appeal to the SCA.[1048]

II. The Doctrine of Procedural Legality

444. South African criminal procedure is largely based upon the doctrine or principle of procedural legality. An appeal or review court must set aside a conviction or sentence if it finds that a *failure of justice* has resulted from a procedural irregularity committed in relation to the trial.[1049] This aspect is dealt with more fully in Chapter 5 *infra,* which deals with review and appeal. The important point to note at this stage is that the appeal or review court must on the basis of an irregularity which has resulted in a failure of justice set aside the conviction *even if otherwise convinced of the factual guilt of the accused.* This principle is well illustrated in *S v. Mushimba,*[1050] *S v. Zulu,*[1051] *S v. Ebrahim*[1052] and *S v. Lwane.*[1053]

445. The doctrine of procedural legality may however be undermined where there is a less-than-vigorous evidential rule of exclusion in respect of evidence illegally obtained by the police in the course of their investigation. The inclusionary approach as followed in the Anglo-South African law of evidence, in the light of the Constitutional precepts, is discussed in paragraph 469 *infra.*

1040. Criminal Procedure Act 51 of 1977, s. 108 as read with s. 106(4).
1041. Criminal Procedure Act 51 of 1977, s. 175(1); *S v. Mabote* 1983(1) SA 745 (O).
1042. Criminal Procedure Act 51 of 1977, s. 274(2); *S v. Leso* 1975 (3) SA 694 (A).
1043. *S v. Glegg* 1973 (1) SA 34 (A).
1044. *R v. Kirsten* 1950 (3) SA 659 (C).
1045. P.J. Schwikkard & T.B. Mosaka, *Principles of Evidence* 5th ed. (Juta, Cape Town 2023) 11ff.
1046. Criminal Procedure Act 51 of 1977, s. 309, subject to s. 309B, which sets out the requirements for application of leave to appeal.
1047. Criminal Procedure Act 51 of 1977, s. 316.
1048. Criminal Procedure Act 51 of 1977, s. 316(8).
1049. Criminal Procedure Act 51 of 1977, s. 322; *see S v. Carter* 2007 (2) SACR 415 (SCA).
1050. 1977 (2) SA 829 (A).
1051. 1990 (1) SA 655 (A).
1052. 1991 (2) SA 553 (A).
1053. 1966 (2) SA 433 (A).

III. Principles Concerning Trial Procedures

446. Criminal trial procedure in South Africa can be described as a sui generis procedure. Judicial examination (an inquisitorial feature) is employed to determine the issues between the accused and the prosecution. Once the issues have been determined, it is left to the opposing parties to adduce evidence in support of their respective cases (an accusatorial feature). Oral evidence is normally required. At this stage, the presiding judicial officer plays a passive role, except in so far as he should ask questions to clarify matters and except in so far as he is in terms of case-law required to assist an undefended accused.[1054] The court may not descend into the arena.[1055]

447. In terms of section 186 of the Criminal Procedure Act 1977, the court may, however, at any stage of criminal proceedings subpoena any person as a witness at such proceedings, and the court shall so subpoena a witness if the evidence of such witness appears to the court essential to the just decision of the case. This introduces an inquisitorial feature into the adversarial process but is considered necessary in order to promote an accurate fact-finding process.

§5. Rights of the Suspect and His or Her Lawyer

I. The Right to a Lawyer

448. Detainees and accused (and inevitably arrested persons who are detained at the moment of arrest) have the right to choose and to consult with a legal practitioner, and to be informed of this right promptly,[1056,1057] and must also be informed of the right to have a legal practitioner assigned to them by the state and at state expense, if substantial injustice would otherwise result.[1058]

In terms of section 73(2A) of the Criminal Procedure Act, every accused must be informed of his or her right to be represented at his or her own expense by a legal adviser of his or her own choice, or if he or she cannot afford legal representation, that he or she can apply for legal aid from the state, and further how this may be done. The arrested person should be informed of this right not only at the time of the arrest but also at every other stage of the investigation where his or her cooperation is sought.[1059]

1054. *S v. Rudman*; *S v. Johnson*; *S v. Xaso*; *Xaso v. Van Wyk* 1989 (3) SA 368 (E); N.C. Steytler, *The Undefended Accused on Trial* (Juta, Cape Town 1988) 146–147.
1055. *S v. Rall* 1982 (1) SA 828 (A).
1056. *See* P.J. Schwikkard, 'Arrested, Detained and Accused Persons' in I. Currie & J. de Waal, *Bill of Rights Handbook* 6th ed. (Juta, Cape Town 2013) 744 769; J.J. Joubert et al., *Criminal Procedure Handbook* 13th ed. (Juta, Cape Town 2020) 104.
1057. Constitution, 1996, ss 35(2)(*b*) and 35(3)(*f*); Criminal Procedure Act 51 of 1977, s. 73(1).
1058. Constitution, 1996, ss 35(2)(*c*) and 35(3)(*g*).
1059. Section 73(2A) provides that this duty to inform arises at the time of arrest of the accused, when he or she is served with a summons, when a written notice is handed to him or her, when an indictment is served on him or her, and at the time of the first appearance in court.

II. Prison Service Regulations Governing a Lawyer's Access to an Inmate

449. A lawyer's access to an inmate is regulated by the correctional service regulations,[1060] which provide, *inter alia*, that an inmate may consult with his or her legal practitioner in connection with legal matters subject to the conditions determined by the Commissioner of Correctional Services. Such a consultation is subject to the following:

a. A legal practitioner must lodge proof of his or her identity and status as legal practitioner at the request of the Head of Correctional Centre.
b. Such a consultation must take place only between 8 AM and 3:30 PM unless the Head of Correctional Centre, due to the existence of urgent or exceptional circumstances, has given his or her prior permission.
c. The consultation must take place in sight but out of earshot of a correctional official.
d. The legal practitioner may be allowed to utilise his or her own interpreter, secretary or typist.
e. If a particular legal practitioner is refused access to the inmate, the inmate may request to consult with another legal practitioner.

III. Legal Professional Privilege

450. All confidential oral or written communications made between the suspect (accused) and his legal representative in the latter's professional capacity and which are made for the purpose of obtaining or giving legal advice are privileged and may not be disclosed in a court of law unless the client (as the holder of the privilege) has expressly or impliedly waived such privilege.[1061] Protection of this legal professional privilege is an important component of the right to a fair trial, and the breach thereof may constitute a grave irregularity vitiating the proceedings.[1062] It has been held that any claim to the relaxation of legal professional privilege must be approached with the greatest circumspection.[1063] Legal representation is extremely desirable in view of the adversarial trial system in South Africa. Such representation has, furthermore, been described as a corollary of the right of access to the courts.[1064] Legal representation as a trial right is further discussed in paragraph 595 *infra*.

1060. Correctional Services Regulations (as amended): Government Notice R323 of 25 Apr. 2012, reg. 12.
1061. P.J. Schwikkard & T.B. Mosaka, *Principles of Evidence* 5th ed. (Juta, Cape Town 2023) 160ff.
1062. *S v. Mushimba* 1977 (2) SA 829 (A). It should be noted however that a breach of the privilege will not automatically render a trial unfair – *see Bennett v. Minister of Safety and Security* 2006 (1) SACR 523 (T).
1063. *S v. Safatsa* 1988 (1) SA 868 (A).
1064. *Mandela v. Minister of Prisons* 1983 (1) SA 938 (A) 957D.

§6. SYSTEM AND FORMS OF EVIDENCE

I. The System of Evidence

451. The English law of evidence serves as the common law of the South African law of evidence in respect of all evidentiary matters for which no specific statutory provision exists locally.[1065] Section 252 of the Criminal Procedure Act 1977 provides, for example, that the law as to the admissibility of evidence, which was in force on 30 May 1961, shall apply in any case not expressly provided for by the Criminal Procedure Act or any other law. The common law of evidence that was in force on 30 May 1961 was the English law of evidence. It is therefore appropriate to speak of the 'Anglo-South African law of evidence.' It is a system which also belongs to the broader category known as the Anglo-American system,[1066] that is, the system found in common law countries where much emphasis is put on the so-called concentrated trial during which witness is examined orally and evidence is received in terms of rules of exclusion originally designed to keep certain evidence away from lay finders of fact (the jury).

452. Rules of exclusion comprise the main part of the law of evidence. The system of evidence can therefore be described as a strict system, as opposed to the free system of evidence found in Continental countries.[1067]

453. The evidentiary system in criminal trials is also governed by adversarial principles: oral evidence is largely received (the principle of orality applies) and parties have the right to cross-examine witnesses called by their opponents.

454. The accused is presumed to be innocent. The prosecution must as a rule prove its case beyond reasonable doubt.

The accused has the fundamental right to refuse to testify. He cannot be compelled to cooperate. But his silence in court is a factor that may count against him once the prosecution has managed to establish a prima facie case against him.[1068]

455. There are some exceptions to the principle that the prosecution must prove its case beyond a reasonable doubt. At common law, an accused who raises a defence of criminal non-responsibility on the basis of his mental abnormality at the time of the commission of the crime has the duty to prove this defence on a balance of probability.[1069] Proof on a balance of probability is a lesser standard than proof beyond reasonable doubt.

1065. C.W.H. Schmidt, *Bewysreg* 3rd ed. (Butterworths, Durban 1989) 14ff.; P.J. Schwikkard & T.B Mosaka, *Principles of Evidence* 5th ed. (Juta, Cape Town 2023) 6ff.
1066. S.E. van der Merwe, 'Die evolusie van die mondelinge karakter en uitsluitingsreëls van die Engelse gemene bewysreg' 1991 *Stell L.R.* 281.
1067. S.E. van der Merwe, 'Accusatorial and Inquisitorial Procedures and Restricted and Free Systems of Evidence', in A.J.G.M. Sanders (ed.), *Southern Africa in Need of Law Reform* (Butterworths, Durban 1981) 141 145–146.
1068. *S v. Khoza* 1982 (3) SA 1019 (A) 1043C–E.
1069. *S v. Mahlinza* 1967 (1) SA 408 (A) 419.

456. A distinction is drawn between the *admissibility* and the *weight* of the evidence. Evidence is admissible if the court may lawfully receive it in determining the issues. Once admissible, the question concerning weight arises. There are no degrees of admissibility and evidence cannot therefore be more or less admissible. Weight,however varies according to the circumstances of the case. Admissibility is largely a question of law, whereas weight is largely a question of fact.

II. Forms of Evidence

457. Evidence may take various forms, including oral, documentary, real or electronic evidence.

458. Oral (*viva voce*) evidence is evidence given in court by a witness who has taken the oath or who has affirmed that he would speak the truth or who has been warned to speak the truth.[1070] Affirmation *in lieu* of the oath may be permitted on one of several grounds, for example, where the witness objects to taking the oath at all or to taking the oath as required, in its prescribed form. A witness may also be warned to speak the truth if such witness is on the basis of ignorance arising from youth or defective education or any other cause, found not to understand the nature of the oath or the affirmation.

459. Documentary evidence may in exceptional circumstances also be received. A 'document' includes everything that contains the written or pictorial proof of something. Authenticity must be proved, and the contents of the document must be proved by production of the original. There are certain common-law and statutory exceptions to the rule requiring production of the original.

460. Real evidence consists of material objects such as clothing and weapons. Real evidence can also be furnished in terms of a procedure known as the inspection *in loco* which takes place when the court adjourns in order physically to inspect the actual scene of the crime in the presence of the parties.

461. Rapid developments in technology over the past few decades have posed challenges for evidence law, specifically in respect of the admissibility of electronic evidence and its evidential weight.[1071] While the term 'electronic evidence' is nowhere defined in any law relating to the admissibility of electronic evidence, regulation takes place by way of provisions in various legal sources, including the Electronic Communications and Transactions Act of 2002.[1072] This Act is based on the Model Law on Electronic Commerce, which flows from the resolution adopted by the General Assembly of the United Nations Commission on International Trade

---

1070. *See* Criminal Procedure Act 51 of 1977, ss 161–164.
1071. N. Singh, 'Electronic Evidence' in P.J. Schwikkard & T.B. Mosaka, *Principles of Evidence* 5th ed. (Juta, Cape Town 2023) 471ff.
1072. Electronic Communications and Transactions Act 25 of 2002.

Law (UNCITRAL).[1073] In terms of admissibility, it is provided that in any legal proceedings, the rules of evidence must not be applied so as to deny the admissibility of a data message, that is, the output of information by/in an electronic medium, in evidence on the mere grounds that it is constituted by a data message, or if it is the best evidence that the person adducing it could reasonably be expected to obtain, on the grounds that it is not in its original form.[1074] Whether the rules exclude hearsay evidence, which is evidence, the probative value of which is dependent upon the credibility of any other person than the person giving evidence, has been a matter of debate in South African law.[1075] The courts have favoured an approach which subjects the inclusive approach to electronic evidence in the Act, to the ordinary rules of evidence, including hearsay, as regards admissibility.[1076] Whether electronic evidence should be regarded as real evidence and thus be admissible on the grounds of relevance or as documentary evidence, which would make all the rules for admissibility of documents (including hearsay) applicable to the evidence, has been debated in the courts.[1077]

Due evidential weight must be afforded a data message,[1078] and the Act further provides that in assessing evidential weight, a court must take account of the following factors: the reliability of the manner in which the data message was generated, stored or communicated; the reliability of the manner in which the integrity of the data message was maintained; the manner in which its originator was identified; and any other relevant factor.[1079] Expert evidence may be employed to assess evidential weight, which may be challenged on the grounds of reliability or authenticity.[1080]

462. The term 'probative material' includes oral, documentary and real evidence. But it also covers other means of furnishing proof, such as formal admissions, judicial notice and presumptions.

Oral argument by the parties or their legal representatives is also received. However, oral argument is not evidence. It is a persuasive comment in respect of the weight that the court should attach to the probative material in deciding the ultimate question concerning guilt or innocence.

1073. *See* GA Resolution 2205 (XXI) of 17 Dec. 1966, referred to as the Model Law on Electronic Commerce; N. Singh, 'Electronic Evidence' in P.J. Schwikkard & T.B. Mosaka, *Principles of Evidence* 5th ed. (Juta, Cape Town 2023) 477.
1074. Electronic Communications and Transactions Act 25 of 2002, s. 15(1).
1075. N. Singh, 'Electronic Evidence' in P.J. Schwikkard & T.B. Mosaka, *Principles of Evidence* 5th ed. (Juta, Cape Town 2023) 479–481.
1076. N. Singh, 'Electronic Evidence' in P.J. Schwikkard & T.B. Mosaka, *Principles of Evidence* 5th ed. (Juta, Cape Town 2023) 479–481.
1077. N. Singh, 'Electronic Evidence' in P.J. Schwikkard & T.B. Mosaka, *Principles of Evidence* 5th ed. (Juta, Cape Town 2023) 485–487.
1078. Electronic Communications and Transactions Act 25 of 2002, s. 15(2).
1079. Electronic Communications and Transactions Act 25 of 2002, s. 15(3).
1080. N. Singh, 'Electronic Evidence' in P.J. Schwikkard & T.B. Mosaka, *Principles of Evidence* 5th ed. (Juta, Cape Town 2023) 482.

§7. Exclusion of Evidence

463. In terms of section 210 of the Criminal Procedure Act 1977, no evidence as to any fact, matter or thing shall be admissible if it is irrelevant or immaterial in the sense that it cannot conduce to prove or disprove any point or fact at issue in criminal proceedings.[1081] The basic evidential canon is therefore that all irrelevant evidence must be excluded.[1082] But this does not mean that all relevant evidence is admissible. There are also several other rules which govern the admissibility of *relevant* evidence, like rules pertaining to hearsay, privilege and confessions. What of 'expert evidence' coming from an artificial intelligence (AI) system: could the machine be seen as a true expert witness on the basis of its knowledge, or would such evidence not be accepted in court unless supported by an 'independent' human expert?[1083]

I. The Exclusion of Irrelevant Evidence: The Previous Convictions and Bad Character of an Accused

464. Proof of the previous convictions and bad character of an accused is permitted for purposes of determining an appropriate sentence but may as a rule not be furnished on the merits of the case, that is, on the question of whether there should be a conviction or an acquittal. Previous convictions and bad character are deemed irrelevant – and therefore inadmissible. This is a rule of the Anglo-South African common law and it has also been reinforced by statutory law. Section 211 of the Criminal Procedure Act 1977 provides that – except where otherwise expressly provided for by the Criminal Procedure Act or the Child Justice Act 2008, or except where the fact of a previous conviction is an element of any offence with which an accused is charged – no evidence shall be admissible to prove that an accused had previously in South Africa or elsewhere been convicted of any offence. Section 211 should be read with section 197, which provides that an accused who gives evidence at criminal proceedings shall neither be asked nor required to answer any question tending to show that he has committed or has been convicted of or has been charged with any offence other than the offence with which he is charged, or that he is of bad character. However, this protective shield is lifted where an accused (or his legal representative) asks any question of any witness with a view to establishing the good character of the accused, or where the accused gives evidence of his own good character, or where the nature or conduct of the defence is such as to involve an attack on the character of the complainant or any other witness for the prosecution.[1084] There are also three further situations where the protection against proof of previous convictions and bad character is destroyed:[1085] where the accused

1081. *S v. Shabalala* 1986 (4) SA 734 (A).
1082. P.J. Schwikkard & T.B. Mosaka, *Principles of Evidence* 5th ed. (Juta, Cape Town 2023) 45ff.
1083. This matter is unresolved in South African law. For a general discussion, *see* DP van der Merwe, 'Legal Aspects of the Fourth Industrial Revolution (4iR) – (With Specific Reference to ChatGPT and Other Software Purporting to Give Legal dvice)' 2024 *Obiter* 939 955.
1084. Criminal Procedure Act 51 of 1977, s. 197(*a*).
1085. Criminal Procedure Act 51 of 1977, s. 197(*b*)–(*d*).

gives evidence against a co-accused charged with the same offence or an offence in respect of the same facts; where the accused is charged with receiving stolen property and proper advance notice as required by sections 240(1) and 241 of the Criminal Procedure Act has been given to him by the prosecution; and, finally, where the proof that he has committed or has been convicted of such other offence is admissible to show that he is guilty of the offence with which he is charged. This latter situation deals with the vexed problem of so-called similar fact evidence, that is, evidence which refers to an accused's activities (including his illegal activities) on an occasion or occasions other than the one that is in dispute, but which is in time, place, method or circumstance so closely linked to the subject matter of the charge, that it is of sufficient relevance to be admissible. Similar facts can become admissible on account of their high probative value – and they will be admissible despite the fact that they might involve proof of previous convictions or bad character.[1086] This approach does not conflict with the fundamental rule that irrelevant evidence is inadmissible. It merely confirms the fundamental rule, namely that relevant evidence is admissible. It must be noted, however, that similar fact evidence admitted in criminal proceedings must have a strong degree of probative force.[1087]

465. Protection of the accused against unwarranted imputations on his character is also evident in the following rules: if an accused is brought into court in leg-irons, the presiding judicial officer should recuse himself, that is, withdraw from the case;[1088] the appearance in court of an accused dressed in prison garb is also improper unless the trial involves an offence committed in prison, or one related to his imprisonment, for example, escaping from custody;[1089] an alias may not be used in the indictment or charge;[1090] and, finally, it may not be alleged in any indictment or charge that an accused has previously been convicted in South Africa or elsewhere – except where the fact of a previous conviction is an element of the offence charged.[1091]

II. The Exclusion of Hearsay Evidence

466. The common-law hearsay rule and its exceptions have been replaced by the Law of Evidence Amendment Act 45 of 1988. It is generally accepted that this Act is a vast improvement over the rigidity which prevailed at common law. The Act defines hearsay and confirms the inadmissibility thereof. However, it also creates certain exceptions and grants a discretion to the court to admit hearsay evidence if the court is satisfied – after having considered certain prescribed factors[1092] – that such admission would be in the interests of justice.

1086. *R v. Pharenque* 1927 AD 57.
1087. P.J. Schwikkard & T.B. Mosaka, *Principles of Evidence* 5th ed. (Juta, Cape Town 2023) 71–84.
1088. *S v. Pakkies* 1985 (4) SA 592 (Tk); *S v. Stevens* 1961 (3) SA 518 (C).
1089. *S v. Mthembu* 1988 (1) SA 145 (A).
1090. *S v. Langa* 1972 (4) SA 260 (T).
1091. Criminal Procedure Act 51 of 1977, s. 89.
1092. The following factors are identified in s. 3(1)(*c*)(i) to 3(1)(*c*)(vi) of the Law of Evidence Amendment Act 45 of 1988: the nature of the proceedings; the nature of the evidence; the purpose for

Hearsay is statutorily defined as written or oral evidence, which is of such a nature that its probative value depends upon the credibility of someone other than the person giving such evidence.[1093] This is a declarant-orientated definition: Does the court have to rely upon the credibility of a non-witness, that is, someone who has not taken the oath, is not available for cross-examination and whose demeanour cannot be observed by the trier of fact? The evidence is admissible if the person upon whose credibility the probative value of such evidence depends does indeed testify at the proceedings.[1094]

An accused may consent to the admission of hearsay.[1095] He may therefore waive his right to confront (cross-examine) the witnesses against him. However, in the absence of legal representation, the court must be satisfied that such a waiver is made voluntarily, knowingly and intelligently.[1096]

South African courts have shown a marked reluctance to exercise their discretion to admit hearsay against an accused.[1097]

III. Confessions

467. The term 'confession' has a technical meaning. It is a self-incriminatory extra-curial statement in which an accused admits all the elements of the crime and which – if proved in a court of law – would be tantamount to a plea of guilty. A confession has been described as 'an unequivocal acknowledgement of guilt, the equivalent of a plea of guilty before a court of law'.[1098] A confession made to a peace officer may never be received in a court of law unless such confession is confirmed and reduced to writing in the presence of a magistrate or justice of the peace.[1099]

A confession can also only be received if the prosecution can prove beyond reasonable doubt that the accused made his confession whilst in his sound and sober senses[1100] and that he did make the confession freely and voluntarily[1101] and without undue influence.[1102]

---

which the evidence is tendered; the probative value of the evidence; the reason why the evidence is not given by the person upon whose credibility the value of such evidence depends and, further, any prejudice to a party where hearsay is admitted. Section 3(1)(*c*)(vii) of the relevant Act also refers to 'any other factor which should in the opinion of the court be taken into account'.

1093. Law of Evidence Amendment Act 45 of 1988, s. 3(4).
1094. Law of Evidence Amendment Act 45 of 1988, s. 3(1)(*b*).
1095. Law of Evidence Amendment Act 45 of 1988, s. 3(1)(*a*).
1096. *S v. Ngwani* 1990 (1) SACR 449 (N).
1097. *Metedad v. National Employers' General Insurance Co* 1992 (1) SA 494 (C) 499H. For discussion of hearsay evidence, *see* P.J. Schwikkard & T.B. Mosaka, *Principles of Evidence* 5th ed. (Juta, Cape Town 2023) 285ff.
1098. *R v. Becker* 1929 AD 167, 171.
1099. Criminal Procedure Act 51 of 1977, s. 217(1)(*a*).
1100. *See generally*, *R v. Ramsamy* 1954 (2) SA 491 (A).
1101. *See generally*, *S v. Yolelo* 1981 (1) SA 1002 (A).
1102. *See generally*, *R v. Barlin* 1926 AD 459 462. Section 35(1)(*c*) of the Constitution provides that an arrested person shall have the right 'not to be compelled to make a confession or admission that could be used in evidence against' him.

Where a confession is made to a magistrate and reduced to writing by him or is confirmed and reduced to writing in the presence of a magistrate, the confession shall, upon the mere production thereof at criminal proceedings, be admissible in evidence against the accused if it appears from the document in which the confession is contained that the confession was made by a person whose name corresponds to that of the accused and, where an interpreter was used, if a certificate by the interpreter appears on such document to the effect that he interpreted truly and correctly and to the best of his ability when the confession was recorded.[1103] It has also been held that a magistrate who records the confession is under a duty to investigate the possibility that the police might have threatened or assaulted the accused in order to induce him to confess to the magistrate.[1104] But this is a notoriously difficult task as there is very often a 'veil between the previous interrogations by the police and the subsequent appearance of the interrogated persons before the magistrate'.[1105]

468. There are two further important rules governing confessions. First, a confession by an accused is inadmissible as evidence against his co-accused even if such co-accused are implicated in the confession.[1106] Second, a confession which is found admissible on its own is insufficient for purposes of a conviction. There must be *aliunde* evidence of the commission of the crime or evidence confirming the confession in a material respect.[1107]

IV. Unconstitutionally Obtained Evidence

469. Section 35(5) of the Constitution provides that evidence obtained in a manner that violates any right in the Bill of Rights must be excluded if the admission of that evidence would render the trial unfair or otherwise be detrimental to the administration of justice. This section operates as a qualified exclusionary rule in that evidence unconstitutionally obtained *must* be excluded (in this sense, it is peremptory), but this only operates where admission of such evidence *would* render the trial unfair or *would* otherwise be detrimental to the administration of justice.[1108] The court must exercise a value judgment in ascertaining whether either of these two conditions for exclusion exists, and in this sense, the rule is discretionary.[1109] The

1103. Criminal Procedure Act 51 of 1977, s. 217(1). In *S v. Zuma* 1995 (1) SACR 568 (CC), the Constitutional Court declared the presumption (contained in s. 217(1)(*b*)(ii)) that a confession made in terms of this section was presumed to be made freely and voluntarily by the accused in his sound and sober senses, without undue influence, to be an unconstitutional infringement of the right to a fair trial.
1104. *S v. Jakatyana* 1990 (1) SACR 420 (Ck).
1105. *R v. Gumede* 1942 AD 398, 433.
1106. Criminal Procedure Act 51 of 1977, s. 219; *R v. Baartman* 1960 (3) SA 535 (A).
1107. Criminal Procedure Act 51 of 1977, s. 209.
1108. P.J. Schwikkard & T.B. Mosaka, *Principles of Evidence* 5th ed. (Juta, Cape Town 2023) 228.
1109. P.J. Schwikkard, 'Arrested, Detained and Accused Persons' in I. Currie & J. de Waal, *The Bill of Rights Handbook* 6th ed. (Juta, Cape Town 2013) 806.

court must take into account competing factors in determining whether the admission of evidence will render a trial unfair.[1110] Such factors include competing societal interests of due process and crime control;[1111] the type and degree of breach;[1112] type and degree of prejudice to the accused – if any;[1113] and public policy.[1114] As regards when the admission of evidence will be otherwise detrimental to the administration of justice, the court would have to consider the need for a balance between respect for the Bill of Rights and respect for the judicial process.[1115] Important factors in this regard include the 'good faith' (or 'bad faith') conduct of the police;[1116] public safety and urgency;[1117] the nature and seriousness of the violation;[1118] the availability of lawful means or methods of securing the evidence;[1119] whether the evidence is real evidence or testimonial communications;[1120] and inevitable discovery or discovery on the basis of an independent source.[1121]

Where the conduct involved in the setting of a trap goes beyond providing an opportunity to commit an offence, the evidence thus obtained may be excluded.[1122]

V. Privilege as the Basis for Excluding Evidence

470. Relevant and otherwise admissible evidence can be excluded on the basis that it is privileged.[1123] The most important privileges are the privilege against self-incrimination, witness statement privilege, marital privilege, the police informer's privilege, the privilege governing the investigative methods of the police and, finally, legal professional privilege. The latter privilege was discussed in paragraph 450 *supra.*

1110. P.J. Schwikkard, 'Arrested, Detained and Accused Persons' in I. Currie & J. de Waal, *The Bill of Rights Handbook* 6th ed. (Juta, Cape Town 2013) 808.
1111. In *Lawrie v. Muir* 1950 SC (J) 16 26–27, the court identified 'the interest of the citizen to be protected from illegal or irregular invasions of his liberties by the authorities' as opposed to 'the interest of the State to secure that evidence bearing upon the commission of the crime and necessary to enable justice to be done shall not be withheld from Courts of law on merely formal or technical ground'.
1112. *S v. Seseane* 2000 (2) SACR 225 (O).
1113. *S v. Soci* 1998 (2) SACR 275 (E); *S v. Lottering* 1999 (12) BCLR 1478 (N).
1114. *S v. Soci supra; S v. Lottering supra.*
1115. *S v. Mphala* 1998 (1) SACR 654 (W) 657g-h, *see also* note 1111 *supra.*
1116. *S v. Naidoo* 1998 (1) SACR 479 (N); *S v. Mphala* 1998 (1) SACR 388 (W).
1117. *S v. Madiba* 1998 (1) BCLR 38 (D).
1118. *S v. Mark* 2001 (1) SACR 572 (C); *S v. Tandwa* 2008 (1) SACR 613 (SCA).
1119. *S v. Mkhize* 1999 (2) SACR 632 (W) 638e.
1120. *S v. Mkhize supra* 637g–h.
1121. For discussion of all these factors, *see* P.J. Schwikkard & T.B. Mosaka, *Principles of Evidence* 5th ed. (Juta, Cape Town 2023) 259ff.
1122. Criminal Procedure Act 51 of 1977, s. 252A(3).
1123. *See generally*, S.J. van Niekerk, S.E. van der Merwe & A.J. van Wyk, *Privilegies in die Bewysreg* (Butterworths, Durban 1984) 1ff.; P.J. Schwikkard & T.B. Mosaka, *Principles of Evidence* 5th ed. (Juta, Cape Town 2023) 133ff.

A. The Privilege Against Self-Incrimination: The Witness

471. A witness may refuse to answer a question if the answer to such a question could directly or indirectly expose such a witness to a criminal charge.[1124] The privilege is not available if the answer would merely establish civil liability on the part of the witness.[1125]

472. There is a special procedure in terms of which a witness may lawfully be required to furnish incriminating answers. This procedure must be set in motion by the prosecution and is governed by section 204 of the Criminal Procedure Act 1977. Whenever the prosecution informs a court that a prosecution witness will be required by the prosecution to furnish incriminating answers with regard to an offence specified by the prosecutor, the court shall inform such witness:

1. that he is obliged to give evidence at the proceedings in question;
2. that questions may be put to him which may incriminate him with regard to the offence specified by the prosecutor;
3. that he will be obliged to answer any question put to him, whether by the prosecution, the accused or the court, notwithstanding that the answer may incriminate him with regard to the offence so specified or with regard to any offence in respect of which a verdict of guilty would be competent upon a charge relating to the offence so specified;
4. that if he answers frankly and honestly all questions put to him, he shall be discharged from prosecution with regard to the offence so specified and with regard to any offence in respect of which a verdict of guilty would be competent upon a charge relating to the offence so specified.

Having been so informed, the witness shall be required to give evidence and answer any question put to him, whether by the prosecution, the accused or the court, notwithstanding that the reply thereto may incriminate him with regard to the offence so specified by the prosecutor or with regard to any offence in respect of which a verdict of guilty would be competent upon a charge relating to the offence so specified. If at the end of the trial,[1126] the court is of the opinion[1127] that the witness had answered 'frankly and honestly'[1128] all questions put to him, such witness shall be granted indemnity from prosecution for the offence initially specified by the prosecutor and for any other offence in respect of which a verdict of guilty would be competent upon a charge relating to the offence so specified.

No indemnity is granted where the witness has failed to answer all questions frankly and honestly.[1129] But in the subsequent prosecution of the witness, the

1124. Criminal Procedure Act 51 of 1977, s. 203.
1125. Criminal Procedure Act 51 of 1977, s. 200.
1126. *S v. Mnyamana* 1990 (1) SACR 137 (A).
1127. *S v. Lubbe* 1981 (2) SA 854 (C).
1128. *R v. McMillan* 1958 (4) SA 461 (A); *Mahomed v. Attorney-General of Natal* 1996 (1) SACR 139 (N).
1129. Criminal Procedure Act 51 of 1977, s. 204(3).

incriminating evidence given by the accused in his capacity as a witness in the earlier proceedings may not be used against him – except in respect of perjury arising from the giving of the evidence in question.

B. The Privilege Against Self-Incrimination: The Accused

473. The accused has a privilege against self-incrimination[1130] which can be described as his right to silence[1131] or passive defence right.[1132] This common-law privilege is underpinned by the right to a fair trial, set out in section 35 of the Constitution. The accused may exercise his right during pre-trial,[1133] plea[1134] and trial proceedings.[1135] However, an accused who wishes to testify in his own defence at the conclusion of the case for the prosecution cannot successfully rely on his privilege against self-incrimination in respect of questions relating to the offence or offences charged.[1136]

474. An accused also cannot rely upon his privilege against self-incrimination in order to avoid the ascertainment of his physical features (like fingerprints) or bodily conditions or characteristics (like the taking of blood or hair samples).[1137] South African criminal procedure and evidence rely in this regard upon the so-called Wigmorean orthodoxy[1138] in terms of which the ambit of the privilege against self-incrimination is restricted to *communications*.[1139] This means that voice identification, that is, where the suspect or accused is not required to 'communicate' but merely to say a few words – does not amount to a breach of the privilege against self-incrimination.[1140] There is no communication.

1130. *See generally*, S.J. van Niekerk, S.E. van der Merwe & A.J. van Wyk, *Privilegies in die Bewysreg* (Butterworths, Durban 1984) 169ff.
1131. S.E. van der Merwe, *Handleiding tot Artikels 112 en 115 van die Strafproseswet 51 van 1977* (Butterworths, Durban 1980) 86.
1132. S.E. van der Merwe, 'Kommissies en selfinkriminasie: Ter verdediging van die passiewe verdedigingsreg' 1991 *Stell LR* 102.
1133. *S v. Waite* 1978 (3) SA 896 (O); *S v. Maritz* 1974 (1) SA 266 (NC).
1134. *S v. Daniëls* 1983 (3) SA 275 (A).
1135. Criminal Procedure Act 51 of 1977, s. 196(1)(*a*).
1136. Criminal Procedure Act 51 of 1977, s. 197.
1137. *Ex parte Minister of Justice: in re R v. Matemba* 1941 AD 75 82–83; *Nkosi v. Barlow* 1984 (3) SA 148 (T) 154 and s. 37 of the Criminal Procedure Act 51 of 1977. It may be argued that although s. 37 infringes s. 35(1)(*c*) of the Constitution, this limitation may be justifiable in terms of s. 36 of the Constitution – P.J. Schwikkard & T.B. Mosaka, *Principles of Evidence* 5th ed. (Juta, Cape Town 2023) 147–151. *See Levack v. Regional Magistrate Wynberg* 2003 (1) SACR 187 (SCA).
1138. B.M. Dann, 'The Fifth Amendment Privilege Against Self-Incrimination: Extorting Physical Evidence from a Suspect' 1970 *Southern California LR* 597.
1139. E. du Toit et al., *Commentary on the Criminal Procedure Act* (Juta, Cape Town 1987) 3–4; S.J. van Niekerk, S.E. van der Merwe & A.J. van Wyk, *Privilegies in die Bewysreg* (Butterworths, Durban 1984) 159ff.
1140. Decisions like *R v. Gericke* 1941 CPD 211 and *S v. M* 1963 (3) SA 183 (T) must be interpreted in this light.

Provision is made in the Electronic Communications and Transactions Act[1141] for a cyber inspector, appointed in terms of the Act[1142] and having obtained the requisite warrant[1143] to, *inter alia*, have access to and inspect the operation of any computer or equipment forming part of all information systems, and any associated apparatus or material, which the cyber inspector has reasonable cause to suspect is or has been used in connection with any offence.[1144] In terms of the Cybercrimes Act,[1145] provision is made for access, search and seizure of articles. For these provisions, *see* paragraph 527 *infra*.

C. Witness Statement Privilege

475. The written statements obtained by the police from possible witnesses are privileged until after the conclusion of the trial.[1146] This is known as 'witness statement privilege'.[1147] The privilege belongs to the prosecutor[1148] and he may waive it. In certain circumstances, the prosecutor *must* abandon the privilege, for example, where the written statement is used to refresh the memory of the prosecution witness in the witness box.[1149] And the prosecutor *must* also hand the written statement over to the defence if there is a serious discrepancy between the written statement of the prosecution witness and his oral testimony.[1150]

476. A policeman's pocketbook is not a privileged document,[1151] unless the relevant entries can be classified as falling under witness statement privilege, that is, where it forms part of the prosecution's brief[1152] in the sense that it contains information originally compiled for the benefit of the prosecution and with a view to prosecution.[1153]

477. An accused who has made a statement to the police is, prior to and during his trial, entitled to a copy of this statement.[1154]

1141. Electronic Communications and Transactions Act 25 of 2002.
1142. Section 80.
1143. In terms of s. 83(1).
1144. Section 82(1)(*f*). In terms of s. 82(2), refusal to cooperate with such lawful search and seizure constitutes an offence.
1145. Cybercrimes Act 25 of 2020.
1146. *Ex parte Minister of Justice: In re S v. Wagner* 1965 (4) SA 507 (A); *R v. Steyn* 1954 (1) SA 324 (A) 335A; *S v. Mavela* 1990 (1) SACR 582 (A); *Zweni v. Minister of Law and Order* (1) 1991 (4) SA 166 (W).
1147. *S v. Jifa* 1991 (2) SACR 52 (E) 64.
1148. *Van den Berg v. Streeklanddros, Van der Bijlpark* 1985 (3) SA 960 (T).
1149. *R v. Elijah* 1963 (3) SA 86 (SR) and S.E. van der Merwe, 'Refreshing the Memory of a Witness' 1991 *Stell LR* 62 75–76.
1150. *S v. Kamte* 1992 (1) SACR 677 (A).
1151. *S v. Mayo* 1990 (1) SACR 659 (E).
1152. *S v. Mavela* 1990 (1) SACR 582 (A).
1153. *S v. Majikela* 1991 (1) SACR 509 (E).
1154. Criminal Procedure Act 51 of 1977, s. 335.

478. Statements obtained by the defence from prospective defence witnesses are also privileged.[1155]

D. Marital Privilege

479. A spouse has the right to refuse to disclose *communications* received from the other spouse.[1156] 'Marriage' includes a customary marriage or customary union concluded under indigenous law and custom or any marriage concluded under any system of religious law,[1157] as well as a civil union.[1158]

E. The Police Informer's Privilege

480. An 'informer' is somebody who secretly reports criminal activities to the police and who does so on the understanding that his identity will not be disclosed.[1159] In court evidence which reveals the identity of the informer or the nature of his information may not be received. There is, however, a so-called *in favorem innocentiae*-exception, that is, where in the opinion of the presiding judicial officer, it is likely that the evidence would tend to establish the innocence of the accused.[1160]

F. Privilege Governing Investigative Methods of the Police

481. Closely related to the informer's privilege is a privilege in terms of which evidence, which relates to the methods employed by police in order to investigate crime, is also protected from disclosure.[1161]

VI. Competence and Compellability of Witnesses

482. Everyone is presumed to be competent and compellable to testify. The most important exceptions are dealt with in A to D *infra.*

1155. S.J. van Niekerk, S.E. van der Merwe & A.J. van Wyk, *Privilegies in die Bewysreg* (Butterworths, Durban 1984) 222–223.
1156. Criminal Procedure Act 51 of 1977, s. 198.
1157. Criminal Procedure Act 51 of 1977, s. 195(2).
1158. Civil Union Act 17 of 2006, s. 13.
1159. A.J. van Wyk & S.E. van der Merwe, 'Die aanbrengersprivilegie' 1983 *SACC* 145 146; P.J. Schwikkard & T.B. Mosaka, *Principles of Evidence* 5th ed. (Juta, Cape Town 2023) 187–189.
1160. *Ex Parte Minister of Justice: In re R v. Pillay* 1945 AD 653; *R v. Van Schalkwyk* 1938 AD 543.
1161. *R v. Abelson* 1933 TPD 227; P.J. Schwikkard & T.B. Mosaka, *Principles of Evidence* 5th ed. (Juta, Cape Town 2023) p. 186, who point out that such a claim to privilege should not merely be an attempt to cover up the fact that evidence was unconstitutionally obtained.

A. Mentally Disordered or Intoxicated Persons

483. No person appearing or proved to be afflicted with mental illness or to be labouring under any imbecility of mind due to intoxication or drugs or the like, and who is thereby deprived of the proper use of reason, shall be competent to testify whilst he is so disabled or affected.[1162]

B. Children

484. Children may only testify if the court is satisfied that they appreciate the duty to speak the truth, have sufficient intelligence and can communicate effectively. There is no age below which a child automatically becomes incompetent to testify.

Children may testify against their parents. But the High Court has stated that it is in principle undesirable that children should be compelled to do so.[1163]

The matter really rests in the discretion of the prosecutor and the calling of a child to testify against a parent will depend upon the availability of other witnesses, the seriousness of the offence and whether the child happens to be the victim.[1164]

C. The Accused's Spouse as a Prosecution Witness

485. The spouse of an accused is a competent but generally non-compellable *prosecution* witness. The spouse can only be compelled to testify *for the prosecution* in respect of certain crimes, for example, bigamy, incest, abduction and any offence committed against the person or a child of the spouse or the accused.[1165] A further exception is where the accused committed an offence against the person of his or her spouse.[1166]

D. The Accused and Spouse of the Accused as Defence Witnesses

486. An accused and the wife or husband of an accused shall be a competent witness *for the defence* at every stage of criminal proceedings, whether or not the accused is jointly charged with any other person.[1167] However, an accused shall not

1162. Criminal Procedure Act 51 of 1977, s. 194. In s. 194A, provision is made for the evaluation of the competency of witnesses due to state of mind.
1163. *R v. Zulu and Zulu* 1947 (2) PH H302 (N).
1164. P.J. Schwikkard & T.B. Mosaka, *Principles of Evidence* 5th ed. (Juta, Cape Town 2023) pp. 494–495.
1165. Criminal Procedure Act 51 of 1977, s. 195.
1166. Criminal Procedure Act 51 of 1977, s. 195(1)(a).
1167. Criminal Procedure Act 51 of 1977, s. 196.

be called as a witness except upon his own application.[1168] He may therefore lawfully refuse to testify in his own defence. A co-accused cannot compel an accused or the latter's spouse to testify.[1169]

§8. Prescription of the Right to Prosecute

487. The right to institute a prosecution for any offence[1170] lapses after the expiration of a period of twenty years from the time when the offence was committed, unless some other period is expressly provided by law.[1171]

1168. Criminal Procedure Act 51 of 1977, s. 196(1)(a).
1169. Criminal Procedure Act 51 of 1977, s. 196(1)(b).
1170. Other than murder; treason committed in times of war; robbery, where aggravating circumstances were present; kidnapping; child-stealing; the common-law crime of bribery; the corruption offence contained in s. 1 of the Corruption Act 92 of 1994; offences referred to in Parts 1 to 4, or ss 17, 20 or 21 (as related to these offences) of Ch. 2 of the Prevention and Combating of Corrupt Activities Act 12 of 2004; any sexual offence in terms of the common law or statute; a Convention offence as defined in s. 1 (*supra*, para. 354); the terrorism offence referred to in s. 2; and an offence associated with terrorist activities referred to in ss 3, 13 or 14, of the Protection of Constitutional Democracy against Terrorist and Related Activities Act 33 of 2004; genocide, crimes against humanity and war crimes (s. 4 of the Implementation of the Rome Statute of the International Criminal Court Act 27 of 2002); trafficking in persons for sexual purposes (ss 4, 5, 7 and 10 of the Prevention and Combating of Trafficking in Persons Act 7 of 2013); or torture, as contemplated in s. 4 of the Prevention and Combating of Torture of Persons Act 13 of 2013.
1171. Criminal Procedure Act 51 of 1977, s. 18.

Chapter 2. Investigation

§1. The Division of Power: Police, Prosecution and Judicial Officers

I. The Police

488. The Republic of South Africa has a national police force, which is an independent government department headed by the National Commissioner of Police, who is under the ultimate control of a member of the Cabinet, the Minister of Law and Order. The structure and responsibilities of the department[1172] are governed by statute. The SAPS Act was enacted: (a) to ensure the safety and security of all persons and property in the national territory; (b) to uphold and safeguard the fundamental rights of every person as guaranteed by the Constitution; (c) to ensure cooperation between the Service and the communities it serves in the combating of crime; (d) to reflect respect for victims of crime and an understanding of their needs; and (e) to ensure effective civilian supervision over the Service and to provide for a Directorate in the Service to combat national priority offences.[1173]

There are several statutes which in certain circumstances grant extraordinary investigative powers to members of the police force, for example, section 25 of the Criminal Procedure Act 51 of 1977 and sections 11 and 12 of the Drugs and Drug Trafficking Act 140 of 1992.

II. The Police and the Prosecuting Authorities

489. There is, in practice, some loose form of cooperation between the police and prosecutors in the investigation of a case and its preparation for trial. The initial investigation is done by the police. They do so upon their own initiative or as a result of a complaint received from the public or in consequence of instructions received from the prosecuting authorities. They prepare a docket (file, dossier) for submission to the public prosecutor, who takes the decision on whether to prosecute or not. The prosecutor – in the exercise of her discretion to prosecute – examines the witness's statements and documentary evidence contained in the docket, together with such real evidence as might be available. At this stage, the prosecutor may also direct and control the investigation by giving specific instructions to the investigating officer, that is, the police official charged with the investigation of the crime. The prosecutor may, for example, call for statements from further potential witnesses, or she may direct that an identification parade be held. But she does not personally partake in any investigative work. If finally satisfied that on all the available evidence, there is a reasonable prospect of a successful prosecution and if satisfied that there is no other compelling reason to decline to prosecute, the prosecutor will institute a criminal action and take such further steps as are legally required

1172. *See supra,* para. 37.
1173. South African Police Service Act 68 of 1995, preamble.

(such as issuing a summons) and legally permitted (such as having a personal pretrial interview with prospective prosecution witnesses). The prosecutor determines the charges and is in this respect *dominus litis.*

III. The Prosecuting Authority

490. A single prosecuting authority, structured in terms of an Act of Parliament, is provided for in section 179(1) of the Constitution. The pre-constitutional system of attorneys-general based at various divisions of the High Court, acting independently of each other, has now fallen away. The prosecuting authority has the power to institute criminal proceedings on behalf of the state and to carry out any necessary functions incidental to instituting criminal proceedings.[1174] The prosecuting authority can also withdraw charges[1175] and stop prosecutions which have already begun.[1176] The Constitution guarantees the professional independence of the prosecuting authority.[1177]

491. The President appoints the NDPP[1178] and, after consultation with the Minister of Justice and the NDPP, appoints no more than four persons as Deputy National Director of Public Prosecutions (DNDPP).[1179] In terms of section 9 of Act 32 of 1998, a person appointed as NDPP or DNDPP must be a fit and proper person to be entrusted with the responsibilities of the office and qualified to practice in all courts in the Republic, as well as a South African citizen. Whilst the NDPP holds office for a non-renewable ten-year period, a DNDPP is not subject to this restriction. Both are required to retire at the age of 65.[1180] The President may provisionally suspend the NDPP or DNDPP from office, pending such inquiry into fitness to hold office as the President deems fit, and may remove him or her from office for: (i) misconduct; (ii) on account of continued ill-health; (iii) on account of incapacity to carry out his or her duties of office efficiently; or (iv) on account thereof that he or she is no longer a fit and proper person to hold the office concerned.[1181] Any DNDPP may exercise or perform any of the functions, powers or duties of the NDPP which he or she has been authorised by the NDPP to exercise or perform.[1182] The NDPP, as head of the prosecuting authority, has authority over all the duties and functions of all members of the prosecuting authority; determines prosecution policy; may intervene in any prosecution process when policy directives are not

1174. Constitution of the RSA, 1996, s. 179(2).
1175. Criminal Procedure Act 51 of 1977, s. 6(*a*).
1176. Criminal Procedure Act 51 of 1977, s. 6(*b*).
1177. *S v. Yengeni* 2006 (1) SACR 405 (T) para. 51.
1178. National Prosecuting Authority Act 32 of 1998, s. 10, read with s. 179(1)(*a*) of the Constitution.
1179. National Prosecuting Authority Act 32 of 1998, s. 11(1).
1180. National Prosecuting Authority Act 32 of 1998, ss 12(1) & (2).
1181. National Prosecuting Authority Act 32 of 1998, s. 12(6). In terms of s. 12(6)(*a*A), this period of suspension terminated by the decision whether or not to remove the NDPP or DNDPP may not exceed twelve months.
1182. National Prosecuting Authority Act 32 of 1998, s. 23.

complied with; and may review a decision to prosecute or not to prosecute.[1183] The prosecuting authority is accountable to Parliament[1184] and the Minister of Justice has the final responsibility over the prosecuting authority.[1185]

492. After consultation with the Minister of Justice and the NDPP, the President may appoint a Director of Public Prosecutions (DPP) at the seat of each High Court,[1186] applying the same criteria as those for appointment as the NDPP, apart from South African citizenship.[1187] A DPP is responsible for the management of any DDPP or prosecutor under his or her control and has the power to: (i) institute and conduct criminal proceedings and carry out functions incidental thereto; (ii) supervise, direct and coordinate the work and activities of all DDPP's and prosecutors in his or her office; (iii) supervise, direct and coordinate specific investigations; and (iv) carry out all duties and functions and exercise all powers assigned to him or her.[1188]

IV. The Prosecutors

493. Prosecutors are appointed on the recommendation of the NDPP or his or her representative, subject to the laws governing the public service.[1189] A prosecutor is required to exercise the powers, carry out the duties and perform the functions set out by Act 32 of 1998 or any other law or by the head of the office or investigating directorate where he or she is employed or by the DPP in whose jurisdiction the lower court where he or she is employed is situated.[1190] Such powers must be exercised in the context of 'maximum compliance with constitutional obligations'.[1191] A prosecutor normally institutes a criminal case at his or her own discretion, subject to any instructions or guidelines which might have been given by the DPP. In difficult or controversial cases, the public prosecutor can – and at times should – approach the DPP to take a final decision. There are certain scattered statutory provisions which require the written authority of a DPP before a prosecution may be instituted for a particular offence. Such an example is found in sections 16(2)(*a*) and 38(1)(*c*) of the Criminal Law (Sexual Offences and Related Matters)

1183. National Prosecuting Authority Act 32 of 1998, s. 22.
1184. National Prosecuting Authority Act 32 of 1998, s. 35.
1185. National Prosecuting Authority Act 32 of 1998, s. 33.
1186. National Prosecuting Authority Act 32 of 1998, s. 13(1)(*a*).
1187. Similar criteria also apply to term of office and removal from office – *see* J.J. Joubert et al., *Criminal Procedure Handbook* 13th ed. (Juta, Cape Town 2020) 63.
1188. National Prosecuting Authority Act 32 of 1998, s. 24. Any power, duty or functioned by a DDPP is regarded as that of the DPP concerned.
1189. National Prosecuting Authority Act 32 of 1998, s. 16. Prosecutors may be appointed to the office of the NDPP; the office of the prosecuting authority at the seat of the High Court; the investigating directorates; and the lower courts in the Republic. A member of the SAPS may be required to act as a prosecutor in the lower court – s. 13(5) of the South African Police Service Act 68 of 1995.
1190. National Prosecuting Authority Act 32 of 1998, s. 25.
1191. *Jaipal v. S* 2005 (4) SA 581 (CC) para. 56.

Amendment Act 32 of 2007. In such an instance, any prosecution instituted without the DPP's written authority is null and void.

494. There is an important ethical facet to the duties of public prosecutors. They may not suppress any evidence which might be favourable to an accused.[1192] They are officers of the court and must at all times seek to ensure that justice is done.

V. Private Prosecutions

495. Private prosecutions are permitted in certain limited circumstances.[1193] A private prosecution is a very rare phenomenon in South Africa[1194] and is one in which a private individual[1195] and not the State prosecutes. It is permitted in order to avoid illegal retaliation by an individual who feels aggrieved by a DPP's decision not to prosecute. A private prosecutor must show a peculiar and substantial interest in the issue of the trial.[1196] The result is that a private prosecution can in principle not take place in respect of so-called victimless crimes. A private prosecution can only take place after all the facts have been considered by a DPP and after he or she has declined to prosecute. Upon the application of the person who wishes to pursue a private prosecution, the DPP concerned must issue a *nolle prosequi* certificate.[1197] This certificate entitles the private prosecutor to have the necessary summons issued even though the trial court will ultimately decide whether he or she has the necessary interest.

VI. Magistrates and Judges: Their Role in the Investigation of Crime

496. Magistrates (presiding judicial officers in lower courts) and judges (presiding judicial officers in the Supreme Court) perform a judicial function – as opposed to an investigative or prosecutorial function. South Africa does not make use of investigating magistrates or examining judges.

497. Magistrates may at times issue arrest or search warrants on the basis of statements submitted to them by the prosecution or police.[1198] But this is seen as a judicial function.

1192. *S v. Van Rensburg* 1963 (2) SA 343 (N); J.J. Joubert et al., *Criminal Procedure Handbook* 13th ed. (Juta, Cape Town 2020) 80.
1193. Criminal Procedure Act 51 of 1977, s. 7.
1194. *Black v. Barclays Zimbabwe's Nominees (Pty) Ltd.*, 1990 (1) SACR 433 (W).
1195. Who must be a natural person: *Black v. Barclays Zimbabwe's Nominees (Pty) Ltd.*, 1990 (4) SA 720 (A); *National Society for the Prevention of Cruelty to Animals v. Minister of Justice and Constitutional Development* 2016 (1) SACR 308 (SCA).
1196. Criminal Procedure Act 51 of 1977, s. 7(1)(*a*).
1197. Criminal Procedure Act 51 of 1977, s. 7(2)(*a*).
1198. *See* e.g., Criminal Procedure Act 51 of 1977, s. 43, and s. 43(1A) relating to terrorism offences, which provides for extended jurisdiction for the magistrate or justice.

498. Potential witnesses who unlawfully refuse to make statements to the police in the course of the latter's investigation of crime can be compelled to appear before a judge or magistrate. In terms of section 205 of the Criminal Procedure Act 51 of 1977, a judge or magistrate may, upon the request of a DPP or prosecutor authorised thereto in writing by the DPP, require the attendance before him or any other judge or magistrate, for examination by the DPP or prosecutor authorised thereto, of any person who is likely to give material and relevant information[1199] as to any alleged offence, whether or not it is known by whom the offence was committed. In this respect, judges and magistrates do indirectly participate in the investigation of crime. It should be noted that the potential witness may refuse to answer on the basis of any lawful excuse, for example, possible privileges or where it is humanly intolerable for the person concerned to disclose the required information.[1200] Such examination may be conducted privately at a place designated by the judicial officer and need not be held in court.[1201] This procedure is not inconsistent with any of the provisions in the Bill of Rights.[1202]

499. There is also a practice in terms of which magistrates and judges direct that the record of trial proceedings, which have been concluded, should be submitted to the DPP concerned because of the fact that other criminal activities which were not the subject of the trial proceedings had come to light. But this does not mean that magistrates or judges investigate or prosecute crime. It merely means that they report crimes which come to their attention in the performance of their official duties.

§2. Infiltration and Deceptive Forms of Investigation

I. Infiltration

500. Infiltration as an investigative method employed by the police must in the context of the present discussion be understood as systematic and deliberate investigation through the use of undercover operatives, like spies or *agent provocateurs*. There are no *specific* rules regulating this kind of infiltration. The permissible scope of infiltration is therefore determined by the ordinary rules of substantive criminal and private law. Infiltration per se is not prohibited. But common law or statutory crimes committed by the police as part of an overall scheme to infiltrate, can be prosecuted. And from a private law perspective, certain police actions executed as part of an infiltration may amount to actionable invasions of personal rights, such as the right to privacy.[1203] An aggrieved citizen may also obtain an order (interdict) from court restraining the police from performing or going ahead with activities

---

1199. *See generally*, *S v. Russell* 1977 (4) SA 291 (C).
1200. *Attorney-General, Transvaal v. Kader* 1991 (4) SA 727 (A).
1201. Criminal Procedure Act 51 of 1977, s. 205(3).
1202. *Nel v. Le Roux* 1996 (3) SA 562 (CC).
1203. *See generally*, D.J. McQuoid-Mason, *The Law of Privacy in South Africa* (Juta, Cape Town 1978) 147.

which infringe or might infringe his rights. However, in the final analysis, the victim of *infiltration, as such*, is not adequately protected because of the absence of specific and comprehensive rules governing infiltration. Too much is left at the discretion of the police. It has repeatedly been pointed out that there is a clear need for public officially enforced guidelines specifying the criteria for the use of undercover operatives.[1204]

Police infiltration will not be tolerated when it comes to the confidential relationship between legal representative and client.[1205]

II. The 'Police Trap' (Entrapment)

501. A trap has been judicially described as 'a person who, with the view to securing the conviction of another, proposes certain criminal conduct to him, and himself ostensibly takes part therein'.[1206] The trap is not an accomplice even though he creates the occasion for someone else to commit the offence. A policeman in plain clothes might act as a trap. But often ordinary citizens act as traps at the request of the police and for financial reward from the authorities.

502. In terms of section 252A of the Criminal Procedure Act, a trap may be used for law enforcement purposes to detect or uncover the commission of a crime, and the evidence obtained by means of the trap will be admissible, provided that the conduct of the trap does not go beyond providing an opportunity to commit an offence.[1207] In deciding whether the conduct did go beyond providing an opportunity to commit an offence, the court may take into account such factors as the nature of the crime, the availability of other law enforcement techniques, the degree of persistence of the law enforcement official, the type of inducement used, and whether the conduct exploited emotions, sympathy, friendship or a particular vulnerability.[1208] If the court determines that the conduct of the trap was improper, such evidence obtained from the trap may be excluded if the evidence was obtained in an improper or unfair manner and the admission of such evidence would render the trial unfair or would be otherwise detrimental to the administration of justice.[1209] A police official who participates in a trap to detect or uncover the commission of a crime shall not be criminally liable in respect of any act which constitutes an offence and which relates to the trap if it was performed in good faith.[1210]

1204. A.S. Matthews, *Freedom, State Security and the Rule of Law* (Juta, Cape Town 1986) 190–191.
1205. *S v. Mushimba* 1977 (2) SA 829 (A).
1206. *S v. Malinga* 1963 (1) SA 692 (A) 693; *S v. Ohlenschlager* 1992 (1) SACR 695 (T). *See also*, J.M.T. Labuschagne, 'Die lokvink en lokvinkbetrapte in die strafregspleging' 1976 De Jure 16.
1207. Criminal Procedure Act 51 of 1977, s. 252A(1).
1208. Criminal Procedure Act 51 of 1977, s. 252A(2).
1209. Criminal Procedure Act 51 of 1977, s. 252A(3).
1210. Criminal Procedure Act 51 of 1977, s. 252A(5).

III. The Police Informer

503. The use of a police informer is a deceptive form of investigation. This form of investigation and the evidential privilege which exists in this regard were discussed in paragraph 480 *supra.*

§3. Electronic Eavesdropping

504. The Regulation of Interception of Communications and Provision of Communication-Related Information Act 70 of 2002 authorises the interception and monitoring of communications and conversations in respect of certain serious offences and if the security of the Republic is threatened.

505. Sections 16 and 18 of the Act provide that a judge may approve, on application, an interception direction, which authorises the interception, at any place in the Republic, of any communication, direct or indirect, in the course of its occurrence or transmission, or in respect of archived communication. A judge may also, in terms of sections 17 and 18 of the Act, authorise, on application, a real-time communication-related direction, in terms of which a telecommunication service provider must provide real-time communication-related information in respect of a customer on an ongoing basis, as it becomes available. If only archived communication-related information is required, a magistrate, regional court magistrate, or a judge may, in terms of sections 18 and 19 of the Act, consider an application for an archived communication-related direction, in terms of which a telecommunication service provider is directed to provide archived communication-related information in respect of a customer. In terms of section 21 of the Act, application can be made to a judge for a decryption direction, in terms of which a decryption key holder is directed to either disclose a decryption key, that is, any key, mathematical formula, code, password, algorithm or any other data, which is used to allow access to encrypted information or facilitate the putting of encrypted information into intelligible form, or to provide decryption assistance in respect of encrypted information. Any law enforcement officer may execute a direction issued under the Act in terms of section 26.

506. An interception direction may only be issued if the judge is satisfied, on the facts alleged in the application, that there are reasonable grounds to believe that:

1. a serious offence has been or is being or will probably be committed;
2. the gathering of information concerning an actual threat to the public health or safety, national security or compelling national economic interests of the Republic is necessary;
3. the gathering of information concerning a potential threat to the public health or safety or national security of the Republic is necessary;
4. the making of a request for the provision, or the provision to the competent authorities of a country or territory outside the Republic, of any assistance in

connection with, or in the form of, the interception of communications relating to organised crime or any offence relating to terrorism or the gathering of information relating to organised crime or terrorism is in accordance with an international mutual assistance agreement, or the interests of the Republic's international relations or obligations; or

5. the gathering of information concerning property which is or could probably be an instrumentality of a serious offence or is or could probably be the proceeds of unlawful activities is necessary.[1211]

§4. Arrest, Search and Seizure

I. Arrest

A. *Purpose and Effect of Arrest*

507. Arrest is a method of securing an accused's attendance at trial.[1212] The effect of an arrest is that the person arrested shall be in lawful custody and shall be detained in custody until he is lawfully released from custody,[1213] for example, where he is released on bail,[1214] or on warning,[1215] or is discharged upon final acquittal. An arrest may be effected with or without a warrant[1216] by persons identified[1217] in the Criminal Procedure Act or other legislation. Arrest is regulated by statutory provisions. But these provisions are interpreted in the light of the common-law principle favouring the personal liberty of the individual and must be seen in the context of the accused's right not to be deprived of his freedom arbitrarily or without just cause or his right to freedom of movement.[1218]

B. *Basic Principles Governing a Lawful Arrest*

508. The arrestor must take physical control of the body of the arrestee[1219] by actually touching the latter's body, unless the arrestee submits to custody.[1220] Reasonable force may be used in effecting an arrest.[1221] In certain limited

1211. Regulation of Interception of Communications and Provision of Communication-Related Information Act 70 of 2002, s. 16(5)(*a*). The same considerations apply to a real-time communication-related direction (s. 17(4)) and to an archived communication-related direction (s. 19(4)).
1212. Criminal Procedure Act 51 of 1977, s. 38.
1213. Criminal Procedure Act 51 of 1977, s. 39(3).
1214. Criminal Procedure Act 51 of 1977, s. 60.
1215. Criminal Procedure Act 51 of 1977, s. 72.
1216. Criminal Procedure Act 51 of 1977, s. 39(1).
1217. *See* e.g., Criminal Procedure Act 51 of 1977, ss 40 and 47.
1218. Constitution, 1996, ss 12(1)(*a*) and 21(1) respectively.
1219. *R v. Tiro* 1951 (3) SA 390 (T).
1220. Criminal Procedure Act 51 of 1977, s. 39(1). *See also S v. Thamaha* 1979 (3) SA 487 (O) 490.
1221. *See* Criminal Procedure Act 51 of 1977, s. 49; *Macu v. Du Toit en 'n ander* 1983 (4) 629 (A).

circumstances – which are more fully discussed below – lethal force may be employed where a suspect takes flight.[1222]

An arrestor must, at the time of the arrest or immediately after having effected the arrest, inform the arrestee of the cause of the arrest,[1223] that is, the alleged criminal conduct forming the basis of the arrest. At this stage, it is not required that a detailed description of the charge, which will in court be put to the accused, should be given[1224] – especially not in those circumstances where the arrestee has been caught *in flagrante delicto* and is therefore probably fully aware of the circumstances which led to his arrest.[1225] In the case of arrest on the basis of a warrant, the arrestee is entitled to a copy of such warrant.[1226]

An improper motive does not make *an otherwise lawful* arrest unlawful.[1227] But the purpose of an arrest must at all times be to bring the arrestee before a court of law to be charged and tried.[1228] A Director of Public Prosecution's decision to refuse to prosecute does not mean that the earlier lawful arrest must *ex post facto* be deemed unlawful. Any detention which follows upon an unlawful arrest is unlawful.[1229] An arrestee who challenges the lawfulness of his arrest or detention does not carry any burden of proof. The burden of proving lawfulness is upon the arrestor.[1230] An arrest must take place on the basis of a reasonable suspicion. It is an objective test. This requirement applies to arrests without warrant as well as arrests executed on the basis of a warrant. Detention, which follows upon a lawful arrest, becomes unlawful if the accused is not as soon as possible brought to a police station or, in the case of an arrest by warrant, to any other place expressly mentioned in the warrant. The detention also becomes unlawful if an accused is denied his right to a first appearance in court within forty-eight hours after having been arrested or such other period as prescribed by law.[1231]

C. Warrant of Arrest by Magistrate or Justice of the Peace

509. Any magistrate or justice of the peace may, upon the written application of an attorney-general, public prosecutor or commissioned officer of police, issue a warrant for the arrest of any person. The written application must set out the alleged offence, must claim jurisdiction and must state that from evidence taken upon oath

1222. Criminal Procedure Act 51 of 1977, s. 49(2).
1223. Criminal Procedure Act 51 of 1977, s. 39(2); *Brand v. Minister of Justice* 1959 (4) SA 712 (A). A suspect who makes it practically impossible for the arrestee to inform him of the reason for the arrest cannot complain that he was never properly informed in terms of s. 39(2). *See R v. September* 1959 (4) SA 256 (C).
1224. *Minister of Law and Order v. Kader* 1991 (1) SA 41 (A).
1225. *Minister of Law and Order v. Parker* 1989 (2) SA 633 (A).
1226. Criminal Procedure Act 51 of 1977, s. 39(2).
1227. *Minister van die Suid-Afrikaanse Polisie v. Kraatz* 1973 (3) SA 490 (D) and *Tsose v. Minister of Justice and others* 1951 (3) SA 10 (A) 17.
1228. *Wiesner v. Molomo* 1983 (3) SA 151 (A).
1229. *Minister of Law and Order, KwaNdebele and others v. Mathebe and others* 1990 (1) SA 114 (A) 122D.
1230. *Minister of Law and Order v. Parker* 1989 (2) SA 636 (A).
1231. *See generally*, Criminal Procedure Act 51 of 1977, s. 50.

there is a reasonable suspicion that the person in respect of whom the warrant is applied for has committed the offence.[1232]

D. Arrest by Peace Officer Without a Warrant

510. In terms of section 40(1) of the Criminal Procedure Act 51 of 1977, a peace officer (all police officers are peace officers) may, without warrant, arrest any person:

a. who commits or attempts to commit any offence in his presence;[1233]
b. whom he reasonably suspects of having committed an offence referred to in Schedule 1 of the Act;
c. who has escaped or who attempts to escape from lawful custody;
d. who has in his possession any implement of housebreaking or car breaking as contemplated in section 82 of the General Law Amendment Act 129 of 1993, and who is unable to account for such possession to the satisfaction of the peace officer;
e. who is found in possession of anything which the peace officer reasonably suspects to be stolen property or property dishonestly obtained, and whom the peace officer reasonably suspects of having committed an offence with respect to such thing;
f. who is found at any place by night in circumstances which afford reasonable grounds for believing that such person has committed or is about to commit an offence;
g. who is reasonably suspected of being or having been in unlawful possession of stock or produce as defined in any law relating to the theft of stock or produce;
h. who is reasonably suspected of committing or of having committed an offence under any law governing the making, supply, possession or conveyance of intoxicating liquor or of dependence-producing drugs or the possession or disposal of arms or ammunition;
i. who is found in any gambling house or at any gambling table in contravention of any law relating to the prevention or suppression of gambling or games of chance;
j. who wilfully obstructs him in the execution of his duty;
k. who has been concerned in or against whom a reasonable complaint has been made or credible information has been received or a reasonable suspicion exists that he has been concerned in any act committed outside the Republic which, if committed in the Republic, would have been punishable as an offence, and for which he is, under any law relating to extradition or fugitive offenders, liable to be arrested or detained in custody in the Republic;
l. who is reasonably suspected of being a prohibited immigrant in the Republic in contravention of any law regulating entry into or residence in the Republic;

1232. Criminal Procedure Act 51 of 1977, s. 43. 'Attorney-general' is interpreted as Director of Public Prosecutions in terms of s. 45 of Act 32 of 1998.
1233. On the term 'presence', *see generally, Areff v. Minister van Polisie* 1977 (2) SA 900 (A) 908–909.

m. who is reasonably suspected of being a deserter from the South African National Defence Force;
n. who is reasonably suspected of having failed to observe any condition imposed in postponing the passing of sentence or in suspending the operation of any sentence under this Act;
o. who is reasonably suspected of having failed to pay any fine or part thereof on the date fixed by order of the court under this Act;
p. who fails to surrender himself in order that he may undergo periodical imprisonment when and where he is required to do so under an order of court or any law relating to prisons;
q. who is reasonably suspected of having committed an act of domestic violence as contemplated in section 1 of the Domestic Violence Act 116 of 1998, which constitutes an offence in respect of which violence is an element.

E. Arrest by Private Person Without a Warrant

511. In terms of section 42(1), any private person may without a warrant arrest any person:

a. who commits or attempts to commit in his presence (or whom he reasonably suspects of having committed) an offence referred to in Schedule 1 of the Criminal Procedure Act;
b. whom he reasonably believes to have authority to arrest that person for that offence;
c. whom he is by any law authorised to arrest without warrant in respect of any offence specified in that law; and
d. whom he sees engaged in an affray.

512. Every male inhabitant of the Republic between 16 and 60 years of age is required, when called upon by any police official, to assist in arresting any person or in detaining any person so arrested.[1234]

F. Breaking Open Premises for Purposes of an Arrest

513. Any person who may lawfully arrest another in respect of any offence and who knows or reasonably suspects such other person to be on any premises may, if he first audibly demands entry into such premises and notifies the purpose for which he seeks entry and fails to gain entry, break open, enter and search such premises for the purpose of effecting the arrest.[1235]

1234. Criminal Procedure Act 51 of 1977, s. 47(1).
1235. Criminal Procedure Act 51 of 1977, s. 48.

G. The Use of Force (Including Lethal Force) in Effecting an Arrest

514. This aspect is a controversial issue in South African criminal procedure[1236] and is regulated by section 49 of the Criminal Procedure Act 51 of 1977. Since arrest is a drastic method of securing the presence of an accused at his trial, and use of force in order to effect such arrest is even more drastic, it is required that this area of the law be strictly regulated.[1237] Section 49(2) provides that if any arrestor[1238] attempts to arrest a suspect[1239] and the suspect resists the attempt or flees, or resists the attempt and flees when it is clear that an attempt to arrest him or her is being made, and the suspect cannot be arrested without the use of force, the arrestor may, in order to effect the arrest, use such force as may be reasonably necessary and proportional in the circumstances to overcome the resistance or to prevent the suspect from fleeing. In addition to the requirement that the force must be reasonably necessary and proportional in the circumstances, the arrestor may use deadly force[1240] only if: (i) the suspect poses a threat of serious violence to the arrestor or any other person; or (ii) the suspect is suspected on reasonable grounds of having committed a crime involving the infliction or threatened infliction of serious bodily harm, and there are no other reasonable means of effecting the arrest, whether at that time or later.

The requirement that the force used be 'reasonably necessary and proportional in the circumstances' entails a consideration of all the circumstances in order to determine whether the use of the degree of force was justified.[1241] The previous formulation of section 49(2), which allowed for the killing of a person, who was to be arrested for an offence referred to in Schedule 1 of the Criminal Procedure Act but who could not be arrested or prevented from fleeing by any other means, to be regarded as justifiable homicide, was struck down as unconstitutional by the Constitutional Court in *Ex Parte Minister of Safety and Security and Others: In Re S v.*

1236. *See generally*, J.R.L. Milton, 'Ultima Ratio Legis: The Use of Deadly Force in Effecting Arrests', in J.A. Coetzee (ed.), *Gedenkbundel H.L. Swanepoel* (Butterworths, Durban 1976) 140; S.V. Hoctor, *Snyman's Criminal Law* 7th ed. (LexisNexis, Durban 2020) 108ff.; J. Burchell, *South African Criminal Law and Procedure,* Vol 1 *General Principles* 4th ed. (Juta, Cape Town 2011) 198ff.

1237. This is particularly so given that the suspect retains his constitutional rights to freedom and security of the person, including the right to be free from all forms of violence (s. 12) and the right to a fair trial, including the right to be presumed innocent (s. 35(3)).

1238. Criminal Procedure Act 51 of 1977, s. 49(1) provides that 'arrestor' means any person authorised under the Act to arrest or to assist in arresting a suspect.

1239. Criminal Procedure Act 51 of 1977, s. 49(1) provides that 'suspect' means any person of whom an arrestor has or had a reasonable suspicion that such person is committing or has committed an offence.

1240. Criminal Procedure Act 51 of 1977, s. 49(1) defines 'deadly force' as force that is likely to cause serious bodily harm or death and includes, but is not limited to, shooting at a suspect with a firearm.

1241. *Govender v. Minister of Safety and Security* 2001 (4) SA 273 (SCA) 293; S.V. Hoctor, *Snyman's Criminal Law* 7th ed. (LexisNexis, Durban 2020) 109; J. J. Joubert et al., *Criminal Procedure Handbook* 13th ed. (Juta, Cape Town 2020) 168ff.

Walters and Another.[1242] The law with regard to use of force in order to effect an arrest was set out as follows in the *Walters* case:[1243]

a. The purpose of arrest is to bring before court for trial persons suspected of having committed offences.
b. Arrest is not the only means of achieving this purpose, nor is it always the best.
c. Arrest may never be used to punish a suspect.
d. Where arrest is called for, force may be used only where it is necessary in order to carry out the arrest.
e. Where force is necessary, only the least degree of force reasonably necessary to carry out the arrest may be used.
f. In deciding what degree of force is both reasonable and necessary, all the circumstances must be taken into account, including the threat of violence the suspect poses to the arrester or others and the nature and circumstances of the offence the suspect is suspected of having committed; the force being proportional in all these circumstances.
g. Shooting a suspect solely in order to carry out an arrest is permitted in very limited circumstances only.
h. Ordinarily, such shooting is not permitted unless the suspect poses a threat of violence to the arrester or others or is suspected on reasonable grounds of having committed a crime involving the infliction or threatened infliction of serious bodily harm and there are no other reasonable means of carrying out the arrest, whether at that time or later.
i. These limitations in no way detract from the rights of an arrester attempting to carry out an arrest to kill a suspect in self-defence or in defence of any other person.

515. Whilst previous formulations of this provision have placed a burden of proof on the accused, on a balance of probabilities, to establish that his conduct may be statutorily justified, in the light of the protection of the right to be presumed innocent, and the associated judicial antipathy for reverse onus provisions, it seems that at most an evidential burden would rest on the accused, to adduce evidence to create a reasonable doubt that his conduct complied with the provisions of the section.[1244]

II. Entry, Search and Seizure

A. Seizure by the State

516. The state may seize anything:

1242. *Ex Parte Minister of Safety and Security and Others: In Re S v. Walters and Another* 2002 (4) SA 613 (CC).
1243. *Ex Parte Minister of Safety and Security and Others: In Re S v. Walters and Another* 2002 (4) SA 613 (CC) para. 54.
1244. S.V Hoctor, *Snyman's Criminal Law* 7th ed. (LexisNexis, Durban 2020) 111–112.

a. which is concerned in or is on reasonable grounds believed to be concerned in the commission or suspected commission of an offence, whether within the Republic or elsewhere;
b. which may afford evidence of the commission or suspected commission of an offence, whether within the Republic or elsewhere; or
c. which is intended to be used or is on reasonable grounds believed to be intended to be used in the commission of an offence.[1245]

The gist of the procedures to be followed is set out in B to H *infra.*

B. Seizure under Search Warrant

517. An article may as a rule only be seized by virtue of a search warrant issued, *first*, by a magistrate or justice, if it appears to such magistrate or justice from information on oath that there are reasonable grounds for believing that any such article is in the possession or under control of or upon any person or upon or at any premises within his area of jurisdiction; or, *second*, by a judge or judicial officer presiding at criminal proceedings, if it appears to such judge or judicial officer that any such article in the possession or under the control of any person or upon or at any premises is required in evidence at such proceedings.[1246]

A search warrant shall be executed by day, unless the person issuing the warrant has authorised the execution thereof by night.[1247] The warrant must be clearly worded[1248] and must have been issued in advance of the search and seizure. The warrant must authorise search as well as seizure before any lawful seizure can take place.[1249] The police official executing the warrant must at all times act reasonably and may only act as authorised by the warrant.[1250]

518. Documents falling within the ambit of legal professional privilege cannot be seized in terms of a warrant.[1251] It has been suggested that the police should afford the lawyer and his client an opportunity to approach the court on this issue and have the warrant set aside.[1252]

C. Search and Seizure Without a Warrant

519. An arrested person may be searched without a search warrant. This is authorised by section 23 of the Criminal Procedure Act 51 of 1977.

1245. Criminal Procedure Act 51 of 1977, s. 20.
1246. Criminal Procedure Act 51 of 1977, s. 21.
1247. Criminal Procedure Act 51 of 1977, s. 21(3)(*a*).
1248. *World Wide Film Distributors v. Divisional Commander, South African Police* 1971 (4) SA 312 (C).
1249. *Nusas v. Divisional Commander, South African Police* 1971 (2) SA 553 (C).
1250. *Divisional Commissioner, South African Police v. SAAN* 1966 (2) SA 503 (A).
1251. *Sasol III (Edms) Bpk v. Minister van Wet en Orde* 1991 (3) SA 766 (T).
1252. *Cheadle, Thompson and Hayson v. Minister of Law and Order* 1986 (2) SA 279 (W).

520. A police official may also without a search warrant search any person or container or premises for the purpose of seizing any article referred to in section 20 of the Criminal Procedure Act 51 of 1977, if the person concerned consents to the search for and the seizure of the article in question, or if the person who may consent to the search of the container or premises consents to such search and the seizure of the article in question.[1253] A police official may also act without a search warrant if he on reasonable grounds believes that a search warrant will be issued to him if he applies for such warrant and if he on reasonable grounds believes that the delay in obtaining such warrant would defeat the object of the search.[1254]

521. The question of whether reasonable grounds were present is an objective one.[1255] The official concerned must show that reasonable grounds existed at the time when he decided to act without a warrant.[1256]

D. Search of Premises Where Police Official Is Not Readily Available

522. Any person who is lawfully in charge or in occupation of any premises and who reasonably suspects that stolen stock or produce, as defined in any law relating to the theft of stock or produce, is on or in the premises concerned, or that any article has been placed thereon or therein, or is in the custody or possession of any person upon or in such premises in contravention of any law relating to intoxicating liquor, dependence-producing drugs, arms and ammunition or explosives, may at any time, *if a police official is not readily available*, enter such premises for the purpose of searching such premises and any person thereon or therein, and if any such stock, produce or article is found, he shall take possession thereof and forthwith deliver it to a police official.[1257]

E. Power of Police to Enter Premises

523. Section 26 of the Criminal Procedure Act 51 of 1977 provides that where a police official in the investigation of an offence or alleged offence reasonably suspects that a person who may furnish information with reference to any such offence is on any premises, such police official may without warrant enter such premises for the purpose of interrogating such person and obtaining a statement from him. However, this section also contains a proviso to the effect that the police official concerned shall not enter any private dwelling without the consent of the occupier thereof.

1253. Criminal Procedure Act 51 of 1977, s. 22(*a*).
1254. Criminal Procedure Act 51 of 1977, s. 22(*b*).
1255. *See generally, Ndabeni v. Minister of Law and Order* 1984 (3) SA 500 (D).
1256. *Alex Cartage (Pty) Ltd v. Minister of Transport* 1986 (2) SA 838 (E); *see also Magobodi v. Minister of Safety and Security* 2009 (1) SACR 355 (Tk), *NDPP v. Starplex 47 CC and others: In re Ex parte NDPP v. Mamadou & others* 2009 (1) SACR 68 (C).
1257. Criminal Procedure Act 51 of 1977, s. 24.

Section 25(1) of the Criminal Procedure Act makes provision for the issuing of warrants in certain limited circumstances granting a police official the power to enter premises (including private dwellings) and to carry out such investigations and to take such steps *as such police official* may consider necessary for the preservation of the internal security of the Republic or for the maintenance of law and order or for the prevention of any offence. This is a peculiar provision. The normal objective standard (what would the reasonable police official do in the prevailing circumstances) is statutorily displaced by a subjective standard, namely the standard of the police official concerned. It has rightly been pointed out that it 'is hardly necessary to underline the folly of placing such ill-defined power in the hands of a policeman'.[1258] The position is exacerbated by the fact that entry, search and seizure as provided for in section 25(1) can also take place without a warrant if a police official on reasonable grounds believes, first, that a warrant would be granted if applied for and, second, that the delay in obtaining it would defeat the purpose of the entry, search and seizure.[1259] However, the issue of whether there are reasonable grounds to proceed without a warrant is an objective one.[1260] But thereafter, a subjective test applies in respect of the steps to be taken.

F. Search to Be Conducted in Decent and Orderly Manner

524. A search of any person or premises shall be conducted with strict regard to decency and order. A woman shall be searched by a woman only. If no female police official is available, the search shall be made by any woman designated for this purpose by a police official.[1261]

G. Entry, Search and Seizure in Terms of the SAPS Act 68 of 1995

525. The National or a Provincial Commissioner of the SAPS may, in terms of section 13(8) of this Act, where it is reasonable in the circumstances in order to exercise a power or perform a function of the Service, in writing, authorise a member under his or her command to set up a roadblock or roadblocks on any public road in a particular area or to set up a checkpoint or checkpoints at any public place in a particular area. Any member of the Service may, without a warrant, search any vehicle and any person in or on such vehicle at such roadblock or checkpoint and seize any article referred to in section 20 of the Criminal Procedure Act found by him or her upon such person or in or on such vehicle.[1262]

1258. A.S. Mathews, *Freedom, State Security and the Rule of Law* (Juta, Cape Town 1986) 187. However, in *Goqwana v. Minister of Safety and Security NO* 2016 (1) SACR 384 (SCA), it was held that abuse may be safeguarded against by requiring a high degree of specificity in respect of identifying by name the specific police official in the search warrant in question.
1259. Criminal Procedure Act 51 of 1977, s. 25(3).
1260. *S v. Boshoff* 1981 (1) SA 393 (T).
1261. Criminal Procedure Act 51 of 1977, s. 29.
1262. South African Police Service Act 68 of 1995, s. 13(8).

Members of the SAPS are also empowered to conduct a search without a warrant for the purposes of border control[1263] and in a cordoned-off area to ensure public safety.[1264]

H. Search Without Warrant in Terms of the Drugs and Drug Trafficking Act 140 of 1992

526. In terms of section 11(1) of the above Act, a police official may, if he has reasonable grounds to suspect that an offence under the Act has been or is about to be committed by means or in respect of any scheduled substance, drug or property, at any time enter or board and search any premises, vehicle, vessel or aircraft on or in which any such substance, drug or property is suspected to be found or search any container or other thing in which any such substance, drug or property is suspected to be found.

I. Search and Seizure in Terms of the Electronic Communications and Transactions Act 25 of 2002 and the Cybercrimes Act 19 of 2020

527. In terms of the Electronic Communications and Transactions Act, cyber inspectors, who must be duly authorised,[1265] have powers of monitoring and inspection with specific regard to websites, cryptography service providers and authentication service providers,[1266] which include the right to enter a premises or access an information system on the authority of a warrant,[1267] in order to engage in a search of such premises or that information system or, on reasonable grounds, any person, and to seize any information for an investigation.[1268]

1263. South African Police Service Act 68 of 1995, s. 13(6).
1264. South African Police Service Act 68 of 1995, s. 13(7).
1265. Electronic Communications and Transactions Act 25 of 2002, s. 80.
1266. Electronic Communications and Transactions Act 25 of 2002, s. 81. In terms of s. 1: 'web site' means any location on the Internet containing a home page or web page; 'cryptography service' means any service provided to a sender or a recipient of a data message or to anyone storing a data message, and which is designed to facilitate the use of cryptographic techniques; and 'authentication services or products' means products or services designed to identify the holder of an electronic signature to others.
1267. Electronic Communications and Transactions Act 25 of 2002, s. 83.
1268. Electronic Communications and Transactions Act 25 of 2002, s. 82. Failure to cooperate with such a lawful search and seizure is an offence (s. 82(2)). The Criminal Procedure Act 51 of 1977 applies *mutatis mutandis* to searches and seizures in terms of Act 25 of 2002 (s. 82(3)). For purposes of Act 25 of 2002, any reference in the Criminal Procedure Act 51 of 1977 to 'premises' and 'articles' includes an information system as well as data messages.

The Cybercrimes Act provides that a police official may search for, access,[1269] or seize[1270] any article within the Republic, in terms of the Act.[1271] An article may be searched for, accessed or seized under the authority of a search warrant,[1272] and this investigative process may be assisted by a duly appointed investigator.[1273] Where a police official arrests a person without a warrant,[1274] a search and seizure may follow, where there are reasonable grounds for belief on the part of the police official that a search warrant will be granted, and where it is not reasonably practicable, on grounds of urgency, to make a written application.[1275] Criminal offences target both unlawful conduct on the part of persons hindering an investigation[1276] and unlawful conduct by police officials or others who misuse their powers in this context.[1277]

§5. Identification Procedures

I. Section 37 of the Criminal Procedure Act 51 of 1977

528. The above section contains extensive provisions concerning the ascertainment of the bodily features of an arrested person or someone who has already been formally charged in court. The purpose of these provisions is to facilitate identification and to secure real evidence which may be important for purposes of any subsequent trial.

1269. In terms of s. 25 of the Cybercrimes Act 25 of 2020, 'access' includes without limitation to make use of: (i) a computer data storage medium, or a computer system, or their accessories and components or any part thereof or any ancillary device or component thereto; and (ii) data or a computer program held in a computer data storage medium or a computer system.
1270. In terms of the Cybercrimes Act 25 of 2020, s. 25, 'seize' includes to: (i) remove a computer data storage medium or any part of a computer system; (ii) render inaccessible, data, a computer program, a computer data storage medium or any part of a computer system in order to preserve evidence; (iii) make and retain a copy of data or a computer program; or (iv) make and retain a printout of the output of data or a computer program.
1271. Cybercrimes Act 25 of 2020, s. 28. The Criminal Procedure Act 51 of 1977 applies in addition to the provisions of the Cybercrimes Act unless inconsistent with the provisions of the Cybercrimes Act (s. 27).
1272. Cybercrimes Act 25 of 2020, s. 29.
1273. Where it is not reasonably practicable to make a written application for a warrant, an oral application may be made (s. 30) and a search warrant may be dispensed with where the consent of the person who has lawful authority to consent has been obtained or where there is reasonable belief on the part of the police official performing the search and seizure that the warrant would be granted, and that any delay would thwart the object of the search and seizure (s. 32).
1274. In terms of s. 40 of the Criminal Procedure Act 51 of 1977. *See supra* para. 510.
1275. Cybercrimes Act 25 of 2020, s. 33.
1276. Failure to assist a police official or investigator (s. 34); obstructing or hindering a police official or investigator (s. 35).
1277. Wrongful search, access or seizure and restriction on use of instrument, device, password or decryption key or information to gain access (s. 37); providing false information under oath or by way of affirmation (s. 38); unauthorised disclosure of information (s. 39). In addition, the Act provides that the powers conferred upon a police official or investigator must be conducted in a decent and orderly manner with due regard to the rights of other persons (s. 36).

Fingerprints, palm prints, footprints and photographs may be taken by any police official.[1278] Identification parades – including the so-called voice-identification parade – may also be held by any police official.

This section should be approached bearing in mind the requirements of the Constitution.[1279] The taking of fingerprints does not violate the accused's right to remain silent or his right to dignity.[1280] However, this section does not authorise the removal of a bullet under general anaesthetic.[1281]

II. Blood Samples

529. Police officials may not take blood samples.[1282] Authority to take blood samples is confined to medical officers of any prison and district surgeons, that is, medical practitioners employed by the state. But there are two exceptions to this rule. *First*, any registered medical practitioner or registered nurse may take a blood sample if requested thereto by a police official.[1283] *Second*, if any registered medical practitioner attached to any hospital is on reasonable grounds of the opinion that the contents of the blood of any person admitted to such hospital for medical attention or treatment may be relevant in any later criminal proceedings, such medical practitioner may take a blood sample of such person or cause such sample to be taken.[1284]

III. Identification Parades

530. The specific procedure to be adopted in conducting an identification parade is not regulated by statute, even though the power to hold one is granted by statute. South African courts, however, have laid down certain rules in terms of which a parade should be conducted. These rules are not rules of law but merely rules of practice aimed at enhancing the weight of the evidence of identification.[1285] Non-compliance with these rules does not render the evidence of identification inadmissible but can make it worthless.

The following rules of practice are the most important:[1286]

1278. The Criminal Law (Forensic Procedures) Amendment Act 6 of 2010 regulates the taking, usage, storage, retention and destruction of finger-prints, body-prints and photographic images and the keeping of databases, and authorises comparative searches against other databases and security measures relating to the integrity of information stored on the databases.
1279. J.J. Joubert et al., *Criminal Procedure Handbook* 13th ed. (Juta, Cape Town 2020) 185. In particular, the right to dignity (s. 10) and the right to freedom and security of the person (s. 12) fall to be considered.
1280. *S v. Huma* 1995 (2) SACR 411 (W).
1281. *Minister of Safety and Security v. Xaba* 2004 (1) SACR 149 (D).
1282. Criminal Procedure Act 51 of 1977, s. 37(1)(*c*).
1283. Criminal Procedure Act 51 of 1977, s. 37(2)(*a*).
1284. Criminal Procedure Act 51 of 1977, s. 37(2)(*b*).
1285. *See generally*, *S v. Mlati* 1984 (4) SA 629 (A); *R v. Kola* 1949 (1) PH H100 (A).
1286. *See* E. du Toit et al., *Commentary on the Criminal Procedure Act* (Juta, Cape Town 1987) 3–18ff.

1. The police official in charge of the parade should not be the investigating official, that is, the official who is charged with the investigation of the crime in respect of which the parade is held.
2. The suspect and the persons on the parade should be more or less of the same build, height, age and appearance.
3. The parade ('line-up') should in principle consist of at least eight to ten persons, and a greater number is desirable.
4. The police official in charge of the parade should inform the suspect that he may initially take up any position in the line-up and may change his position before any other identifying witness is called.
5. Identifying witnesses should be kept apart from each other and should not be able to see the line-up being formed or re-formed.

IV. Destruction of Certain Evidence

531. In certain cases, any relevant body-prints or photographic images collected in terms of section 37 must be destroyed within thirty days of notification being made to the relevant authority.[1287] This is required in the following circumstances: where a decision was made not to prosecute a person, or where the person is found not guilty at his or her trial, or if his or her conviction is set aside by a superior court, or if he or she is discharged at a preparatory examination, or if no criminal proceedings were instituted against the person concerned, or if the prosecution declines to prosecute.

V. Furnishing of Name and Address

532. A peace officer may call upon any person whom he has power to arrest or who is reasonably suspected of having committed or of having attempted to commit an offence or who, in the opinion of the peace officer, may be able to give evidence in regard to the commission or suspected commission of any offence, to furnish him with his full name and address. If such person fails to comply, the peace officer may arrest him.[1288] It is an offence to fail to furnish a name and address or to furnish a false or incorrect name and address.[1289]

§6. Interrogation of Witnesses and Suspects

I. Witnesses

533. A potential witness who refuses to make a statement to the police in the course of the latter's investigation of a crime or alleged crime can be compelled to

1287. Criminal Procedure Act 51 of 1977, s. 37(6)(*a*)(iii).
1288. Criminal Procedure Act 51 of 1977, s. 41(1).
1289. Criminal Procedure Act 51 of 1977, s. 41(2).

appear before a judicial officer to answer questions put by a prosecutor. This procedure takes place in terms of section 205 of the Criminal Procedure Act 51 of 1977 and is discussed in paragraph 498 *supra*. The witness who refuses to respond when asked relevant questions before the magistrate and who does so in the absence of a lawful excuse commits an offence.[1290] The witness is entitled to legal representation.[1291]

A lawful excuse exists where it is humanly intolerable for the witness concerned to disclose the required information[1292] or where he can legitimately rely on an evidential privilege,[1293] including the privilege against self-incrimination. However, where the witness relies on his privilege against self-incrimination, the prosecutor may invoke section 204 of the Criminal Procedure Act 51 of 1977. This section was discussed in paragraph 472. In terms of section 204, the witness is made an offer of indemnity to prosecution and is then required to answer questions. He commits an offence if he persists in his refusal to disclose information after having been warned by the court in terms of section 204 of the Criminal Procedure Act 1977 that he is obliged to answer, has prospects of indemnity, and cannot rely on the privilege against self-incrimination.

II. Police Questioning of Suspects: The Judges' Rules

534. Police questioning of suspects should in principle proceed in terms of the so-called Judges' Rules. However, these rules are not rules of law – despite the fact that they are known as the 'Judges' Rules'. These rules were compiled by South African judges in 1931 and were issued by the Executive as administrative directives to guide the police and to provide some protection to suspects. The failure of the police to comply with the Judges' Rules in their questioning of a suspect does not mean that the suspect's statement is automatically inadmissible in a court of law. Failure to comply with the Judges' Rules is only one factor to be taken into account in determining whether a statement was made freely and voluntarily and without undue influence.[1294] But in at least one Supreme Court decision, it was stated that serious consideration should be given to declaring that the Judges' Rules impose a duty on the police and that material non-observance of this duty should ordinarily render the incriminating statement inadmissible.[1295]

535. The Judges' Rules consist of the following ten rules:

Rule (1): Questions may be put by policemen to persons whom they do not suspect of being concerned in the commission of the crime under investigation, without any caution being first administered.

1290. Criminal Procedure Act 51 of 1977, s. 205(2) as read with s. 189. In terms of s. 205(4), such witness shall not be sentenced to imprisonment unless the judicial officer is of the opinion that the information is necessary for the administration of justice or the maintenance of law and order.
1291. *S v. Nkosi* 1990 (1) SACR 509 (N).
1292. *Attorney-General, Transvaal v. Kader* 1991 (4) SA 727 (A).
1293. *See generally*, *Smit v. Van Niekerk* N.O. 1976 (4) SA 304 (E).
1294. *R v. Kuzwayo* 1949 (3) SA 761 (A) 767–768.
1295. *S v. Mpetha (2)* 1983 (1) SA 576 (C).

Rule (2): Questions may be put to a person whom the police have decided to arrest or who is under suspicion where it is possible that the person by his answers may afford information which may tend to establish his innocence, as, for instance, where he has been found in possession of property suspected to have been stolen, or of an instrument suspected to have been used in the commission of the crime, or where he was seen in the vicinity about the time when a crime was committed. In such a case, caution should first be administered. Questions, the sole purpose of which is that answers may afford evidence against the person suspected, should not be put.

Rule (3): The caution to be administered in terms of Rule 2 should be to the following effect: 'I am a police officer. I am making inquiries (into so and so) and I want to know anything you can tell me about it. It is a serious matter and I must warn you to be careful what you say.' Where there is any special matter as to which an explanation is desired, the officer should add words such as: 'You have been found in possession of . . . and unless you can explain this I may have to arrest you.'

Rule (4): Questions should not be put to a person in custody with the exception of questions put in terms of Rule (7).

Rule (5): Where a person in custody wishes to volunteer a statement, he should be allowed to make it, but he should first be cautioned.

Rule (6): A statement made by a prisoner before there is time to caution him is not rendered inadmissible in evidence, merely by reason of no caution having been given prior to the commencement of his statement, but in such a case he should be cautioned as soon as possible.

Rule (7): A prisoner making a voluntary statement must not be cross-examined, but questions may be put to him solely for the purpose of removing elementary or obvious ambiguities in voluntary statements. For instance, if he has mentioned an hour without saying whether it was morning or evening or has given a day of the week and day of the month which do not agree, or has not made it clear to what individual or what place he intended to refer in some part of his statement, he may be questioned sufficiently to clear up the point.

Rule (8): The caution to be administered to a person in custody should be to the following effect:

a. Where he is formally charged: 'Do you wish to say anything in answer to the charge? You are not obliged to do so, but whatever you say will be taken down in writing and may be used in evidence.'
b. Where a prisoner volunteers a statement otherwise than on a formal charge: 'Before you say anything (or, if he has already commenced his statement, "anything further"), I must tell you that you are not obliged to do so, but whatever you say will be taken down in writing and may be given in evidence.'

Rule (9): Any statement made in accordance with the above rules should, whenever possible, be taken down in writing and in the language in which it was made. It should be read over to the person making it, and he should be given full opportunity to make any corrections there in that he may wish to and should then be invited to sign it.

Rule (10): When two or more persons are charged with the same offence, and a voluntary statement is made by any one of them, the police, if they consider it desirable, may furnish each of the other persons with a copy of such statement, but nothing should be said or done by the police to invite a reply. The police should not read such statement to a person furnished, unless such person is unable to read it and desires that it be read over to him. If a person so furnished desires to make a voluntary statement in reply, the usual caution should be administered.

The fact that the Judges' Rules do not have the force of a rule of law 'does not mean that they are to be ignored'.[1296]

536. A person's silence after he had been warned by the police in his capacity as a suspect that he was not obliged in terms of the Judges' Rules to say anything in answer to a charge put to him during police questioning cannot at his later trial be held against him and cannot be used to rebut any defence raised at the trial.[1297]

III. Other Instances of Detention for Purposes of Interrogation

537. Section 12(1) of the Drugs and Drugs Trafficking Act 140 of 1992 provides that a magistrate may issue a warrant for the arrest and detention of any person whenever it appears to such magistrate from information submitted to him on oath by the Director of Public Prosecutions (DPP) and that there are reasonable grounds for believing that any person is withholding any information as to a drug offence, whether the drug offence has been or is being or is likely to be committed in the Republic or elsewhere.

In terms of section 12(3) of the Drugs and Drugs Trafficking Act, any person arrested and detained in terms of a warrant as described shall be detained until the magistrate orders his release when satisfied that the detainee has satisfactorily replied to all questions at the interrogation or that no useful purpose will be served by his further detention. There is a proviso that the DPP concerned may at any time direct in writing that the interrogation of any particular detainee be discontinued, whereupon that detainee shall be released without delay. The detainee shall be brought before the magistrate within forty-eight hours of his arrest and thereafter not less than once every ten days.

Any person detained in terms of section 12 may at any time make representation in writing to the magistrate relating to his detention or release.

1296. *S v. Sampson and another* 1983 (3) SA 239 (A). The continued application of the Rules in the constitutional era was affirmed in *S v. Nombewu* 1996 (2) SACR 396 (E) at 403.
1297. *S v. Maritz* 1974 (1) SA 266 (NC).

§7. Legal Aid

I. Governmental Structures

538. Legal Aid South Africa, as established by section 2 of the Legal Aid South Africa Act 39 of 2014, renders legal aid to indigent persons. A judge of the High Court is the chairperson of the board which governs this entity.[1298]

II. The *Pro Deo* System

539. All persons, excluding corporate entities, who cannot afford legal representation and who are charged with serious offences in the High Court may be represented by *pro deo* counsel, that is, a legal representative appointed by the High Court and paid by the State.[1299]

The accused may refuse *pro deo* counsel. The trial judge should, however, explain to such an accused that *pro deo* counsel is an independent advocate who is not connected to the police or prosecution.[1300]

540. A major defect in the *pro deo* system is that experienced counsel are normally not available for this kind of appointment and the result is that relatively inexperienced counsel are as a rule called upon to defend an accused in respect of the most serious of offences.

III. The Public Defender System

541. In 1997, Legal Aid South Africa decided to move towards a system of salaried legal practitioners as the primary means by which legal aid would in the future be provided. Legal aid is currently provided throughout South Africa through a network of 128 client-serving offices, of which 64 are local offices and 64 are satellite offices, which are in turn supported by six provincial offices and one national office.[1301]

1298. *See* E. du Toit et al., *Commentary on the Criminal Procedure Act* (Juta, Cape Town 1987) 11–11ff.

1299. *See S v. Ndlovu; S v. Sibisi* 2005 (2) SACR 645 (W) 655e-f; J.J. Joubert et al., *Criminal Procedure Handbook* 13th ed. (Juta, Cape Town 2020) 112–114.

1300. *S v. Tyebela* 1989 (2) SA 22 (A).

1301. www.legal-aid.co.za (last accessed 30 Jun. 2016).

Chapter 3. Pre-trial Proceedings

§1. The Decision to Prosecute

I. The Discretion to Prosecute

542. The principle of compulsory prosecution (also referred to as the principle of legality in some legal systems) does not apply in the South African criminal justice system. Directors of Public Prosecutions and their prosecutors who are controlled by them have a discretion whether or not to prosecute.

A public prosecution is instituted if the public prosecutor is satisfied that the police investigation is complete, that there are reasonable prospects of success and that there is no compelling reason to decline to prosecute. Any decision taken by a local public prosecutor can be overruled by the DPP concerned.[1302]

543. A compelling reason for declining to prosecute may be the triviality of the offence (*de minimis non curat lex*), the ill-health of the accused, the antiquated nature of the offence or the advanced age (or relatively young age) of the accused concerned. One former attorney-general has described the discretion as 'a very valuable safeguard, because one has to take into account ... what the consequences to [an accused] may be, apart from any penalty which a court of law might inflict. If, in our view, the consequences are out of all proportion to the gravity of the offence committed, we are permitted to exercise our discretion and decline to prosecute'.[1303]

There is a rule of practice in terms of which any accused, or his legal representative acting upon his instructions, may make representations to a DPP to decline to prosecute.

II. The Discretion and the Executive

544. The executive authority cannot interfere with any decision taken by the DPP. However, the Minister of Justice has the statutory authority to request the NDPP to furnish him or her with information or a report with regard to any case, matter or subject dealt with or handled by the NDPP or a DPP in the performance of their duties or the exercise of their powers and, further, to provide him or her with the reasons for any decision taken by the DPP concerned in the performance of his duties or the exercise of his discretion.[1304]

1302. *See* para. 490 *supra*.
1303. P. Yutar, 'The Office of Attorney-General in South Africa' 1977 *SACC* 136.
1304. National Prosecuting Authority Act 32 of 1998, s. 33(2).

III. The Discretion and the Judiciary

545. Courts have on occasion expressed their disapproval of the fact that a prosecution was instituted. However, they cannot interfere with the prosecution. They can, at most, in the event of a conviction, impose a lenient sentence reflecting their opinion that the prosecution was unwarranted. If convinced of the triviality of the case, the court may acquit the accused.[1305] But this is done on the basis of substantive criminal law principles, and not as a way of interfering with the prosecution.

On the whole, courts are reluctant to comment on the discretion exercised by the prosecuting authority.[1306]

546. Courts have refused to issue a *mandamus* (i.e., a particular court order) to compel the prosecuting authority to prosecute.[1307] And a court will not as a rule interdict the prosecuting authority from prosecuting where it has decided to do so.[1308] It has also been held that a court cannot compel the prosecuting authority to decide within a specified period whether it intends to prosecute certain accused.[1309]

547. A court can intervene where the prosecuting authority exercises its discretion to prosecute improperly.[1310]

IV. Withdrawal of the Charge

548. A Director of Public Prosecutions (DPP) or public prosecutor may, *before an accused has pleaded to a charge*, withdraw that charge. However, the accused is then not entitled to a verdict or acquittal.[1311] He may at a later stage be re-charged, for example, where new evidence comes to light. A public prosecutor may withdraw a charge without the consent of the DPP, as the latter has the residual power to prosecute the accused afresh if dissatisfied with the prosecutor's withdrawal of the charge.

V. Stopping the Prosecution

549. A Director of Public Prosecutions may at any time, *after an accused has pleaded but before conviction*, stop the prosecution in respect of that charge. If this

1305. *See supra*, para. 237.
1306. *See generally*, F.G. Richings, 'The Prosecutor's Discretion: A Plea for Circumspection' 1977 *SACC* 143, 144.
1307. *Gillingham v. Attorney-General* 1909 TS 572.
1308. *Allen v. Attorney-General* 1936 CPD 302.
1309. *Wronsky v. Prokureur-Generaal* 1971 (3) SA 292 (SWA).
1310. *Highstead Entertainment (Pty) Ltd t/a 'The Club' v. Minister of Law and Order* 1994 (1) SA 387 (C). *See Freedom under Law v. National Director of Public Prosecutions* 2014 (1) SA 254 (GNP) para. 124, where it was held that a court may interfere where the discretion is improperly exercised, *mala fide* or deployed for ulterior purposes.
1311. Criminal Procedure Act 51 of 1977, s. 6(*a*).

is done, the accused is entitled to an acquittal[1312] and can in any subsequent prosecution in respect of the same facts successfully rely on a plea of previous acquittal (*autrefois acquit*).

However, a public prosecutor may not stop a prosecution without the consent of the DPP or someone properly authorised by the DPP to consent thereto.[1313] In the absence of such consent, the DPP is in the general interest of the community entitled to prosecute again.[1314]

VI. Acceptance by a Prosecutor of an Accused's Plea

550. A prosecutor may in the exercise of his discretion accept an accused's plea of guilty to a lesser offence than the one charged, for example, a plea of *guilty* to culpable homicide, which is a lesser offence to a charge of murder. It has been held that acceptance of a plea of guilty to a lesser offence limits the ambit of the dispute between the accused and the prosecution.[1315] Only in limited circumstances can the main charge be revived.[1316]

The prosecutor's acceptance of an accused's plea of *not guilty* does, however, amount to a stopping of the prosecution and the trial court may then enquire from the prosecutor whether he has the necessary consent of the Director of Public Prosecutions to stop the prosecution.[1317]

§2. Committal Proceedings

551. The elaborate preparatory examination provided for in sections 123–143 of the Criminal Procedure Act 51 of 1977 has virtually become obsolete. The present situation is that the prosecution relies on other sections[1318] in the same Act, which make provision for summary trials and which are aimed at expediting committal proceedings. What follows is a broad outline.

552. In the vast majority of cases, an accused's first appearance is in the magistrates' court. The case can be disposed of in the magistrates' court if this court has the necessary territorial, penal and substantive jurisdiction. If territorial jurisdiction is lacking, the court must refer the case to the court which has such jurisdiction.[1319]

553. If the magistrates' court lacks penal or substantive jurisdiction and the charge is therefore only justiciable in the regional or High Court, the accused may

1312. Criminal Procedure Act 51 of 1977, s. 6 (*b*).
1313. *See*, the proviso in s. 6(*b*) of the Criminal Procedure Act 51 of 1977.
1314. *S v. Van Niekerk* 1985 (4) SA 550 (B); *S v. Tengo* 2003 (1) SACR 162 (SCA).
1315. *S v. Ngubane* 1985 (3) SA 677 (A).
1316. Criminal Procedure Act 51 of 1977, s. 113(2).
1317. *S v. Van Niekerk* (*supra*).
1318. *See generally*, Criminal Procedure Act 51 of 1977, s. 115A to s. 122D.
1319. Criminal Procedure Act 51 of 1977, s. 110.

nevertheless be called upon to plead in the magistrates' court.[1320] He is then questioned in terms of section 112(1)(*b*) in the event of a plea of guilty and in terms of section 115 in the event of a plea of not guilty. The purpose, nature and ambit of the questioning are the same as if the accused is on trial. Judicial examination of the accused is discussed in paragraphs 629 and 635 *infra*. Questioning that takes place in respect of a charge justiciable in the regional or High Court is known as the 'abbreviated preparatory examination'.

554. Two important principles apply during the proceedings of the abbreviated preparatory examination: first, an accused who has pleaded not guilty must be informed that he need not respond to any questions put by the court. Second, neither the prosecutor nor the accused leads any evidence at this stage. The accused, who wishes to respond to the court's questioning, is not under oath. His explanation is therefore not 'evidence' in the true sense of the word. He may not be questioned by the prosecutor.

555. Upon completion of the so-called abbreviated preparatory examination, the proceedings are adjourned pending the decision of the Director of Public Prosecutions as regards the final charges and the appropriate forum where the accused will stand trial – subject to the fact that treason is only triable by the High Court.

556. The record of the proceedings in the magistrates' court may be proved in the court in which the accused is finally arraigned for trial.[1321] However, the accused has the right to dispute the record. He may, for example, dispute the plea or any admission made by him during the abbreviated preparatory examination.

557. The accused has the right to be represented by a lawyer at every stage of committal proceedings.

§3. Indictments and Charges

I. Terminology

558. The first step in the process of prosecuting a criminal charge is the initial investigation by the police,[1322] following a complaint received by the public, or on their own initiative, or following instructions received from the prosecuting authority.[1323] Police prepare a docket (a file or dossier), which is submitted to the prosecutor, who makes the decision whether or not to prosecute, exercising the prosecutorial discretion in this regard by examining the available evidence, both documentary and real, and if deemed necessary, requiring the investigating police

1320. *See* e.g., Criminal Procedure Act 51 of 1977, s. 119.
1321. *See* e.g., Criminal Procedure Act 51 of 1977, s. 121(5)(*a*).
1322. J.J. Joubert et al. (eds), *Criminal Procedure Handbook* 13th ed. (Juta, Cape Town 2020) 73.
1323. National Prosecuting Authority Act 32 of 1998, s. 24(4)(*c*)(i).

officer assigned to the matter to engage in further investigations.[1324] The prosecutor does not however personally engage in any investigation, which facilitates objectivity and the possible independent evaluation of the police investigation.[1325] Once a prosecutor is satisfied that there is enough evidence to provide reasonable prospects of a conviction, a prosecution typically follows.[1326]The document stating the offence(s) that the accused is allegedly guilty of is known as an 'indictment' for purposes of a High Court trial[1327] and as a 'charge' for purposes of a lower court trial.

II. Rules Peculiar to an Indictment

559. The rules which govern an indictment and charge are the same except for the following rules, which are peculiar to an indictment:

1. An indictment must be lodged with the registrar of the superior court and must be signed by the Director of Public Prosecutions concerned.
2. An indictment must be accompanied by a summary of the salient facts of the case[1328] as well as a list of the names and addresses of witnesses whom the prosecution intends to call.[1329]
3. Service of the indictment and notice of trial must take place at least ten days before trial unless the accused agrees to a shorter period.[1330]

III. Indictments and Charges: Rights of the Accused

560. The term 'charge' as used in the rest of this discussion includes 'indictment'.

A. *The Right to Be Informed*

561. Section 84 of the Criminal Procedure Act 51 of 1977 determines that a charge shall set forth the relevant offence in such manner and with such particulars as to the time and place at which the offence is alleged to have been committed and the person, if any, against whom and the property, if any, in respect of which the

---

1324. J.J. Joubert et al. (eds), *Criminal Procedure Handbook* 13th ed. (Juta, Cape Town 2020) 73.
1325. J.J. Joubert et al. (eds), *Criminal Procedure Handbook* 13th ed. (Juta, Cape Town 2019) 73.
1326. Unless public policy demands otherwise – *see* para. 4(*c*) of the Prosecution Policy issued by the National Director of Public Prosecutions, read with the National Prosecuting Authority Act 32 of 1998, s. 21(1)(*a*).
1327. Criminal Procedure Act 51 of 1977, s. 144(1).
1328. Criminal Procedure Act 51 of 1977, s. 144(3)(*a*).
1329. In certain circumstances, the DPP may withhold names and addresses. *See* Criminal Procedure Act 51 of 1977, s. 144(3)(*a*)(ii).
1330. Criminal Procedure Act 51 of 1977, s. 144(4)(*a*).

offence is alleged to have been committed, as may be *reasonably sufficient* to inform the accused of the nature of the charge.[1331]

Before evidence is led, an accused may in writing request further particulars from the prosecution, and the court may order delivery of such particulars.[1332] The test in determining the need for further particulars is whether the accused requires information (in addition to that contained in the charge) in order to adequately prepare for his trial.[1333] Whenever further particulars are furnished, the prosecution must prove the charge as particularised.[1334]

B. The Right to Examine Charge

562. An accused has an absolute right to examine the charge at any stage of the relevant criminal proceedings.[1335]

C. The Right to Object to the Charge

563. An accused may – before pleading – object to the charge on one or more of the following grounds:[1336] that the charge does not comply with the provisions of the Criminal Procedure Act 51 of 1977; that an essential element of the offence is not averred; that no offence is disclosed; that insufficient particulars are furnished; or that he (the accused) is incorrectly identified or described in the charge. The court may in its discretion quash the charge.[1337]

D. The Right to Have Character Protected

564. It may not in any charge be alleged that an accused has previously been convicted of an offence, whether in South Africa or elsewhere.[1338] The only exception is where the fact of a previous conviction is an element of the offence charged, for example, where the charge is one of escaping from lawful custody.

IV. Statutory Provisions Favouring the Prosecution

A. Defect in Charge Cured by Evidence

565. Where a charge is defective for the want of an averment which is an essential ingredient of the relevant offence, the defect shall, unless brought to the notice

1331. *See also generally*, *Levenstein v. S* [2013] 4 All SA 528 (SA) para. 98; *S v. Rosenthal* 1980 (1) SA 65 (A) 98E–G; *S v. Hugo* 1979 (4) SA 536 (A) 540E.
1332. Criminal Procedure Act 51 of 1977, s. 87.
1333. *R v. Mokgoetsi* 1943 AD 622.
1334. *R v. Verity-Amm* 1934 TPD 416 422.
1335. Criminal Procedure Act 51 of 1977, s. 80.
1336. Criminal Procedure Act 51 of 1977, s. 85.
1337. Criminal Procedure Act 51 of 1977, s. 85(2)(b).
1338. Criminal Procedure Act 51 of 1977, s. 89.

of the court before judgment, be cured by evidence at the trial proving the matter which should have been averred.[1339] The courts insist, however, that in applying this rule, there must be no prejudice to the accused.[1340]

B. Charges Where It is Doubtful What Offence Was Committed

566. If by reason of any uncertainty as to the facts which can be proved or if, for any other reason, it is doubtful which of several offences is constituted by the facts which can be proved, the accused may be charged with the commission of all or any of such offences, and any number of such charges may be tried at once, or the accused may be charged in the alternative with the commission of any number of such offences.[1341] However, when it comes to verdict, the rule against double jeopardy applies and there may therefore be no duplication of convictions in respect of the same criminal conduct.[1342]

C. Charge Need Not Specify or Negative Certain Defences

567. In criminal proceedings, any exception, exemption, proviso, excuse or qualification, whether it does or does not accompany in the same section the description of the offence in the law creating the offence, may be proved by the accused but need not be specified or negatived in the charge and, if so specified or negatived, need not be proved by the prosecution.[1343] This means that on a charge of, for example, illegal possession of a drug, the state need not allege and need not prove that the accused had no permit to possess such a drug. But the accused may of course raise possession of a permit as a defence to the charge.

§4. Plea Bargaining and Other Transactions

568. Plea bargaining as a negotiating process between the defence and prosecution – and which does not involve the bench – has always taken place.[1344] As a result of these negotiations, the prosecutor might accept a plea of guilty to a lesser charge, or the defence might plead guilty in respect of certain charges upon the withdrawal by the prosecution of others. There is no involvement of the bench as regards the

1339. Criminal Procedure Act 51 of 1977, s. 88.
1340. *S v. Slabbert* 1968 (3) SA 318 (O).
1341. Criminal Procedure Act 51 of 1977, s. 83.
1342. *See generally*, E. du Toit, et al., *Commentary on the Criminal Procedure Act* (Juta, Cape Town 1987) 14–5 to 14–14A.
1343. Criminal Procedure Act 51 of 1977, s. 90.
1344. *See generally*, D. van Zyl Smit & N.M. Isakow, 'The Decision on How to Plead: A Study of Plea Negotiation in Supreme Court Criminal Matters' 1986 *SACC* 3.

appropriate sentence. The prosecution and defence cannot agree on the appropriate sentence. It is the duty of the court to impose sentence.[1345]

It is generally recognised that any form of plea negotiation may not be of such a nature that the accused's right to tender a plea freely and voluntarily is infringed.[1346] The lawyer for the defence must ensure that his client is not put under undue pressure to tender an incorrect plea of guilty merely to gain the advantage of having other charges withdrawn.

Plea bargaining was formalised at the end of the 1970s in South African law. Section. 105A of the Criminal Procedure Act essentially codifies the practice, also providing for the prosecutor to reach an agreement with the defence on sentence. The plea agreement takes place between an 'authorised in writing' prosecutor and a legally represented accused and does not involve the judicial officer. Section 105A is intended to be utilised for those 'matters of some substance' which if disposed of will serve the purpose of 'decongesting or reducing the court rolls' without sacrificing the demands of justice and or the public interest.[1347] While statistics on plea agreements are hard to come by, these considerations are intended to determine the matters dealt with under section 105A.

The judicial officer must question the accused on the contents of the agreement in court in order to satisfy herself whether the accused is admitting all elements of the offence. If so satisfied, the court proceeds to the matter of sentence without, for the moment, recording a conviction. If, upon consideration of the sentencing agreement, the court is satisfied that it is just, the court will accordingly convict the accused and sentence him accordingly. If the court deems that the sentence agreement is not just, it informs the parties what it considers to be just, and the parties can either elect to abide by the agreement on the merits, allowing the court to consider sentence in the normal way, or one of the parties can withdraw from the agreement, requiring that the trial begins *de novo* before another judicial officer, a judge or magistrate, as the case may be. Although in respect of the latter scenario it is prohibited to plea bargain in terms of section 105A in respect of a charge arising from the same facts,[1348] traditional plea bargaining as it exists in practice may still take place in respect of either scenario, although this would be in terms of an informal agreement rather than the formal agreement regulated by statute.[1349]

569. In respect of certain minor offences (largely statutory offences), a special procedure applies whereby an accused may pay an admission of guilt fine without

1345. On traditional plea bargaining, *see* J.J. Joubert et al., *Criminal Procedure Handbook* 13th ed. (Juta, Cape Town 2020) 310.
1346. E. du Toit et al., *Commentary on the Criminal Procedure Act* (Juta, Cape Town 1987) 15–18.
1347. In terms of the directives issued by the NDPP and tabled before Parliament on 22 Oct. 2010. *See*, further, M.B. Rodgers, 'The Development and Operation of Negotiated Justice in the South African Criminal Justice System' 2010 *SACJ* 239 248.
1348. Criminal Procedure Act 51 of 1977, s. 105A(10).
1349. J.J. Joubert et al., *Criminal Procedure Handbook* 13th ed. (Juta, Cape Town 2020) 310.

appearing in court.[1350] Upon payment, the accused is deemed to have been convicted and sentenced by a court of law.[1351] The clerk of the court enters the admission of guilt in the criminal record book of the court. The so-called fine may not exceed ZAR 10,000.00 (at exchange rates applicable at time of writing: GBP 420/USD 550/EUR 500) and is determined by the prosecuting authorities and is subject to review by the magistrate of the district concerned. As is the case for plea bargaining, the payment of the admission of guilt fine must be ratified by the relevant judicial officer. Appearance in court is necessary where the accused refuses to pay the admission of guilt or where the payment of the fine is held to be insufficient or not in accordance with justice by the magistrate concerned. The prosecution is then required to prove its case in the ordinary way.

Provision is also made for a prosecutor to, by way of endorsement delivered to the accused, allow the accused to admit guilt and pay a fine after appearing in court, before the accused has entered a plea, and if the prosecutor on reasonable grounds believes that a magistrate's court upon conviction will not impose a fine exceeding the amount determined by the Minister.[1352] The Minister may further, after consultation, *inter alia,* with the NDPP, declare any offence or category of offences as an offence that does not result in a previous conviction of an accused.[1353] Where a person obtains a criminal record, having paid an admission of guilt fine for such an offence, the criminal record will be automatically expunged by the Criminal Record Centre of the SAPS.[1354]

570. Compounding of certain minor offences (largely traffic offences) is also possible in the South African criminal justice system.[1355] This means that upon payment of a sum of money to the authorities, no prosecution will be instituted. The amount may not exceed the amount that a court would probably have imposed as a fine.

1350. Criminal Procedure Act 51 of 1977, s. 57.

1351. *See generally*, S.E. van der Merwe & J.J. Büchner, 'The Admission of Guilt Fine' 1986 *SACC* 49; *see NGJ Trading Stores (Pty) Ltd v. Guerreiro* 1974 (4) SA 738 (A). An admission of guilt is regarded as a previous conviction for the purposes of all offences.

1352. Criminal Procedure Act 51 of 1977, s. 57A.

1353. Criminal Procedure Act 51 of 1977, s. 57B. The following grounds or criteria must be considered in this determination: (i) the offence must statutory in nature and punishable with a fine, without or with an alternative sentence of imprisonment not exceeding six months in default of payment of a fine; (ii) the offence must not: contain an element of violence, involve the infliction of mental, psychological or physical harm on another person, involve damage to property, involve an element of dishonesty, involve cruelty to animals, be an offence against the administration of justice, or cause pecuniary or economic loss to another person; and (iii) where a criminal record cannot be regarded as an appropriate mechanism to encourage compliance with the law.

1354. Criminal Procedure Act 51 of 1977, s. 57C, read with s. 57B(1).

1355. Criminal Procedure Act 51 of 1977, s. 341.

§5. Pre-trial Detention

I. Witnesses

A. *Pre-trial Detention of Witness on Application by Director of Public Prosecutions (DPP)*

571. In exceptional circumstances, a DPP may apply to a judge in chambers to have a prospective prosecution witness detained pending the proceedings in which the witness will testify.[1356]

The consent of the witness is not required. The DPP may only bring such an application in respect of certain serious offences and if he is from information placed before him of the opinion that the personal safety of such person is in danger, or that he may abscond or be tampered with or intimidated. The application is made *in camera*. A witness may only be detained in terms of a warrant issued by a judge, except for an initial seventy-two-hour period of detention, which may be ordered by the DPP if he is satisfied that there should be no delay in detaining the witness.

The period of detention, in terms of a judge's warrant, terminates on the day on which the relevant criminal proceedings are concluded unless proceedings are not commenced within six months from the date on which the witness was detained, in which case the accused shall be released after the expiry of such period. The DPP may also order an earlier release.[1357]

572. A lawyer is only permitted access to a detained witness with the consent of and subject to such conditions as determined by a DPP or other state official delegated by the DPP.[1358] A magistrate must visit the witness in private at least once a week.[1359]

B. *Pre-trial Detention of a Witness on His Own Application*

573. In terms of the Witness Protection Act of 1998, any witness who has reason to believe that his or her safety or the safety of any related person is or may be threatened by any person or persons whether known to him or not may report to a designated person and apply in the prescribed manner that he or she or any related person be placed under protection.[1360] The Director of the Office for Witness Protection may approve or refuse an application for protection.

1356. Criminal Procedure Act 51 of 1977, s. 185. Section 185(9) determines that a 'judge in chambers' means a judge sitting behind closed doors when hearing the relevant application.
1357. Criminal Procedure Act 51 of 1977, s. 185(4).
1358. Criminal Procedure Act 51 of 1977, s. 185(5).
1359. Criminal Procedure Act 51 of 1977, s. 185(6).
1360. Witness Protection Act 112 of 1998, s. 7.

II. Accused

574. There are several ways in which an accused who is in custody pending trial may be released on condition that he will attend his trial.

An accused who is under the age of 18 and who is in custody in respect of any offence may be placed in an appropriate child and youth care centre or a police cell or lock-up, in terms of the Child Justice Act of 2008.[1361]

In certain circumstances, a court may release an accused on warning pending his trial.[1362]

A. Bail: Nature, Purpose and Effect

575. The most important method of pre-trial release of an accused is by granting bail to him. The effect[1363] of bail is that an accused who is in custody shall be released from custody upon payment of, or the furnishing of a guarantee to pay, the sum of money determined for his bail and that he shall appear at the place and on the date and at the time appointed for his trial or to which the proceedings relating to the offence in respect of which the accused is released on bail are adjourned.[1364] The accused's release shall, unless sooner terminated, endure until a verdict is given by a court in respect of the charge to which the offence in question relates, or, where sentence is not imposed forthwith after verdict and the court in question extends bail, until sentence is imposed.

576. Bail has been described as 'an ordinary contract by which an accused undertakes to appear on a particular day, failing which the money deposited can be forfeited ... .'[1365]

577. The purpose of bail is to strike a balance between, on the one hand, the interests of society (the accused should stand his trial and there should be no interference with the administration of justice) and, on the other hand, the liberty of the accused (who, pending the outcome of his trial, is presumed to be innocent).[1366]

1361. Child Justice Act 75 of 2008, s. 27, provides that the police official must give consideration to detaining any child 12 years or older, but under 14 years, or any child 14 years or older charged with a Schedule 1 or 2 offence in an appropriate child or youth care centre, if available, and if unavailable in a police cell or lock-up. A child 14 years or older charged with a Schedule 3 offence must be detained in a police cell or lock-up.

1362. Criminal Procedure Act 51 of 1977, ss 63A, 72.

1363. Criminal Procedure Act 51 of 1977, s. 58.

1364. Constitution, 1996, s. 35(1)(*f*) states that everyone who is arrested for allegedly committing an offence has the right to be released from detention if the interests of justice permit, subject to reasonable conditions.

1365. *Da Costa v. The Magistrate, Windhoek* 1983 (2) SA 732 (SWA) 747H. Bail is non-penal in character – *S v. Acheson* 1991 (2) SA 805 (Nm) 822A.

1366. *See* E. du Toit, et al., *Commentary on the Criminal Procedure Act* (Juta, Cape Town 1987) 9–1ff.; J.J. Joubert et al., *Criminal Procedure Handbook* 11th ed. (Juta, Cape Town 2014) 210ff.

B. Bail Granted by Police or Authorised by DPP

578. In respect of certain minor offences, any police official of or above the rank of non-commissioned officer may release an accused on bail prior to the latter's first court appearance.[1367] An action for damages will lie if the refusal is malicious.[1368]

579. A Director of Public Prosecutions (or a prosecutor authorised by her) may authorise the release of an accused, charged with an offence contained in Schedule 7 of the Criminal Procedure Act, on bail.[1369]

C. Bail Application in Court

580. An accused who is in custody in respect of any offence shall, subject to the provisions of section 50(6) of the Criminal Procedure Act, be entitled to be released on bail at any stage preceding his conviction in respect of such offence, if the court is satisfied that the interests of justice so permit.[1370] If aggrieved by the refusal of a lower court to admit him to bail or by the imposition by such court of a condition of bail, an accused may appeal to the High Court having jurisdiction.[1371] If unsuccessful, a further appeal against the decision of the High Court is possible, with the leave of that court, to the SCA. If the High Court was the Court of First Instance, there is a right of appeal without prior leave to the SCA. A DPP may appeal to the High Court against the decision of a lower court to release an accused on bail or a condition thereof[1372] and may also appeal to the SCA against the decision of a High Court to release an accused on bail.[1373] A successful appeal will result in the issuing of a warrant of arrest.

581. A bail application should be treated as a matter of urgency.[1374]

582. Bail may not be fixed at an amount so high as to amount to a refusal of bail.[1375] Bail must be fixed at an amount which the accused can pay[1376] but which is also high enough to serve as an incentive for him to stand trial and not have the amount forfeited to the state.[1377]

1367. Criminal Procedure Act 51 of 1977, s. 59.
1368. *See generally*, *Shaw v. Collins* 1883 SC 389.
1369. Criminal Procedure Act 51 of 1977, s. 59A.
1370. Criminal Procedure Act 51 of 1977, s. 60(1). Section 50(6)(a) provides that an accused is at his first appearance in court entitled to apply for release on bail, and s. 50(6)(d) provides that a lower court may postpone bail proceedings of a person brought before court for a period not exceeding seven days at a time. An accused is not entitled to bring a bail application outside ordinary court hours – s. 50(6)(b). For release of a child on bail, *see* s. 25 of the Child Justice Act 75 of 2008.
1371. Criminal Procedure Act 51 of 1977, s. 65(1). *See* J.J. Joubert et al., *Criminal Procedure Handbook* 13th ed. (Juta, Cape Town 2020) 216–217.
1372. Criminal Procedure Act 51 of 1977, s. 65A(1)(*a*).
1373. Criminal Procedure Act 51 of 1977, s. 65A(2)(*a*).
1374. *Magistrate, Stutterheim v. Mashiya* 2003 (2) SACR 106 (SCA) 113*c-d*.
1375. *S v. Ho* 1979 (3) SA 734 (W).
1376. *S v. Mohamed* 1977 (2) SA 531 (A).
1377. *R v. Du Plessis* 1957 (4) SA 463 (W).

D. Evidential Rules Governing Bail Applications

583. The burden of proof in bail applications is on the prosecution on a balance of probabilities, unless section 60(11) is applicable.[1378] Section 60(11) provides that where an accused is charged with an offence referred to: (a) in Schedule 6 of the Criminal Procedure Act, the court must order that the accused be detained in custody until dealt with in accordance with the law, unless the accused, having been given a reasonable opportunity to do so, adduces evidence which satisfies the court that exceptional circumstances exist which in the interests of justice permit his release; or (b) in Schedule 5, but not Schedule 6, of the Criminal Procedure Act, the court must order that the accused be detained in custody until dealt with in accordance with the law, unless the accused, having been given a reasonable opportunity to do so, adduces evidence which satisfies the court that the interests of justice permit his release; or (c) contemplated in section 59(1)*(a)*(ii) or (iii), the court shall order that the accused be detained in custody until he or she is dealt with in accordance with the law, unless the accused, having been given a reasonable opportunity to do so, adduces evidence which satisfies the court that the interests of justice permit his or her release.[1379]

584. The strict rules of evidence which apply to trial proceedings are not applicable to bail applications. The principle of orality need not be applied.[1380] Hearsay can readily be received,[1381] as well as the opinion of the investigating police official on the likelihood of the accused absconding if released on bail.[1382] Proof of previous convictions may be proved by the state during the course of a bail application. The accused is compelled to inform the court whether he has previously been convicted of an offence.[1383] The record of the bail proceedings forms part of the record of the trial of the accused following such bail proceedings, so that the trial court will as a rule have access to all evidence led at the bail application.[1384]

1378. *S v. Tshabalala* 1998 (2) SACR 259 (C).
1379. The Constitutional Court held that s. 60(11)(*a*) is constitutional despite placing a burden of proof on the accused to adduce evidence in *S v. Dlamini; Dladla and Others; Joubert; Schietekat* 1999 (2) SACR 51 (CC). Given that the court found a bail application in terms of s. 60(11)(a), more gravely invasive of the accused's right to liberty than that in s. 60(11)(*b*), the latter procedure would be regarded as acceptable. Section 60(11A) facilitates proof of the jurisdictional fact, i.e., the fact necessary to bring a bail applicant within the ambit of s. 60(11).
1380. *S v. Pienaar* 1992 (1) SACR 178 (W).
1381. *S v. Maharaj* 1976 (3) SA 205 (D) 208E.
1382. *S v. Hlongwa* 1979 (4) SA 112 (D).
1383. Criminal Procedure Act 51 of 1977, s. 60(11B)(*a*)(i).
1384. Criminal Procedure Act 51 of 1977, s. 60(11B)(*c*) read with (*a*). If the accused elects to testify during bail proceedings, then in order to protect the accused's fair trial rights, the court is required to inform him that anything he says may be used against him at his subsequent trial, and is admissible in any subsequent proceedings – *see S v. Snyman* 1999 (8) BCLR 931 (C). This section is not unconstitutional – *S v. Dlamini; Dladla and Others; Joubert; Schietekat* 1999 (2) SACR 51 (CC) para. 99.

E. Factors a Court Must Consider in a Bail Application

585. In the exercise of its discretion to grant or refuse bail, there is one all-embracing issue: Will the interests of justice be prejudiced if the accused is granted bail? In assessing this question, it must be borne in mind that if an accused is refused bail in circumstances where he will stand his trial, the interests of justice are also prejudiced.[1385] In terms of section 60(4) of the Criminal Procedure Act, the refusal to grant bail and the detention of an accused in custody shall be in the interests of justice where one or more of the following grounds are established:[1386]

a. where there is the likelihood that the accused, if released on bail, will endanger the safety of the public, any person against whom the offence was allegedly committed or any particular person or will commit a Schedule 1 offence;[1387]
b. where there is the likelihood that the accused, if released on bail, will attempt to evade trial;[1388]
c. where there is the likelihood that the accused, if released on bail, will attempt to influence or intimidate witnesses or to conceal or destroy evidence;[1389]
d. where there is the likelihood that the accused, if released on bail, will undermine or jeopardise the objectives or the proper functioning of the criminal justice system, including the bail system;[1390] or
e. where in exceptional circumstances, there is the likelihood that the release of the accused will disturb the public order or undermine the public peace or security.[1391]

F. Bail Conditions

586. The *general conditions* of bail are that the accused should stand his trial on the date and at the time and place determined by the court granting bail. However, the court may also set further additional conditions. Section 62(*e*) of the Criminal

1385. *S v. Pineiro* 1992 (1) SACR 577 (Nm) 580c-d.
1386. It was held in *S v. Dlamini; Dladla and Others; Joubert; Schietekat* 1999 (2) SACR 51 (CC) that ss 60(4)–(9) are not unconstitutional. In addition to the specific guidelines relating to each of the factors listed in s. 60(4), s. 60(9) sets out guidelines in relation to the weighing up of the interests of justice against the right of the accused to freedom and in particular the prejudice the accused is likely to suffer if detained in custody. In addition, the absence of reasonable prospects of success on appeal may justify refusal of bail – J.J. Joubert et al., *Criminal Procedure Handbook* 13th ed. (Juta, Cape Town 2020) 223.
1387. The guidelines by which this factor must be evaluated are set out in Criminal Procedure Act 51 of 1977, s. 60(5).
1388. The guidelines by which this factor must be evaluated are set out in Criminal Procedure Act 51 of 1977, s. 60(6).
1389. The guidelines by which this factor must be evaluated are set out in Criminal Procedure Act 51 of 1977, s. 60(7).
1390. The guidelines by which this factor must be evaluated are set out in Criminal Procedure Act 51 of 1977, s. 60(8).
1391. The guidelines by which this factor must be evaluated are set out in Criminal Procedure Act 51 of 1977, s. 60(8A).

Procedure Act 51 of 1977 specifically grants the court the power to add such conditions which, in the opinion of the court, will ensure that the proper administration of justice is not placed in jeopardy by the release of the accused. Practical examples of such conditions are that the accused must hand his passport over to the police, that he must report to the police station once a day at a specified time or that he may not leave a specific magisterial district.

Any bail conditions set by the court must be practically feasible[1392] and may not be *ultra vires*[1393] or *contra bonos mores*[1394] or vague and ambiguous.[1395]

587. If an accused is released on bail and the prosecutor applies to the court concerned to lead evidence to prove that the accused has failed to comply with a condition, the court shall, in terms of section 66 of the Criminal Procedure Act, if the accused is present and denies that he failed to comply with such condition or denies that his failure to comply with such condition was due to fault on his part, proceed to hear such evidence as the prosecutor and the accused may place before it. If the accused is not present when the prosecutor applies to the court, the court may issue a warrant for the arrest of the accused, and shall, when the accused appears before the court and denies that he failed to comply with the condition in question or that his failure to comply with such condition was due to fault on his part, proceed to hear such evidence as the prosecutor and the accused may place before it. If the accused admits that he failed to comply with the condition in question or if the court finds that he failed to comply with such condition, the court may, if it finds that the failure by the accused was due to fault on his part, cancel the bail and declare the bail money forfeited to the state.[1396] The accused then remains in custody pending the outcome of his trial.

G. Cancellation of Bail

588. Any court before which a charge is pending in respect of which bail has been granted may, whether the accused has been released or not, issue a warrant for the arrest of the accused and make such order as it may deem proper, including an order that bail is cancelled and that the accused be imprisoned until the conclusion of the relevant criminal proceedings, upon information on oath that:

1. the accused is about to evade justice or is about to abscond in order to evade justice;
2. the accused has interfered or threatened or attempted to interfere with witnesses;
3. the accused has defeated or has attempted to defeat the ends of justice;

1392. *R v. Fourie* 1947 (2) SA 547 (O) 577.
1393. *R v. Conradie* 1907 TS 455.
1394. *See generally*, *De Jager v. Attorney-General, Natal* 1967 (4) SA 143 (D).
1395. *S v. Budlender* 1973 (1) SA 264 (C) 271 A.
1396. Criminal Procedure Act 51 of 1977, s. 66(3).

4. the accused poses a threat to the safety of the public, a person against whom the offence was allegedly committed or any other particular person;
5. the accused has failed to disclose previous convictions or where previous convictions have come to light after release on bail;
6. further information has come to light relating to factors which might have affected the decision to grant bail;
7. the accused has contravened any prohibition, condition, obligation or order imposed in terms of any law that was issued by a court to protect the person against whom the offence in question was allegedly committed from the accused;
8. the accused has not disclosed that an order was issued in terms of any law by a court to protect the person against whom the offence in question was allegedly committed from the accused and whether such an order is still of force;
9. the accused has not disclosed or correctly disclosed that he or she is or was, at the time of the alleged commission of the offence, a sentenced offender who has been placed under correctional supervision, day parole, parole or medical parole as contemplated in section 73 of the Correctional Services Act, 1998;
10. it is in the interests of justice to do so.[1397]

Bail may also be cancelled on the basis of the accused's culpable failure to appear as required at trial.[1398]

1397. Criminal Procedure Act 51 of 1977, s. 68(1). In terms of s. 68(2) where it is not practicable to obtain a warrant of arrest (as in sub-s. (1)) a magistrate may, where there is a statement on oath from a peace officer setting out one or more of the grounds in sub-s. (1), issue a warrant of arrest for the accused, and if satisfied that the ends of justice may be defeated if the accused is not placed in custody, cancel the bail and commit the accused to prison until the conclusion of the relevant criminal proceedings.
1398. Criminal Procedure Act 51 of 1977, s. 67.

Chapter 4. The Trial Stage

§1. Order of Proceedings

589. The following is a broad outline of the successive main stages in criminal trial proceedings: the accused's plea which is followed by judicial questioning of the accused; the presentation of evidence by the prosecution and closure of the case for the prosecution; the (possible) discharge of the accused at the closure of the case for the prosecution; the optional presentation of evidence by the defence if there is no discharge; closure of the case for the defence; argument by the prosecution and defence on the merits of the case, that is, whether the court should convict or acquit; judgment by the court on the merits; and, finally, the sentencing stage which follows in the event of a conviction.

§2. Presence and Representation of an Accused

I. Presence of Accused

A. Methods of Securing Attendance of the Accused in Court

590. The methods of securing the attendance of an accused who is 18 years or older in court for purposes of his trial are:[1399] arrest,[1400] summons,[1401] written notice[1402] and indictment.[1403] An earlier warning to appear in court may in certain instances also be used[1404] and the mechanism known as 'bail' (described in paragraphs 575 et seq. *supra*) is also an indirect way of securing an accused's attendance.

B. Right of Accused to Be Present

591. Section 158 of the Criminal Procedure Act 51 of 1977 provides that all criminal proceedings in any court shall take place in the presence of the accused except as otherwise expressly provided for in the Act[1405] or any other law. The right

---

1399. Criminal Procedure Act 51 of 1977, s. 38. In terms of the Child Justice Act 75 of 2008, the Director of Public Prosecutions may direct that the young offender be dealt with by way of the preliminary inquiry procedure (set out in ss 5(2) to (4) of this Act; the methods for securing attendance at such preliminary inquiry are set out in s. 17 of this Act).
1400. *See* e.g., Criminal Procedure Act 51 of 1977, s. 39.
1401. Criminal Procedure Act 51 of 1977, s. 54. A summons is a document setting out the charge(s) against the accused and ordering him to appear at a specific date and time in a specified lower court. It is signed by the clerk of the court and is personally served upon an accused.
1402. Criminal Procedure Act 51 of 1977, s. 56. This notice also gives an accused the option to pay and admission of guilt without appearing in court.
1403. Criminal Procedure Act 51 of 1977, s. 144.
1404. Criminal Procedure Act 51 of 1977, s. 72.
1405. *See* e.g., Criminal Procedure Act 51 of 1977, ss 159(2) and 160.

to be present is fundamental[1406] and is a natural result of an adversarial trial system where an accused has the right to confront witnesses against him.[1407] This basic principle of criminal procedure is underpinned by sections 34 and 35(*c*) and (*e*) of the Constitution, which set out the right of access to courts and the right to a public trial before an ordinary court and to be present when so tried, respectively.

The fundamental right of an accused to be present is well illustrated by the Supreme (now High).[1408] Court decisions to the effect that it is irregular for a trial court to conduct an inspection *in loco* in the absence of the accused,[1409] to discuss the case out of court in the absence of the accused[1410] or to change the accused's sentence in his absence.[1411]

C. Limitations on the Right to Be Present

592. If an accused behaves in a manner which makes the continuance of the proceedings impracticable, the court may direct that he be removed and that the proceedings continue in his absence.[1412] Any serious and persistent disruptive behaviour would constitute sufficient ground for a court to order removal of the accused. However, an accused must be given a prior warning by the court to the effect that his conduct might lead to his being removed.[1413] Such a warning must be recorded.[1414] An accused who has been removed may at a later stage, depending upon his conduct, again attend the proceedings in question. He may then, unless he was legally represented during his absence, examine any witness who testified during his absence. He may also inspect the record of the proceedings or require the court to have such record read over to him.[1415]

Where there are co-accused, a court may in certain limited circumstances authorise the absence of one accused on account of the tragic personal circumstances of this accused, like the death of a family member.[1416] This provision is hardly ever employed. The practice is to postpone the whole case to a date convenient to all parties.

593. It is possible to proceed with a trial where one accused in a joint trial has absconded. Section 160(3)(*b*) of the Criminal Procedure Act 51 of 1977 provides that if it appears to the court that the presence of an absent accused cannot reasonably be obtained, the court may direct that the proceedings in respect of the accused who are present be concluded as if such proceedings had been separated from the

---

1406. *R v. Blackbeard* 1925 TPD 965.
1407. *See generally*, S.E. van der Merwe, 'Die evolusie van die mondelinge karakter en uitsluitingsreëls van die Engelse gemene bewysreg' 1991 *Stell LR* 281 290–291.
1408. *See supra,* para. 413.
1409. *R v. Makiep* 1948 (1) SA 947 (A).
1410. *S v. Lewis* 1950 (1) SA 623 (E).
1411. *S v. Radebe* 1973 (4) SA 244 (O).
1412. Criminal Procedure Act 51 of 1977, s. 159.
1413. *R v. Pauline* 1928 TPD 643.
1414. *R v. Mokoa* 1985 (1) SA 350 (O).
1415. Criminal Procedure Act 51 of 1977, s. 160(1).
1416. Criminal Procedure Act 51 of 1977, s. 159(2)(*a*)(ii).

proceedings at the stage at which the accused concerned became absent from the proceedings. When such absent accused is again in attendance, the proceedings against him shall continue from the stage at which he became absent, and the court shall not be required to be differently constituted merely by reason of such separation. It has been held that in the exercise of its discretion, the court should consider the following facts and factors:[1417]

a. The stage of the trial when the absent accused was no longer in attendance at the proceedings.
b. The duration of the trial up to the stage when the absent accused no longer attended the proceedings.
c. The possible future duration of the trial if evidence in respect of all the charges and all the accused was tendered.
d. The possible future duration of the trial if evidence was adduced only in respect of the accused in attendance and their involvement in the charges.
e. The question whether the accused still present are busy testifying or are under cross-examination.
f. The number of accused who originally appeared and the number of them who are absent from the proceedings.
g. The possible prejudice which the accused still present or the state or witnesses might suffer if no, or a particular, direction is issued.
h. The possible benefit to the accused still present or the state or the absent accused if no, or a particular, direction is issued.
i. The possibility that some or all of the absent accused will again appear in the proceedings and, if so, how soon after the court is asked to issue a direction.
j. The seriousness of the charge against the accused still present and possible consequences should a conviction follow.
k. Whether the accused still present have been released on bail and, if not, what the possibility of bail is.
l. The period for which the accused still present has already been in custody.

D. Absence During Verdict

594. When, in a trial, the evidence on behalf of all the accused has been concluded and any accused is absent when the verdict is to be delivered, the verdict may be delivered in respect of all the accused or be withheld until all the accused are present or be delivered in respect of any accused present and withheld in respect of the absent accused until he is again in attendance.[1418]

1417. *S v. Toka* 1990 (1) SACR 553 (T).
1418. Criminal Procedure Act 51 of 1977, s. 160(3)(*c*).

II. Representation by a Legal Representative

595. An accused is entitled to be represented by a legal representative.[1419] 'Legal practitioner' is the generic term used for attorneys (solicitors) and advocates (barristers).[1420] Though an attorney has right of appearance in all courts, typically, he or she would perform legal administrative work.[1421] An advocate is a specialist litigator and may appear in all courts, usually upon the instruction of an attorney.

A. Legal Representation as a Trial Right

596. A court must promptly inform an accused of his right to legal representation.[1422] Such right must therefore be explained to the unrepresented accused by a judicial officer.[1423] Failure to do so can lead to a failure of justice.[1424] Where the accused facing a serious charge persists, after such explanation, with the choice to appear in person, the court should seek to establish whether this is indeed an informed choice.[1425] The accused should also be promptly informed of his or her right to legal representation at state expense.[1426]

B. Reasonable Opportunity to Obtain Legal Representation

597. An accused has a right to a reasonable opportunity to obtain legal representation.[1427] He may ask for a remand to brief a lawyer. Postponement of the trial is at the discretion of the court. It is a discretion that must be exercised judicially,[1428] taking into account the interests of the accused and the prosecution, and having regard to the accused's right to choose and be represented by a legal practitioner and to be promptly informed of such right.[1429] In the exercise of its discretion, the court should consider several factors.[1430] It has been held that the absence of any fault on the part of the accused in obtaining legal representation timeously is an important consideration.[1431] Liberty pending trial and the time that was available

1419. Criminal Procedure Act 51 of 1977, s. 73(1).
1420. The Legal Practice Act 28 of 2014 has instituted a new legal framework for the legal profession, aimed at its transformation and restructuring in line with constitutional imperatives.
1421. *See supra,* para. 43.
1422. Constitution, 1996, s. 35(2)(*b*); Criminal Procedure Act 51 of 1977, s. 73(2A).
1423. *S v. Pienaar* 2000 (2) SACR 143 (NC).
1424. *S v. Mabaso* 1990 (3) SA 185 (A) 204.
1425. *S v. Nkondo* 2000 (1) SACR 538 (W); *S v. Manale* 2000 (2) SACR 666 (NC).
1426. Constitution, 1996, s. 35(3)(*g*).
1427. Criminal Procedure Act 51 of 1977, s. 73(2B).
1428. *R v. Zackey* 1945 AD 505 511.
1429. Constitution, 1996, s. 35(3)(*f*).
1430. *See generally*, E. Du Toit et al., *Commentary on the Criminal Procedure Act* (Juta, Cape Town 1987), 11–26ff.; J. van den Berg, 'Legal Representation: Right or Privilege?' 1984 *THRHR* 447 452.
1431. *See generally*, E. Du Toit et al., *Commentary on the Criminal Procedure Act* (Juta, Cape Town 1987), 11–28; J. van den Berg, 'Legal Representation: Right or Privilege?' 1984 *THRHR* 452.

to an accused are also relevant considerations.[1432] If an accused refuses or fails to appoint a legal adviser of his own choice within a reasonable time and his failure to do so is due to his own fault, the court may order that the trial proceed without legal representation, unless the court is of the view that in doing so substantial injustice would result, in which case the court may order that a legal advisor be assigned to the accused at state expense.[1433]

C. *Main Duties of Legal Representative in Defending an Accused*

598. A legal representative is for the duration of his mandate in control of the mode of presentation of the defence case.[1434] But he must ensure that his client (the accused) is aware of his procedural rights.[1435] The client himself must, for example, take the final decision on whether to testify or not after having been advised by the legal representative.[1436]

The Appellate Division has held that cross-examination of a prosecution witness, partly by the legal representative and partly by the accused, is unacceptable.[1437]

During cross-examination, the legal representative has a procedural duty to put the essence of the accused's defence to prosecution witnesses who are able to comment thereon.[1438]

599. It is against public policy for a legal representative to testify *against* a former client even if the latter has directly or impliedly waived legal professional privilege.[1439]

Legal professional privilege – which was discussed in paragraph 450 *supra* – must at all times be respected and protected by a legal representative[1440] and he must on behalf of his client object to any question which might elicit information in breach of such privilege.[1441]

D. *Duty of Counsel in Defending the Admittedly Guilty*

600. A legal representative may not in defending an accused assert that which he knows to be untrue. This means that where a client has confessed to the legal representative, the latter may not set up a defence which he knows is inconsistent

---

1432. *R v. Bikitsha* 1960 (4) SA 181 (E).
1433. Criminal Procedure Act 51 of 1977, s. 73(2C). The accused may nevertheless refuse such representation – *see S v. Tandwa* 2008 (1) SACR 613 (SCA) para. 8.
1434. *R v. Matonsi* 1958 (2) SA 450 (A).
1435. *S v. Majola* 1982 (1) SA 125 (A).
1436. *S v. Majola* (*supra*); *S v. Louw* 1990 (3) SA 116 (A); E. Morris, *Technique in Litigation* 2nd ed. (Juta, Cape Town 1985) 273.
1437. *R v. Baartman* 1960 (3) SA 535 (A); *S v. Nkwanyana* 1990 (4) SA 735 (A).
1438. *S v. Nkomo* 1975 (3) SA 598 (N).
1439. *S v. Boesman* 1990 (2) SACR 389 (E).
1440. *S v. Mushimba* 1977 (2) 829 (A).
1441. *Schlosberg v. Attorney-General* 1936 WLD 59.

with the confession. However, objection may still be taken to technical matters like the court's lack of jurisdiction or the form and contents of the charge or indictment.[1442]

E. Withdrawal by Legal Representative

601. If a legal representative appears for two or more accused who happen to accuse each other, the legal representative must terminate his service in respect of *all* the accused.[1443] He cannot retain his brief in respect of one accused as he might consciously or unconsciously use against the other accused information obtained during their former lawyer-client relationship.[1444] Legal professional privilege should not be placed in jeopardy.

A legal representative should also withdraw where a client persists in furnishing him with irreconcilable instructions.

It has been held though that upon a legal representative's withdrawal from a case, the court should ask an accused whether he wishes to instruct another legal representative and – if the accused does not want such an opportunity – he should be asked whether he is in a position to undertake his own defence.[1445]

III. Assistance to Accused by Someone Who Is Not Legally Qualified

A. Assistance to Adult Accused

602. A person who *represents* an accused must be legally qualified to do so.[1446] However, section 73(3) of the Criminal Procedure Act 51 of 1977 provides, *inter alia*, that any accused who, in the opinion of the court, requires the *assistance* of another person at criminal proceedings may with permission of the court be so assisted. The person who renders such assistance may not cross-examine prosecution witnesses[1447] and may not decide on behalf of the accused how to exercise certain procedural rights.[1448] In one decided case, the judge rightly called upon the legislature to clarify what is meant by 'assistance' in section 73(3).[1449]

1442. E.A.L. Lewis, *Legal Ethics: A Guide to Professional Conduct for South African Attorneys* (Juta, Cape Town 1982) 204.
1443. *S v. Moseli* (1) 1969 (1) SA 646 (O).
1444. *S v. Dintwe* 1985 (4) SA 539 (BG) 541.
1445. *S v. Khoali* 1990 (1) SACR 276 (O).
1446. *S v. Mkhize*; *S v. Mosia*; *S v. Jones*; *S v. le Roux* 1988 (2) SA 868 (A) 875G.
1447. *S v. Masithlela* 1986 (3) SA 402 (O).
1448. *See generally*, *S v. L* 1988 (4) SA 757 (C).
1449. *S v. L* (*supra*) 761C.

B. Assistance to Accused under Eighteen Years

603. An accused under the age of 18 may be assisted by his or her parent, guardian or an appropriate person.[1450] Unless exempted from doing so, a parent, guardian or appropriate person who fails to attend the proceedings in question after having been duly warned to do so commits an offence.[1451]

The court must give a juvenile accused the opportunity to contact his parents or guardian in order to secure their presence,[1452] and he must also be informed of his right to be assisted by a parent or guardian.[1453]

It has been held that the assistance which a parent or guardian may render in terms of section 73(3) is not the same as legal representation and that such a parent or guardian has at any rate no greater right than a legal representative and can merely advise the juvenile accused.[1454] It is improper for the court to order the juvenile accused to act in accordance with the advice of his parent or guardian.[1455]

§3. ARRAIGNMENT AND PLEA

604. An accused stands arraigned when the prosecution has finalised its charges and the accused is called upon to plead to these charges in the court which has the necessary jurisdiction to dispose of the case.

The charge or charges must be put to the accused by the prosecutor.[1456] This must be done before any evidence is led. An accused has a right to demand a verdict once he has pleaded.[1457] The plea of an accused must be tendered freely and voluntarily.[1458]

605. A juvenile accused who has legal representation need not plead personally.[1459] It has been suggested that the same rule should apply to an adult accused.[1460] However, in practice, an adult accused is generally called upon to plead personally – and thereafter, his legal representative should indicate to the court whether the plea is in accordance with his instructions.[1461]

606. The plea serves an important purpose in the sense that it assists the court and the prosecution in determining the ambit of the *lis*. But an accused who refuses

1450. Criminal Procedure Act 51 of 1977, s. 73(3). *See* ss 3(*g*), 38(2), 44(1)(*b*), 65 of the Child Justice Act 75 of 2008.
1451. Child Justice Act 75 of 2008, s. 65(7).
1452. *S v. Khumbusa* 1911 (1) SA 391 (N).
1453. *S v. H* 1978 (4) SA 385 (E) 387A.
1454. *S v. Assel* 1984 (1) SA 402 (C).
1455. *S v. Assel* (*supra*) 405F.
1456. Criminal Procedure Act 51 of 1977, s. 105.
1457. Criminal Procedure Act 51 of 1977, s. 108.
1458. *S v. Mbothoma* 1978 (2) SA 530 (O).
1459. *S v. Mpongoshe* 1980 (4) SA 593 (A).
1460. S.E. van der Merwe, G.A. Barton & K.J. Kemp, *Plea Procedures in Summary Criminal Trials* (Butterworths, Durban 1984) para. 8 2.
1461. E. du Toit et al., *Commentary on the Criminal Procedure Act* (Juta, Cape Town 1987) 15-2A.

to plead does not commit the crime known as contempt of court.[1462] The court is simply required to record a plea of not guilty on behalf of an accused who refuses to plead.[1463] This procedure should be seen as indirect confirmation of an accused's common-law passive defence right, namely his right to refuse to cooperate through oral communications until such time as it is necessary for him to put his defence to prosecution witnesses during the cross-examination of such witnesses.

I. The Various Possible Pleas upon Arraignment

607. Section 106(1) of the Criminal Procedure Act 51 of 1977 provides that when an accused pleads to a charge, he may plead:

a. that he is guilty of the offence charged or of any offence of which he may be convicted on the charge; or
b. that he is not guilty; or
c. that he has already been convicted of the offence with which he is charged; or
d. that he has already been acquitted of the offence with which he is charged; or
e. that he has received a free pardon under section 327(6) from the State President for the offence charged; or
f. that the court has no jurisdiction to try the offence; or
g. that he has been discharged under the provisions of section 204 from prosecution for the offence charged; or
h. that the prosecutor has no title to prosecute; or
i. where the accused has not yet pleaded, that the prosecution may not be resumed or instituted, owing to an order by a court that due to unreasonable delays in completing proceedings, the case be struck off the roll and not be resumed or instituted *de novo* without the written instruction of the Director of Public Prosecutions (DPP) (in terms of section 342A(3)(*c*)).

608. The plea known as *lis pendens* (the matter is pending in another court) is not mentioned in section 106(1) or anywhere else in statutory law. However, it is, in terms of common law, possible for the accused to draw the trial court's attention to the fact that the same matter is pending against him in another court[1464] which is also a criminal court.[1465]

609. Two or more pleas may be pleaded together, except that a plea of guilty may not be pleaded with any other plea to the same charge.[1466]

610. An accused is required to give reasonable notice to the prosecution of his intention to rely on a plea other than the plea of guilty or not guilty and shall in

1462. *S v. Monnanyane* 1977 (3) SA 976 (O).
1463. Criminal Procedure Act 51 of 1977, s. 109.
1464. *S v. Motsepa* 1982 (1) SA 304 (O).
1465. *R v. Setchell* 1907 TS 611.
1466. Criminal Procedure Act 51 of 1977, s. 106(2).

such notice state the ground on which he bases his plea. However, the requirement of such notice may be waived by the DPP or the prosecutor, as the case may be, and the court may, on good cause shown, dispense with such notice or adjourn the trial to enable such notice to be given.[1467]

II. Mental Illness of the Accused

611. Issues concerning the mental illness of an accused can be raised at any stage of criminal proceedings. In practice, however, issues of this nature are most frequently raised when the accused is called upon to plead – even though there is no specific provision for a plea of 'not guilty on account of mental illness'.[1468]

A. *The Distinction Between Non-triability on Account of Mental Illness and Lack of Criminal Capacity on Account of Mental Illness*

612. The issue of the mental condition of an accused is relevant in two different situations. One involves the procedural issue of whether the accused is mentally fit to stand trial; the other is whether the accused's mental condition at the time of the crime excuses him from liability.

As regards triability, the test is whether the accused is by reason of mental illness or intellectual disability not capable of understanding the proceedings so as to make a proper defence.[1469] As regards the matter of responsibility, the question is, was the accused at the time of the commission or omission constituting the alleged offence suffering from a mental illness or intellectual disability which made him incapable:

a. of appreciating the wrongfulness of his or her act or omission; or
b. of acting in accordance with an appreciation of the wrongfulness of his or her act or omission.[1470]

Mental illness as a substantive criminal law defence is discussed in paragraph 217 *supra*.

613. The prosecution has the burden of proving triability beyond a reasonable doubt if an accused alleges non-triability on account of mental illness.[1471] But different rules apply where an accused alleges lack of criminal capacity on account of mental illness. In this instance, the accused must prove his defence on a balance of

1467. Criminal Procedure Act 51 of 1977, s. 106(3).
1468. Since the issue of mental illness at the plea stage either amounts to the issue of triability or non-liability on the basis of pathological incapacity, and the latter plea is in essence a plea of 'not guilty' (s. 106(1)(*b*)), this issue will be dealt with here for sake of convenience.
1469. Criminal Procedure Act 51 of 1977, s. 77(6).
1470. Criminal Procedure Act 51 of 1977, s. 78(1); *S v. Kavin* 1978 (2) SA 731 (W).
1471. *R v. Mashimbi* 1958 (1) SA 390 (T) 392D–E; *S v. Ebrahim* 1973 (1) SA 868 (A) 871.

probability.[1472] This shift in the incidence of the ordinary burden in criminal trials must be understood in the light of the common-law rebuttable presumption that all people are for substantive law purposes presumed to be of sound mind.

B. The Psychiatric Enquiry and Report

614. If the court is satisfied that some factual or speculative medical basis has been laid for an allegation of non-triability or lack of criminal responsibility on account of mental illness or intellectual disability,[1473] the court must direct that the matter be enquired into and be reported on in terms of the provisions of section 79 of the Criminal Procedure Act 51 of 1977. The court may for the purpose of the relevant enquiry commit the accused to a psychiatric hospital, or to any other place designated by the court, for such periods, not exceeding thirty days at a time, as the court may from time to time determine. Where an accused is in custody when he is so committed, he shall, whilst he is so committed, be deemed to be in the lawful custody of the person or the authority in whose custody he was at the time of such committal.[1474]

615. Where the accused is charged with murder or culpable homicide or rape or compelled rape or a charge involving serious violence (or where the court in any particular case so directs), the enquiry shall be conducted and be reported on:

1. by the head of the designated health establishment or by a psychiatrist delegated by the head concerned; and
2. by a psychiatrist appointed by the court; and
3. by a psychiatrist appointed by the court upon application and on good cause shown by the accused for such appointment; and
4. by a clinical psychologist where the court so directs.[1475]

In respect of all other offences, the enquiry need only be conducted and reported on by the head of the designated health establishment designated by the court or by a psychiatrist delegated by the head concerned.[1476]

The report must be in writing and copies must be made available to the court, accused and prosecutor. The report must include a description of the nature of the enquiry as well as a diagnosis of the mental condition of the accused. It must, furthermore, include a psychiatric finding on triability or criminal capacity or both, as the case may be.[1477]

1472. *S v. Mahlinza* 1967 (1) SA 408 (A) 419. *See* para. 222 *supra*.
1473. *S v. Mokie* 1992 (1) SACR 430 (T).
1474. Criminal Procedure Act 51 of 1977, s. 79(2).
1475. Criminal Procedure Act 51 of 1977, s. 79(1)(*b*).
1476. Criminal Procedure Act 51 of 1977, s. 79(1)(*a*).
1477. Criminal Procedure Act 51 of 1977, s. 79(3) and (4).

616. If the finding contained in the relevant report is the unanimous finding of the persons who enquired into the mental condition of the accused and the finding is not disputed by the prosecutor or the accused, the court may determine the matter on such report without hearing further evidence.[1478] However, if the finding is not unanimous or, if unanimous, is disputed by the prosecutor or the accused, the court shall determine the matter after hearing evidence. The prosecutor and the accused may for this purpose present evidence to the court, including the evidence of any person who under section 79 enquired into the mental condition of the accused.[1479]

617. Where the psychiatric finding is disputed, the party disputing the finding may subpoena and cross-examine any person who under section 79 has enquired into the mental condition of the accused.[1480]

618. If the court finds that the accused is capable of understanding the proceedings so as to make a proper defence, the proceedings shall be continued in the ordinary way.[1481] Proceedings must also be continued in the ordinary way if the defence of lack of criminal capacity on account of mental illness is rejected by the court. But any statement made by the accused during the psychiatric enquiry may not be used against him in the course of his continued trial.[1482] The purpose of this exclusionary rule is to ensure that an accused who has been sent for psychiatric observation and enquiry should feel free frankly and honestly to discuss the case with the psychiatrists concerned without the fear of any incriminating statements being used against him at his trial for any other purpose than to report on his mental state.[1483]
It has been held that public policy requires such an approach.[1484] The rule is in the final analysis in the best interests of the administration of justice.

619. The psychiatric report may, however, ultimately have an important effect in respect of sentencing: if the court finds that the accused at the time of the commission of the act in question was criminally responsible for the act but that his capacity to appreciate the wrongfulness of the act or to act in accordance with an appreciation of the wrongfulness of the act was diminished by reason of mental illness or intellectual disability, the court may take the fact of such diminished responsibility into account when sentencing the accused.[1485]

1478. Criminal Procedure Act 51 of 1977, ss 77(2), 78(3).
1479. Criminal Procedure Act 51 of 1977, ss 77(3), 78(4).
1480. Criminal Procedure Act 51 of 1977, ss 77(4), 78(5).
1481. Criminal Procedure Act 51 of 1977, s. 77(5).
1482. Criminal Procedure Act 51 of 1977, s. 79(7).
1483. S.J. van Niekerk, S.E. van der Merwe & A.J. van Wyk, *Privilegies in die Bewysreg* (Butterworths, Durban 1984) 15.
1484. *S v. Forbes* 1970 (2) SA 594 (C).
1485. Criminal Procedure Act 51 of 1977, s. 78(7).

C. The Finding of Non-triability: Effect and Consequences

620. It is provided in the Criminal Procedure Act[1486] that if the court which has jurisdiction to try the case[1487] finds that the accused is not capable of understanding the proceedings so as to make a proper defence, the court may, if it is of the opinion that it is in the interests of the accused, and unless it can be proved on a balance of probabilities that, on the limited evidence available the accused committed the act in question, order that such information or evidence be placed before the court as it deems fit so as to determine whether the accused has committed the act in question. In the case of a charge of murder or culpable homicide or rape or compelled rape, or a charge involving serious violence or if the court considers it to be necessary in the public interest, where the court finds that the accused has committed the act in question, or any other offence involving serious violence, the court may direct that the accused be: (i) detained in a psychiatric hospital; (ii) temporarily detained in a correctional health facility of a prison where a bed is not immediately available in a psychiatric hospital and be transferred where a bed becomes available, if the court is of the opinion that it is necessary to do so on the grounds that the accused poses a serious danger or threat to himself or herself or to members of the public, pending the decision of a judge in chambers;[1488] (iii) admitted to and detained in a designated health establishment stated in the order as if he or she were an involuntary mental health care user;[1489] (iv) released subject to such conditions as the court considers appropriate; or (v) referred to a Children's Court,[1490] and pending such referral be placed in the care of a parent, guardian or other appropriate person or, failing that, placed in temporary safe care.[1491]

Where, in similar circumstances, the court finds that the accused has committed an offence other than the one contemplated above or that he or she has not committed any offence, the court may direct that the accused be:[1492] (i) admitted to and detained in a designated health establishment stated in the order as if he or she were an involuntary mental health care user;[1493] (ii) released subject to such conditions as the court considers appropriate; (iii) released unconditionally; or (iv) referred to a Children's Court,[1494] and pending such referral be placed in the care of a parent, guardian or other appropriate person or, failing that, placed in temporary safe care.[1495]

1486. Criminal Procedure Act 51 of 1977, s. 77(6)(*a*)(i).
1487. In terms of s. 75 of Act 51 of 1977.
1488. In terms of s. 47 of the Mental Health Care Act 17 of 2002.
1489. As contemplated in s. 37 of the Mental Health Care Act 17 of 2002.
1490. As contemplated in s. 64 of the Child Justice Act 75 of 2008.
1491. As defined in s. 1 of the Children's Act 38 of 2005.
1492. Criminal Procedure Act 51 of 1977, s. 77(6)(*a*)(ii).
1493. As contemplated in s. 37 of the Mental Health Care Act 17 of 2002.
1494. As contemplated in s. 64 of the Child Justice Act 75 of 2008.
1495. As defined in s. 1 of the Children's Act 38 of 2005.

If the court makes a finding of non-triability after the accused has been convicted of the offence charged but before sentence is passed, the court shall set the conviction aside, and if the accused has pleaded guilty, it shall be deemed that he or she has pleaded not guilty.[1496]

621. Where a direction is issued in terms of section 77(6) as set out above, the accused may, at any time thereafter, when he or she is capable of understanding the proceedings so as to make a proper defence, be prosecuted and tried for the offence in question.[1497] He cannot, therefore, at a later trial in respect of the same facts successfully rely on a plea of previous acquittal. The reason for this is that the earlier finding of non-triability was a procedural issue and not one of substantive criminal law. He was not acquitted at the first trial.

The accused who is convicted after having unsuccessfully raised non-triability on account of mental illness may appeal.[1498]

D. The Finding of Lack of Criminal Capacity: Effect and Consequences

622. If the court finds that the accused committed the act in question and that he or she at the time of such commission was by reason of mental illness or intellectual disability not criminally responsible for such act, the court shall find the accused not guilty, or if the court so finds after the accused has been convicted of the offence charged but before sentence is passed, the court shall set the conviction aside and find the accused not guilty, by reason of mental illness or intellectual disability, as the case may be. The court shall further direct, in a case where the accused is charged with murder or culpable homicide or rape or compelled rape, or another charge involving serious violence, or if the court considers it to be necessary in the public interest that the accused be:[1499] (i) detained in a psychiatric hospital; (ii) temporarily detained in a correctional health facility of a prison where a bed is not immediately available in a psychiatric hospital and be transferred where a bed becomes available, if the court is of the opinion that it is necessary to do so on the grounds that the accused poses a serious danger or threat to himself or herself or to members of the public, pending the decision of a judge in chambers;[1500] (iii) admitted to and detained in a designated health establishment stated in the order and treated as if he or she were an involuntary mental healthcare user;[1501] (iv) released

1496. Criminal Procedure Act 51 of 1977, s. 77(6)(*b*).
1497. Criminal Procedure Act 51 of 1977, s. 77(7). The court may act in the same way, in terms of the result contemplated in s. 77(9), where the court overturns a finding of competence to stand trial.
1498. Criminal Procedure Act 51 of 1977, s. 77(8).
1499. Criminal Procedure Act 51 of 1977, s. 78(6)(i).
1500. In terms of s. 47 of the Mental Health Care Act 17 of 2002.
1501. As contemplated in s. 37 of the Mental Health Care Act 17 of 2002.

subject to such conditions as the court considers appropriate; (v) released unconditionally; or (vi) referred to a Children's Court,[1502] and pending such referral be placed in the care of a parent, guardian or other appropriate person or, failing that, placed in temporary safe care.[1503]

In any other case,[1504] the court shall direct that the accused be: (i) admitted to and detained in a designated health establishment stated in the order and treated as if he or she were an involuntary mental healthcare user;[1505] (ii) released subject to such conditions as the court considers appropriate; (iii) released unconditionally; or (iv) referred to a Children's Court,[1506] and pending such referral be placed in the care of a parent, guardian or other appropriate person or, failing that, placed in temporary safe care.[1507]

An accused against whom such a finding is made may appeal against such finding if the finding is not made in consequence of an allegation by the accused that he is not criminally responsible for the offence charged.[1508] He may also appeal if his defence was rejected and he was convicted.

III. The Plea of Previous Acquittal (Autrefois Acquit) or Previous Conviction (Autrefois Convict): Policy Considerations

623. These pleas derive from the right to a fair trial.[1509] Moreover, they are based on the fundamental common-law principle that the individual should be protected from the inconvenience, anxiety and embarrassment of repeated prosecutions in respect of the same criminal conduct: *Nemo debet bis vexari pro una et eadem causa.* It is, furthermore, also in the interest of the administration of justice that there should be finality in criminal matters – or any other litigation. *Interest rei publicae ut sit finis litium.* In respect of the plea of previous conviction, it is also true that sound penal policy demands that a person should not be punished twice in respect of one and the same offence.[1510] It has rightly been held that reasonableness and fairness form the basis of the pleas of previous acquittal and previous conviction.[1511]

624. These pleas will only be successful if the previous acquittal or conviction was by a court of competent jurisdiction and if it can be said that there is substantial identity between the offences charged. There is a third requirement in respect of the

1502. As contemplated in s. 64 of the Child Justice Act 75 of 2008.
1503. As defined in s. 1 of the Children's Act 38 of 2005.
1504. Criminal Procedure Act 51 of 1977, s. 78(6)(ii).
1505. As contemplated in s. 37 of the Mental Health Care Act 17 of 2002.
1506. As contemplated in s. 64 of the Child Justice Act 75 of 2008.
1507. As defined in s. 1 of the Children's Act 38 of 2005.
1508. Criminal Procedure Act 51 of 1977, s. 78(8).
1509. Constitution of the RSA, s. 35(3)(*m*).
1510. *S v. Kgatlane* 1978 (2) SA 10 (T) 11D.
1511. *R v. Manazewitz* 1933 AD 165.

plea of previous acquittal, namely that the acquittal must have been on the merits.[1512] This means that a second prosecution is permitted where an accused's previous acquittal was not based on evidence or the lack thereof but on an irregularity which made the previous proceedings a nullity and inevitably resulted in an acquittal.[1513]

A. *Court of Competent Jurisdiction*

625. The plea of previous acquittal or conviction can be upheld in respect of a verdict delivered by a foreign court[1514] which was properly constituted in terms of the laws of the foreign country concerned.

B. *The Same Offence or Offence Substantially Identical*

626. It has been held that it is too narrow a test merely to ask whether the accused was at his first trial in jeopardy of being convicted of the offence with which he is charged in the second trial.[1515] A wider test is necessary in order to protect the individual, namely, whether there is substantial identity of subject matter between the first and second trials.[1516] The result is that a person who, for example, has been acquitted in an earlier trial on a charge of uttering can successfully plead previous acquittal if later charged on the same facts with theft.[1517] His plea must be sustained despite the fact that he was at his first trial not in jeopardy of being convicted of theft.[1518]

627. However, there is a rule that someone convicted of a crime can at a later stage be charged again with a more serious crime arising out of the same incident if it was not possible at the time of the first trial to have preferred the more serious charge.[1519] This means that an accused who has been convicted of attempted murder (his victim was still alive at the time of the trial) may later be charged with murder if his victim dies as a result of the unlawful attack, which was also the subject of the first trial.[1520] Obviously, if at his first trial he had been acquitted on the merits, he could successfully plead previous acquittal at the second trial.

1512. *S v. Mthetwe* 1970 (2) SA 310 (N).
1513. *S v. Moodie* 1962 (1) SA 587 (A).
1514. *S v. Pokela* 1968 (4) SA 702 (E).
1515. *Ex parte Minister of Justice: In re R v. Moseme* 1936 AD 52 60.
1516. *S v. Ndou* 1971 (1) SA 668 (A) 680F.
1517. *S v. Davidson* 1964 (1) SA 192 (T).
1518. *See also generally, S v. Nkosi* 1990 (1) SACR 653 (T) for a similar argument.
1519. *R v. Dayzell* 1932 WLD 157.
1520. *S v. Gabriel* 1971 (1) SA 646 (RA).

IV. Conviction Solely on a Plea of Guilty

628. In respect of certain minor statutory offences as well as certain minor common-law offences,[1521] an accused may be convicted solely on the basis of his plea of guilty.[1522] After conviction, evidence may be received for purposes of sentencing.[1523] The court may then impose any sentence *other than* a fine exceeding ZAR 5,000 (GBP 210/USD 275/EUR 250) or imprisonment (including any other form of detention)[1524] without the option of a fine.[1525] It is the duty of the presiding officer to decide whether the offence is of such a trivial nature that it calls for conviction solely on the basis of the plea of guilty tendered by the accused.[1526] However, the court may not in the exercise of its discretion ignore minimum sentences prescribed by statute.[1527]

V. The Plea of Guilty and Peremptory Judicial Questioning of the Accused

629. Upon a plea of guilty, the court *must*, if it is of the opinion that the offence merits punishment of imprisonment or any other form of detention without the option of a fine or of a fine exceeding the amount of ZAR 5,000 (GBP 210/USD 275/EUR 250), question the accused with reference to the alleged facts of the case in order to ascertain whether he admits the allegations in the charge to which he has pleaded guilty.[1528] The court may then, if satisfied that the accused is guilty of the offence to which he has pleaded guilty, convict the accused on his plea of guilty of that offence and impose any competent sentence. Questioning of the accused is also peremptory where the prosecutor requests the court to do so.[1529] However, the prosecutor himself has no power to question the accused to test the validity of the plea of guilty.

The court can convict without evidence having been led by the prosecution, provided that the court is satisfied that the answers given by the accused adequately

1521. *See generally*, *S v. Mia* 1962 (2) 718 (N) 719C.
1522. Criminal Procedure Act 51 of 1977, s. 112(1)(*a*). *See generally*, S.E. van der Merwe, *Handleiding tot Artikels 112 en 115 van die Strafproseswet* (Butterworths, Durban 1980) 10; S.E. van der Merwe, G.A. Barton & K.J. Kemp, *Plea Procedures in Summary Criminal Trials* (Butterworths, Durban 1984) 21–25.
1523. *S v. Phundula* 1978 (4) SA 855 (T) 859. A plea of not guilty must be recorded if evidence led for purposes of sentencing should indicate innocence. *See also*, Criminal Procedure Act 51 of 1977, s. 112(3) as read with s. 113.
1524. In *S v. Tolmay* 1980 (1) SA 182 (NC) it was held that committal to a rehabilitation centre is a form of detention without the option of a fine.
1525. Criminal Procedure Act 51 of 1977, s. 112(1)(*a*). In terms of the Criminal Procedure Act 51 of 1977, s. 287, a fine may be imposed either on its own as a primary penalty, or with imprisonment as an alternative.
1526. *S v. Mangwegape* 1979 (3) SA 1210 (O) 1212C–D. *See also*, *S v. Phundula* (*supra*) 859.
1527. *S v. Mkhafu* 1978 (1) SA 665 (O).
1528. Criminal Procedure Act 51 of 1977, s. 112(1)(*b*).
1529. *See generally*, S.E. van der Merwe, G.A. Barton & K.J. Kemp, *Plea Procedures in Summary Criminal Trials* (Butterworths, Durban 1984) 43–44.

support his plea of guilty and that it is therefore not necessary to correct the plea of guilty to one of not guilty and to require the prosecution to prove its case.[1530]

The accused is not under oath or affirmation when questioned by the court.

630. If an accused or his legal adviser hands a written statement by the accused into court, in which the accused sets out the facts which he admits and on which he has pleaded guilty, the court may, *in lieu* of questioning the accused, convict the accused on the strength of such statement and sentence him as provided if the court is satisfied that the accused is guilty of the offence to which he has pleaded guilty.[1531] However, the court may in its discretion also put any question to the accused in order to clarify any matter raised in the statement.

631. Nothing prevents the prosecutor from presenting evidence on any aspect of the charge, or the court from hearing evidence, including evidence or a statement by or on behalf of the accused, with regard to sentence, or from questioning the accused on any aspect of the case for the purposes of determining an appropriate sentence.[1532]

632. The correction of a plea of guilty to one of not guilty is governed by section 113 of the Criminal Procedure Act 51 of 1977. This section provides that if the court, at any stage of the proceedings and before sentence is passed, is in doubt whether the accused is in law guilty of the offence to which he has pleaded guilty or is satisfied that the accused does not admit an allegation in the charge or that the accused has incorrectly admitted any such allegation or that the accused has a valid defence to the charge, the court shall record a plea of not guilty and require the prosecutor to proceed with the prosecution. However, all admissions correctly and validly made by the accused up to the stage at which the court records a plea of not guilty shall stand as proof of the facts admitted. The prosecution need then only attempt to prove the remaining facts.

A. *After a Plea of Guilty*

633. The court may not cross-examine the accused,[1533] should avoid asking leading questions[1534] and may not attempt to persuade an accused that his denial of an incriminatory fact is incorrect or invalid.[1535] Factual information must be elicited[1536] and legal terminology should be avoided.[1537] The object of the questioning

---

1530. Criminal Procedure Act 51 of 1977, s. 113.
1531. Criminal Procedure Act 51 of 1977, s. 112(2). *See also generally*, *S v. Hlangothe* 1979 (4) SA 199 (B); *S v. Soci* 1986 (2) SA 14 (A) 18A–B; *S v. Khiba* 1978 (2) SA 540 (O).
1532. Criminal Procedure Act 51 of 1977, s. 112(3). *See also S v. Quinta* 1979 (2) SA 326 (O) and *S v. Balpile* 1979 (1) SA 702 (NC).
1533. *S v. Jacobs* 1978 (1) SA 1176 (C) 1177C.
1534. *S v. Mkhize* 1981 (3) SA 585 (N) 586H.
1535. *S v. Jacobs (supra); S v. Somyali* 1979 (2) 274 (E) 276.
1536. *S v. Lebokeng* 1978 (2) SA 674 (O).
1537. *S v. Phikwa* 1978 (1) SA 397 (E) 393.

would be defeated if admissions of unlawfulness and intent are obtained in the absence of *facts* which can support a finding of unlawfulness and intent.[1538]

B. Procedure in Favorem Innocentiae

634. The purpose of judicial questioning is to protect an accused and especially one who is illiterate and unsophisticated – from the adverse consequences of an ill-considered or incorrect plea of guilty.[1539] Courts are required to lean in favour of innocence when evaluating the answers of the accused.[1540] A plea of not guilty must be recorded if the accused's answers raise the possibility of a defence, for example, where his replies indicate that he might have acted under compulsion[1541] or in private defence.[1542] The judicial examination is, in the final analysis, a method of testing the validity of the plea of guilty.[1543]

VI. The Plea of Not Guilty and Judicial Questioning of the Accused: The Explanation of Plea

635. Where an accused pleads not guilty to the offence charged, the presiding judge, regional magistrate or magistrate, as the case may be, may ask him whether he wishes to make a statement indicating the basis of his defence.[1544] Where the accused does not make a statement or does so and it is not clear from the statement to what extent he denies or admits the issues raised by the plea, the court may question the accused in order to establish which allegations in the charge are in dispute.[1545] The court may in its discretion put any question to the accused in order to clarify any matter and shall enquire from the accused whether an allegation which is not placed in issue by the plea of not guilty may be recorded as an admission by the accused of that allegation.[1546] If the accused so consents, such admission shall be recorded and shall be deemed to be a formal admission which dispenses with the need of proving such a fact.[1547] Where the legal adviser of an accused on behalf of the accused replies, whether in writing or orally, to any question by the court, the accused shall be required by the court to declare whether he confirms such reply or not.[1548]

1538. *S v. Witbooi* 1978 (3) SA 590 (T) 595B–C.
1539. *S v. Baron* 1978 (2) SA 510 (C) 512G.
1540. *S v. Mkhize* 1978 (1) SA 264 (N) 268A–B.
1541. *S v. Van Deventer* 1978 (3) SA 97 (T).
1542. *S v. Tshumi* 1978 (1) SA 128 (N).
1543. *See generally*, *S v. Naidoo* 1989 (2) 114 (A) 121F.
1544. Criminal Procedure Act 51 of 1977, s. 115(1).
1545. Criminal Procedure Act 51 of 1977, s. 115(2)(*a*).
1546. Criminal Procedure Act 51 of 1977, s. 115(2)(*b*).
1547. Criminal Procedure Act 51 of 1977, s. 115(2)(*b*) as read with s. 220.
1548. Criminal Procedure Act 51 of 1977, s. 115(3).

636. The procedure as described above is known as the 'explanation of plea'. The accused is not under oath or affirmation during the explanation of plea and may not be questioned by the prosecutor.

A. Procedural Rights of the Accused and Judicial Warnings

637. The court must inform the accused that he is under no obligation to make a statement in response to the court's invitation to do so.[1549] He must, furthermore, be warned that he need not answer any questions put by the court.[1550] These warnings are aimed at protecting an accused's right to silence.[1551] He may lawfully refuse to respond.[1552] The statutory power of the court to question him does not place any duty upon the accused to respond.[1553]

An accused should also be warned that the effect of a formal admission is that the state need not prove the fact which has been formally admitted. And the accused should be informed that he need not consent to the recording of formal admissions.[1554] This rule stems from the fact that an accused is under no duty to assist the prosecution in proving its case against him.

B. Purpose, Manner and Ambit of Judicial Questioning During the Explanation of Plea

638. The purpose of judicial questioning is to establish what the defence of the accused is and to eliminate issues that are really common causes between the accused and the prosecution.[1555] The questioning must take place before any evidence is led by the prosecution.[1556] It is also irregular to question the accused without having first invited him to make a statement indicating the basis of his defence.[1557]

The court is not entitled to cross-examine the accused.[1558] It may therefore not ask questions which are directed – or which appear to be directed at refuting the defence put forward by the accused.[1559] The judicial officer may not descend into the arena, despite his statutory powers to question the accused.

It is irregular for the court to question an accused on matters which neither directly nor indirectly appear in the charge.[1560]

1549. *S v. Daniëls* 1983 (3) SA 275 (A).
1550. *S v. Daniëls* (*supra*) 299F–H.
1551. *See generally*, *S v. Evans* 1981 (4) SA 52 (C).
1552. *S v. Mabaso* 1990 (3) SA 185 (A) 211C–D.
1553. J.J. Joubert et al., *Criminal Procedure Handbook* 13th ed. (Juta, Cape Town 2020) 324.
1554. *S v. Daniëls* (*supra*) 299H–300A.
1555. *S v. Moloyi* 1978 (1) SA 516 (O) 520E.
1556. *S v. Mayedwa* 1978 (1) SA 509 (E) 512A.
1557. *S v. Philander* 1977 (2) PH H214 (NC).
1558. *S v. Seleke* 1980 (3) SA 745 (A) 574A.
1559. *S v. Herbst* 1980 (3) SA 1026 (E) 1031D.
1560. *S v. Novuka* 1978 (2) PH H120 (O) and *S v. Molelekeng* 1992 (1) SACR 604 (T).

Once an accused has made a statement which clearly indicates his defence, it is irregular for the court to persist in questioning the accused.[1561]

§4. Presentation, Examination and Confrontation of Evidence

639. The prosecution is required to lead evidence where the accused has pleaded not guilty or where the accused's plea of guilty was corrected to a plea of not guilty.[1562]

I. The Presentation of the Case for the Prosecution

A. The Opening Address and General Provisions

640. The prosecutor may, before any evidence is adduced, address the court for the purpose of explaining the charge and indicating, without comment, to the court what evidence he intends to adduce in support of the charge.[1563] An opening address is as a rule only delivered in complicated cases.

The prosecutor may then examine the witnesses for the prosecution and adduce such evidence as may be admissible to prove that the accused committed the offence referred to in the charge or that he committed an offence of which he may be convicted on the charge.[1564]

Where any document may be received in evidence by any court upon its mere production, the prosecutor shall read out such document in court unless the accused is in possession of a copy of such document or dispenses with the reading out thereof.[1565] In several instances, however, it is necessary to call witnesses to identify and hand in documents.

B. Examination and Confrontation of Prosecution Witnesses

641. Every witness called to testify on behalf of the prosecution is first questioned by the prosecutor. This is known as 'examination-in-chief'. The prosecutor questions the witness on the basis of the latter's written statement made to the police during the investigation of the crime. As a rule, the prosecutor may not prove the written statement of the witness. Oral evidence is required. And the court and the defence may as a rule not have any access to the written statement. The statement is privileged.[1566] But in certain circumstances, access must be allowed, for example,

1561. *S v. Muzikayifani* 1979 (2) SA 516 (D) 517G.
1562. Criminal Procedure Act 51 of 1977, s. 113.
1563. Criminal Procedure Act 51 of 1977, s. 150(1).
1564. Criminal Procedure Act 51 of 1977, s. 150(2)(*a*).
1565. Criminal Procedure Act 51 of 1977, s. 150(2)(*b*).
1566. *S v. Mavela* 1990 (1) SACR 582 (A).

where the prosecutor uses the written statement to refresh the memory of his witness[1567] or where there is a serious discrepancy between the written statement and the oral evidence of the witness.[1568]

642. The prosecutor may not ask leading questions on matters in dispute and may not cross-examine (attack the credibility) his own witness unless the witness has been declared hostile by the court upon the application of the prosecutor.[1569] An application of this nature is not easily granted.[1570]

The prosecutor has a duty not to elicit inadmissible evidence from his witness – and if he does so, the defence may intervene by way of an objection to be ruled upon by the court. The court may also intervene *mero motu* and must do so where the accused has no legal representative.

643. The accused or his legal representative has a right to cross-examine the prosecution witness upon completion of the latter's evidence-in-chief.[1571] In fact, there is a duty to cross-examine if the evidence of the prosecution witness is disputed.[1572] The cross-examiner is not restricted to matters which were covered by the prosecutor during examination-in-chief. The purpose of cross-examination is to elicit facts favourable to the cross-examiner's case, to attack the credibility of the witness concerned or to show that the witness is mistaken. Leading questions may be asked by the cross-examiner. But the court might eventually attach little weight to answers given to leading questions.[1573]

A cross-examiner may not put misleading statements to a witness[1574] and may not be abusive or discourteous.

A prosecutor has a right to re-examine his witness upon completion of cross-examination.[1575] The purpose of re-examination is to clear up any points or misunderstandings which may have occurred during cross-examination. It follows that re-examination must be confined to matters touched upon during cross-examination. Fresh matters can only be covered with leave of the court – and then the defence has a right to cross-examine on these new points raised in re-examination.

Where it appears to the court that any cross-examination is being unreasonably protracted, it may request the cross-examiner to disclose the relevancy of any line of examination and may impose reasonable limits on such examination.[1576]

The court may within limits ask questions during evidence-in-chief, cross-examination and re-examination.

1567. *R v. Elijah* 1963 (3) SA 86 (SR).
1568. *S v. Kamte* 1992 (1) SACR 677 (A).
1569. Criminal Procedure Act 51 of 1977, s. 190.
1570. *See generally*, *S v. Steyn* 1987 (1) SA 353 (W).
1571. Criminal Procedure Act 51 of 1977, s. 166(1); this is also a constitutional right in terms of s. 35(3)(i) of the Constitution – *see S v. Msimango* 2010 (1) SACR 544 (GSJ).
1572. *S v. Malelele* 1975 (4) SA 128 (T).
1573. *R v. Milne and Erleigh* (7) 1951 (1) SA 791 (A).
1574. *S v. Khubeka* 1982 (1) SA 534 (W) 536.
1575. Criminal Procedure Act 51 of 1977, s. 166(1).
1576. Criminal Procedure Act 51 of 1977, s. 166(3).

C. Closure and the Application for Discharge of the Accused

644. The prosecution closes its case when it has in its discretion presented all the necessary oral, documentary and real evidence supporting its case. At this stage, the defence or the court[1577] may raise the question of whether the accused should not be discharged in terms of section 174 of the Criminal Procedure Act 1977. This section provides that if, at the close of the case for the prosecution, the court is of the opinion that there is no evidence that the accused committed the offence, it may return a verdict of not guilty. The basis of this provision is that an accused need not be called upon to defend himself if the prosecution has failed to make out a case against him. It is just another illustration of the passive defence right of the accused.

The courts employ the following test when they have to decide whether a discharge in terms of section 174 of the Criminal Procedure Act 51 of 1977 is warranted:[1578] Is there evidence upon which a reasonable man may convict? If the answer is yes, a discharge must be refused. If the answer is no, it must be asked whether there is a reasonable possibility that the evidence of the prosecution might be supplemented by the defence. In a decision in the post-constitutional era,[1579] the SCA has held, taking into account the privilege against self-incrimination and the rights to human dignity and freedom, that an accused must be discharged at the end of the State's case if a conviction would only be possible if the accused were to testify and incriminate himself. Where there are co-accused, and the State's case against one accused may be supplemented by the evidence of a co-accused, this approach would not apply.

645. An application for discharge must be made and considered before any evidence is led by the defence.[1580]

II. The Presentation of the Case for the Defence

A. Opening Address

646. If an accused is not discharged at the close of the case for the prosecution, the court must ask him whether he intends to adduce any evidence on behalf of the defence. If he answers in the affirmative, he may address the court for the purpose of indicating to the court, without comment, what evidence he intends adducing on behalf of the defence.[1581]

1577. *S v. Amerika* 1990 (2) SACR 480 (C); *S v. Maliga* 2015 (2) SACR 202 (SCA).
1578. *S v. Schuping* 1983 (2) SA 119 (B); *S v. Zimmerie* 1989 (3) SA 484 (C).
1579. *S v. Lubaxa* 2001 (2) SACR 703 (SCA).
1580. *See also generally, S v. Phuravhatha* 1992 (2) SACR 545 (V).
1581. Criminal Procedure Act 51 of 1977, s. 151 (1)(*a*).

B. The Order in Which Witnesses Should Be Called

647. The court shall also ask the accused whether he himself intends to give evidence on behalf of the defence.[1582] If the accused answers in the affirmative, he shall, except where the court on good cause shown allows otherwise, be called as a witness before any other witness for the defence.[1583] If the accused answers in the negative but decides, after other evidence has been given on behalf of the defence, to give evidence himself, the court may draw such inference from the accused's conduct as may be reasonable in the circumstances.[1584]

648. There are no statutory provisions regulating the order in which accused who are tried jointly must testify.[1585] The practice is that they should testify in the numerical order in which they are listed in the charge or indictment. But the court may order a departure from this practice if none of the parties would be prejudiced and if fairness so requires.[1586] It has also been held that if all the co-accused agree that they should present their cases in an order which differs from the numerical order, then they may do so.[1587]

C. Examination and Confrontation of the Accused and Other Defence Witnesses

649. The accused who wishes to testify and all other witnesses called to testify on behalf of the defence are each individually taken through the three basic stages known as evidence-in-chief, cross-examination and re-examination. And the rules which apply in respect of the examination of prosecution witnesses and which were described in paragraph 642 *supra* are *mutatis mutandis* applicable to the accused and other defence witnesses.

Cross-examination is conducted by the prosecutor as well as the co-accused who did not call the witness. The High Court has often disapproved of rude and unfair cross-examination by a prosecutor.[1588] An accused may also not be cross-examined on the basis of inadmissible evidence, for example, an inadmissible confession.[1589]

D. Closure of the Case for the Defence

650. The defence closes its case when satisfied that all available evidence supporting its case has been led.

1582. Criminal Procedure Act 51 of 1977, s. 151(1)(*b*).
1583. Criminal Procedure Act 51 of 1977, s. 151(1)(*b*)(i).
1584. Criminal Procedure Act 51 of 1977, s. 151(1)(*b*)(ii).
1585. *See generally*, *S v. Swanepoel* 1980 (2) SA 81 (NC) 83.
1586. *S v. Ngobeni* 1981 (1) SA 506 (B).
1587. *S v. Mpetha* (1) 1983 (1) SA 493 (C).
1588. *S v. Omar* 1982 (2) SA 357 (N).
1589. *S v. Nkwanyana* 1978 (3) SA 404 (N) 406.

III. Witnesses Called by the Court

651. The court may *at any stage of criminal proceedings* subpoena or cause to be subpoenaed any person as a witness at such proceedings, and the court shall so subpoena a witness or so cause a witness to be subpoenaed if the evidence of such witness appears to the court essential to the just decision of the case.[1590]

652. The prosecutor and the accused may, with leave of the court, examine or cross-examine any witness called by the court at criminal proceedings.[1591]

653. The court may *at any stage of criminal proceedings* examine any person, other than the accused, who has been subpoenaed to attend such proceedings or who is in attendance at such proceedings and may recall and re-examine any person, including an accused, already examined at the proceedings, and the court shall examine, or recall and re-examine, the person concerned if his evidence appears to the court essential to the just decision of the case.[1592]

IV. Address by Parties at Conclusion of All the Evidence

654. After all the evidence has been adduced, the prosecutor may address the court and thereafter the accused may address the court.[1593] It is an irregularity to deviate from this order.[1594]

The prosecutor may reply on any matter of law raised by the accused in his address and may, with leave of the court, reply on any matter of fact raised by the accused in his address.[1595]

§5. Judgment, Verdict and Sentence

I. Judgment

655. Judgment may be given immediately or may be deferred.[1596] In High Court trials, reasons must be given;[1597] though a magistrate or regional magistrate does *not have to* give reasons, in practice, reasons are required in every case where legal or factual disputes have arisen.[1598] The reasons must, where necessary, deal with questions of fact as well as law. The fundamental question is whether the court is satisfied that the guilt of the accused has been proved beyond reasonable doubt.

1590. Criminal Procedure Act 51 of 1977, s. 186.
1591. Criminal Procedure Act 51 of 1977, s. 166(2).
1592. Criminal Procedure Act 51 of 1977, s. 167.
1593. Criminal Procedure Act 51 of 1977, s. 175(1).
1594. *S v. Dlamini* 1992 (2) SACR 533 (N).
1595. Criminal Procedure Act 51 of 1977, s. 175(2).
1596. Criminal Procedure Act 51 of 1977, s. 177.
1597. Criminal Procedure Act 51 of 1977, s. 146.
1598. Magistrates' Court Act 32 of 1944, s. 93*ter*(3)(*c*)–(*e*); *S v. Maake* 2011 (1) SACR 263 (SCA).

II. Competent Verdicts

656. If the court finds that the offence as specified in the charge or indictment has not been proved, the accused must be acquitted of this offence. However, this is not the end of the matter. The court must also consider the question of a so-called competent verdict.[1599] A 'competent verdict' is a verdict of guilty in respect of an offence not specifically mentioned in the charge or indictment but in respect of which the court is authorised by statute to convict if such an offence – and not the one specifically mentioned in the charge – is eventually proved. For example, where it is alleged that the accused intentionally and unlawfully killed a human being, the indictment need only allege murder. If intention to kill is not proved, but negligence is, then the court may convict the accused of culpable homicide because section 258(*a*) of the Criminal Procedure Act 51 of 1977 provides that a verdict of guilty of culpable homicide can be a competent verdict on a charge of murder where murder is eventually not proved but culpable homicide is. The court must during the course of the trial give an undefended accused a timeous warning of the possibility that a competent verdict might be returned against him.[1600] The basis of this rule is that the accused must not be taken by surprise. Competent verdicts are not mentioned in the charge or indictment and the accused might be prejudiced in his defence if he is not fully aware of all the possible 'implied' charges against him.[1601]

A. *Attempts*

657. If the evidence in criminal proceedings does not prove the commission of the offence charged but proves an attempt to commit that offence or an attempt to commit any other offence of which an accused may be convicted on the offence charged, the accused may be found guilty of an attempt to commit that offence or, as the case may be, such other offence.[1602]

B. *Accessory after the Fact*

658. If the evidence in criminal proceedings does not prove the commission of the offence charged but proves that the accused is guilty as an accessory after that offence or any other offence of which he may be convicted on the offence charged, the accused may be found guilty as an accessory after that offence or, as the case may be, such other offence, and shall, in the absence of any punishment expressly provided by law, be liable to punishment at the discretion of the court.[1603] However,

1599. Competent verdicts are regulated by ss 256–270 of the Criminal Procedure Act 51 of 1977.
1600. *S v. Fielies* 2006 (1) SACR 302 (C) paras 7–9.
1601. S.E. van der Merwe, '"Skuldig" maar ontoerekeningsvatbaar dronk – Prosesregtelike aangeleenthede rakende die Strafregwysigingswet 1 van 1988' 1990 *Stell LR* 94 103–104.
1602. Criminal Procedure Act 51 of 1977, s. 256.
1603. Criminal Procedure Act 51 of 1977, s. 257.

such punishment shall not exceed the punishment which may be imposed in respect of the offence with reference to which the accused is convicted as an accessory.

III. Sentencing Procedures

A. *Proof of Previous Convictions*

659. The prosecution may, after an accused has been convicted but before sentence has been imposed upon him, produce to the court for admission or denial by the accused a record of previous convictions alleged against the accused. The court must then ask the accused whether he admits or denies any previous conviction as alleged by the prosecutor. If the accused denies such previous conviction, the prosecution may tender evidence that the accused was so previously convicted. If the accused admits such previous conviction or such previous conviction is proved against the accused, the court shall take such conviction into account when imposing any sentence in respect of the offence of which the accused has been convicted.[1604] However, certain minor previous convictions expire after ten years and must be ignored by the court.[1605]

B. *Evidence for Purposes of Determining an Appropriate Sentence*

660. Section 274(1) of the Criminal Procedure Act 51 of 1977 provides that the court may before passing sentence receive such evidence as it thinks fit in order to inform itself as to the proper sentence to be passed. It is an established rule of practice that the court must call for a pre-sentence report,[1606] where a juvenile has been convicted of a serious crime.[1607]

The accused may testify and call witnesses on the matter of sentencing. The prosecutor may also call witnesses.

661. The ordinary strict rules of evidence do not apply when the court requires information for purposes of sentencing.[1608] Hearsay is readily received[1609] and both the accused and the prosecutor may make statements from the bar. However, the SCA has held that any procedure which is for any reason unfair to the accused is irregular.[1610]

1604. Criminal Procedure Act 51 of 1977, s. 271.
1605. Criminal Procedure Act 51 of 1977, s. 271A.
1606. *See generally*, S.E. van der Merwe, 'The Contents and Evidential Aspects of a Pre-sentence Report' 1980 *SACC* 126.
1607. *S v. Jansen* 1975 (1) SA 425 (A). In addition, a child justice court imposing a sentence must request a pre-sentence report prepared by a probation officer prior to the imposition of sentence – s. 71(1)(*a*) of the Child Justice Act 75 of 2008.
1608. S.S. Terblanche, *Guide to Sentencing in South Africa* 3rd ed. (LexisNexis, Durban 2016) 95ff.
1609. *S v. Rooi* 1980 (1) 363 (C).
1610. *S v. Jabavu* 1969 (2) SA 466 (A) 472.

C. Final Right to Address

662. Section 274(2) gives the accused a statutory right to address the court on any evidence received for purposes of sentencing and on the matter of sentence. The prosecution has a similar right.

663. The accused may then be sentenced by the court, either immediately or at a later date, if the court needs time to consider the matter. The competent sentences and related matters are dealt with in Part III *infra.*[1611]

1611. *See also* Ch. 7 of Part I *supra* for further discussion.

Chapter 5. Appeal and Review

§1. Post-Trial Remedies

664. The important post-trial remedies are appeal and review. These are judicial remedies in the sense that they require the intervention of a court of law. The right to a fair trial set out in section 35 of the Constitution specifically guarantees the right of review or appeal by a court of higher instance.[1612] Other post-trial remedies are linked to the Executive, for example, the power of the President to extend mercy,[1613] to grant a free pardon[1614] or to substitute a verdict.[1615]

§2. The Distinction Between Appeal and Review

665. Appeal and review are different procedures which seek to attain the same goal, namely, to convince a higher court that the trial court's conviction and sentence should be set aside or that only the sentence should be set aside or reduced.

Appeal is the correct procedure to follow where the allegation is that the trial court came to an incorrect conclusion on the facts (the evidence) or on the law. An appeal is in principle argued on the record of the proceedings in the trial court. Only in most exceptional circumstances will a party be permitted to lead further evidence. An appeal must be lodged within fourteen (High Court) or fifteen (Full Court or SCA) days after the trial court's verdict. But on good cause shown, a court may condone the late filing of an appeal.

666. Review is the correct procedure where the allegation is that irregularities were committed by the trial court. A review court is entitled to receive affidavits[1616] in addition to the record of the trial proceedings. There is no specific time limit for review. But it must be brought within a reasonable period.[1617]

§3. The Right to Appeal

I. The Accused

667. Any person convicted of any offence by any lower court (including a person discharged after conviction) may, subject to the provisions of section 84 of the Child Justice Act of 2008, and subject to leave to appeal being granted in terms of

1612. Constitution of the RSA, s. 35(3)(*o*).
1613. Section 84(2)(*j*) of the Constitution empowers the President, subject to and in accordance with the Constitution, to pardon or reprieve offenders and to remit any fines, penalties or forfeitures. This prerogative is, *ex abundanti cautela*, also set out in the Criminal Procedure Act 1977, s. 325.
1614. Criminal Procedure Act 51 of 1977, s. 327(6)(*a*)(i).
1615. Criminal Procedure Act 51 of 1977, s. 327(6)(*a*)(ii).
1616. That is a statement a person makes in which he or she promises (by way of oath or affirmation) that he or she will only make truthful statements.
1617. *Zwane v. Magistrate of Maphumulo* 1980 (3) SA 976 (N).

section 309B or section 309C of the Criminal Procedure Act, appeal against such conviction and against any resultant sentence or order to the High Court having jurisdiction.[1618] Section 309B provides that any accused who wishes to note an appeal against conviction or sentence must apply to that court for leave to so appeal.[1619] If any application for leave to appeal (or for further evidence or for condonation of late appeal) is refused by a lower court, the accused may by petition apply to the Judge President of the High Court having jurisdiction.[1620] A person convicted and sentenced in a case heard by a single High Court judge may apply to that court for leave to appeal against conviction or against any resultant sentence or order.[1621] The Court of Appeal in such cases will be the SCA, unless the court or judge granting the application directs that the matter be heard by a full court of that High Court.[1622] If any application for leave to appeal (or for further evidence or for condonation of late appeal) is refused by a High Court, the accused may by petition apply to the President of the SCA to grant such application.[1623] The accused may further apply (to the High Court) for a special entry to be made on the record stating that the High Court proceedings were irregular or not according to law.[1624]A question of law may further be reserved by the trial (High) court for the consideration of the SCA.[1625]

II. The Prosecution

668. The prosecution cannot appeal against an acquittal on the facts. However, when a trial court has in any proceedings given a decision in favour of the accused on any *question of law*, the Director of Public Prosecutions may require that court

1618. Criminal Procedure Act 51 of 1977, s. 309(1)(*a*). The exception, when an appeal may be noted without having to apply for leave to appeal, is where the convicted person was, in terms of s. 84 of the Child Justice Act 75 of 2008, at the time of the commission of the offence, either below the age of 16 years, or 16 years or older but under 18 years and sentenced to any form of imprisonment not wholly suspended.
1619. Subject to s. 84 of Act 75 of 2008. The procedure for such application is set out in s. 309B. In terms of s. 309B(5), an application for leave to appeal may be accompanied by an application to adduce further evidence relating to the conviction or sentence.
1620. Criminal Procedure Act 51 of 1977, s. 309C(2).
1621. Criminal Procedure Act 51 of 1977, s. 316(1)(*a*); Superior Courts Act 10 of 2013, s. 16. The exception, when an appeal may be noted without having to apply for leave to appeal, is where the convicted person was, in terms of s. 84 of the Child Justice Act 75 of 2008, at the time of the commission of the offence, either below the age of 16 years, or 16 years or older but under 18 years and sentenced to any form of imprisonment not wholly suspended.
1622. Criminal Procedure Act 51 of 1977, s. 315. No appeal lies against the judgment or order of a Full Court on appeal unless with the special leave of the SCA – s. 316(3)(*a*). In terms of s. 316(5)(*a*), an application for leave to appeal may be accompanied by an application to adduce further evidence relating to the prospective appeal. A full court, in relation to any division of the High Court, means a court consisting of three judges of the division of the High Court, in terms of the Superior Courts Act 10 of 2013, s. 1.
1623. Criminal Procedure Act 51 of 1977, s. 316(8)(*a*); Superior Courts Act 10 of 2013, s. 17.
1624. Criminal Procedure Act 51 of 1977, ss 317, 318. Where such application for a special entry is refused, the SCA may be approached by way of petition addressed to the President of the SCA.
1625. Criminal Procedure Act 51 of 1977, s. 319.

to state a case for the Court of Appeal, setting forth the question of law and its decision thereon and, if evidence has been heard, its findings of fact in so far as these findings are material to the question of law.[1626] If the prosecution's appeal to the High Court on a point of law is unsuccessful, it may with leave of the High Court appeal to the SCA.

669. The Director of Public Prosecutions may appeal to the High Court against a sentence imposed by a lower court, provided leave to appeal was granted by a judge in chambers and, with leave, to the SCA in respect of a sentence imposed by the High Court.[1627]

§4. Powers of Court of Appeal

670. The Court of Appeal may confirm, alter or quash the conviction; may confirm, alter, reduce or increase the sentence imposed by the trial court; may in exceptional circumstances hear further evidence before reaching its verdict; and, finally, may remit the case to the trial court with instructions to deal with certain matters as the Court of Appeal may think fit.[1628] Where, for example, a conviction and sentence are set aside by the Court of Appeal on the ground that a failure of justice has in fact resulted from the admission against the accused of evidence otherwise admissible but not properly placed before the trial court by reason of some defect in the proceedings, the Court of Appeal may remit the case to the trial court with instructions to deal with any matter, including the hearing of such evidence, in such manner as the Court of Appeal may think fit.

It must also be pointed out that, notwithstanding that the Court of Appeal is of opinion that any point raised might be decided in favour of the accused, no conviction or sentence shall be set aside or altered by reason of any irregularity or defect in the record or proceedings, unless it appears to the Court of Appeal that a failure of justice has in fact resulted from such irregularity or defect.

§5. Special Entry

671. There are no review procedures in respect of alleged irregularities in High Court trials. However, section 317 of the Criminal Procedure Act 51 of 1977 makes provision for a so-called special entry on the grounds of which the aggrieved accused may take his case to the SCA. Leave to approach the SCA by way of special entry must be obtained from the trial judge or other available judge. If an application for a special entry is refused, the accused may within twenty-one days of such refusal (or within such further period as may on good cause be permitted) apply, by way of petition addressed to the President of the SCA, for a special entry to be made on the record.

1626. Criminal Procedure Act 51 of 1977, s. 310.
1627. Criminal Procedure Act 51 of 1977, s. 310A, s. 316B.
1628. J.J. Joubert et al., *Criminal Procedure Handbook* 13th ed. (Juta, Cape Town 2020) 517–520.

§6. REVIEW

I. Grounds of Review

672. The High Court has the power to review the proceedings of any lower court. The grounds on which the proceedings may be brought for reviewing purposes are the following:[1629] absence of jurisdiction on the part of the trial court; interest in the cause, bias,[1630] malice or corruption on the part of the presiding officer; gross irregularity in the proceedings; and, further, the admission of inadmissible or incompetent evidence[1631] or the rejection of admissible or competent evidence.[1632]

II. Automatic Review

673. The record of certain cases tried in the magistrates' courts *must* be sent to the High Court regardless of the accused's attitude. This is known as automatic review and applies to the following cases:[1633] where a sentence of more than three months imprisonment (including compulsory residence in a child and youth care centre in a programme provided for in section 191(2)(*j*) of the Children's Act 38 of 2005) or a fine in excess of ZAR 6,000 (GBP 252/USD 330/EUR 300) has been imposed by a magistrate who has not yet held the rank of magistrate for a period of seven years; where a sentence of more than six months imprisonment (including compulsory residence in a child and youth care centre in terms of Act 38 of 2005) or a fine in excess of ZAR 12,000 (GBP 504/USD 660/EUR 600) has been imposed by a magistrate who has held the rank of magistrate for seven years or longer. A review of this nature is considered by a judge in chambers, but he may also call for the matter to be argued in court. Automatic review only takes place if the accused had no legal representation at the trial.

III. Review of Proceedings Before Sentence

674. If a magistrate or regional magistrate after conviction but before sentence is of the opinion that the proceedings in respect of which he or she brought in a conviction are not in accordance with justice or that doubt exists whether the proceedings are in accordance with justice, he or she shall, without sentencing the accused,

---

1629. Superior Courts Act 10 of 2013, s. 22(1).
1630. *See generally*, *S v. Nameng* 1967 (2) SA 201 (T); *S v. Bam* 1972 (4) SA 41 (E).
1631. *R v. Mocke* 1949 (4) SA 95 (T).
1632. *R v. Grieve* 1947 (2) SA 264 (T).
1633. Criminal Procedure Act 51 of 1977, s. 302. In addition, in terms of s. 85 of the Child Justice Act 75 of 2008, children convicted in terms of this Act have their sentences automatically reviewed provided that at the time of the commission of the offence the convicted child was below the age of 16 years, or was at least 16 but below the age of 18 years and was sentenced to any form of imprisonment not wholly suspended or any sentence of compulsory residence in a child and youth care centre providing a programme as per s. 191(2)(*j*) of the Children's Act 38 of 2005.

record the reasons for his or her opinion and transmit them, together with the record of the proceedings, to the registrar of the provincial division having jurisdiction, and such registrar shall, as soon as practicable, lay the same for review in chambers before a judge.[1634] The judge may then deal with the matter in the same way as any other review.

IV. Powers of High Court as Court of Review

675. On review, the High Court may:

1. confirm, alter or quash the conviction, and in the event of the conviction being quashed where the accused was convicted on one of two or more alternative charges, convict the accused on the other alternative charge or on one or other of the alternative charges;
2. confirm, reduce, alter or set aside the sentence or any order of the magistrates' court;
3. set aside or correct the proceedings of the magistrates' court;
4. generally give such judgment or impose such sentence or make such order as the magistrates' court ought to have given, imposed or made on any matter which was before it at the trial of the case in question; or
5. remit the case to the magistrates' court with instructions to deal with any matter in such manner as the provincial or local division may think fit; and
6. make any such order in regard to the suspension of the execution of any sentence against the person convicted, or the admission of such person to bail, or, generally, in regard to any matter or thing connected with such person or the proceedings in regard to such person as to the court seems likely to promote the ends of justice.[1635]

§7. Institution of Proceedings De Novo Where Conviction Set Aside on Appeal or Review

676. An accused whose conviction was set aside on appeal or review may as a rule not be prosecuted again in respect of the same facts. A second prosecution is, however, permitted where the Court of Appeal or review had set aside the conviction on the ground that the trial court was not a competent court or that the charge document ('charge' in lower courts, and 'indictment' in the High Court) was invalid or that there was any other technical irregularity or defect in the trial court proceedings.[1636] In these instances, the accused is considered not to have been acquitted on the merits of the case, and a second prosecution is possible.

1634. Criminal Procedure Act 51 of 1977, s. 304A.
1635. Criminal Procedure Act 51 of 1977, s. 304(2)(*c*).
1636. Criminal Procedure Act 51 of 1977, s. 324.

Part III. Execution and Extinction of Sentence

Chapter 1. Sources of Penitentiary Law and Nature of Regulations

677. The correctional system in South Africa is governed by the Correctional Services Act of 1998,[1637] as informed by the Bill of Rights, which forms part of the Constitution. In this regard, the following rights are particularly pertinent: the right to dignity;[1638] the right to freedom and security of the person, including the right not to be subjected to cruel, inhuman and degrading punishment or treatment;[1639] and the right of detained, arrested and accused persons.[1640] Prisoners retain all their rights upon detention, subject to the criteria for limitation of such rights in section 36 of the Constitution.[1641] The Correctional Services Act is supplemented by subordinate legislation in the form of general Regulations made in terms of the Act by the Minister of Correctional Services.[1642] Other Acts, such as the Criminal Procedure Act 51 of 1977, contain important provisions relating to the manner in which sentences such as fines and compensation orders must be implemented.

678. The purpose of the Correctional Services Act, which came into force in July 2004, was to change the law relating to the correctional system and to give effect to the Bill of Rights in the Constitution, in particular, relating to prisoners. Thus, the Act recognises international principles on correctional matters, sets out certain mandatory minimum rights applicable to all prisoners, provides for independent monitoring systems in the form of the judicial inspectorate and independent prison visitors and makes provision for private sector involvement in the correctional system. In trying to foreground rehabilitation in all the activities of the Department of Correctional Services and taking into account the constitutional rights of prisoners,

1637. Correctional Services Act 111 of 1998. The previous piece of legislation governing correctional matters, Act 8 of 1959, has almost entirely been repealed. For general discussion of the law governing the correctional system, *see* J.A. Faris, 'Prisons' in W.A. Joubert (ed.), *LAWSA* vol. 33 3rd ed. (LexisNexis, Durban 2020).
1638. Constitution, 1996, s. 10.
1639. Constitution, 1996, s. 12.
1640. Constitution, 1996, s. 35.
1641. *S v. Makwanyane* 1995 (2) SACR 1 (CC) para. 143.
1642. Correctional Services Regulations as amended (GN R323 in GG 35277 of 25 Apr. 2012), made in terms of s. 134 of Act 111 of 1998.

some of the language of the previous legislation has been amended by the Correctional Services Amendment Act 25 of 2008.[1643] A number of regional and international instruments governing the rights of detained persons apply to South Africa, including the United Nations Convention on Civil and Political Rights, the United Nations Convention against Cruel, Inhuman and Degrading Treatment or Punishment, the African Charter on Human and People's Rights, along with various instruments dealing with the rights of detained children,[1644] and various non-binding standards and principles relating to detained persons.[1645]

1643. Thus a prisoner is now to be referred to as an 'inmate', a prison is now referred to as a correctional centre, and sentenced or unsentenced prisoner referred to as 'sentenced' or 'unsentenced offender' (in terms of s. 1 of Act 111 of 1998). A 'remand detainee' is a person detained in a remand detention facility awaiting the finalisation of his or her trial, if such person has not commenced serving a sentence or is not already serving a prior sentence; and a 'remand detention facility' is a place established under the Act for the reception, detention or confinement of a person liable to detention in custody (s. 1).

1644. The United Nations Convention on the Rights of the Child (1989); the United Nations Rules for Juveniles Deprived of their Liberty (adopted by the UN General Assembly resolution 45/113 on 14 Dec. 1990) and the United Nations Standard Minimum Rules for the Administration of Juvenile Justice (The Beijing Rules) adopted by (UN General Assembly resolution 40/33 of 29 Nov. 1985).

1645. For example, the Body of Principles for the Protection of all Persons under any form of Detention or Imprisonment (UN General Assembly resolution 43/173 of 9 Dec. 1988); and the Code of Conduct for Law Enforcement Officials (UN General Assembly resolution 34/169 of 17 Dec. 1979).

Chapter 2. General Principles Concerning the Purposes and Functioning of the Correctional System

679. The Department of Correctional Services is required to fulfil the purpose of the correctional system as set out in the Correctional Services Act of 1998: to contribute to maintaining and protecting a just and safe society by enforcing sentences of the courts in the manner prescribed by the Act, detaining all inmates in safe custody whilst ensuring their human dignity, and promoting the social responsibility and human development of all sentenced offenders.[1646] The department is under the control of the national commissioner.[1647]

680. Every inmate is required to accept the authority and obey the lawful instructions of the commissioner and correctional officials, and the department must in turn take steps to ensure the safe custody of every inmate and maintain security and good order in the correctional centre, but in doing so must not unduly infringe inmates' rights.[1648] No person may be admitted to a correctional centre without a valid warrant for his or her detention.[1649] On admission to a correctional centre, each inmate should be promptly informed of his or her right to consult with a legal practitioner or to have a legal practitioner assigned to him or her at state expense if substantial injustice would otherwise result.[1650] Inmates should be duly provided with necessary information about their incarceration and must be medically examined.[1651]

1646. Correctional Services Act 111 of 1998, s. 2.
1647. Correctional Services Act 111 of 1998, s. 3.
1648. Correctional Services Act 111 of 1998, s. 4.
1649. Correctional Services Act 111 of 1998, s. 6(1)(*a*).
1650. Correctional Services Act 111 of 1998, s. 6(3).
1651. Correctional Services Act 111 of 1998, s. 6(4), 6(5).

Chapter 3. The Correctional System

§1. Organisational Structure

I. Administration

681. The Minister is required to appoint a National Council for Correctional Services, the primary function of which is to advise in developing policy in regard to the correctional system and the sentencing process.[1652]

682. The Act provides that the department and every correctional official must strive to fulfil the purpose of the Act, and to that end, each official must perform his or her duties under the Act.[1653] The Minister may delegate any of the powers vested in him or her by the Act to the National Commissioner.[1654] The National Commissioner may delegate any of the powers vested in him or her by the Act or any other Act and may sub-delegate any power delegated by the Minister.[1655]

683. Provision has been made in the Act for private sector involvement in prisons. The Minister may enter into a contract with a private party for the design, construction, financing and operation of a correctional centre or part thereof.[1656]

684. Each correctional centre is required to have one or more case management committees made up of correctional officials.[1657] The role of the committee is to ensure that each sentenced offender is assessed and that there is a correctional service plan for each sentenced offender serving more than twenty-four months' imprisonment.[1658] To this end, the committee must at regular intervals interview such offenders to review such plans and make preliminary arrangements for the possible placement of a sentenced offender under community corrections. Moreover, the committee is required to submit a report, along with all relevant documents, to the correctional supervision and parole board, with regard to the offence or offences for which the sentenced offender was convicted, together with the following documents and information:

- the judgment on the merits and any remarks made by the court in imposing sentence;
- the sentenced offender's previous criminal record;
- the conduct, disciplinary record, adaptation, training, aptitude, industry, physical and mental state of such sentenced offender;

1652. Correctional Services Act 111 of 1998, ss 83, 84.
1653. Correctional Services Act 111 of 1998, s. 96(1).
1654. Correctional Services Act 111 of 1998, s. 97(1). The exception is the power to make regulations, in terms of s. 134.
1655. Correctional Services Act 111 of 1998, s. 97(2).
1656. Correctional Services Act 111 of 1998, s. 103. *See* further Ch. XIV of the Act.
1657. Correctional Services Act 111 of 1998, s. 42(1).
1658. Correctional Services Act 111 of 1998, s. 38(1A).

- the likelihood of relapse into crime; the risk posed to the community and the manner in which such risk can be reduced;
- the assessment results and the progress with regard to the correctional sentence plan contemplated in section 38;
- the possible placement of an offender under correctional supervision in terms of a sentence provided for in section 276(1)(*i*) or 287(4)(*a*) of the Criminal Procedure Act, or in terms of the conversion of such an offender's sentence into correctional supervision under section 276A(3)(*e*)(ii) or 287(4)(*b*) of the said Act, and the conditions for such placement;
- a certified copy of the offender's identity document and, in the case of a foreign national, a report from the Department of Home Affairs on the residential status of such offender;
- the possible placement under correctional supervision or release of an offender who has been declared a dangerous criminal, in terms of section 286B(4)(*b*) of the Criminal Procedure Act;
- the possible placement of such sentenced offender on parole or day parole or medical parole and the conditions for such placement;
- and information regarding such other matters as the Correctional Supervision and Parole Board may request.[1659]

II. Classification of Inmates

685. All sentenced offenders are allocated a security classification. Security classification is determined by the extent to which the inmate presents a security risk and so as to determine the correctional centre or part of a correctional centre in which he or she is to be detained.[1660] Offenders may be held in maximum, medium and minimum security prisons. The security classification is linked to the concomitant 'privilege' classification in correctional centres, which ranges from Group C with minimum privileges to Group A with maximum privileges within each security classification.

686. In addition to the formal classification systems, male and female inmates are also separated,[1661] as are adults and juveniles.

1659. Correctional Services Act 111 of 1998, s. 42(2). The phrase 'such other matters' allows the Board to request any information which it believes pertains to the offender's incarceration. For discussion of 'correctional supervision and parole board' *see* para. 697 *infra*.

1660. Correctional Services Act 111 of 1998, s. 29. In terms of Reg. 22 of the Correctional Services Regulations (GN R323 in GG 35277 of 25 Apr. 2012), the security risk classification is determined by the Commissioner in accordance with the following principles: (*a*) individual classification in so far as the period of sentence permits and an analysis and assessment of the prisoner's previous record, aptitude, qualification or previous training, ability and other personal factors; (*b*) the maintenance of regular contact with, spouse, partner and next of kin; and (*c*) insofar as the duration of sentence permits, the application of progressive and flexible reclassification.

1661. Correctional Services Act 111 of 1998, s. 7. The term 'inmate' includes both convicted and unconvicted persons detained in custody in any correctional centre or remand detention facility (s. 1).

§2. Correctional Centre Regime

I. Minimum Requirements for Treatment of Inmates

687. The Act makes provision for the accommodation of inmates to be consistent with the conditions of human dignity.[1662] Sentenced offenders must be separated from persons awaiting trial or sentence, and male inmates must be separated from female inmates and inmates who are children must be kept separate from adult inmates and in accommodation appropriate for their age.[1663] Moreover, the National Commissioner may detain inmates of specific age, health or security risk categories separately and may accommodate inmates in single or communal accommodation depending on the availability of accommodation.[1664] As regards nutrition, each inmate must be provided with clean drinking water and an adequate diet to promote good health, which must take account of special dietary needs, religious requirements and cultural preferences, where reasonably practicable.[1665] Every inmate is required to keep his or her person, clothing, bedding and cell clean and tidy, and the department must provide the means to do so.[1666] Every inmate must be supplied with clothing and bedding to meet the requirements of hygiene and climactic conditions.[1667] The opportunity to exercise sufficiently in order to remain healthy must be available to each inmate, and a minimum of one hour daily must be allowed, weather permitting, in the open air.[1668] The department is required to provide adequate healthcare within its resources to each inmate, and each inmate should be encouraged to undergo treatment where necessary, subject to the principles of informed consent.[1669]

688. Every detained person has the right to communicate with, and be visited by, that person's spouse or partner, next of kin, chosen religious counsellor, and chosen medical practitioner.[1670] Inmates must be encouraged by the department to maintain contact with the community and keep abreast of current affairs, and thus, they must be given the opportunity of being visited, for a minimum of one hour of visits per month.[1671]Freedom of conscience, religion, thought, belief and opinion must be allowed each inmate, including being able to freely and voluntarily attend

1662. Correctional Services Act 111 of 1998, s. 7(1). The requirements apply to floor space, cubic capacity, lighting, ventilation, sanitary installations and general health conditions.
1663. Correctional Services Act 111 of 1998, s. 7(2)(*a*), (*b*), (*c*).
1664. Correctional Services Act 111 of 1998, s. 7(2)(*d*), (*e*).
1665. Correctional Services Act 111 of 1998, s. 8.
1666. Correctional Services Act 111 of 1998, s. 9.
1667. Correctional Services Act 111 of 1998, s. 10(1). A remand detainee is required to wear a prescribed uniform which distinguishes him or her from a sentenced offender, and remand detainees, who are not permitted to appear in court in such uniform, must be provided with clothing at State expense if he or she does not have adequate clothing (s. 48).
1668. Correctional Services Act 111 of 1998, s. 11.
1669. Correctional Services Act 111 of 1998, s. 12.
1670. Constitution, 1996, s. 35(2)(*f*).
1671. Correctional Services Act 111 of 1998, s. 13.

religious services, and to possess religious literature.[1672] The department must provide or give access to as full a range of programmes and activities as is practicable to meet the educational and training needs of sentenced offenders,[1673] and where it does not, the National Commissioner must inform inmates of services available from other sources and must put inmates in touch with appropriate agencies.[1674] Inmates are further entitled to consult on any legal matter with a legal practitioner of his or her choice at his or her own expense.[1675] Access to appropriate available reading material of his or her choice must be afforded by an inmate, whether from a correctional centre library or from outside the correctional centre.[1676]

689. Every inmate who is a child and is subject to compulsory education must attend and have access to such educational programmes.[1677] The National Commissioner must provide every inmate who is a child with social work services, religious care, recreational programmes and psychological services, and must, if practicable, ensure that inmates who are children remain in contact with their families through additional visits and by other means.[1678] A female inmate may be permitted, subject to such conditions as may be prescribed by regulation, to have her child with her until such child is 2 years of age or until such time that the child can be appropriately placed, taking into consideration the best interest of the child.[1679] The Department is responsible for food, clothing, healthcare and facilities for the sound development of the child for the period that such child remains in correctional centre.[1680]

II. The Privilege System

690. A privilege system is used to encourage good behaviour in sentenced offenders, to engender a sense of responsibility in them, and to ensure their interest and cooperation in reintegration and development programmes.[1681] Individual prisoners are divided into three privilege groups: A, B and C, with A constituting the highest privilege group. Prisoners are awarded B-group privileges on admission to

1672. Correctional Services Act 111 of 1998, s. 14. Where practicable, places of worship must be provided at every correctional centre for inmates.
1673. Correctional Services Act 111 of 1998, s. 41(1).
1674. Correctional Services Act 111 of 1998, s. 16(2). Inmates with disabilities must be accommodated – s. 16(3).
1675. Correctional Services Act 111 of 1998, s. 17. Remand detainees in a remand detention facility must be provided with the opportunities and facilities to prepare their defence. *See supra,* para. 678 for definitions.
1676. Correctional Services Act 111 of 1998, s. 18.
1677. Correctional Services Act 111 of 1998, s. 19(1). Where practicable, all children who are inmates not subject to compulsory education must be allowed access to educational programmes.
1678. Correctional Services Act 111 of 1998, s. 19(2), (3).
1679. Correctional Services Act 111 of 1998, s. 20(1).
1680. Correctional Services Act 111 of 1998, s. 20(2).
1681. Service order (SO) 3 of 1 Nov. 1998. The National Commissioner may issue such orders in terms of s. 134(2) of Act 111 of 1998.

prison and thereafter are assessed and re-graded at six monthly intervals.[1682] Group privileges include musical and radio programmes, musical instruments, showing of films, videos and television sets, sports and games, recreational meetings, concerts and choirs.[1683] Such amenities must be prescribed by regulation and available to all sentenced offenders as far as possible.[1684] Where, for economic or practical reasons, such amenities can only be introduced in some prisons, their partial introduction should be on a non-discriminatory basis.[1685]

III. Other Aspects of Living Conditions

A. Labour

691. Every sentenced offender, in addition to the obligations which apply to all inmates, must participate in the assessment process and must perform any labour which is related to any development programme unless unfit to do so.[1686] As full a range of programmes and activities as is practicable must be provided by the department, in order to give effect to the educational and training needs of sentenced offenders.[1687] It is not required that unsentenced offenders perform labour.

B. Disciplinary Measures and Security

692. The Correctional Services Act of 1998 provides that discipline and order must be maintained, but with no greater measure than is necessary for security purposes and for the good order of the correctional centre.[1688] If an inmate is convicted of an offence in a court of law, the department may take disciplinary action against such inmate without any further inquiry.[1689] Disciplinary action may also be taken where criminal proceedings are still pending against the inmate.[1690] There are a range of acts detailed in the Correctional Services Act, which constitute disciplinary infringements.[1691]

693. The right of every prisoner to personal integrity and privacy is subject to the limitations reasonably necessary to ensure the security of the community, safety

1682. SO V(3)(e). Privileges are further classified as 'primary privileges' aimed at the retention and furtherance of family ties and 'secondary privileges' which are aimed at leisure time activities, such as participation in sports and television (SO V(3)(*b*)(aa)).
1683. SO V(3)(*b*)(bb). These are also regarded as secondary privileges.
1684. *Strydom v. Minister of Correctional Services* 1999 (3) BCLR 342 (W).
1685. Correctional Services Act 111 of 1998, s. 37(3).
1686. Correctional Services Act 111 of 1998, s. 37. *See* further ss 38, 40.
1687. Correctional Services Act 111 of 1998, s. 41.
1688. Correctional Services Act 111 of 1998, s. 22(1).
1689. Correctional Services Act 111 of 1998, s. 22(2).
1690. Correctional Services Act 111 of 1998, s. 22(3).
1691. Correctional Services Act 111 of 1998, s. 23. The procedures relating to disciplinary hearings are set out in s. 24.

of correctional officials and the safe custody of all inmates.[1692] Thus, the Act provides for searches,[1693] and for steps to be taken to identify an inmate.[1694] The security classification is determined by the extent to which the inmate presents a security risk in order to determine the correctional centre or part of the correctional centre in which the inmate is to be detained.[1695] Provision is also made for the segregation of an inmate,[1696] for the restraint of an inmate by means of mechanical restraints[1697] and the use of minimum force to detain all inmates in safe custody.[1698] Restrictions imposed on remand detainees should be limited to what is necessary for the maintenance of security and good order in the remand detention facility and must, where practicable, allow such detainees all the amenities to which they could have access outside the remand detention facility.[1699]

C. Location and Leave

694. A sentenced offender must, where possible, be housed at the correctional centre closest to the place where he or she is to reside after release, and the same considerations apply to transfer of an offender.[1700] The National Commissioner may grant permission in writing to a sentenced offender to leave the correctional centre temporarily for the purposes of compassionate leave, treatment, development or support programmes, preparation for release or any other reason related to the reintegration of a sentenced offender into the community.[1701]

§3. Complaints Procedures and Judicial Controls

695. Every inmate must, on admission and on a daily basis, be given the opportunity to make complaints or requests to the Head of the Correctional Centre or an authorised correctional official.[1702] Such official must record all such complaints and requests and any steps taken in dealing with them; deal with complaints and requests promptly and inform the inmate of the outcome; and if the complaint concerns an alleged assault, ensure that the inmate undergoes an immediate medical examination and receives the treatment prescribed by the correctional medical practitioner.[1703] If an inmate is not satisfied with the response to his or her complaint or request, the inmate may indicate this together with the reasons for the dissatisfaction to the Head of the Correctional Centre, who must refer the matter to the

1692. Correctional Services Act 111 of 1998, s. 26(1).
1693. Correctional Services Act 111 of 1998, s. 27.
1694. Correctional Services Act 111 of 1998, s. 28.
1695. Correctional Services Act 111 of 1998, s. 29.
1696. Correctional Services Act 111 of 1998, s. 30.
1697. Correctional Services Act 111 of 1998, s. 31.
1698. Correctional Services Act 111 of 1998, s. 32.
1699. Correctional Services Act 111 of 1998, s. 46.
1700. Correctional Services Act 111 of 1998, s. 43.
1701. Correctional Services Act 111 of 1998, s. 44.
1702. Correctional Services Act 111 of 1998, s. 21(1).
1703. Correctional Services Act 111 of 1998, s. 21(2).

National Commissioner.[1704] The response of the National Commissioner must be conveyed to the inmate.[1705] If not satisfied with the response of the National Commissioner, the inmate may refer the matter to the independent correctional centre visitor, who must deal with it in terms of the procedures laid down in the Act.[1706]

696. Independent oversight over the correctional services is provided by the Correctional Services Act. Provision is made for the establishment of an independent inspectorate through the establishment of the Judicial Inspectorate for Correctional Services under the control of the inspecting judge.[1707] The object of the judicial inspectorate is to facilitate the inspection of correctional centres so that the inspecting judge can report on the treatment of inmates and on conditions in correctional centres.[1708] The inspecting judge, who is either a judge of the High Court in active service or a judge discharged from active service, is appointed by the President.[1709] The inspecting judge is given the power to inspect or arrange for the inspection of correctional centres and remand detention facilities in order to report on the treatment of inmates in these correctional centres and remand detention facilities and on conditions and any corrupt or dishonest practices in correctional centres and remand detention facilities.[1710] In doing so, the inspecting judge may hold an inquiry, assign functions to inspectors, and make rules for the efficient functioning of the inspectorate. The inspecting judge is required to identify a suitably qualified and experienced person as the chief executive officer of the inspectorate.[1711] Apart from assuming full financial and administrative responsibility for the inspectorate, the chief executive officer must, in consultation with the inspecting judge, appoint an independent correctional centre visitor for each correctional centre.[1712] Such visitor is required to deal with inmates' complaints through visits, interviews, monitoring complaints and discussion.[1713]

1704. Correctional Services Act 111 of 1998, s. 21(3).
1705. Correctional Services Act 111 of 1998, s. 21(4).
1706. Correctional Services Act 111 of 1998, s. 21(5).
1707. Correctional Services Act 111 of 1998, s. 85(1).
1708. Correctional Services Act 111 of 1998, s. 85(2).
1709. Correctional Services Act 111 of 1998, s. 86.
1710. Correctional Services Act 111 of 1998, s. 90.
1711. Correctional Services Act 111 of 1998, s. 88A.
1712. Correctional Services Act 111 of 1998, s. 92.
1713. Correctional Services Act 111 of 1998, s. 93.

Chapter 4. Community Corrections

697. The object of community corrections is to afford sentenced offenders an opportunity to serve their sentences in a non-custodial manner and to lead a socially responsible and crime-free life during their sentence period and thereafter, thus providing for rehabilitation of the offender and reintegration into society on release.[1714] The following persons are placed under community corrections: those placed under correctional supervision in terms of the Act; sentenced offenders who have been granted temporary leave; sentenced offenders placed on day parole; sentenced offenders placed on parole in terms of section 73 of the Act; and sentenced offenders placed under the supervision of a correctional official. In each case, the person to be subjected to such corrections must agree to the stipulated conditions and undertake to cooperate in meeting those conditions.[1715]

The following conditions may be attached to community corrections by a court or other competent authority: house detention; community service; seeking employment; remaining in employment; paying compensation to the victim; taking part in treatment, development or support programmes; participation in victim-offender mediation or family group conferencing; making a financial contribution towards the cost of his or her community corrections; restriction to one or more magisterial districts; residing at a fixed address; refraining from alcohol or illegal drugs; refraining from committing a criminal offence; refraining from visiting a particular place; refraining from making contact with particular persons; refraining from threatening a particular person; being subject to monitoring; or subject to such limitations as appropriate in the circumstances.[1716] Failure to comply with any such condition may have consequences, including, at the behest of the National Commissioner, a change in the conditions of community corrections.[1717] All forms of community corrections must be supervised in the community by correctional officials and should not invade the privacy of the person concerned more than necessary to ensure compliance.[1718]

Under the Act, a correctional supervision and parole board receives reports from the case management committee regarding any sentenced offender at the correctional centre served by the committee.[1719] Having received such report, the board may place a sentenced offender serving a determinate sentence of more than twenty-four months under correctional supervision or day parole or grant parole or set the conditions of community corrections imposed on a sentenced offender.[1720] Correctional supervision or parole may be granted on medical grounds.[1721] The President may authorise that a sentenced offender be placed on correctional supervision or parole.[1722]

1714. Correctional Services Act 111 of 1998, s. 50(1)(*a*).
1715. Correctional Services Act 111 of 1998, s. 51.
1716. Correctional Services Act 111 of 1998, s. 52. Where the offender is a child, attendance of educational programmes may also constitute a condition.
1717. Correctional Services Act 111 of 1998, ss 70–71.
1718. Correctional Services Act 111 of 1998, s. 57.
1719. Correctional Services Act 111 of 1998, s. 42(2)(*d*).
1720. Correctional Services Act 111 of 1998, s. 75(1)(*a*).
1721. Correctional Services Act 111 of 1998, s. 79.
1722. Correctional Services Act 111 of 1998, s. 82.

Chapter 5. The Release of Sentenced Prisoners

§1. Constitutional Powers of Pardon and Reprieve

698. In theory, sentences are disposed of by their being carried out in the manner prescribed by the court which imposed them. Thus, the sentenced person, having paid the fine or having served the term of imprisonment, is free of the sanction imposed by the court. In practice, the position is more complicated. The serving of the sentence alone is not the end of the matter, for the conviction and sentence of the accused may be recorded by the police.[1723] Moreover, a criminal record may have many negative consequences for an individual. Thus, for example, someone convicted of a crime involving an element of dishonesty may not be a director of a company or a curator of an insolvent estate.[1724] Certain criminal convictions only cease to be recognised as previous convictions after a period of ten years has elapsed, during which the person concerned has not been sentenced to a further term of imprisonment of more than six months without the option of a fine.[1725]

699. The one way in which a sentence can be erased completely is by the President exercising his or her constitutional power to pardon an offender.[1726] The President also has a constitutional power to grant reprieve, that is, the power to substitute a lighter sentence for a heavier one.

700. In cases where all the appellate procedures have been exhausted, an accused person may petition the Minister of Justice if he believes that new evidence has come to light which might materially affect his conviction.[1727] The Minister has the discretion to refer the matter to a court, which will hear the evidence and make a finding which it reports to the President. The President may then exercise his or her powers of pardon or reprieve in the light of this finding or advice from the court.

§2. Release Procedures

I. Mode of Release

701. A sentenced offender must be prepared for placement, release and reintegration into society by participating in a pre-release programme.[1728] Material and

1723. For the practice in respect of previous convictions, *see* E. Du Toit et al., *Commentary on the Criminal Procedure Act* (Juta, Cape Town 1987) 27–1ff.
1724. On the influence of criminal convictions on status, *see* B. van Heerden, A. Cockrell & R. Keightley, *Boberg's Law of Persons and the Family* 2nd ed. (Juta, Cape Town 1999) 229; F. du Bois, 'Convicted Persons' in F. du Bois (ed.), *Wille's Principles of South African Law* 9th ed. (2007) 134.
1725. Criminal Procedure Act 1977, s. 271A.
1726. Constitution, 1996, s. 84(2)(*j*).
1727. Criminal Procedure Act 1977, s. 327.
1728. Correctional Services Act 111 of 1998, s. 45(1).

financial support is provided at release to sentenced offenders.[1729] Where a sentenced offender is to be placed under correctional supervision or to be released on parole, he must be properly informed of the conditions imposed.[1730]

702. Having considered the report on a sentenced offender serving a determinate sentence of more than twenty months submitted to it by the Case Management Committee, along with any other information before it, a Correctional Supervision and Parole Board may:[1731]

a. place such sentenced offender under correctional supervision or day parole or grant parole or medical parole, and set the conditions of community corrections imposed on such offender;
b. in respect of any sentenced offender declared a dangerous criminal in terms of section 286A of the Criminal Procedure Act, make recommendations to the court on the granting of the placement under correctional supervision or day parole or parole or medical parole and on the period for and the conditions of community corrections imposed on the sentenced offender; and
c. in respect of any sentenced offender serving a sentence of life imprisonment, make recommendations to the Minister on the granting of day parole or parole or medical parole and the conditions of community corrections to be imposed on such an offender.

The Board may also act to cancel correctional supervision, day parole or parole which has been granted or amend the conditions under which community corrections have been imposed after consideration and on the request of the National Commissioner.[1732]

703. The National Commissioner may place a sentenced offender serving a sentence of twenty-four months or less under correctional supervision, day parole, parole or medical parole and prescribe conditions. He or she may further cancel correctional supervision, day parole or medical parole and alter the convictions for community corrections relating to such offender.[1733]

704. The Minister may grant parole or day parole or prescribe the conditions of community corrections for a person serving a sentence of life incarceration in respect of whom this has been recommended by the National Council, flowing from

1729. Correctional Services Act 111 of 1998, s. 45(3).
1730. Correctional Services Act 111 of 1998, s. 55(3).
1731. Correctional Services Act 111 of 1998, s. 75(1), subject to the provisions of s. 52. With regard to certain specified offences, input must be sought from the Department of Justice and the South African Police Service (s. 75(1A), (1B)). Decisions of the Board (composed in terms of s. 74) are subject to review by the Correctional Supervision and Parole Review Board (ss 75(8), 76, 77).
1732. Correctional Services Act 111 of 1998, s. 75(2). When the board cancels correctional supervision, day parole or parole, it must reconsider the decision within two years (s. 75(6)).
1733. Correctional Services Act 111 of 1998, s. 75(7). The requirements set out in s. 79 of the Act must however be met before such discretion is triggered – *National Commissioner for Correctional Services v. Democratic Alliance* 2023 (2) SA 530 (SCA).

the proceedings of the Board. Where the Board recommends that in respect of such person's day parole or parole be withdrawn or community corrections amended, the Minister, on the advice of the National Council, may do so.[1734] The Minister may further, on the recommendation of the National Council, advance the approved date for the placement of any sentenced offender or group of sentenced offenders under community corrections, where overcrowding is materially affecting the safety, dignity and care of offenders at a particular correctional centre or in general.[1735]

705. Leaving aside the power to pardon or reprieve sentenced offenders, the President may authorise the placement on correctional supervision or parole of any sentenced offender, subject to such conditions recommended by the Board having jurisdiction, or in the case of a person serving a life sentence, the Minister.[1736]

706. The Correctional Supervision and Parole Board may, on the recommendation of the National Commissioner, grant special remission for 'highly meritorious service'.[1737]

707. Prison legislation also provides that any offender serving a sentence in a correctional centre who, based on the written evidence of the medical practitioner treating that offender, is diagnosed as suffering from a terminal disease or condition, or if such offender is rendered physically incapacitated as a result of injury, disease or illness, so as to severely limit daily activity or intimate self-care, may be considered for placement under correctional supervision or on parole, by the National Commissioner, Correctional Supervision and Parole Board or the Minister. In addition to the medical condition being diagnosed, appropriate arrangements must be in place for the inmate's supervision, care and treatment within the community into which he is released, and there must be a low risk of re-offending.[1738]

II. Length and Form of Sentences

708. A sentenced offender remains in a correctional centre for the full period of sentence, and a sentenced offender sentenced to life incarceration remains in a correctional centre for the rest of his or her life.[1739] Upon expiry of the term of incarceration, the sentenced offender is released from the correctional centre and from

1734. Correctional Services Act 111 of 1998, s. 78. When the Minister cancels correctional supervision, day parole or parole, he or she must reconsider the decision within two years.
1735. Correctional Services Act 111 of 1998, s. 81.
1736. Correctional Services Act 111 of 1998, s. 82.
1737. Correctional Services Act 111 of 1998, s. 80. A person serving a life sentence or a sentence under s. 286A of the Criminal Procedure Act does not qualify for such remission.
1738. Correctional Services Act 111 of 1998, s. 79.
1739. Correctional Services Act 111 of 1998, s. 73(1), subject to the provisions of the Act relating to release, *see supra* paras 701 et seq.

any form of community corrections imposed in lieu of part of a sentence of incarceration.[1740] However, a sentenced offender may be placed under correctional supervision or day parole or parole before the expiration of his term of incarceration.[1741] Subject to the sentenced offender accepting the conditions for placement, the date on which such sentenced offender is placed under correctional supervision or on day parole or parole is determined by the Correctional Supervision and Parole Board, whilst in the case of a sentenced offender sentenced to life incarceration, the date of placement on day parole or parole is determined by the Minister.[1742]

709. A sentenced offender serving a determinate sentence or cumulative sentences of more than twenty-four months may not be placed on day parole or parole until such sentenced offender has served either the stipulated non-parole period, or if no non-parole period was stipulated, half of the sentence, but day parole or parole must be considered whenever a sentenced offender has served twenty-five years of a sentence or cumulative sentences. An offender serving a determinate sentence or cumulative sentences of not more than twenty-four months may not be placed on parole or day parole until such offender has served either the stipulated non-parole period or, if no non-parole period was stipulated, a quarter of the sentence. A person sentenced to:

1. periodical incarceration must be detained periodically in a correctional centre as prescribed by regulation;
2. life incarceration may not be placed on day parole or parole until he or she has served at least twenty five years;
3. any term of incarceration, excluding persons declared dangerous criminals in terms of section 286A of the Criminal Procedure Act, may be placed on day parole or parole on reaching the age of 65 years provided that he or she has served at least fifteen years of such sentence.[1743]

710. A person declared a habitual criminal may be detained in a correctional centre for a period of fifteen years and may not be placed on day parole or parole until after a period of at least seven years.[1744]

711. If sentenced to incarceration under section 276(1)(*i*) of the Criminal Procedure Act, an offender must serve at least one-sixth of his or her sentence before being considered for placement under correctional supervision.[1745] A person sentenced to incarceration for a period not exceeding five years as an alternative to a

1740. Correctional Services Act 111 of 1998, s. 73(2). Where such release may lead to the death or impairment of the health of the inmate, or a source of infection to others, the inmate will be dealt with in terms of the applicable legislation (s. 73(3)).
1741. Correctional Services Act 111 of 1998, s. 73(4).
1742. Correctional Services Act 111 of 1998, s. 73(5).
1743. Correctional Services Act 111 of 1998, s. 73(6)(*a*), (*a*A), (*b*). The dual system of assessment of parole based on date of sentence was declared unconstitutional in *Phaahla v. Minister of Justice and Correctional Services* 2019 (2) SACR 88 (CC).
1744. Correctional Services Act 111 of 1998, s. 73(6)(*c*).
1745. Correctional Services Act 111 of 1998, s. 73(7)(*a*), unless the court directs otherwise.

fine under section 287(4)(*a*) of the Criminal Procedure Act may be considered for placement under correctional supervision by the National Commissioner or the Correctional Supervision and Parole Board as soon as possible after admission to a correctional centre subject to the confirmation of a suitable support system, unless the court has directed otherwise.[1746] A person sentenced to incarceration for a period exceeding five years as an alternative to a fine under section 287(4)(*b*) of the Criminal Procedure Act may be recommended to a court for placement under correctional supervision, except if the court has directed otherwise, in circumstances where such an offender has completed at least one-quarter of the sentence and the remainder of the sentence until sentence expiry does not exceed five years.[1747]

712. A person sentenced to incarceration for a definite period in terms of section 276(1)(*b*) of the Criminal Procedure Act may not be placed under correctional supervision unless such sentence has been converted into correctional supervision in accordance with section 276A(3) of the said Act.[1748] A person sentenced to incarceration for a definite period under section 276(1)(*b*) of the Criminal Procedure Act may be referred to a court in accordance with section 276A(3)(*a*) of that Act, if the offender has completed at least a quarter of the effective sentence and the remainder of the sentence until sentence expiry does not exceed five years.[1749]

1746. Correctional Services Act 111 of 1998, s. 73(7)(*b*).
1747. Correctional Services Act 111 of 1998, s. 73(7)(*c*).
1748. Correctional Services Act 111 of 1998, s. 73(7)(*d*). In terms of s. 276A(3), where a person has been sentenced by a court to imprisonment for a period, either not exceeding five years, or exceeding five years, but his date of release is not more than five years in the future, and such a person has already been admitted to a prison, the Commissioner or a parole board may, if he or it is of the opinion that such a person is fit to be subjected to correctional supervision, apply to the clerk or registrar of the court, as the case may be, to have that person appear before the court *a quo* in order to reconsider the said sentence.
1749. Correctional Services Act 111 of 1998, s. 73(7)(*e*).

General Conclusion

713. South African criminal law is thus founded on both common-law and statutory sources, with the substantive criminal law comprising general principles which are derived from both Roman-Dutch and English Common Law antecedents and which have been further refined through the case-law, as well as specific crimes, which are either common-law or statutory in nature. The procedural criminal law is largely codified in the form of the Criminal Procedure Act 51 of 1977, although common-law sources still play a role with regard to certain aspects. The trial on the merits is accusatorial in nature, governed by strict rules of evidence. This may be contrasted with the sentencing phase of the trial, where the rules of evidence are more flexible and where the judicial officer enjoys a more active role, thus incorporating a more inquisitorial approach. All aspects of the South African criminal law are required to conform to the precepts of the Bill of Rights contained in the 1996 Constitution.

714. In respect of future developments in South African criminal law, there are some pertinent issues and developments which may be noted. With regard to the substantive criminal law, questions still remain regarding the status of the defence of non-pathological incapacity after the opaque judgment of the SCA in *S v. Eadie*[1750] and in the context of the development of the common-law rules of liability to accord with the rights and values in the Constitution,[1751] with regard to issues such as whether one is entitled to kill in defence of property,[1752] or whether a person under duress may rely on the necessity defence to justify taking the life of an innocent third party.[1753] With regard to criminal procedure, the recent long-awaited changes to the law relating to use of force in arrest will inevitably continue to spark debate as to the appropriate limits to be placed on the conduct of police officers and, concomitantly, the limitation of the rights of suspected offenders.[1754] The impact of the new rules governing the procedure to be employed in respect of children suspected of committing a crime in the Child Justice Act[1755] will continue to be felt. International and transnational criminal law will continue to influence domestic South African law, both in respect of the need for cooperation between states in combating certain forms of crime and in respect of the enactment of laws under the

1750. *S v. Eadie* 2002 (1) SACR 663 (SCA); *see supra*, para. 228.
1751. *See supra*, para. 70.
1752. *See supra*, para. 191.
1753. *See supra*, para. 194.
1754. *See supra*, para. 514 for the present position.
1755. Child Justice Act 75 of 2008.

influence of international instruments.[1756] With regard to sentencing, once again the changes brought about by the Child Justice Act in respect of child offenders fall to be fully assessed,[1757] along with the concomitant rise in significance of restorative justice considerations in South African courts.[1758] The minimum sentencing legislation will continue to challenge the courts to strike a balance between crime control policy concerns and the rights of convicted offenders.[1759] Ultimately, all these changes and potential changes fall to be carried out in the context of the rights protected in the Bill of Rights and the overarching values of the Constitution.

1756. *See* discussion in J. Burchell, *South African Criminal Law and Procedure,* Vol. I *General Principles of Criminal Law* 4th ed. (Juta, Cape Town 2011) 6–8; *see*, e.g., *supra* para. 371.
1757. *See* S.V. Hoctor, 'Sentencing' in W.A. Joubert (ed.), *The Law of South Africa* Vol. 24 2nd ed. (LexisNexis, Durban 2010) paras 528–529.
1758. *See S v. Thabethe* 2011 (2) SACR 567 (SCA); *S v. Seedat* 2015 (2) SACR 612 (GP); *S v. Seedat* 2017 (1) SACR 141 (SCA).
1759. *See* S.V. Hoctor, 'Sentencing' in W.A. Joubert (ed.), *The Law of South Africa* Vol. 24 2nd ed. (LexisNexis, Durban 2010) paras 538–539; S.S Terblanche, *A Guide to Sentencing in South Africa* 3rd ed. (2016) 45ff.

Selected Bibliography

A. Bibliographies

Rabie M.A., Bibliography of South African Criminal Law-General Principles (Juta, Cape Town 1987).

B. Legislation

Statutes of the Republic of South Africa (Butterworths, Durban 1965, loose-leaf and kept up to date).
Statutes of South Africa (Juta, Cape Town, CD-ROM updated bi-annually).

C. Cases

All South African Law Reports (LexisNexis, Durban, since 1996) (abbreviated as All SA).
South African Law Reports (Juta, Cape Town, since 1910) (abbreviated as SA).
South African Criminal Law Reports (Juta, Cape Town, since 1990) (abbreviated as SACR).
Prentice Hall Weekly Legal Services (Prentice Hall, Durban, 1930–1995) (abbreviated as PH).
Burchell J.M., *Cases and Materials on Criminal Law* 4th ed. (Juta, Cape Town 2016).
Snyman C.R. *Criminal Law Casebook* 5th ed. (Juta, Cape Town 2013).
Visser P.J. & Vorster J.P., *General Principles of Criminal Law Through the Cases* 3rd ed. (Butterworths, Durban 1990).

D. Journals

Annual Survey of South African Law (1947–2017).
Crime Punishment and Correction (1972–1976).
South African Journal of Criminal Law and Criminology (1977–1987).
South African Journal of Criminal Justice (since 1988).

E. Reports

Report of the ad hoc Committee of the Presidents Council on the Immorality Act (PC 1/1985).
Report of the Commission of Enquiry into the Penal System of the Republic of South Africa RP 78/1976.
Report of the Commission of Enquiry into the Responsibility of Mentally Deranged Persons and Related Matters RP 60/1967.

South African Law Commission Report on the Investigation into the Application of Mens Rea in Statutory Offences (1982).
South African Law Reform Commission Money Laundering and Related Matters (1996).
South African Law Reform Commission Report on Sentencing (2000).
South African Law Reform Commission Application of the Bill of Rights to Criminal Procedure, Criminal Law, the Law of Evidence and Sentencing (2001).
South African Law Reform Commission Sexual Offences Report (2002).
South African Law Reform Commission Stalking (2008).
South African Law Reform Commission Trafficking in Persons (2008).
South African Law Reform Commission Sexual Offences: Adult Prostitution (2017).
South African Law Reform Commission Report on the Review of the Law of Evidence (2019).
South African Law Reform Commission Report on Sexual Offences: Pornography and Children (2022).

F. Books

Burchell J., South African Criminal Law and Procedure Vol. 1 General Principles of Criminal Law, 4th ed. (Juta, Cape Town 2011).
Burchell J., Principles of Criminal Law 5th ed. (Juta, Cape Town 2016).
De Wet J.C. & Swanepoel H.L., Die Suid-Afrikaanse Strafreg 4th ed. (Butterworths, Durban 1985).
Du Toit E., Straf in Suid-Afrika (Juta, Cape Town 1981).
Du Toit E., et al., Commentary on the Criminal Procedure Act (Juta, Cape Town 1987, loose-leaf and kept up to date).
Dugard C.J.R., South African Criminal Law & Procedure, Vol. IV Introduction to Criminal Procedure (Juta, Cape Town 1977).
Gardiner F.G., & Lansdown C.W.H., South African Criminal Law and Procedure, 6th ed. (Juta, Cape Town 1957).
Hoctor S.V., Snyman's Criminal Law 7th ed. (LexisNexis, Durban 2020).
Hoctor S.V., 'Criminal Law' 3rd ed. in Joubert W. A. (ed.), The Law of South Africa Vol. 11 (LexisNexis, Durban 2023).
Hoctor S.V., 'Sentencing' 2nd ed. in Joubert W.A. (ed.), The Law of South Africa Vol. 24 (LexisNexis, Durban 2010).
Joubert J.J. (ed.), Criminal Procedure Handbook 13th ed. (Juta, Cape Town 2020).
Kemp G. (ed.), Criminal Law in South Africa 4th ed. (Oxford University Press, Cape Town 2022).
Kruger A., Hiemstra's Criminal Procedure (LexisNexis, Durban 2008, loose-leaf).
Lansdown A.V. & Campbell J., South African Criminal Law & Procedure, Vol. V Criminal Procedure and Evidence (Juta, Cape Town 1982).
Loubser M.M., Theft of Money in South African Law (1978).
Mathews A.S., Freedom, State Security and the Rule of Law (Juta, Cape Town 1986).
Matthaeus A., On Crimes: A Commentary on Books XLVII & XLVIII of the Digest translation by M.L. Hewett & B.C. Stoop Vol. 1 (Juta, Cape Town 1987).

Milton J.R.L., Hoctor S.V. & Cowling M.G., South African Criminal Law & Procedure, Vol. III Statutory Offences (Juta, Cape Town 1988, loose-leaf and kept up to date).

Milton J.R.L., South African Criminal Law & Procedure, Vol. II Common-law Crimes, 3rd ed. (Juta, Cape Town 1996).

Rabie M.A. & Strauss S.A., Punishment: An Introduction to Principles (Lex Patria, Pretoria 1985).

Schwikkard P.J. & Mosaka T.B., Principles of Evidence 5th ed. (Juta, Cape Town 2023).

Terblanche S.S., Guide to Sentencing in South Africa 3rd ed. (LexisNexis, Durban 2016).

Van der Merwe, D.P., Sentencing (Juta, Cape Town 1991, loose-leaf).

Van Zyl Smit D., South African Prison Law and Practice (Butterworths, Durban 1992).

Selected Bibliography

Index

The numbers here refer to paragraph numbers.

Index

www.ingramcontent.com/pod-product-compliance
Ingram Content Group UK Ltd.
Pitfield, Milton Keynes, MK11 3LW, UK
UKHW020135290926
15471UKWH00003B/508

9 789403 5446